At age 27, L. Ron Hubbard clinically "died" only to discover that he could "remote view." From this state of consciousness, which would later be called "exterior," he was able to access what he termed the answers to all of the questions that had ever puzzled philosophers or the minds of men. Transcribing this information into a work entitled Excalibur, which is still under lock and key to this day, he developed one of the most controversial movements in history: Dianetics and Scientology.

The truth and import of the above can only be evaluated *by the all out war which was waged by governmental forces and spy agencies to obtain the legally construed rights to the above mentioned work and all of the developments and techniques that ensued from it.*

The Montauk Book of the Dead is the personal story of *Peter Moon which not only pierces the mystery of death but gives an unbiased behind-the-scenes look at one of the most controversial figures in history and the bizarre legacy of his death. Read this book and expect to learn more than you ever thought possible.*

THE MONTAUK BOOK OF THE DEAD

BY PETER MOON

NEW YORK

The Montauk Book of the Dead
Copyright © 2005 by Peter Moon
First printing, March 2005

Cover art and illustration by Jill Bauman
Typography by Creative Circle Inc.
Published by: Sky Books
             Box 769
             Westbury, New York 11590
             email: skybooks@yahoo.com
             website: www.skybooksusa.com

Library of Congress Cataloging-in-Publication Data

Moon, Peter
    The Montauk Book of the Dead
by Peter Moon
    456 pages
    ISBN 978-0-9678162-3-4
1. Biography and Autobiography 2. Religion 3. Moors
Library of Congress Control Number 2005921593

To Hardy and Libby

Other titles from Sky Books

by Preston Nichols and Peter Moon

The Montauk Project: Experiments in Time
Montauk Revisited: Adventures in Synchronicity
Pyramids of Montauk: Explorations in Consciousness
Encounter in the Pleiades: An Inside Look at UFOs
The Music of Time

by Peter Moon

The Black Sun: Montauk's Nazi-Tibetan Connection
Synchronicity and the Seventh Seal

by Joseph Matheny with Peter Moon

Ong's Hat: The Beginning

by Stewart Swerdlow

Montauk: The Alien Connection
The Healer's Handbook: A Journey Into Hyperspace

by Alexandra Bruce

The Philadelphia Experiment Murder:
Parallel Universes and the Physics of Insanity

by Wade Gordon

The Brookhaven Connection

CONTENTS

PRELUDE

All Hallows Eve, Autumn 1960

The year was 1960 and it was the 29th of October. Most people's minds were occupied with the presidential race between Kennedy and Nixon which was the main topic of conversation. It seemed that everyone had an opinion about who should win. As a seven-year-old boy, I was more excited that it was Saturday and Halloween was only two days away. As I fooled around in my front yard on an overcast autumn day in Southern California, the Lackson family surprisingly and suddenly appeared in my front yard. Riding bicycles, they were on their way to the Lakewood Center Shopping Mall to buy decorations for a Halloween party to be held in their house the following evening. I was told I could come along, but I would have to get permission and hurry up. Bill Lackson was about two years older than I and his sister, Sandra, was even older. Their mother, Ann, was a widow. As I was considerably younger than everyone, I had to struggle just to keep up with them on my bike as they were certainly not slowing down to accommodate me.

When we finally reached Lakewood Center, I realized it was the first time I had ever been there without my parents, and I found the experience quite exhilarating. It was one of those small hallmarks of growing up. Our first destination was the basement of a dime store where they had a holiday department where Ann began buying different things for the party. Then, she stopped what she was doing, called us together and bought each of us a grab bag. For a nickel, each of us received a bag with various surprises in it. We all agreed the surprises were rather worthless, but it was great fun that only a kid could appreciate. At the time, I thought it was very kind of her to buy me the bag as I knew she was a widow

11

and had to struggle to make ends meet. I was too young to have any sort of rational perspective on the relative value of a nickel.

When we finished and returned to our block, Ann had me go see my mother and ask for permission to eat lunch at their house. I remained there for the entire day as I helped them decorate for the Halloween party to be held the following evening.

This was not the first Halloween I remember, but it was definitely the most memorable. My mind waxed poetic as I learned about ghosts, witches, bats, black cats, and goblins. At that age, I was the best artist in my class and was particularly adept at drawing bats against a yellow moon and black cats with arched backs. I was learning my first bit of lore about the different spirits and forms that represented them. I could feel the color of the holiday. It was orange and black with some yellow sprinkled in now and then.

Although Ann was a devout Catholic and her children attended the local Catholic school, she explained a bit of the old holiday and how the Church celebrated All Saints Day on November 1st in what was originally a counter-maneuver against the old ways. This was the first time I was old enough to really appreciate the legends of Halloween. I was soon bolstered in my shallow interest to understand these potentially frightening spirits through the comic books of that era which included *Caspar, the Friendly Ghost; Wendy, the Good Little Witch;* and my personal favorite, *Hot Stuff, the Good Little Devil.*

Although the experiences of this particular Saturday might seem rather mundane, I was struck very deeply on the inside. It was not only an opportunity to engage in make-believe and create art but it was also my first bit of learning with regard to the legends and lore of Halloween. When I told Ann I was going to be a black cat for Halloween, I remember her telling me that a cat has nine lives. I do not know if any us really thought that it was true, but we all believed it for the moment. It was fun and the lore made it so. Although my understanding was somewhat shallow, this was the first time I had ever grasped the inner meaning of any holiday. Christmas was still the preferred holiday by reason of the gifts one would receive, but no other holiday ever remained so poetic in my imagination as Halloween. Perhaps you can imagine my inspiration years later when I was introduced to the writings of Ray

Bradbury, an author who excited my mind with images of October and Mars. Immediately after reading two chapters of Bradbury's poetic prose, I was inspired to become a writer. Had it not been for this early Halloween, I do not know that the inspiration would have been the same.

Besides serving as the seed for my future as a writer, this particular Halloween season was to reach out across the time line decades later and grab me in a most particular and peculiar manner. But no matter what has happened since or what may happen in the future, the innocence of that day can never be lost.

13

THE DREAM

Human beings are often at their best when they exercise their creative dynamics by indulging in legends and pretending. If mythology is not the direct work of the gods, it is sometimes the closest conduit we have to working with the Creative Force that is known as the Author of the Universe. There is, however, a junction point where real events and circumstances weave their way into the fabric of mythology and vice versa. As a result of my sojourn into the world of the imagination and the occult, which began with my early interest in Halloween, I have found myself strangely positioned at the threshold where real world events mix with synchronicity and incredible phenomena. The book you are about to read was never meant to be written, at least as far as I was concerned. It was, however, deemed necessary by experiences of synchronicity with regard to my "first" Halloween.

Halloween is a fun time, but the Tooth Fairy is also a prime example where mythology enters the human experience. As one grows up and loses a tooth, people tend to fawn over you as if you had accomplished something when all you have really done is just grow a bit older. At this time, in some strange way, parents give a love and attention that they might not otherwise express. As we grow and lose our baby teeth, we are not only heralded but are also met with a reward in the physical word: a coin or pentacle.* As I grew, I collected my baby teeth and kept them in a plastic casing.

---

* The pantacle or pentacle is also the symbol for "coins" or earth-based reality and commerce in the Tarot. The suit of pentacles has been represented by a five pointed star or pentagram, the top point of which represents *shin*, a word which means "spirit" as in the Japanese word *Shinto* (made up of the words *shin* and *Tao*) and while this definition of *shin* is recognized by many Hebrew scholars, *shin* is more commonly defined as "tooth." For further information on this concept and its applications, including how these concepts were transliterated into the English word *Jesus*, read *Synchronicity and the Seventh Seal* by Peter Moon.

As a kid, I remember looking at my old teeth years afterwards and silently recognizing where I had been. The teeth meant little to me as I had no use for them, but they spoke a truth that was beyond words. They were a testament to my physical history but also represented my emergence from innocence. It came as a total shock to me in later life, well into my middle age, when the Tooth Fairy struck again.

Deep in my slumber, I knew that I had emerged from trying times in my own life. A horrible divorce was followed by a struggle to regain what had been lost. I was therefore not surprised to be greeted by a sparkle of magic in the dream state, but the intensity and virtual reality of it was quite unsuspected.

I dreamt I had woken to see a dark blue sky with no stars whatsoever. "Where are the stars?" I thought. Suddenly, a fairy appeared with a magic wand. Although nothing was said, I knew she was the Tooth Fairy as she waved her wand and a cascade of pentagram-shaped stars followed in her wake. The stars were glorious and began to find their place as they filled the night sky. It was Midsummer Night's Eve as I heard chirping outside my open window. In the park behind my house, creatures that sounded like munchkins were giggling and talking at a feverish pitch. A wood sprite nearby motioned me to follow. As I climbed out my window, there were all sorts of creatures on an exodus through the park and into the woods. There was no choice but to follow and find out. As I followed the crowd, which was growing in size and momentum every minute, I heard a munchkin-type creature say that the Bard of Bards would soon be appearing in the glen. Another said that the Bard of Bards was the last in a long line of troubadours. He was the story teller of story tellers.

I was aware that there are many definitions and descriptions of bards. They were considered vital sources of information in the Middle Ages. With no newspapers, they travelled from town to town and absorbed the various cultures and information. Kings, nobleman, and the populace depended upon them for news, much of which was directly connected to survival. They were well-taken-care-of and afforded luxuries beyond the commoners. Bards were extremely popular until the time of John Dee. Queen Elizabeth I issued a declaration against them and stated them to be the worst sort of people who incited insurrection. Ever since, their position in society has never recovered. Bards were musicians, lyricists, and balladeers. The most exciting function they possessed, however, was that they were advertisers of adventure. Any young lad who wanted to go out and make a name for himself or just pursue the spirit of adventure would listen to the bard in order to find the way to his destiny. In the Middle Ages, there was no more exciting time than the arrival of a bard in town.

I was no exception to this excitement as I found myself following this crowd so that I could sit and listen to this great bard, the man they called the Bard of Bards. I knew this must be a very special story or piece of news because the elemental spirits were out in droves. What was he going to say? I was enthralled.

As I travelled with the crowd, the night wore thin and I began to see the first vestiges of day break. Seeing a glen in the clearing, I had to pass a narrow path in the woods which was guarded by those who looked like the Merry Men of Robin Hood. As I passed, one man held up his hand.

"Do you be of Scota?" he asked me.

"Yes," I said, knowing this answer was like a password which referred to the fact or legend that all Celtic people derive their heritage from Scota, the daughter of an ancient Pharaoh of Egypt.

"Then, welcome to the Emerald Isle!" he said as I passed.

The elemental spirits and little people were not asked such questions as they scurried to the glen ahead. The morning was now becoming quite bright as hordes of creatures of all types seated themselves amidst the dew-filled grass around a small lake with a large flat stone in front. There were dwarves, elves, undines, salamanders, and every kind of creature or little person you might imagine, except for hobbits. There were no signs of hobbits anywhere; unless, of course, they were invisible or watching from a hiding place. There were plenty of men and women around, too, and they began to cheer as a large group of bards approached from the distance. This was the moment they had all been waiting for. The bards were all dressed somewhat similar, most in buckskin of various colors and shades. They carried their various instruments as well. In the center of them was the Bard of Bards who was dressed in the most faded and drab buckskin garment of them all. He was, however, the most vibrant for he wore a very colorful foolscap with bells. I knew that this represented the Hebrew letter *shin* with its three flames. Over his buckskins, he wore a vest or breastplate which was studded with extremely ornate jewels and crystals. It was as if his drab dress was to offset the spectacular color of this jeweled garment. He also carried a mandolin. I sat near a patch of grass not far from where his entourage was now beginning to sit. I wanted to hear everything he had to say.

When everyone had taken their seats, all became silent. The Bard of Bards was seated as well, and this surprised me. It was as if everyone here was part of a congregation who were saying silent prayers, and I needed to get up to speed. As they sat quietly, a naked blue lady emerged from the small lake. She was perfectly shaped but littered with sprigs and the slime of nature. There was no mistaking, however, that she was of great beauty. As all the creatures held their heads down, I was the only one looking up at her. I felt that maybe I was doing something wrong and should not be looking, but she met my gaze and came toward me. There was no need for conversation as I could read her mind as she grabbed me by the hand and escorted me to the flat stone where I had expected the Bard of Bards to begin speaking at any time. I was completely taken by surprise. The message in her eyes was clear, but it did not completely dawn on me until all the creatures raised their heads and the Bard of Bards looked at me straight in the eyes. I thought I had come here to listen to him, but it was the other way around. It became most apparent that he and everyone else wanted to hear my story. I knew that, as a bard, he would immerse himself in my story, integrate it, and see that it would be absorbed into the world. After all, that is what bards do.

Standing before this teaming crowd, I was dumbstruck. It seemed as if every creature in heaven and on Earth had come to hear me. Beyond the creatures and surrounding the entire lake were black and white clouds of energy, some of which shaped themselves into devils and angels. Outside of these clouds were a host of all my ancestors who had ever lived before me. Alongside them were countless other souls who had lived upon the Earth. The message was very clear without anyone saying a word. It was time to tell my story, ready or not. It seemed as if the very universe would hang in the balance. Everyone wanted to know what I had to say.

INTRODUCTION

As this book is called *The Montauk Book of the Dead*, some explanation is due with regard to the title. Death is defined as "the total and permanent cessation of all the vital functions of a plant or animal." If you really think about it, this definition is oxymoronic and says more about the persons who composed the definition than it does about that state of existence that we commonly refer to as "death." Auspiciously absent from the above definition are the words *soul, spirit,* and *human being.* The word *animal* itself means "spirit." Of course, we all know that the dictionary definition is referring to physical death. The "vital functions" refer to the common medical definition of death, but there are certainly vital functions of life within the context of the morphogenetic grid that supercede normal biological functions. Since the beginning of time, there has always been a mysterious concourse between the living and the dead. Although the doors between these two worlds are sometimes very obscure, they are always there.

Traditionally, two of the most heralded books concerning death are *The Tibetan Book of the Dead* and *The Egyptian Book of the Dead.* Both of these books are dedicated to the proposition that your personal consciousness survives physical death.

The title of *The Tibetan Book of the Dead* is really a misnomer. Its original translation reads more like "The Way of the Great Liberation." It is generally considered by its fans to be a series of procedures for navigating your way to and through the various states of existence that come with the process of physical death. The most popular translation is aggravated by the fact that it is a Buddhist amalgamation based upon the original doctrines of the Bon tradition that are not easily translated to a Western mind. There are also those who would boldly tell you that *The Tibetan Book of the Dead* is a series of procedures designed to keep you in a controlled state of either virtual imprisonment or patriarchal servitude or something even worse. Whatever the case, the idea of a way of "great liberation" is certainly inspiring to the degree it suggests a state of beingness that is akin to a freedom beyond what we might ordinarily experience in a human body.

There is also *The Egyptian the Book of the Dead* which is a different book altogether. Based upon much rigmarole and ritual concerning embalming, the popular translation by Wallace Budge is either alarmingly misleading or more likely misdirected by a complete ignorance of what he is dealing with. Although blatant references in his own work suggest that the ancient Egyptians transmuted metals into gold by separating it from its native ore and producing a black powder with marvelous powers, the author never really explains what the ancient Egyptians were preoccupied with when it came to transcending or superceding the death state.

In Abydos, Egypt, the ground near the river was well known for its black dirt which possessed special properties. When this certain black ore was placed against gold, it was transmuted, by nature of the superconductivity present, into a powdered form. The ancients knew this as "occultum" because it had unseen (*occult* means unseen or hidden) properties which, to the uninitiated, seemed magical or miraculous. The preparation of this "magical" powder was known as "khemeia" which basically means black. It is from this process that we get the word *alchemy* (from *Al-Khemeia*) and the phrase "black magic." *

While the above easily becomes a separate study in itself, there is a much more important point that is to be gleaned from the original texts which would more properly constitute an "Egyptian Book of the Dead." First, the consumption of such powder, under advantageous circumstances, was eventually supposed to result in the activation of superconductive properties in the brain to the point where both hemispheres of the brain would link up and create a fully activated human being who could thereby access the full potential of human consciousness. Second, and perhaps more importantly, this activation led to a composed spiritual state that would even better serve the idea of that which could be called true immortality.

---

* More information on these subjects can be found in *The Black Sun: Montauk's Nazi-Tibetan Connection* by Peter Moon.

Whether or not these so-called "Books of the Dead" are right, wrong, good, or bad, they offer, at the very least, the prospect of a life after death. More than that, each suggests that a continuity of consciousness is possible.

Various authors and commentators have suggested that these ancient Egyptians and Tibetans knew a considerable more about death than we do today. If this is true, they certainly did not know how to or wish to communicate it in a preservable format that could be readily digestible to future generations for use as a handbook for finding one's way into and through the afterlife. The reason for this is that the process of death itself has been convoluted by various unconscious processes which have made the death experience perplexing for most of the human race. It is a grim subject. This book is designed to put you in concert with some of the natural rhythms of life and death so that you might awaken to your own inherent genetic memories. The more familiar that life and death become to you, the more natural will be your reactions and responses to Death, one of the most intimidating elements of existence.

There are also many other books about dying and the dead, some of which might prove helpful in dealing with the inevitable and others that are designed to spin you in. We are all going to meet our maker someday so perhaps it is a good idea to learn something about that state which we will someday transit to.

I think that one of the easiest ways to explain the principle of death is through the archetypal images used in astrology. In that reference frame, death is assigned to the Eighth House* of the zodiac which is the constellation known as Scorpio. This sign not only represents death but also sex, regeneration, and taxation. In astrology, subjects such as accounting, sex (including the sex trade), and morticians are all ruled by Scorpio. This is particularly interesting when you consider that conspiracy theorists will tell you, not incorrectly, that populations are controlled and manipulated through sex, death, and taxation. The Catholic Church is an excellent example in this regard. They tell people how and when to have sex and seek compliance through the threat of eternal

---

* In astrology, there are twelve signs of the zodiac and each represents a different division of the zodiac. Each division is called a house and represents different aspects of life.

damnation. Taxation comes in the form of tithes but also in payments for dispensation and absolution.

When you stand back and look through the lens of astrology, it is obvious that there are archetypal forces ruling the sinister aspects of churches that having nothing to do with what might be termed angelic elements. We get further insight when we realize that the "ruler" of the Eighth House of Scorpio is the planet Pluto which also represents the god of the same name.

Pluto, the ruler of the underworld or Hades (also the Greek name for him), is one of the most intimidating gods in the pantheon. When Pluto abducted Perosephene to his domain, not even Zeus, the most powerful of the gods, could have his way with him. Eventually, Zeus worked out a compromise whereby Perosephene would spend part of the year in the daylight.

Often misunderstood, Pluto is not really an evil god but is completely ruthless and merciless in carrying out his aims. When you have Pluto on the horizons, there is no fighting back because he represents the inevitable. The wisdom of Pluto teaches you to yield and deal with the unavoidable destiny of the situation.

The upside of Pluto is that he affords transmutation. In other words, he takes you from a situation where you are stagnant and no longer need to be and into a new situation where you can learn and eventually prosper from. This is regeneration. It could mean a new job, a new spouse or even a new life. It should not go unnoticed that, in Christian mythology, not even Christ himself could escape the realm of Pluto. Three days in hell were experienced before rising from the dead. He was purged of the sins of Mankind. Pluto, in that instance as well as others, stands at the gateway to "heaven." With Pluto, the principle of regeneration is invoked.

Pluto is not only considered to be one of the most powerful gods but one of the busiest. He purges and gets rid of elements in yourself that do not need to be there; hence, the concept of purgatory. It is not hard to imagine a cluster of souls who have just left the earth plane and made their way across the river Styx to the realm of Pluto. They are waiting in long lines as Pluto looks at their karma and does a mix and match. His ledger lists their assets and liabilities with regard to good deeds and bad ones. It is this hurried and chaotic mixture of energies at the gates of Hades that makes justice a sometimes haphazard commodity in the ordinary stream of life. Pluto looks at the ledger and assigns a particular individual to another or others who might balance the ledger, but there can be problems. Who shows up at the gate with you is determined by timing and various other factors which are sometimes random. Pluto has many ledgers to account for, and they do not necessarily get balanced in an instant or even in one life. Pluto is known as the plodding planet and the god of the same name certainly takes his time. While these unbalanced accounts might make for severe injustices on the earth plane, Pluto will eventually get around to balancing the scales. It is sometimes a very brutal truth, but it is the way this universe works.

It is this chaotic balancing of the ledger which also makes Pluto the ruler or the criminal underworld, secret societies, and anything that might be considered nefarious. This includes psychic crime as well for Pluto rules psychic ability. If you look around at the various injustices in the world that do not resolve themselves by routine or simple appeal to the duly appointed authorities, then look to the realm of Pluto. Doing this might not instantly resolve the situation, but you will at least understand the nature of what you are dealing with.

In this book, I will not only be giving you an initiation into the process of death but life as well. There is considerably more data to offer on the subject than what I have included here, but it is a tale to give you a new and different perspective. Hopefully, you will find it useful in your own process.

For those of you who are not already familiar with me, I burst onto the literary shelves in 1992 when I authored *The Montauk Project: Experiments in Time* with Preston Nichols. That is a bizarre story of both legendary and real events that took place at the Montauk Point Air Force Station in the 1970's and early 1980's. It dealt with all sorts of psychic phenomena which included one of the most spectacular nuts and bolts accounts of time travel to ever reach ink and paper. On the negative side, this time travel project exploited the mental and physical well being of many of the participants. Torture and brutality were utilized as a means by which to open up an individual's psychic powers.

Through bizarre twists and turns of synchronicity, I ended up as the scribe of the Montauk Project. In the past, however, I have only been able to offer abbreviated accounts of my personal life as well as the circumstances which brought me into a position to begin cleaning up the literal spiritual and physical holocaust that has occurred at Montauk Point. Since many people are preoccupied with thinking they were involved in such an endeavor as the Montauk Project, there have been many questions and even consternation over the fact that I have not claimed to be a part of it. There are, quite admittedly, aspects of myself that reach far beyond the bounds of most people's common references. The reason for many of these questions is that I have only been able to offer brief sketches of my past. This book will explain not only many of the odd angles that you do not know about but also the underlying theme of how I became involved with Montauk. Besides that, it will tell you a story that the world has not heard.

In addition to the Montauk Project, there is a whole other issue with regard to Montauk Point and that has to do with the fact that it is sacred ground that once housed ancient pyramids belonging to the Montauk Indians. Despite the vehement protests of the Montauks, the New York State Supreme Court declared the tribe extinct and colluded in an attempt to appropriate their most sacred land. Ironically, this very same land was used to house these unusual and ghoulish experiments. To this day, the land has not been returned to the Montauks.

Montauk Point is not the only sacred realm upon this earth to have suffered the consequences of trespassing or violation. In actual fact, most of you have suffered severe forms of this yourself. Much of this violation, however, is so subtle and insidious that you are not even aware of the full extent to which this has taken place. The story of Montauk Point is a grandiose illustration of the very worst elements that have peen perpetrated upon humanity, by "forces unknown," that have attempted to choke the highest aspects of consciousness. If you have the latitude to look into the depths of your own soul, you will certainly discover that these very same "forces unknown" have also reduced your own psychic abilities and personal power. This book is a story of how I came to recognize these "forces unknown" and, to a significant extent, overcame them. Death is man's greatest intimidator. It is something we all have to face. I hope this book increases your understanding of what should be a natural process and that it makes the process of death less intimidating for you.

1

IN DEATH'S GRIP

My story begins on the 15th day of December in 1974. I was living and working aboard a ship which was docked at Pier 59 in Los Angeles Harbor in San Pedro. It was a bright and sunny morning in the harbor and I was enjoying it, but I had no idea it would be one of the most riveting and influential days of my entire life. On that particular day, I was engaged in an activity that was an extreme rarity for me. In fact, I never recall ever having done it before. I was giving some people a tour of the ship. As I guided some people up a series of ladders to the ship's bridge, I was accosted by Dick Glass, a man I hardly knew at all. Dick told me that there were some people on the dock who wanted to see me. I told him that it would have to wait until I finished the tour, but he made it very clear that whatever I was doing would have to stop and that I must make my way down the gangway to see these people. As the tour was not really all that important, I relented. I had absolutely no idea who these people might be, but as soon as I arrived on the dock, I immediately recognized my father's cousin, Jacquie, and her husband, Tommy Anast. They lived only a short distance away in Palos Verdes and knew I lived on the ship, but there was no reason for them to visit me. I primarily remembered them from visiting their house on New Year's Day or at other times when I was a young child. Tommy then grabbed me, almost as if using a wrestling hold to keep me in a secure position.

"Son, your parents were in an automobile accident last night. They both died immediately."

There was complete finality in what he said and no mention of hospitals or gasping for their last breath. Looking back, I cannot imagine news that would have been much more shocking or devastating than that. Although I was in a state of shock, I was not in complete shock. Before I could react to Tommy's words, I heard a voice run through my head.

"I knew it!" were the words that went through my mind.

This was an unusual response, but I cannot explain it other than the fact that it was my response. In some strange way, it was as if my brain circuitry had expected it. Pluto was balancing the ledgers and this was the fallout. I did not think in astrological terms in those days, but on some level, my intuition told me that this was my destiny and that I should not be surprised. Perhaps it was sobering or fortunate that this moment afforded me a brief window into the fields of destiny, but there was also a very human situation to deal with and this included my emotions and that of everyone else who might be involved. I was only twenty-one years old and felt that this was the biggest slap in the face the universe could have given me. The two people who had loved me and cared most about my welfare were now gone. It was all over. My most immediate analytical thought was to realize how lucky I was that this had not happened at a time when I was younger and unprepared to deal with the rest of my life. I was now on my own, but it was, nevertheless, like receiving a knockdown blow — and a hard knockdown blow — in only the third round of a fight.

Death had not only arrived at my door but had arrived on his horse and reared at me. Not one death but two. No, it was not really like being hit with a knockdown blow. It was like being hit with two different fists at the same time and being hit hard.

Since that time, I was keenly aware that I began to view life different than most people. I have been extremely thankful for every minute and have never taken my day-to-day survival for granted. I have found this to be a big advantage in dealing with the changes and surprises that come your way in life.

My parents were gone, but I knew I still had a lot of living to do. There was no question of carrying on as I had a deep reservoir of energy inside of me. I knew my destiny made for a bright future, but no details were supplied. I had no idea, however, that I would end up, in some strange way, carrying my parents with me.

2

DAD

Although what is to be said here are long and distant memories, my interaction with my father helped shape my outlook and interests that would play a role in my later life.

If there is a simple way to describe my father in a few words, it would probably be "outgoing and friendly." People not only liked him, they liked him a lot, and I was no exception. My mother once said to me that she had never seen a boy like their father as much as I did. His work kept him from home a lot. He was a petroleum engineer for a French company known as Schlumberger (pronounced Shlum-ber-jay) and, consequently, one of the first things I learned about my fellow Americans was that they could not pronounce words too well. Everyone pronounced it "Shlumburger." Basically, this company was a competitor of Haliburton and serviced oil wells. My father's expertise was in evaluating drill sites to determine whether oil would be found or not.

As a rule, my dad did not get weekends off and was on call twenty-four hours a day and would often leave the house at two or three in the morning. His days off were scheduled to some extent, but they were staggered. As a young kid, I remember impatiently counting the days, waiting for him to be around. I missed him when he was gone. Although he was not around every day or weekend, he would make the most of his time with me. Consequently, I got to see a lot of Southern California. On the rare occasions when he could, he would take me with him on his job. That was always a great adventure.

27

More than anything, my father loved the ocean. He was a Scorpio. Growing up in La Jolla (pronounced *la-hoya* which means "the jewel" in Spanish) near San Diego, he spent much of his childhood on the beach where he surfed and rowed out on his small little skif to view the gray whales during their migrations. He took me fishing often and also to Marineland of the Pacific, the original aquatic park (now defunct), where he taught me the name and characteristics of any fish I could find in the tank. He rarely watched television; but when he was around in the early morning, he encouraged me to watch *Kingdom of the Sea*, a documentary style show about the ocean. At an early age, I knew a lot more about the ocean than most kids and even most adults. His interest in the ocean gave me an interest in the ocean.

Although he seemed to despise television, he did not forbid it in the household. There were only a handful of movies which I might somewhat facetiously refer to as "required viewing" by him. By this, I mean that he became so excited that he acted as a live commercial for watching them. His interest in television was so rare that you could not help from being infected by his enthusiasm. It also meant that you got to stay up late so that acted as an added enticement. These movies were *Moby Dick, Captain's Courageous, Mutiny on the Bounty*, and *The Endless Summer*. All were movies about the sea. The first three were classics while the latter was sort of a modern classic about two surfers who follow summer across the globe seeking to catch the perfect wave.

He also took me on several all-day fishing trips to Catalina Island where you would board a commercial boat just before midnight and go to sleep. When you woke up, it was just about five o'clock in the morning, the time when schools of large tuna would feed just off the northern part of the island. I was usually the only kid on board unless it was my best friend and next door neighbor, Greg Arcuri. On the return trips from Catalina, I remember sitting on the bow of the ship and enjoying the crashing of the waves, especially when it got rough. My father would come to the bow to make sure I knew to hold onto the rail so as not to be swept overboard. I also remember old salts coming up to the bow and standing there with me for a while. It was terribly rocky, but I was having the time of my life like it was a roller-coaster ride. They would look at me like I was crazy because they would start to get sick. It was the sort of fun that only a kid could enjoy.

When I was about nine, Greg and I would stay up late on Friday nights to watch reruns of *Sea Hunt* with Lloyd Bridges. It was our favorite show. Greg taught me to splash water on my eyes to keep from falling asleep. One of the biggest highlights of our youth was when our fathers took us to a tuna processing plant and a man told us we had just missed Lloyd Bridges. He was shooting a scene at the pier and had left about ten minutes earlier. Even though we missed him, we were very excited just to have been so close. When I finally had the opportunity to see Greg for the first time in about twenty years, he remembered the incident just as well as I, and we still laugh about it.

My father also spurred my interest in writing when he entered a writing contest and submitted a true story about his real life adventures with the sea. I do not remember the specific parameters of the contest, but it was supposed to be about real life experiences with fishing. To my family's surprise, he won the contest, and I remember going down with him to Pierpoint Landing in Long Beach to retrieve two free tickets for a fishing boat excursion. Even though I was pretty young, I remember thinking that my father probably won the contest for two reasons. First and foremost, he had a very rich history of real experience to draw from when it came to writing about the ocean. Second, I could not help but thinking that the fisherman I had seen might not be too literate or expressive in a literary fashion. My dad, who was a science major in college, told me that his only English class at U.C. Berkeley had been "bonehead English," the required minimum for all university students. I think that early conversations with him about "bonehead English" might have had a slight subconscious effect on the fact that I never entered college. I always thought of "boneheaded" people in an English class. I was not sure what a "bonehead" was at the time, but it did not sound like anything I wanted to be a part of.

While having a bowl of soup with him at a restaurant at Pierpoint Landing, I remember gawking at all the decor of the sea which included mounted fish, buoys, extensive netting, a mermaid or two, and other iconography of the sea. I enjoyed the mock atmosphere which I realized was far more suggestive than the sea itself. What most caught my eye, however, was a large and prominent statue of King Neptune himself. That completely captured my imagination. Asking him what it was, my father told me that Neptune was the King of the Sea. He knew all about Greek mythology as well as a host of other subjects.

If there was any early indication that I was to eventually become a story teller, it was through the sea. One day, my fourth grade class was given the assignment to read a book and give a verbal report on it. As this was not long after I had watched the "required" *Moby Dick* with my father, I came across a book called *The Story of Yankee Whaling* which was full of artistic depictions of the New England whaling days. I brought the book home but was not able to read it right away as he scooped it up and read the whole thing with utter enthusiasm. Most ardently, he shared with me the story of the *Essex*, a true life vessel which was purposely stoved (crashed into and sunk) by a killer sperm whale. This was the true story upon which Herman Melville based *Moby Dick*. The *Essex*, however, was stoved by a black sperm whale and not a white one. Only a few of the sailors survived, but they told a gripping tale of months at sea and how enforced cannibalism enabled them to stay alive. In the end, my father had inadvertently, through his own enthusiasm, done most of my homework. I did not have to read the whole book — I only had to give a talk on this subject. I got up in front of the class and just started relaying what was really a fascinating story. The class was completely spellbound. Looking back, I was simply relaying facts in an understandable manner. They just happened to be very interesting facts which involved high adventure with struggle and survival.

At that time, my father told me that we were now part of a small minority that knew the true history behind the novel *Moby Dick*. The story of the *Essex* was not known well at all at that time period, but it was known. In recent times, the *History Channel* has done a full hour documentary. If he were still alive, my dad would have been glued to the screen when that documentary aired.

After all of this, I decided that I wanted to visit the island of Nantucket, see the whaling museum and become a professional whaler. I wanted to go out on one of those whale boats and go for what was called a Nantucket sleigh ride. I could not imagine a more wonderful or adventurous profession. My father, however, explained that modern whale boats used a mechanized harpoon that did not give the whale an even chance. Saying it was cruel, calculated and brutal, he wanted no part of it and neither did I. I gave up my interest in whaling.

Although I loved the ocean, I loved sports even more. My father was an expert swimmer and was a life guard at the La Jolla beach when he was younger. He was a natural athlete but was not all that interested in other sports. He played football in high school and taught me all the rules. Football became my favorite sport. It was the only sport he ever coached.

My proudest moment with him was, however, during a father-son baseball game. After the little league season was over, we had a picnic and the fathers played the sons. We had a terrible team and had finished second to last, winning only seven out of twenty-one games. I knew, however, that we would cream the fathers. They were pathetic and did not have a chance. That is pretty sad, too, when you consider that we were mostly eleven and twelve-years-old. I am fifty-one now, and I doubt very seriously that my friends and I could be beaten by a team of twelve-year-olds. But, generations get stronger. Anyway, the game got off to a mundane start with us taking an easy lead. Soon, our coach's arm broke down and none of the other fathers could throw the ball over the plate. Again, they were pathetic. Finally, someone suggested my father. I just happened to be the batter when he came in to pitch. Although he was not a pitcher or even someone who had "baseball agility," he was an athlete and could throw the ball over the plate. I was only eleven and was not the best player on our team and was certainly not a power hitter. I hit the ball over everyone's head for a homerun. There was no question about it. Then, a couple of innings later, he came up to bat and hit a homerun in the exact same spot that I had. It went a bit farther and he hit left-handed while I hit right-handed. After he hit it, everyone on the entire field just turned around and looked at me in my position in center field. It was a very strange feeling. We were the only two to hit homeruns the entire day. The game in itself meant nothing to me as they were just a bunch of "old men" who should have been fitted for back braces or remedial exercise programs. He did not really give a damn about baseball, but that did not matter to me. On that team, he clearly stood above the other fathers. I felt I was the only kid who could go home that day with no reason to feel "ashamed."

3

SOUTHERN CALIFORNIA

Growing up in Southern California in the baby boom era was a lot of fun. There were plenty of children around the neighborhood, and I remember all of the fads of the times which included Davey Crockett hats, the Mickey Mouse Club, hula hoops, and the advent of skateboarding. As we outgrew rollerskates, we would nail them to boards and these were the first skateboards. While I can remember vast amounts of my childhood, I will stick to what might be the most relevant and formative events with regard to my life as it concerns the narrative of this book.

There were many kids in the neighborhood and a sense of community that I have never seen since. Many kids would gather, somewhat spontaneously, and play. I, however, was the youngest and was definitely at the bottom of the totem pole in terms of age and physical power. This allowed for a certain amount of abuse from older kids who could sometimes pick on anything smaller than themselves. The first thing I learned was that you were not supposed to "cry to mama." You could do it once, or maybe even get away with it a second time, but if you did it again, you would be ostracized and lose any sort of reputation or standing in the world of little boys. I learned after the first time. As the youngest of my peers, I learned to stay in the background as much as possible and not attract attention. This was my first challenge in dealing with social situations. I did not complain about the older kids and eventually emerged from that situation with a modicum of respect, not only from them but particularly for myself.

33

In baseball, I would always get my turn at bat but was always last and was expected to strikeout. Barely old enough to play, I was allowed to participate. This did not last long though because as I matured, I was very competent in athletics. It was fun to watch older kids change their opinion of you as they watched you literally grow up.

School was a completely different experience. The kids were completely tame compared to what I knew in my neighborhood and were not threatening in the least. They were not, however, particularly friendly. While I had plenty of friends on the block, I felt the kids at school were kind of uninspired. I never was very happy in school until the third grade when I could play kickball. In that game, I did very well and earned my way up a pecking order and became friends with older kids. It gave me a sense of belonging and made life a lot more fun.

In the first grade, we learned how to read. We were divided into five color groups. Red was for the smartest kids and blue was next. These red and blue kids went to school at 10:00 a.m. and left at 3:00 p.m. Reading was in the final hour. The rest of us went to school at 9:00 a.m. and left at 2:00 p.m. For us, reading was in the first hour. I was placed in the Orange group which was the third smartest group. Below that were Yellow and Purple. We all knew that the colors designated how quick we were. The teacher did not hide it. I was thrilled to be learning how to read, and I thought I was doing pretty good. I did, however, stutter something horrible when it came to the word "said." For some reason, I thought it should be "siad" but probably would have had a very easy time of it if the word was spelled "sed." One day, when reading aloud, I had too much trouble with this word and was just having a hard time. The teacher moved me to Yellow.

After school one day, I told my father that I was learning how to read and how excited I was about it. I showed him my school book and wanted to read to him. He did not say a word, but his look told me everything. It was almost a dirty look. Someone, presumably my mother via the teacher, told him that I was not doing very well. I was a remedial case. The family was not celebrating my new found ability to read and certainly not my enthusiasm for it. I did worse in Yellow and the teacher got fed up with my inability to vocalize what I was reading. I was then demoted to Purple and there were only two two kids in that group. Their names were Billy and Chuck and everyone knew they were the dumbest in the class, and now it was my turn to join them. Billy and I even shared the same birthday. Things did not look too good. I knew I had hit bottom, and although I was not pleased about my new status, it did not bother me. Putting me in Purple, however, did not help as I did even worse.

My mother, who was not an assertive person in the least, finally had enough. She heard from me about my adventures in Purple and was not pleased. Telling my teacher I was really a pretty bright kid, it was somehow worked out that I would go to school at 10 a.m. and be part of the Blue group in the afternoon. All of a sudden, I began to thrive. I was not only doing well in the Blue group, I was doing better than everyone. It was not long before I was in the Red group and challenging Laurie Guss for the best reading marks. She was the only Jewish kid in the class. Eventually, I surpassed her.

I was the only kid in the class who traversed all the different reading groups. I knew what it was like to be dumb, smart, and in-between. The only difference in my ability was that I did better when surrounded by intelligent kids and did horrible when surrounded by kids who were not getting it.

Although I eventually did well in reading, my report cards were nothing to brag about — not at all. I sometimes got very good grades in art, but that was about it.

From these experiences, I learned what it was like to be at different spots on the totem pole and not to feel bad or intimidated about my position. Everything, particularly intelligence, was relative.

4

IN TRANSIT

My memories of growing up in Southern California include the baroque architecture that it was so well known for at the time. Route 66, which is now the stuff of legend, was still the main passageway to the west coast. While Route 66 had plenty of baroque architecture itself, Southern California was the ultimate destination or Mecca for everyone who travelled that path. Although I was very young and had not travelled outside of the state other than to Mexico, there was no question that Southern California was the "great country." I heard people talk about it all the time, particularly those who visited our house. Most neighborhoods were routine, and so was ours, but no one could stop talking about the weather, the beach, the mountains and, of course, Disneyland and the various other amusement parks that were not so common in other parts of the country at that time. There was also an abundance of most anything you needed to buy. Your parents did not need to be rich to afford most of it either.

This was also the advent of the Beach Boys and what became known as the surf culture. Everyone idolized this sport and everyone wanted to be a surfer, even those who did not go to the beach. There were three distinctions. Surfer was the most esteemed term and referred to people who actually surfed. A gremi, short for gremlin, was someone who tried to surf but was still learning. They are called gremlins because they do not know proper etiquette and can get in the way or be downright dangerous to surfers or any others in the water. Worst of all was a hodad.

37

These were people who pretended to surf but did not. They were fakes. My father was a bit of a curiosity because it was known throughout the neighborhood that he had actually surfed prolifically as a young man. But, he was well past his surfing years. What was perhaps the most amazing thing about it was that he did it on balsa wood boards that he made himself. There were no skegs or fins on the bottom and they were accordingly hard to control. As for me, I could not even swim so I did not fit into any of the above categories, but I certainly remember them. During those years, one was supposed to wear a white t-shirt with Levis and no shoes. That was the cool dress code. If you had to wear shoes, you wore Parcells or Converse but only if it was necessary.

One of the saddest days in my life was June 27th, 1963, the day my family moved from Lakewood to the San Joaquin Valley desert about one hundred miles to the north. My father had been transferred to a town called Taft. I was well into the eleventh year of my life and was moving from an abundant suburban culture to a redneck oil town. Robin Williams starred in a movie called *The Best of Times* which parodies this town. Although the movie either pretends or seeks to be a parody, it is more like a real life documentary. Taft was originally called Moron until President Taft visited the town. It was named after him. This place was 100° in the summer and their fads or trends were two years behind the times. I noticed this as a kid and could never take the place too seriously. It was, however, in some respects, a haven for kids.

The schools were oil rich, and they hired the best teachers. The sports programs were abundant. As a kid, I never lacked for anything to do or kids to hang out with. My first day in the neighborhood, I was invited to play in a ball game by a kid who is still my friend today. Unfortunately, one of the other kids collapsed after a few innings because the heat was too much for his asthmatic condition. After spending a summer with kids in my new neighborhood, I entered the fifth grade which meant an entire slate of new kids. Fortunately, the kid who ran things when it came to sports took an immediate liking to me and decided I would play quarterback for our room's football team. We did not lose a game, and although I missed my old neighborhood something fierce, I fit right in and was having a great time, particularly from a sports angle. There was always something to do.

Although there were a few nice neighborhoods in the town, many people lived in old and somewhat dilapidated houses. Many of these kids were "inbred" in that their forbearers seemed to have lived in that town for at least a couple of generations and were not the top of the gene pool. There was not one black person in the town when I moved there. It was racist save for the fact that there was no one to be racist against. At one time, a Chinese man came to town and was doing door to door sales. He was an irritant to everyone but only because no one enjoys door to door salesman. One time, some of my friends and I were making mischief in the wee hours of the morning, and the police were called in as a result. While no one knew what we were up to, the police blamed the "Chinaman" and locked him up. We thought it was both sad and funny, but we were not about to volunteer ourselves.

Most of my friends came from decent families who were in the oil business or its related industries, but in Taft, I would sometimes be subjected to the most strange and backward thinking. It taught me a lot about how stupid human beings can be, and this is why I include it in my narrative.

I had a propensity to make fun of some of the backward ways of the townspeople and one day, in the eighth grade, I was offering too many unique opinions for one of my more "intelligent" classmates. I refer to him as "intelligent" because he did well on aptitude tests and got good grades, but he was not very cultured beyond the borders of Taft. Although he had known me and played sports with me for years, he could not deal with my opinions about the town, particularly when I started talking about the backwards ways of the adults. He started looking at me funny as if I were a foreigner and said, "Where do you come from, anyway?"

"L.A.," I said. L.A. referred to the greater Los Angeles area. If you named the individual districts, it could confuse them horribly. L.A. was just a term for "everything down there."

He then bolted away from me as if he was completely rejecting my answer. "No, you don't," he said. "People don't come from L.A."

I could not believe my ears. His horizons could not reach beyond the boundaries of this very small town. I thought his comment was one of the funniest things I can remember from my days there, and I have repeated it often. L.A. was just a place that you heard about or saw on television. It had no reality. In fact, for most people, there was not much reality beyond Taft.

Another time, someone had asked what I had done on a given Saturday. I said that I had gone to Bakersfield on the bus. Actually, I had spent a day there with one of my friends. We took the town bus, which was really a big van, and went to a nice pool hall for most of the day. The kid who had denied that I came from L.A. overheard the conversation and said, "You did not. People don't go to Bakersfield. And they don't take the bus to get there!"

The kid was not joking either. I knew he was not slow academically, but I was concerned about how the backward thinking of this small town had affected him. Some kids were far worse, and experiences outside the context of the town were not real to many of them.

Another very "Taft incident" occurred after I learned how to swim. My old neighbor, Greg, who I still visited at least yearly, got my dad to take him surfing. I was given no choice. Greg had already taught me everything I knew in sports, and now he was going to teach me surfing. I was given stringent lessons in his pool before we went out. Then, he gave me his board while my father guided me out on a rented board beyond the waves. It seemed like I learned an awful lot that day, but there was also a considerable amount of coaching and encouragement. Actually, I was not at all eager to go and was sort of being forced by my father and my peer. After riding a wave in on my belly, a strange thing happened. When I went back to go beyond the breakers, a wave hit me and while it knocked the crap out of me, it also miraculously turned me around and propelled me back towards the beach. Without having to put any effort into catching the wave, I was given a long ride whereupon I could stand up and do pretty much anything I wanted. Other than my first day, I have never experienced this nor seen anyone else experience it. The elements were right that day. It also taught me a valuable lesson. If you are trained to do something and trained to do it right, the elements will usually follow suit and enable you to do whatever it is you were trained to do.

The "Taft incident" I referred to above occurred a few months later when my father took me to the coast to ride some bigger waves. This time I was totally on my own and did very well. The waves were once again on my side. Other days, I did not have the same success. As I was not super proficient, I always thought that it had almost as much to do with the waves as it did with me. When we got home from this successful day at the coast, however, I was not inclined to tell anybody. In fact, I did not say a word to my friends or anyone. You have to realize, surfing was a very glamorized sport at this time. In the middle of the desert, it was even more so because there was no ocean nearby. I did not want to draw attention to myself. My father mentioned to some of the adults in the neighborhood that he had taken me surfing. He was not bragging about me as I was really not all that good, but he did mention it, in addition to the fact that I was proficient. Word got around the neighborhood faster than I could believe.

The next thing I knew, there were all sorts of kids around my house. Some of them were my friends and some were not. I came outside as I was wondering what all the fuss was about. It was like someone had actually touched on alien or something. I was completely taken aback and mystified at what hicks these people were. They were all debating whether I had actually surfed or not, like it was an impossible task as if I had just hit the lotto or been accepted to join the Beatles or something. After much disbelief was directed at me, someone claimed that my dad had said so. Then, they found my dad, asked him and he affirmed it. I was not saying much of anything but was just sort of standing there in disbelief. An adult, however, was somebody to be believed.

After hearing my dad, one kid said, "My brother is a star athlete. He tried it and couldn't. Therefore, he couldn't have."

The kids then pretty much shook their heads and agreed that I did not do it. It was not true. It could not be true. This did not bother me in the least, and I laughed uproariously on the inside. It was sort of like being in a looney bin and having all the inmates laugh at you because you claimed to have watched television when they are not allowed to and "know" that no one watches television.

Although it was funny, the mentality of this town began to weigh upon me. It seemed infectious. It came to a climax in the ninth grade when I was playing on Taft High's lightweight basketball team which consisted mostly of freshmen. We had an excellent team and were vying for the South Sequoia League Championship. Having lost only one game the entire year, a victory over Wasco would pretty much secure the title as they were our primary rivals. After taking the hour or so bus ride to the Wasco gymnasium, we soon found ourselves surrounded by black people for the first time in our lives. Besides us, there was only the varsity and a small contingent of others who had accompanied us. As I said, Taft was a redneck town and this was an unusual experience for all of us. I did not play on the first team and saw no action the entire game except from my perspective on the bench. The game was so close that the coach made only one substitution the entire game.

In the first quarter, one of the Wasco players got way too close to one of my friends, Danny. Danny had a mean streak in him, but worse than that, he had a propensity to come to games drunk. The coach did not notice this, and I was one of only a few who even knew it. Most of the kids in Taft did not start drinking that early, but he was getting a good head-start. When the Wasco player had encroached too far into Danny's space, his inebriated condition, coupled with his mean streak, caused him to significantly over react. Although a foul was immediately called on the other player, Danny pushed the player away vigorously and pulled back his fist, ready to strike. As he stood with his fist in suspended animation, the entire gymnasium, particularly the audience, was riveted with tension-packed emotion. None of the players, however, seemed to be too geared towards fighting at all. Players on both sides seemed intent on just playing basketball. I thought the whole affair was completely ridiculous. Danny had clearly over reacted. On the other hand, none of the Wasco players tried to intimidate our players after that. The Wasco players obviously did not want a fight either because they easily could have had one had they offered the slightest provocation. The game was very close, but we won by only a few points.

After such a game, we would normally watch the varsity compete. For some reason, and possibly to avoid potential altercations in the stands, we took the bus home early. When I returned to Taft, I rapidly made my way to a pizza restaurant because I was hungry. This place was a hangout but mostly for upper classmen. Freshman were to be seen and not heard and most were not expected to come to this place. It was still very early in the evening, and I did not expect any sort of crowd to be there. In fact, I was only planning to eat and depart rapidly. When I entered, I was surprised that the restaurant was full of older students. One of the upper classmen saw me and immediately slapped me on the back as a small cheer emerged from a table nearby.

"I hear you guys had a fight - way to go!"

Someone on the varsity had called and relayed the news about the incident in Wasco with Danny. Apparently, like in any game of telephone tag, the facts had been severely distorted. It had somehow turned into a full-fledged fight and we had gotten the best of them. Taft High also had a reputation that was , "We lost the game but won the fight!"

While there was something nice about being accepted by upper classmen, especially when freshmen were not particularly welcome, the news of a fight had brought out their camaraderie. The implication was clear. My road to becoming an eventual drinking buddy was paved with gold and handfuls of confetti.

Inwardly, another part of me was quite repelled. I could see the mentality of this town and wanted no part of it. After this experience, I realized that I very much wanted to get the hell out of this town. As much as I had enjoyed my life there up to that point, I did not want to be like these people.

As if by magic, I soon got my wish. My father was transferred to his company office in Sacramento. We were going to move once again. This time, I was eager for a new life. My trepidation about the mentality of the town of Taft was punctuated less than a year later. Within months after I left, the first black person in the history of the town was admitted to the high school. He was promptly abused, including physically, and had to leave the school for his own safety. While Alabama and Georgia were making international headlines for racial injustice, no one gave a rat's ass about the San Joaquin Valley, mostly because there were no vast numbers involved. I heard that many of my old class mates were very proud of the way this black person had been jettisoned from the school, but I was more than glad to be gone.

5

DEATH KARMA

Just before I left Taft, there was a peculiar incident that strangely propelled me on to my future destiny. This was actually a very close brush with death that demonstrated that the office of the god Pluto had been aroused.

At the beginning of the eighth grade, we were very much into our noon league football games. These were organized by the coach and we had referees, standings and the works. One day, a bunch of kids told me there was a new kid in school. He had just arrived and was leading a team to victory as he played quarterback. I was beckoned to come and watch him. His name was Mike Pigg. Mike was a good athlete, but I quickly realized everyone was overrating him. He was an oddity to us as the typical new kid was generally inept at athletics. Mike was different and we soon became friends as he was often available to play whatever sports my friends and I had going. We all liked him. There was, however, a very tragic story as to how he ended up in Taft. He had come there to live with his grandmother and go to school because both of his parents had recently died in an automobile accident. Nobody knew the full story, and it was obviously a very charged and sensitive topic. Although he mentioned it now and then, usually to explain to other kids why he lived with his grandmother, nobody dared ask details or circumstances. We were all curious, but no one wanted to push the envelope.

One day, it was either Palm Sunday or Easter Sunday, there was a pickup basketball game at the Catholic school which was located only a few blocks from my house and not far too from his. Around four in the afternoon, all of the other kids departed and it was just Mike and myself. We were both in the ninth grade and had known each other for a year and a half. Playing several games of horse (a variation of the game of basketball) together, we could hear the church bells in the background. We were not churchgoers in any sense of the word, but the topic of religion came up. Mike soon started telling me the entire story of his parents and how they had died in an automobile crash. For the first time, one of us was hearing the whole story. I felt kind of special that he was sharing it with me. When I later filled in some of the missing details for the other kids, they were amazed that he had come to me with the story. To this day, I do not even remember what he told me, only that he was sharing what must have been the most painful experience of his life. I think it made us better friends.

Fate would turn a very strange step soon after when he came to me in great secrecy. He wanted to tell me something very confidential and wanted to talk to me because he believed I was one of few who could keep a secret. He had watched a television show where an underage kid had snuck out in his father's car and went driving around the town. Mike figured that if an idiot like the kid on television could do it then so could he. He had taken out his grandmother's car and had successfully driven around the town. Now, he asked me if I would like to go with him. My father had already given me a few illegal driving lessons of my own at that point, and I was up for it. I decided to go out with him. The first trip was very smooth, and we had a fun time driving around. The second night, however, was fated for disaster.

We had driven way out into the country and picked up one of my old friends. After driving around with him for a good while, we discharged him. Then, we wanted one more drive. We would go to Maricopa, about seven miles away. I made two suggestions to him prior to that. One was very intelligent and the other was doomed. First, I said that we should put on our seat belts. That decision saved our lives. The second decision was that we should take the old road to Maricopa as we would be less likely to be observed. I thought that people might recognize us if they saw us in this small town. As we travelled along at about 60 m.p.h., I told him to turn down the radio and was about to tell him to slow down.

Before I could say a word, he hit a soft shoulder and the car began to whirl off the road and rolled. As the car rolled over and over, I was quite aware. My thinking processes were highly alert, but I had no idea how I would come out of this accident. You feel pretty helpless and in the hands of fate when going through something like that. Eventually, the car rolled to a rest and we were hanging upside down, secured by our seatbelts. It was quite surreal. I was later told the car rolled two and a half complete times. It seemed like more than that. The car was totalled.

As I hung upside down, suspended by my seat belt, my first words to Mike were, "Are you all right?"

As I spoke, the identical words came out of his mouth. He was quite OK. My knee had banged hard against the door handle and it hurt but was not unmanageable. It was a bit of a challenge dislodging the seat belt while hanging upside down. He could use the steering wheel to grab onto and got out much easier. I do not remember if he helped me or not, but I soon got out of the seat belt and fell to the roof of the car. There was plenty of broken glass around, and I had never been so dirty in all of my life.

My knee hurt but that was not about to stop me from walking home the two miles or so we had to cover. As we made our way through the tumbleweeds, we contemplated what story we should tell. Mike swore that he would make no mention of me and that I did not have to tell my parents or anyone else. He would cover for me. While I thought that was quite noble of him, I told him it was not necessary. I did not see any way around it. I was just glad we were both alive. As we departed that evening, his last words to me were that he would cover for me.

When I got home, I immediately told my mother what had happened. I did not even bother to think of an excuse for how else I could have gotten so completely dirty. She was just happy that I was alive and had escaped serious injury or death. A hurt knee was a small price to pay for that.

Within an hour, a highway patrolman came to the door and wanted to talk to both me and my mother. He said that Mike had confessed the whole story to him. I was glad that I had told the truth. The officer was very nice and just wanted to impress upon me the seriousness of what had been done. I needed no lecture at that point.

In what was one of the most bizarre and synchronous events of my entire life, Mike and I had been brought together in time to dance with the fates our own parents would suffer from. His parents had already died in a car crash. Mine were to die some six years later. Oddly, it was I he chose to confide in within earshot of the church bells. The incident would have likely have led to our deaths had it not been for my foresight to strap on the seatbelts.

The local newspaper ran the story as a headline, and I received the most celebrity status I had ever known. It was ridiculous. People on the block would stare at me. Kids at school, all of who knew me or knew who I was, would react with all types of different reactions. Mostly, all I heard was how their parents would have beaten the shit out of them if they had done that. I was even given many details of how their parents would beat them. As I heard these tales, I realized how lucky I was. My parents would not even think about beating me. They were not so stupid.

What my father did do, however, was ground me to the premises for two weeks. The specific rules, set by him, were that I could have friends over but could not go off the property. As most evenings were dedicated to homework and television, this was not a brutal punishment. This grounding actually resulted in a very fun moment when a rather huge gathering of kids came around to my house. I am not sure whether they came to rubberneck at the town's latest celebrity or it was just one of those days when all the kids got together. My driveway was the preferred place to play whiffle ball but never had so many kids showed up to play. We organized the game so I could pitch for my team without being outside of the property line. It worked great, and we were enjoying a tremendous game when my father appeared from the side gate. Everyone became uptight as they feared the game might abruptly end. He looked at me and the entire scene quite carefully. He could obviously see that I was not violating his rules and that I was well within the boundaries he had set. It was clear, however, I had violated the entire spirit of his rules as we were not only having a great time, I was escaping the effects of the pronounced punishment. Nevertheless, he held to his word, and I always admired him for that.

6

DAVIS

Getting my wish to leave the backward town of Taft, my father
decided we should live in Davis, only a ten or twelve minute drive
from his new office in West Sacramento. At that time, Davis was
a small bedroom community but was better known as the location
for one of the premier campuses in the University of California
system. Primarily known for agriculture and animal husbandry,
including genetics, UC Davis was also the second largest pocket
of academic liberalism in the state, Berkeley being the first.

My father's motivation in moving to Davis was that their
school system had an excellent reputation. For me, moving to this
town was an abrupt culture shock. It seemed as if every other kid
at school had a professor for a father and that there had been a
telepathic transfer of data from father to son or daughter. The kids
were unusually smart, but more than that, they parroted tomes of
information about all sorts of cultural phenomena, much of it
having to do with the environment and the politics of the 1960's.
I was not particularly interested in any of these rantings or
information streams, but one thing was exceedingly clear to me.
Never had I seen or been surrounded my so many intelligent people.

Davis was the most snobbish atmosphere I had ever known
and making friends was not just difficult — it seemed literally
impossible. Additionally, I never had such a difficult time in
school. The students had been the recipient of innovative teaching
methods by university professors, but these tended to leave new
students in the dust. As a result, the counselors told me that I was

not expected to do too well. After struggling for a semester, I began to catch on. As a result of no social life, which was an abrupt change for me as well, I began to bury myself in reading. Instead of reading about Mickey Mantle or Willie Mays, I began to read science fiction and that introduced me to philosophy. For the first time, I became seriously interested in something besides sports. My favorite was Ray Bradbury and reading his book, *The Illustrated Man,* gave me my first inspiration to become a writer.

I immensely enjoyed his first story in that book. It was called *The Veldt,* but it was the second story in the book, *The Kaleidoscope,* which changed my life forever. That story is about an astronaut who becomes marooned in space when his equipment fails. He is doomed. Everyone at the control center knows he's doomed and so does he. But, in the meantime, he is being treated to one of the greatest light shows of all time. He is seeing the cosmos with all of its nebulae, comets and stars shows. It is not only the aesthetic view of a lifetime but the greatest show "on Earth." The astronaut chooses not to acknowledge his dire straits and not only enjoys the show but enjoys it with the enthusiasm of a kid. Reading that story gave me my first taste of what immortality must be like. The astronaut knew he was doomed in a physical sense, but he never let it bother him. Bradbury, however, was not stating that the astronaut was immortal, but that is certainly the artistic effect the story had on me. Those experiences told me, in some way or some form, that I could live forever.

I continued to read science fiction and improved in school. As spring time rolled around, one of the kids in my geometry class, Tor, asked me to play to baseball. He had moved to Davis a couple of years earlier and was new to the town as well. Besides being tall and athletic, he was extremely good at organizing games. After the first time I played with him, I remember him telling me that he was surprised at how good I was. Actually, he was far better, at least in terms of demonstrable results. He hit a lot of home runs. At basketball, he had height and strength over me. In football, we one time made the mistake of playing tackle. No one could tackle Tor. There was one thing about him though. I could always tell that if I was playing in a really competitive league that I would end up doing better than him. Why? Because he had no killer instinct. Tor was congenial and very friendly.

The summer of '69 consisted of scrub baseball games punctuated by the lunar landing of Apollo 11. The first man on the moon was very exciting, and I continued reading science fiction. At this time, I was reading *2001: A Space Odyssey*, and I was very interested and excited about Mankind overcoming its ordinary limitations. I was particularly interested in *2001's* author, Arthur C. Clarke, because he took an extremely pragmatic and scientific view in his novels. They were based in the reality of technology and human conditions but also probed probable and possible potentialities as Mankind evolved. *2001* represented, from a conventional world view, the most evolved aspect of man: reaching out to the ultimate frontier as represented by the planets and the stars. The ultimate evolution in that story was the astronaut being subjected to quantum reality and a time-line senior to the ordinary earth experiences we know in three-dimensional reality.

Most of my baseball friends were very interested in the philosophical and social circumstances of life and this included the cutting edge of science fiction. Although I did not read many of the great tomes written on philosophy, I talked and learned about them from others and tried to digest the most sensible elements of existentialism and whatever else was available. I was not at all interested in the power politics of Niccolo Machiavelli. To me, this was a game of corruption and fat cats that I wanted no part of.

As the years progressed, my friend Tor went from being a kid with longer and longer hair to a full-fledged hippie. Well, maybe he was not a real hippie. It is hard to call someone who lives with their parents a real hippie, but he tried hard. In Davis, one was surrounded by hippies, but these were definitely a derivative of the core hippies in San Francisco. To me, hippies will always be familiar entities, but you seldom find them any more. They are almost extinct. I never minded them, but I never wanted to be one either. The problem had to do with what I perceived as a stereotyping of personalities. Most of the people in that era where emulating or conforming to an idealized stereotype of a "hippie" that was permeating the morphogenetic grid at the time. People were not thinking for themselves but were simply following the trends of a subculture. It was chic to be hippie but not if you looked beyond the obvious. Most of the so-called "hippies" of that era have turned into comic parodies of what they once decried.

As Tor aspired to be a hippie, drugs became a part of his life. I smoked marijuana with him on several occasions, but that was as far as I wanted to take it. He was living proof that marijuana was a gateway to other drugs, and I was proof that was not. Eventually, he started taking PCP, also known as angel dust, which is some of the nastiest stuff anyone can take. At that time, we knew it as horse tranquilizer which was in ample supply at the veterinary school at U.C. Davis. It was a popular drug in Davis, but I wanted nothing to do with it.

Tor and I both finished our graduation requirements by January of our senior year so we did not have to attend the second semester. Almost every morning, we jogged to the basketball courts at U.C. Davis and played basketball to keep in shape and have something to do. I had hoped during this time period that I would begin my own writing career, but I soon discovered that this was a tremendous waste of time. I knew that whatever I wrote was not going to meet with any publishing success. I was under no illusions or deceptions. Anything I wanted to write would be too unconventional for a conventional publishing house. Therefore, I wisely gave up the profession of writing, at least for the next twenty years.

One day, shortly after we had graduated in January, Tor asked me to attend a lecture on Scientology. He was curious about it and wanted to know if I would come along. I had only an inkling of what Scientology was at that time. They always announced their weekly lectures in the religious section of the local paper and were a curiosity to me because they were one of the very few religious organizations in Davis that were not Christian. That interested me.

The only other mention I had heard about Scientology was in a magazine article someone at school had shown me a few months earlier. It was a magazine like *Life* or *Time*, but I do not specifically remember. It featured a prominent picture of a pair of soup cans and indicated Scientology was based on a belief of holding soup cans or something like that. I could immediately tell that the article was completely ridiculous and that it was not telling you anything about what Scientology might be. It was common knowledge to high school students in Davis that the media was highly prejudiced and dishonest. I just thought the entire affair was stupid, but I was not interested in reading about soup cans. Whatever Scientology might be, I was not interested in it either, but I was quite sure it had very little to do with soup cans.

Looking back, Tor was probably persuaded to attend that Scientology lecture by Mark Hayward. Mark was our student psychology teacher who was working on his teaching degree. Besides being a university student and a Scientologist, Mark played on the university basketball team. Tor was taller than me and Mark was much taller still. Although I have never really enjoyed the game of basketball too much, I always admired anyone who could be a starter on a college basketball team. It was extremely competitive. Mark was a very upbeat and a successful sort of personality. He was quite likable.

One day, not too long before our graduation, Tor was asking Mark about Scientology. The only thing I remember Mark saying was that they had great procedures to get rid of pain. For example, he was going to have a counseling session in just an hour to prepare him for a trip to the dentist. He indicated that the procedures would take away all the psychic trauma associated with going to the dentist. That not only sounded like a novel idea to me, but a great idea. It did not, however, cause me to be interested in going to a lecture. Only when Tor called me up and asked me to come along with him did I feel interested. If anyone is upset that I eventually became involved in Scientology, it is Tor's fault. If it were not for him, I would never have become involved. Tor never became involved in Scientology himself, and he abruptly died only two years later. I do not know why he came to this planet for such a short time, but it was obvious why he came into my life. Pluto was balancing the ledger and Tor was doing his bidding. I was destined to become a Scientologist. This was not an appellation I would have ever wanted for myself as I am far too much of an individualist to want to be labelled by that or any other tag. Although I regret the appellation, I do not regret the experience.

7

THE THRESHOLD

The first Scientology lecture I attended was given by Robert Vaughan Young, a Ph.D. who had been teaching at U.C. Davis. Vaughan, as he was known, eventually became a prominent figure in Scientology scandals when he had a falling out of rather huge proportions with the Church. I was, however, meeting him two decades before all of that happened. If you want, you can read all about his bitterness on the internet as he has written prolifically about his experiences in Scientology. Some of his bitterness is misplaced and some of it is not. In the end, before he died of prostate cancer, his friends said that he was in relative peace with regard to the subject.

My most poignant memory from that first lecture with Vaughan was this very strange guy in the audience. He had bug-eyes and a very round face and wore long hair. Dressed in overalls, he did not really look like a hippie but more like the crazy or wayward son of a farmer who liked the hippie look. He was not the kind of person you would want to hang out with. When the question and answer period came, this person got a gleam in his eye and said that he heard that the real truth about L. Ron Hubbard was that he came from outer space and that he was here to change the earth or something. Although this character was extremely comical in some regard, I remember thinking he was more "fucking nuts" than anything else.

Vaughan replied that Ron was born in Montana and that he was a regular human being. Actually, Vaughan was wrong about

Montana. Ron was born in Nebraska. Although it is not a very important point at all, I always thought it was odd that Vaughan said Ron was born in Montana and not Nebraska. At the time, I had no idea who Ron was, let alone the place of his birth, but I never forgot what Vaughan said. He seemed to be careless with his facts. Maybe the guy in the overalls is to blame. He created a definite impression on all of us.

After the lecture, I asked Vaughan a few questions, but he would not answer any of them. He just said to read the book *Dianetics: The Modern Science of Mental Health.* Although it was not stated so harshly, Scientology policy states that potential parishioners are not really worth pursuing or bothering with unless they can read that book. If one cannot read or get through that book (at least the first two books within that book), they are not going to be interested enough to even participate in the subject. It is supposed to be a dividing line. Of course, this policy was not always followed. Disreputable people would sometimes tell people all sorts of strange things with false promises. This was never supposed to occur, but human beings have a great way of mucking things up. Scientologists were never an exception. As in any group, there are good and bad people.

I took Vaughan's advice and read the book. The book was all about the theory of an engram, a moment of pain and unconsciousness that shuts down the thinking or analytical part of the mind. Further, it proposed the theory of a Reactive Mind, a part of the mind that operates in a simple stimulus-response fashion. The Reactive Mind is very suitable when it comes to running from a dangerous animal or fire. But, when it is influenced by painful or unconscious moments from the past, it takes on a life of its own and can seriously muck up the analytical functioning of the normal mind.

As a result of reading the book, my entire interest at that point was only in the subject of Dianetics. I would soon learn that Dianetics and Scientology, at least in the mind of Scientologists, were two distinctly different subjects. Dianetics meant "through the mind" and was meant to deal with any psychosomatic illnesses or discomforts. Scientology, on the other hand, dealt with the spiritual aspects of being. Spirituality was a foreign subject to me and of minimal interest. I was, however, readily cognizant that there were hidden areas in the human mind, and I was as curious as hell as to what might be there lurking in my own mind. Dianetics offered a potential answer. This was the first system of theories that I had ever heard of that even approached the subject, let alone offered a system of techniques for getting at the occluded portions of the human mind. Although this could be called occultism because it deals with occluded portions of the human mind, there were no particular occult appearances to the organization itself. There were, however, plenty of hippies and beatnik types, but this was standard fare for this particular town in Northern California at that particular time period.

As I was interested in learning more about Dianetics and receiving their counseling procedures to get at the hidden portions of the mind, I went back to the Scientology center on Olive Drive in Davis and told them I had read the book. I was then told that if I was really interested in pursuing this subject, I should take their introductory Communications Course. It was only fifty dollars then, and I believe it is still fifty dollars to this day. There was no high pressure sales or anything. It was just, "If you're really interested, take this course. Otherwise, don't bother."

Getting onto this course took me no time at all. My mother was happy to give me the fifty bucks for the course. Tor was interested in taking the course, too, but he could not come up with the fifty bucks. As the months rolled by, I found this quite significant. He could easily come up with the money to pay for his burgeoning drug habit, but he could not come up with a lousy fifty dollars which would allegedly improve himself.

The Communications Course was very simplistic. It consisted of learning the basic theory of communication which is basically nothing more than two terminals or viewpoints relaying information back and forth to each other, the proviso being that each actually receives, properly duplicates, and acknowledges that the ideas were actually heard and received. There were many drills dedicated to bringing this home to the student. There was no coercion involved, but one had to exert a considerable amount of discipline in order to break one's own self-ingrained habits with regard to communication. Many of you might think that you or the world have no problems with communication. After all, everybody does it, and there is now all kinds of technology to communicate with; however, a true examination will reveal that most of the world operates at a very low level of communication. Governments across the world are notorious for their inability to communicate with common citizens and address routine concerns. Common courtesy is sometimes the exception rather than the norm.

The most fun aspect of the course was that the supervisors or fellow students would try to make you laugh or break your concentration. This was highly entertaining, and I laughed probably harder and longer than I had ever laughed in my entire life. Although this was not the purpose of the course, it was an absurd and noted highlight.

One of the purposes behind these drills was to enable a counselor or auditor (in Scientology, an auditor is one who asks questions and listens in order to resolve situations) to listen to another without reacting. If a person tells you something horrendous or highly embarrassing about themselves, you had better not laugh or react in any way if you are honestly seeking to help them. The slightest reaction can not only turn them away from wanting to deal with you, it can turn them off subconsciously.

Many people did the Communications Course, enjoyed it and never moved a further step into Scientology. Most everyone I knew who did the course found it tremendously useful in dealing with the ordinary communications in every day life. In my personal life, I noticed that I could all of a sudden get responses out of people that I would not have gotten before. My ability to communicate in situations improved dramatically.

The Communication Course in Scientology was not only designed to teach you to communicate, but it was loaded with references to Scientology and was meant to give you an appreciation of the subject. That was all well and fine I suppose. I do not remember any sales pressure of any kind although you did receive a lot of attention. One was there to learn a subject. The supervisors were primarily there to ensure you understood the communication drills. If opportunities came up when you had questions, they were also quick to help you with answers with regard to Scientology or life in general. Still, this all seemed to be getting in the way of where I wanted to go: getting at those occluded or hidden aspects of the mind. Although I did not appreciate it at the time, this course system was set up to prepare me for such.

8

FREAKOUT

Before I go any further with this narrative, I want to clarify a
very important point with regard to the subject matter being
covered because it can make people react quite viscerally as well
as irrationally. If you are going to penetrate hidden layers of
consciousness, like I was hoping to do, it stands to reason that there
is a censor or something that prevented you from finding out about
them in the first place. Therefore, whatever method is successful
in such an endeavour is going to be subject to a visceral reaction
by reason of the "gray matter" that is working for the censor. It
does not matter whether it is Scientology or something else.

Before I address that point any further, however, I would like
to refer you to some comments made by Joseph Campbell, the late
professor who is best known for his extremely popular video series
where he is interviewed by Bill Moyer on the subjects of mythology and religion. In one of these interviews, Campbell stated how
the divine manifestation we know as God has often been depicted
as a monster force which wrecks all harmony and common
standards of ethics. This is not only true in mythology but can be
read in the Holy Bible when God manifests the flood as well as
many other hardships for man. Campbell does not say that this is
the only manifestation of God but that it is one that humans have
had to contend with since the beginning of Western history.

If we really want to understand this monster force, it behooves
us all to study a little bit about the very nature of monsters or at least
their destructive aspect. While I do not intend to write about

monsters per se in this particular book, it is very important to address certain trigger words and issues which people have often interpreted to either be or act as monsters. By "trigger," I am referring to that which makes people react viscerally. This applies not only to the destructive aspect of God or gods but to anything which might compromise the censorship to the hidden or unfulfilled aspects of your consciousness. It is for this reason alone that the words "Dianetics," "Scientology," and "L. Ron Hubbard" can cause such agita. Whether or not they are fraudulent in themselves is beside the point. Part of the reaction to these words is caused by the fact that they represent that which could destroy the censor. There is also, quite genuinely, a "monster aspect" to these words as numerous people have quite passionately and vehemently complained that they have utterly destroyed people's lives.

While his adherents might either bristle or laugh at the suggestion of Hubbard being a monster, there is no question that he has been portrayed as such by various critics and media sources. L. Ron Hubbard is a name which excites more controversy and opinions than most world leaders. While I cannot personally vouch for the various claims that Hubbard or Scientology have ruined lives, nor is it my role to engage in specific judgements here, we can all easily agree on one thing. These people and/or the media sources who cite such travesties have perceived a destructive or monster force which ruined them of someone else. In public relations, perception is everything. More importantly, we should be more concerned with the actual "monster force" than with what people say about it. If victims understood or correctly perceived this monster force in the first place, it is unlikely that they would have been too adversely affected or perplexed by it.

Personally, I can relate to all of this quite well because my writing career and reputation has been defined by writing about such trigger words and experiences that undermine the censorship to the hidden aspects of consciousness. This encompasses the Montauk Project and mind control as well as a host of controversial figures that not only includes Hubbard but also Preston Nichols, Aleister Crowley, Jack Parsons, and Marjorie Cameron. All of them have been considered "monster forces" in their own right.

In the case of Preston Nichols, his theories and experiences with regard to time phenomena and mind control have either enlightened, amazed, perplexed or offended anyone who has read them. In spite of being one of the more gifted and intelligent people in the military industrial complex, more than a few have referred to him as crazy. The press, however, has primarily ignored him. For the better part of a century, Aleister Crowley has been fanatically described as the wickedest man in the world. Although his most ardent critics will usually concede that he possessed an aptitude for scholarship and occult knowledge, most authors never miss the opportunity to point out that, as an individual, Crowley was prone to petty quarrels or invoking terror, curses, or ill will upon his adversaries. They often refer to him as a satanist, but he is not often, if ever, particularly labeled as insane.

Jack Parsons, who is probably the most idealized and enigmatic of these characters, is generally portrayed as a dark and brooding figure by the popular press. The fact that he was a brilliant rocket scientist who could actually make things work is almost overlooked in comparison to the misperception that he was overwhelmed by dark forces which consumed him or that he succumbed to "devil worship." Despite these portrayals, he is seldom referred to as being insane.

As the forerunner of (and arguably being the reason for) the modern goddess movement, Marjorie Cameron was often portrayed as a witch or suffered from sensationalized reporting which sought to label her as the "Whore of Babalon." Although she was often ostracized, she tended to thrive on this belligerent recognition of herself and her life's artistic statement. She was, however, never really attacked as being "insane."

When we come to the proposition of L. Ron Hubbard, the derisive appellations take on an intensity that is rather unmatched with regard to modern media. We find that the implication and assertion of insanity goes off the meter dial. In fact, if you do a search on the internet, you will find that Hubbard's critics are far more zealous than all of the aforementioned people put together — by far. In fact, I dare you to find anyone on this earth who has been so feverishly and passionately criticized in a public forum. Not even Osama bin Laden or Saddam Hussein have been so zealously sought after in terms of criticism. Part of the reason for this is that Americans have already made up their mind about these individuals and the jury is no longer out on them. Although Hubbard has long since passed away, there is still a considerable amount to be won or lost with regard to his legacy and ultimate judgment. The reason for this is that he left behind a very formidable and powerful movement which is known as Scientology.

Scientology, like any organized religion, is concerned with a battle for men's souls. As that battle concerns your soul, or at least the people in your environment, it might behoove you to learn about it from all angular perspectives. That includes both the positive and the negative. After reading much of what has been said about Hubbard on the internet, I have never seen anyone portrayed as such a complete lunatic. In fact, his critics and non-supporters have created a character that defies any reasonable probability. On the other hand, his supporters and enthusiasts also portray somebody who defies any reasonable probability. Although it would take an encyclopedic volume to make a learned and instructive treatise that would add appropriate relevance to all of the commentaries made about him, that is a worthless endeavor. As far as helping you understand L. Ron Hubbard and who he actually was, I have two characteristics which give me an extreme advantage over typical authors or journalists. First, I actually experienced L. Ron Hubbard. This is something akin to the difference between experiencing warfare on the front line and reading about it in a magazine. Secondly, I do not suffer from any bitterness nor am I in denial about any of his actual or perceived personal shortcomings.

Whether or not Hubbard was a lunatic, there is no question that he has been perceived as such and everyone is entitled to their perceptions. Once again, perception is everything. But, whether or not he was a lunatic, everyone can readily agree that he was an extremely powerful man who built a vast empire and commanded attention in a rather unprecedented manner.

As I want to be sympathetic to all possible viewpoints, I do not feel that it behooves me to convince you that he was either a lunatic or was not one. In either case though, a stern judgment does not really enable one to perceive the whole essence of who this man was. Instead, I would like to focus your attention on how this man attracted millions of followers and why he is the object of much adulation to this very day. Even the densest of his critics would readily admit that he offered a "psychic candy" to lure others away from an ordinary life and into the world of Scientology. For every person who ever entered Scientology, and there have been millions of them, there is a different story to tell. Most authors on this subject tend to have a scatological approach towards this subject. There is plenty of waste matter to go around and while it does have its relevance at times, I am not too interested in it.

Hubbard's confessed admiration of Aleister Crowley and his historical involvement with Jack Parsons and the Babalon Working has caused sensationalistic journalists to attribute him as either being associated with or identified as the Beast of the Apocalypse. This concept makes for an absolutely great cartoon and certainly one that many of you will find very amusing. I have been greatly amused by it myself at times, but it really is a severe distortion of the truth. There is, however, an underlying association and truth behind Hubbard's identification with the Beast that has not receded with the tide nor even been successfully swept under the carpet. Perhaps this is because we are dealing with the "monster force," and the Beast could certainly qualify as a monster.

If you were to do a thorough investigation of all of the people whoever worked with or experienced L. Ron Hubbard or Scientology, you would collect a vast amount of information that would extend to two opposite extremes. Out of this collective would emerge at least two completely different characters. One we could call "Ron," the affable adventure hero and friend to Mankind who developed unprecedented mental technologies that can give man spiritual freedom. The other character could be called the "Anti-Ron," a crazed manic personality who sought total power over others and used the most ruthless and diabolical methods imaginable.

There are plenty of other appellations that could be attached to either "Ron" or the "Anti-Ron," but you get the idea. While others can argue about what his true legacy actually is, the above is the legacy of what others (adherents and detractors) have attributed to him. It is a great lesson in polarity. If we want to extend our sympathies as wide and far as possible, we must realize that all of the experiencers of Ron or the Anti-Ron had a valid experience. They are entitled to their respective viewpoints in the quantum sea of existence. As far as my personal viewpoint goes, I have seen both his adherents and his detractors mis-assess him in the extreme. In either case, however, I do not think that either his critics or his adherents would deny that he fit the definition of Joseph Campbell's description of a monster force that could completely ruin people's concept of harmony and ethics. I know that neither he nor his supporters would have considered that a bad thing because they all believe in radical change. .

The aforementioned people I have written about are interesting because they are all a representative part of a highly complex but very key functionary aspect of our matrix. L. Ron Hubbard's emergence as an integral player in this regard has been noted, but his full role has never been well examined or delineated. The fact that this component part of existence has been, for the most part, obscured from view, explains why the subjects surrounding it have met with such controversy. Scientology, as well as the antecedents from which it came, fit right into this category.

The fact that L. Ron Hubbard emerged from his forays into the occult world with so much temporal power suggests that his role embraced components beyond that of his colleagues. That there was an all-out war to obtain the rights to his legacy is just one testament to the power he is deemed to have possessed.

With this perspective in mind, I will now continue my narrative of how I ended up becoming involved with him.

9

DIANETICS AND SCIENTOLOGY

Personally, I never freaked out about the trigger aspects of Dianetics and Scientology. The theories presented were sometimes very unfamiliar to anything I had ever heard of and hard to swallow, but the psychic candy offered was worth pursuing. After all, I wanted to find out about the hidden aspects of the mind.

At some point during the Communications Course, I learned about what Scientologists call the Gradation and Awareness Chart. This was an elaborate chart of the different levels of training and processing in both Dianetics and Scientology. The left side of the chart was all about training. In Scientology, training refers to the information and learning necessary to become a professional and effective auditor. Processing is depicted on the right side of the chart and this refers to the various levels of procedures or processes that are administered to an individual. Essentially, it was an ornate map of conquering the negative effects of the mind which lead to potential vistas of spiritual empowerment. It was obvious that a lot of thought went into the chart. There was about twenty years of direct experience behind it as well, for better or for worse.

Negative literature on Scientology sometimes admits there are saving graces to the Gradation and Awareness Chart which is known as the Grade Chart to Scientologists. The worst information I have seen with regard to this chart was in an ad for the book *L. Ron Hubbard: Madman or Messiah?* by Bent Corydon. The ad for this book claimed that prospective Scientologists were routinely told that if they did Scientology, they would be able to see 360° around their bodies without the use of their eyes. When I read these ads, it was over four years after I had left the Scientology movement. I did not know if they were more funny or outrageous. When I entered Scientology in 1971, the Grade Chart indicated that one could see while being "fully exterior" from the body. In Scientology, *exterior* is a word which refers to the idea of a person being outside of his body.* By the time I left Scientology, this information had been removed from the Grade Chart.

While *exteriorization*, as it was called, was definitely part of the psychic candy that was offered, I must say, to the credit of the Scientologists who introduced me to the concept, that there was never any guarantee that I nor anyone else could reach such a level. I was only told that we all have the potential to be exterior.

During my twelve years in the Scientology movement, I had occasion to learn of different disreputable things said to people in the name of Scientology. These included false promises and all sorts of nonsense. This was not, however, encouraged. More often, it was severely disciplined. At the entrance level that I experienced, I can only say that most of the people responsible gave a rather honest and sometimes even severe projection of what I could expect. There were no guarantees. Anything good that was going to happen to me in Scientology was going to be as a direct result of me making it happen. There was no silver platter. Auditors and supervisors were only there to guide the way.

After completing the Communications Course, I was told that I could now take the Dianetics Course if I wanted to. It was five hundred dollars which was not a cheap price. The course could take three months or more, but there was no time limit. A colloquial expression for all Scientology courses and procedures was that "it takes as long as it takes."

My parents were not going to spring for five hundred dollars. There was now some concern on their part, but not too much, that I might be getting involved in a cult. As my father had now been abruptly transferred from Sacramento, he was no longer living at home and could not say too much about anything. His company

---

* Scientologists believe that a person is a spirit and not a body. A person is thought to have many lives as he or she goes from body to body during an infinite number of lifetimes.

began transferring him so often that he decided he did not want to move the family away from Davis until he had a permanent tenure. He ended up in Ventura, and as a result, I applied to and was accepted to attend the University of California at Santa Barbara which was only about an hour away from what would be the new family home.

When my father would get a block of days off, he would come back to Davis and generally start bugging me about my interest in Dianetics. Before that, I had been interested in various esoteric paths, and he bothered me about that, too. His sole interest in my life seemed to be getting me interested in a profession. When my interest in doing the Dianetics Course did not relent, he decided to pay a visit to one of my old high school teachers, Mr. Pytell. I had already graduated, but my father wanted to get a beat on me and this Scientology stuff. As we had lived in the same apartment building with Mr. Pytell when we first moved to town, he knew him a little bit and was comfortable with his opinion.

It was clear that my father was very concerned about the possibility of my being involved in a cult, but what Mr. Pytell told him surprised both of us. He told my father that the Scientology center in Davis had an excellent reputation for getting kids off of drugs. In fact, he said it was probably the most successful treatment center in the region.

You have to remember that during the hippie era in Northern California, vast amounts of people were on drugs, particularly at U.C. Davis. Scientology was one of the few ideologies that appealed to the youth of the day that also did not advocate drugs. There were quite a few people who abandoned drugs as a way of enlightenment as a result of their encounters with Scientology in Davis. Further, auditing directly addressed the issues that turned people to drugs in the first place. I realize that many people might not agree with this, and I have no problem with it. I can only say that, in 1971, Scientology Davis had a reputation for such that even extended to my high school teacher. In retrospect, I would have to say that Mr. Pytell was minimizing not only what Scientology actually represented but also any further potential it might have, for better or for worse. He amalgamated it into something that was comfortable for him to accept. Even though he did not believe in Scientology or what it represented, he referred people there if they wanted to get rid of a drug problem because he had seen positive results. This was his testament, not mine. This eased my father's mind somewhat.

Over the years, I had mowed lawns and had been a city paid sports official which included being a Little League umpire. I had saved about $400. As a delayed graduation present, and one that I never expected, my father gave me one hundred dollars. For me, graduation had been in January, and it was now April. I had no idea that kids even received graduation presents so he could have gotten away without one. But, knowing how badly I wanted to do the Dianetics Course, I think he found a way to help me. Thus, in the Spring of 1971, I enrolled in the Dianetics Course which would not only teach me the techniques of how to counsel another, but I would be able to receive free auditing by my fellow students.

Before I was to receive any auditing that was to address my own mind, there were several initiatory or preparatory steps that took place. First, one had to receive an introductory series of auditing sessions which actually oriented one as to what to expect and how one could erase engrams, those moments of pain and unconsciousness in the past that could impinge upon one's normal functioning. Besides this, I was also studying the Dianetics Course and learning how to audit others, but this was only theoretical and practice style. Still, I learned the entire rigmarole of what might be expected to happen from an auditor's viewpoint. I was also absorbing the key components of what might be termed the Scientology belief system. This included the concept of past lives.

I did not believe in past lives when I encountered Scientology. I had thought a little bit about it in my writing and philosophical studies, but the concept had no particular reality to me and certainly no tangibility. The theory of past lives was only being offered as an idea. Referring to the Orient, Hubbard said that a great percentage of the world already believed in past lives and stated that it was a weird idea that we only live but once. This was a unique viewpoint and perhaps a refreshing one, but still, I had no feelings or reality on the subject. I neither rejected it nor did I accept it.

Lest anyone think that I was "a believer" in Scientology, let me correct any potential errors in your system. Well before I ever encountered Scientology, I had already determined that to "believe" anything is erroneous. Belief is basically a suspension of knowledge. You can believe that the ground is beneath your feet, but that does not mean it is so. Only when you test it and prove to yourself that it is there does it become worthy of some form of belief. But, you still do not know that it is really there. You only know that it seems to be there. There need be no investment of belief other than the fact that if you stomp your feet, the ground predictably acts as it should. The ground is really a hypothesis that works, but it should be kept in mind that it only works primarily within the reference frame of the human condition. You might say that more than "believing in the ground," I was viewing it more as a consistent reference point. Belief therefore becomes irrelevant to any true examination of facts and circumstances. In the case of Scientology, past lives, and any other phenomena, it is wise to test concepts for familiar reference points that can be demonstrated to repeat. In this vein, one obtains a familiarization with repeatable phenomena. It is all a matter of existential and experimental observation with reference to repeatable demonstrations of fact. Belief, in and of itself, can be a dangerous or disappointing endeavor. It depends how you define it.

The book that I had read, *Dianetics: The Modern Science of Mental Health,* had no references to past lives in it. Not too many years after that book was written and had become a mass movement, Hubbard observed and reported that people were not really getting rid of all their psychosomatic ills unless they addressed the issue of past lives. This was only his word based upon his studies and experience. I had no experience on the subject. To me, it was only a theory. In the midst of this, I began to consider that I *might* have lived before. Of course, this type of thinking opens the door to suggestibility. I did not contemplate these propositions too much because the course materials sternly warned against self-auditing to discover your own past lives. It was said to cause potential problems.

After studying and being acclimated to the Scientology point of view, it was finally my turn to get some *real* auditing. By this, I mean that I was going to have a psychosomatic ill actually addressed. Feeling I knew what to expect, I went into session.

I was told by my auditor, Tom, that we were going to address "sore throat." This made me very happy because I sometimes had the worst sore throats you could imagine. Nothing was worse to me during my high school days than this repeated and nasty sore throat I would sometimes get. As I expected, I was returned through a precise process of commands to return to present life incidents when I had experienced a sore throat. As I went back into the various incidents, I could feel the sensation of a sore throat returning. This was called restimulating the original engram. In other words, my reactive mind was being invoked. It was not, however, as painful as the original sore throat. It was a mimicry of the real experience. As the incidents went earlier and earlier into my current life, the feeling of pain increased, but this was expected. I was also well aware that I would be faced with the proposition of going before this life. At the same time, I had no actual memory or even fabricated memories of earlier lives.

When you close your eyes and get a mental image picture, it is called *visio* in Dianetics. When you hear a sound or the approximation of a sound, that is called *audio*. In this case, as I recalled the actual somatic (body ailment) and the pain increased, it amplified the *visio* I was experiencing as I recalled the various incidents. In other words, the sore throat had its own attachments that went along with it. In some respects, this is not much different than radio frequency waves. They carry intelligent information and that is why sound and visual representations can be produced on radio and television. In recalling somatics, they carry their own frequency waves which are being reactivated from a "frequency generator" in times past. When a being experiences an engram, a frequency wave is generated from the experience and it reactivates when it is brought to mind. Part of this frequency wave dictates the subject becoming unconscious as the pain becomes unbearable.

During this recall, I theoretically knew that I would have to go earlier than this life if I wanted to heal or erase the problem, at least per the theories of Dianetics. Fortunately, by the time I had restimulated the somatic, I did not have to take a quantum leap to experience visio or audio from previous lives. Pictures came through. They were not necessarily in high fidelity or crystal clear, but they were right there in my quantum field. I knew that I could deny them and "pretend" that they did not exist. Instead, I opted for the idea that they might be real and that it would likely be in my best interest if I experienced them. Subjectively, it was a tad experimental, but I went with it. To this day, I cannot tell you if the experiences were indeed real, but it does not matter. Eventually, I got to the basic engram. The visio turned on very well — in fact, it was rather exceptional. I could see a green field in what appeared to be spring time. I was riding a horse and wearing the armor of a knight covered with a mantle that contained a red cross. Although I had never heard of the Knights Templar in my real life, I later found out that this was the garb that they wore. It does not mean that I was actually a Templar, but I seemed to be wearing their garb. If one accepts the incident as real, it would be a safe bet that I was either a Templar or was impersonating one. It was a rough incident. A bigger and stronger knight, dressed in a blackish armor, approached me and we clashed. In the fight, I did not last too long. His sword was rammed into my throat, right between the helmet and where the armor on the torso ends. It was a vulnerable spot. Eventually, the sword was thrust deep into my throat, and I perished. That was the bad news.

As I recalled the incident and was asked to go through it several times, I could actually feel the sensation of dying and releasing from that body. In the visio, I could quite remarkably see myself looking down from the body. Recovering this memory, or whatever it was, was an exhilarating experience. For the first time, I now had an idea what Scientologists were talking about when they used the term *exterior*. Keep in mind, I was not looking down at my body in the auditing room. I was only exterior in the recalled incident. As I continued to go through the incident again and again, I saw other bits and pieces. The pain in the throat came on strong and dissipated. I kept recalling it and feeling the sword go through the sensitive area. By experiencing and reexperiencing the pain, I could feel it in a way where I was fully conscious of the experience. Soon, the pain and all the mechanics behind it were blown to bits. The frequency generator of this particular pain from the past was now completely inert. Besides the pain, there was a lot of emotional charge that accompanied it. But, this was now releasing, too. It was the emotion of being defeated and thwarted from whatever my mission was. The entire engram had been a great interruption in a stream of consciousness. As it dissipated, I began to feel a relief far beyond the bounds of anything I had ever experienced before. Something very negative had been eradicated.

I began to laugh as I had never laughed before and experienced what Scientologists refer to as erasure of an engram. In fact, this was one of the most spectacular erasures I would ever experience. We addressed other engrams in the session, and I continued to experience more erasures but not quite to the dramatic extent of the first one. Generally, I was having the time of my life. The experience was far beyond anything I had ever expected, and it was only my first auditing session. By the end of the session, I was actually in an exterior state, but I did not know it at the time. I was not, however, "exterior with full perception" which means that one can literally "see" what is going on at a distance without the use of one's eyes. But, it did not matter. It felt like the weight of a thousand years had been lifted.

After all that, I did not give a damn about anything bad anyone said about L. Ron Hubbard or Scientology. I had heard various negative things said about them, but after actually experiencing fantastic results with auditing, that all seemed totally ludicrous. The fact is, I did not owe Ron nor Scientology anything at that point. I could have walked out the door and been just fine and nobody would have bothered me except for perhaps trying to find out what had happened to me. To this day, over thirty years later, that sore throat has never returned.

This was my first taste of the spiritual candy that Scientology had to offer. That experience, however, was a major transition point for me. Prior to that, I had only learned practical skills about communication and dealing with certain psychological aspects of people, but this auditing session had made the more far out aspects of Scientology experiential. These included the concepts of immortality and complete freedom as a spiritual being that is independent from the body. At that point, if I had been a stimulus-response creature like the Frankenstein monster, I would have said, "Pain-ba-a-a-a-d. Dianetics go-o-o-o-d!" This was the type of experience that could hook one on the Scientology stream of consciousness. Actually, for me, the best was yet to come.

10

OLIVE DRIVE

The Scientology center on Olive Drive was known as the Church of Scientology, Mission of Davis. At the time I was there, Olive Drive was the most unique street in the city of Davis. Before the university came to town, in the early 1900's, Olive Drive was the main drive in a rural town that was primarily just a train stop. Although it was the only part of town that was somewhat depressed, it was a bit refreshing in a rural sort of way. Besides that, Olive Drive was challenging to access if you were riding a bike because one had to pass a treacherous underpass to get there. That narrow underpass took more than a few lives over the years.

The Scientology building itself was converted from what had once been a car dealership. One of the garage bays was made into a decent room for the Dianetics Course and the adjacent garage bay was used for the Communications Course. Another garage bay or two had been converted into a hallway of auditing rooms. Besides this, there were administrative offices and a reception area which was used for public lectures and a place to congregate.

Looking back, it is rather ironic that I arrived at the Mission of Davis just prior to what was to become the biggest expansion Scientology had ever known on the public level. It had nothing to do with me personally other than I was to bear witness and become more of an observer than a participant in what happened.

When I got started in Scientology, the proprietors of the Mission of Davis were Martin and Diana Samuels, but they were nowhere around. Both of them were in Los Angeles working on the Scientology OT Levels.* Diana was the first to return, and she went out of her way to make friends with me immediately. She was highly intelligent, pretty, and very good at dealing with people. Diana told me that, when I was on course, I would often interrupt her work as she sometimes ended up laughing hysterically when she heared my voice in the next room. Her office was right next to the course room, and she could not help but hear my outrageous imitations of hillbillies while doing auditing drills. This might sound absurd, but Scientologists are well trained not to laugh when auditing another person. Of course, if you are going to become proficient at not laughing, you are going to have to be subjected to every type of laughter imaginable. The laughter alone I experienced in Scientology was worth the price of the courses. You also acquired some laughing friends along the way.

Not too long after Diana returned, her husband returned. His name was Martin Samuels, and he was the resident czar of the Mission of Davis. He soon began setting up procedures that were to make the Mission of Davis the most successful and popular Scientology center that the world had ever known, at least as far as new public were concerned. Essentially, he would send out trained auditors to the campuses at Davis, Sacramento State College and Sacramento City College. These were very open and liberal times, and these Scientology staffers would approach anyone who might seem interested in having a conversation. There was a specific procedure called the "Dissemination Drill" which centered around finding someone's "ruin." A ruin is what damages you or bothers you in life. It might be your boss, your mother, or the fact that the opposite sex is not nice to you. Most everyone has someone or something that makes their life more difficult than need be. Once this area was addressed in conversation, different theories and plausibilities were offered and demonstrated on how such a ruin

---

* In Scientology, "OT" stands for "Operating Thetan." In Scientology, a thetan is a word for the spirit. An operating thetan is considered to be a being who is unencumbered from restrictions that have been endemic to spirits since the beginning of time. One is supposed to transcend a gradient scale of different levels and abilities towards, ideally, a state of "Full OT" whereby one suffers no restrictions of any kind. This would include freedom from bodily death and also the ability to move, see, hear, and enjoy all possible perceptions without the confines of a human body. An operating thetan, as defined by Scientology, is one of the most bold and ambitious assertions ever made about the potential of human beings.

could be handled through Scientology. But, it was only done through understanding. Duress or coercion was to play no part in the equation. The people Martin hired to do this job were called "disseminators," and they were all very good at what they did. They were all very genuine as well, at least at the time I was there. The Communications Course was held at 8:00 p.m. every evening except for the weekends. As the disseminators did their job, the course became more and more crowded. Eventually, a day time Communications Course was started, and those of us on the Dianetics Course now had companions in the next garage bay during the day. We were all amazed at how rapidly Scientology was expanding in Davis. Except for perhaps the early days, Scientology organizations or churches had NEVER had this sort of expansion going on. The Davis Mission was booming in a fashion that was quite unprecedented.

I remember one day, when I was on a lunch break, I saw a Sea Org* officer drive up and walk rapidly into the reception room. The man had absolutely no subtlety as he blared out to the receptionist, "What's causing the boom?!" He seemed like an idiot to me. I remember that, many years later, Hubbard would castigate this very man for stupidly fouling up a Scientology court case. After this experience, it seemed that Scientology management itself might be clueless as to what could cause a boom. In the case of the Davis Mission, it seemed to be predicated on genuine care and concern, backed up by counseling procedures which actually got excellent results. These procedures, however, did not work out well in all cases. Perhaps I was one of the very many lucky ones.

Another feature of Olive Drive during this period were the constant and consistent testimonials you would hear after people were audited. When people would finish one of the grades or levels of auditing, the course would be interrupted so that they could speak about their "wins" as they were called. A "win," by definition, was doing something that you intended to do but also referred to a success. If someone just said they were happy and did not wish to speak about it, that was fine, too. Nobody would begrudge them for keeping silent, but this was almost never the

---

* The Sea Org, which is short for Sea Organization, refers to the paramilitary management organization that controlled Scientology in 1971. At that time, the Sea Organization had a flotilla (a small fleet) of seven ships.

case. These people were often laughing with great relief as they recounted wonderful tales of vast amounts of emotional charge they had released during auditing. The stories were always heartfelt, often dramatic, but always upbeat and funny. The laughter they evoked in the speakers and the audience spoke for itself. Many of these stories were about Scientology auditing, but that was something I had never really experienced. I had only known Dianetics up to that point. Their genuine successes and stories of spiritual relief and development only served as further candy for me. As I write this, it is thirty-three years later, and those days are very nostalgic to me. It was the time of my spiritual awakening.

Every Friday evening, a graduation was held. All Scientologists who had completed a course or level of auditing would gather together and share their successes. Practically anyone else was invited to chime in as well. I remember one particular evening when everyone got into talking about what a remarkable place Davis was. People were coming up with all sorts of metaphysical hyperbola about Davis and much of it seemed corny, but it was fun. Then, one lady boldly stated that Davis was recognized by a cult in Ohio as being the center of the universe. That seemed to shut everybody up for the most part. It seemed dubious and insignificant, but I never forgot that statement. It would have much more meaning to me later on in my life.

11

EXTERIORIZATION

Although my first auditing was quite spectacular and completely exceeded any expectations, I bogged down after that. In other words, my auditing was not going smoothly, and I was no longer getting the expected results. I was told that I needed Scientology review auditing to get me back on Dianetics. This did not make me happy as Scientology auditing was not familiar, and I felt like a fish out of water. I understood Dianetic auditing backwards and forwards by this time but not Scientology. Review auditing also cost $25 an hour which I did not have so this only exacerbated things. So, I was just bogged.

In the meantime, I had finished the theory part of the Dianetics Course in record time, and it was my turn to audit others. The people I audited had results similar to mine. Maybe some of these results were not quite as spectacular as mine, but all of the preclears had a very good time. Eventually, I had to bring worksheets and folders of the people I had audited to the San Francisco Church so they could be investigated and approved by the Qualifications Division.

After graduating from the Dianetics Course, I was somewhat done with Davis. My next step would have been to co-audit with a fellow Dianetics Course graduate, but, as I said, I was bogged and could not move forward in my own auditing. One of the registrars, Sharon, took me by the hand and told me that the assessment that I needed Scientology review auditing was not correct. A new Case Supervisor had been hired by Martin, and he had reviewed all the case folders at the mission. He had determined that I was bogged due to having gone exterior in my auditing and not being able to "handle" it. I would therefore need what was called an "Interiorization/Exteriorization Rundown." This would cost $125, but there was no time limit on the auditing. All things considered, it was a great deal, but I did not have the money. I was still umpiring Little League games, but this did not amount to much money. Sharon worked with me on a very personal basis with regard to how I could come up with the funds. She was a highly trained auditor, and I sometimes felt that I was being audited in the dialogue with her.

One day, she told me that she had been working with one of my friends who had just abandoned his job as a dishwasher down the street. She asked if I was interested, and I jumped at the chance. My friend set it up, and I reported to the kitchen at midnight and ended up working a very laborious shift with no sleep. I soon became a permanent fixture at Dave and Eddy's Coffee Shop which was then located at the end of Olive Drive. It was my first real job, and I did quite well at it. I was even appointed "Head Dishwasher" which I thought was an extremely humorous title. I was even paid ten cents more per hour than the other dishwashers which I thought was just as comical. I think that the minimum wage then was $1.70 per hour and I was getting $1.80. I worked six days a week and had the money for the Exteriorization/ Interiorization Rundown in no time.

This rundown primarily used Dianetic techniques but was tailored to engrams that involved interiorizing into the body in an unpleasant manner (with pain and unconsciousness). Exteriorization refers to being outside of the body. Interiorization not only refers to being inside the body but being thrust into it in a haphazard and unpredictable way. Most human beings are walking around "interiorized" without having any idea of how they got there except that they were "born" as a body or born into a body. It is very common for people who go exterior by Scientology or other methods to feel a wonderful sense of freedom. This is sometimes, not incorrectly so, associated with manic states of behavior. Interiorization refers to a crash. Drugs can cause an acute interiorization into the body, particularly after a euphoric high.

This was a tremendous rundown, and it totally sorted out the problems I was having in auditing. After this rundown, I now knew what it meant to be "out of the body." Again, this was not with full perception to the point where I could "see" and "hear" outside of the body, but it was a great feeling. It is sort of a spiritual extroversion of looking outward rather than looking inward. I was now able to continue on with my Dianetic auditing and did so.

Right after I finished the Interiorization/Exteriorization Rundown, my parents had sold the house in Davis and were moving to Ventura, California. They were totally taken by surprise when I announced that I would stay in Davis and stay at my job and continue my auditing, too. My parents immediately challenged me as to where I would live, but I had already worked that out. Things were working out just fine. Although I did not think about it at the time, I had moved out of the house and would be on my own for the rest of my life from the age of eighteen onward.

After moving into a new house, I remember going by the graveyard every day after work. Graveyards had always given me the creeps in the past, but now it all seemed different. For the first time in my life, I realized that there were actual spirits attached to the graves. They were only frightening if you let them be so. The whole key was simply acknowledging that there was something there that was not wholly of the corporeal world.

Work continued to go well, and I began saving money for my next level of Scientology. I was planning to become a Scientology auditor, but this would have to be done in San Francisco. I was eventually going to move, but I was not sure when. After a few months of working as a dishwasher, I noticed that the cooks seemed to be rather inept at reporting to work and staying on the job. The turnover rate was incredible, and some of the personnel were better suited for selling caramel popcorn at a wrestling arena. I then proposed to the manager that she should train me to cook. At least, I told her, I was dependable and would show up. During the day, I would work as a dishwasher. Then, I would train for two hours as a cook and get a free meal out of it. My expenses were minimal. After a month of training, I was hired as a cook and worked the graveyard shift from 11:00 p.m. to 7:00 a.m.. Before long, I became very proficient at cooking and could flip eggs as fast as anyone.

As a cook, I was making considerably more money than I had been and got along well with the waitresses and other cooks. As I became more experienced, the head waitress, who was adored by everyone and had been there as long as anyone could remember, began a whispering campaign to make me the manager of the entire restaurant. The owner already liked me, and it was just a matter of time until the manager either quit or was fired. Everyone knew she was a bit batty. If this position was going to be made available to me, and it was apparent that it would be, I would be making a salary commensurate with my father's after being out of school only a year. I know he would have been proud of me, but he would have been more puzzled than proud. I was living completely by the seat of my pants and doing quite well at it. He expected me to follow the program that most of my high school peers followed: go to college so that you could get a good job.

12

RON

During the height of the Vietnam War protests, I attended a "mandatory" concert at the university that was given by Joan Baez. It was either free or offered at a very nominal cost. It was something of a concert but was more of a moratorium protesting the Vietnam War. Although Joan Baez was a beautiful girl and had an excellent singing voice, there was something about her and the movement she was representing that I did not trust. It was not that I thought she was a bad person, but there was something that made me feel that the hordes of protesters were either being used by her or through her. At the same time, my friend Tor was giving me a steady diatribe of information from the Students for a Democratic Society who were even more suspicious. Years later, it was revealed that they were a CIA front group. These encounters with Joan Baez and the SDS made me very suspicious of organizations in general. I made an exception with Scientology only because I found that its precepts and operation were completely "outside of the box."

I bring up Joan Baez because she said something at that concert that I found irritating and still remember. She talked about as much as she sang that night, and one of her favorite diatribes was about her friend, Bob Dylan. She admired him greatly, but she could not stop talking about him. That was not so bad, but she kept saying, "Wait 'til you meet Dylan! Wait 'til you meet Dylan!"

She was talking to everyone on a very familiar basis, but I knew that I was never going to meet Dylan. Further, I had no desire to meet Dylan. It had nothing to do with a dislike for Dylan. I just did not see any personal or potential purpose in communicating with him. It was nothing personal.

This experience was still fresh in my mind some months later when I was on the Communications Course and just becoming interested in Scientology. I had only been on the course a week when members of the Sea Organization came to give a lecture at the Mission of Davis. I had never heard of the Sea Organization or what it was, but it was soon explained to me that they represented the management of Scientology. At the time, they had a flotilla of about seven ships, the largest of which was the *Apollo* and served as the home of L. Ron Hubbard. The *Apollo* was called the Flagship. In nautical terms, a flagship signifies the vessel upon which the admiral of the fleet resides. A flotilla refers to a smaller number of vessels than would normally comprise a fleet. The proper title for a commander of such vessels would be a commodore rather than an admiral. This is why L. Ron Hubbard was referred to as the Commodore by Sea Org members.

Neil Sarfati was the lecturer from the Sea Org that evening, and he was accompanied by his assistant, Ben. They were basically there to recruit new Sea Org members. For the very first time, I was hearing from someone who had actually seen Ron in the flesh. He spoke of Ron with a great deal of familiarity.

"Wait 'til you meet Ron!" said Neil. "He's always laughing and joking around."

Neil made Ron sound like a wonderful person, and I had no reason to doubt this. It retrospect, his statements were a little overblown, but he made Ron sound like a fun and interesting person. Certainly, he did not sound like anyone to be feared. He also said that Ron was working on new procedures and technologies. He told us a little bit about life on the ship and that the Sea Org was a brotherhood dedicated to fixing the planet and getting Scientology into the society so that it could be used to help people. The Sea Org, he said, was designed to be the group "three feet in back of society's head." In Scientology terms, "three feet in back of the head" meant a state of exteriorization. In Sea Org policy, it was boldly stated that the Sea Organization was to operate as if it was three feet in back of society's head in order to guide them to a better world and destination.

Although I was more than interested to hear about Ron, I had absolutely no hopes or intentions of ever meeting him. I did, however, find it odd that I did not resent Neil's comments the way that I had resented those of Joan Baez.

After the lecture, I spoke to Ben, and he told me the circumstances and conditions by which I could join the Sea Org. As I was still a minor, I would need my parents permission although we both knew that this probably would not fly. After that, I corresponded with different Sea Org recruiters from time to time, but it was all rather meaningless.

Although I had no hopes of working with Ron, I did find myself very interested in the Sea Org. It was quite rare for a newcomer to Scientology to be interested in joining the Sea Org. I remember some of the staff members at Davis being incredibly impressed that I was so interested in the Sea Org. They had been studying Scientology for some years and had become quite proficient at it, but the Sea Org was a heavy trip. It was a lifetime commitment of forgoing all temporal pleasures. It was, in fact, a monastic order. Celibacy, however, was not one of the criteria.

At that time, many students in the United States, particularly those in Northern California, thought that the military was a big joke that was merely serving corporate interests. I was no exception, and this was another reason why my interest in the Sea Org was rather remarkable. Paramilitary connoted the same sort of problems there were with the military. Watching the U.S. Government and military choke on itself during the 1960's and early 1970's, I never would have considered a career in the military. When I was younger, I was at one time interested in attending the Air Force Academy but ruled it out when I learned in their literature that they only wanted conformists. Further, they only wanted conformists that conformed.

There are different reasons why the Sea Org appealed to me. It was obviously my destiny, but there was also my early interest and experience with the sea. There was also another factor. I had just studied the novel *Dune* in school, and the Sea Org seemed to be running along the same lines. *Dune* brought home the point that a religion, whether good or bad, was not going to get anywhere unless it was backed by a military operation. At this particular time, CIA agents were quite aware of what they called the "science fiction theme" aspect of the Sea Org. In fact, they were admittedly mystified over how so many young people were attracted to it.

The Sea Org is not the first example on this planet of a religious organization adopting military methods. During the crusades, religious and military conquest went hand-in-hand. Crusaders not only sought out the ultimate religious experience, they created the biggest industry in Europe by protecting pilgrims.

People went on pilgrimages because they were seeking a religious or spiritual advantage as opposed to the economic advantage that came with their profession. One generally needs a modicum of both in order to survive in this world, but there are highly varied opinions as to which is most important and when it is most important. My entire interest in the Sea Org was completely predicated on the idea that the spiritual aspect was the most important; and further, that this organization might provide a workable means to that end.

Although there is no question that the Sea Org was in some ways no different than the fervent religious crusades of the past, my perspective on the entire matter was completely different. I viewed it as the best possible way to access the higher callings of my own pineal gland. My deepest interest was completely along those lines, and the Sea Org appeared as a means to an end. In the final analysis, there was only one way to test the truth of this statement: trial by life.

All of the people I consulted with in the Sea Org had the courtesy to tell me that whatever happened to me was largely the responsibility of myself. In other words, doors would be available, but I would have to make everything work and should not depend upon others to do things for me. It was not an easy ticket. None of this mattered, however, because I was still a minor and not eligible to sign up by California law.

Ambitious beyond belief, the goals and tenets of the Sea Org delineated a path of unlimited human potential. Besides this, what probably appealed to me more than anything was that the Sea Org incorporated this theme in such a way so as to communicate to everyone at a high level of adventure. In retrospect, I must admit that it was one hell of an adventure. For those of you have studied the works of J.R.R. Tolkein, you might recognize it as my invitation to leave the Shire.

13

THE MYSTERY PRINCIPLE

Now that you have been introduced to some of the experiential phenomena which Scientology could produce, perhaps you can better understand the enthusiasm and dedication it has inspired in so many others. I realize there will be some who read this and believe that neither myself nor anyone else could have had some of the experiences previously delineated. To me, such people would be in the same sphere of reference as the redneck hillbillies who had a hard time grasping that anyone could ride a surfboard. It is understandable, however, that many people would be confused or perplexed by reason of the fact that an idea has been presented to them which is completely unfamiliar to their way of thinking or experiencing. By reason of the very nature of what it is addressing, there are also many other unfamiliar elements within the tenets of Dianetics and Scientology. Before one can truly understand the impact that these subjects or L. Ron Hubbard have had upon the world, it is important to examine an interesting rhetorical argument that can be made with regard to this field of study.

First, the purpose of Dianetics was ostensibly to handle psychosomatic ills. Whether it is effective or not is really a secondary point. Although common science has propagated the idea that ninety percent of man's ills are psychosomatic, it offers no viable, prescribed or guaranteed cure for such. Psychiatry is not pretentious about offering real cures. They do not claim to have real cures. Instead, they prescribe drugs in the hopes of alleviating symptoms. When psychiatry tends to pound down hard on anyone who suggests or offers a cure, it moves the institution of psychiatry into a different category entirely.

Psychologists and self-help gurus are nowhere near as inclined not to offer cures. In fact, many of them will claim that psychosomatic ills can be cured; but, they are not particularly known for offering cures, let alone establishing a sizable and significant institution that guarantees and demonstrates it.

Dianetics, as I studied it in 1971, required a deep and involved study before one could sincerely grasp the principles, let alone make them work. Therefore, it becomes disingenuous to claim that Dianetics cannot resolve psychosomatic ills when the people making such assertions have not actually given the procedures a full study and honest effort. Arm chair critics can see failed results by incompetent practitioners and make their comments, but this does not really address the core issue. Is there, somewhere under the sun, a method or means to rid ourselves of psychosomatic ills?

If we rule out Dianetics and hypothesize that it does not work, there is none. If one does exist, it has been effectively suppressed or under-communicated to the point where it is not readily available to the common person. This alone tells us a considerable amount about our human predicament. Science tells us our ills are caused by the spirit or mind but does not even pretend to offer a solution! Rhetorically, this means that the spirit and mind are an unknown zone. Further, when someone makes an academic comment that Dianetics and Scientology do not fulfill this prospect, they could not be coming from a place of actual knowledge; unless, of course, they have a successful model to compare it by. Cases of fraud in Dianetics and Scientology are another matter, but we will touch on that point later.

The fact that the best minds of our universities have no real solutions to our spiritual or mental ills suggests or reflects that the universe itself suffers from an absence of healing or other curative measures. When we add suffering to the equation, we are bringing the ancient dilemma of Buddhism to view: it is a universe of suffering. This, unfortunately, means that we are all sufferers or are prone to suffer. While life may not consist only of suffering, the preoccupation with it brings up an important rhetorical point. If we are all sufferers, it suggests that something or someone is making us suffer.

Is there an escape from suffering? This is a universal question that has been asked many times before. All we can know for certain is that the universe, left to its own devices, has not provided us with an answer. In order to have a sufferer, you need to have someone or something that is making them suffer or precipitating a situation of suffering. This is the universal adversary. Dianetics and Scientology both sought to address this on an individual basis. This brings us to yet another important proposition. Whether or not Dianetics and Scientology work, they operate in a realm or zone which seeks to reverse the energy of the adversary. As was demonstrated earlier, this is an occult zone if only because it is unknown to common man. Anyone working in this zone is going to be subject to the predatory conditions generated by the forces which precipitated the original circumstances of suffering in the first place. Further, anything seeking to emulate this role of the universal healing principle is going to find itself surrounded by the equivalent of great white sharks. If one moves into this realm without at least looking like a shark or something similarly dangerous, they are subject to being consumed.

What exacerbates the above situation is that anyone honestly or desperately seeking a cure is moving into a realm where sharks thrive. It all has to do with the prospect of vulnerability. Sincere healing takes place all the time, but it is largely hidden and unavailable to the average citizen.

I fully realize that the proposition of whether or not Scientology works is controversial. I, and many others I knew, have seen it work countless times. On the other hand, I have also been a firsthand witness to the fact that it has not worked. This brings us to one of the most important and overlooked precepts that can be found in Dianetics and Scientology. Its techniques do not work in an environment of duress, suppression or oppression. This is an actual doctrine of Scientology, and while many people might not believe it, it is the discovery of this doctrine and its derivative corollaries which made Scientology, at one point in its history, the most controversial and dangerous religion on the planet.

If the universe is a prison where we are all subject to suffering, the only salvation would be by means of an escape route. In an analogy where the universe is considered to be a prison, society serves as inmates while the world leaders or secret societies serve as wardens or guardians of the watchtower. As long as you are a good inmate, you can have a reasonably pleasurable life. Sexual furloughs are not frowned upon, and there are plenty of comfortable beds. If one is particularly enterprising, one can manipulate a black market and live high on the hog. As far as prisons go, Earth can be a pretty pleasant prison for many of us. For those who are satisfied with the life of a homo sapien and wish to look no further, it can even be a reasonable substitute for paradise. But, if you want to question the foundation and circumstances, you are prone to being thwarted and severely punished.

The above becomes particularly punctuated with regard to an idea of L. Ron Hubbard which has received much ridicule and derision. He said words to the effect that "Only in this far off corner of a distant galaxy does the fire of freedom burn." By this, he was referring to the idea that the Scientology OT Levels were the only means available on this planet or any other that could literally free beings from entrapment in a human form or from slavish conditions. All of this might seem to be a self-ingratiating and absurd remark, but there is a point about it which is too easily overlooked. There is really no sign of any major institutionalized system that is dedicated to resolving the universal paradigm of oppression that was previously outlined. If Scientology truly works, then Hubbard's words are glaringly true. If it does not work, then we need a system that does work. The adversary, however, holds a major trump card. Most people are so apathetic about and inebriated with the status quo reality that they are not about to do anything.

When Hubbard finished *Dianetics: The Modern Science of Mental Health*, he felt there was a lot more to do. He often quoted a refrain from that book which was "for godsakes, let's build a better bridge." By bridge, he was referring to a means by which people could get rid of all their psychosomatic ills and be completely free from any encumbrances, spiritual or otherwise. You could also define this as a release from suffering. Personally and organizationally, he found the barriers to building a better bridge enormous. People came out of the woodwork to try and stop him. Whether you agree with Hubbard's techniques or not, there is one thing I am sure you will not disagree with: he had his finger on the pulse or trigger of something that is very powerful.

14

PERCEPTION

After finishing the Interiorization/Exteriorization Rundown, I was then able to co-audit Dianetics with one of my fellow graduates. Co-audit means that you audit each other. It was a great way to go because it did not cost anything. We became professional auditors and audited our way to what was called a Dianetic Case Completion. This meant that we had addressed all of our psychosomatic pains and sensations as well as negative emotions and attitudes. If you had a strong distaste for someone or an unpleasant emotion, it was easy. You just addressed it in auditing and "ran out" the engram. This was not brain science but is something that most people would overlook, particularly if they were not part of an institution which was dedicated to helping one alleviate one's ills. It should be mentioned that if one acquired more pains, sensations, emotions or attitudes in the future, one could take up Dianetics again and address the particular issues. It was never considered a closed book.

As I alluded to earlier, all of this only helped my job performance. By the time I had ingrained myself into the infrastructure of Dave and Eddy's coffee shop as a cook, it was 1972 and things were looking up. One day, I received news that there was going to be a big event at the Davis Mission. Yvonne Gillham, the founder of Scientology's Los Angeles Celebrity Center, was paying a visit with her troupe and sidekick movie star, Robert F. Lyons. As strange as it might seem, this was nothing but a goodwill tour. There was no serious recruiting going on that amounted to much.

Yvonne was one of the most loved and successful characters in the history of Scientology. The event featured different performers and a talk by her and "Robert F.," but the stars of the show were an improvisation group of Scientology OTs known as the "Key-out Players." After asking the audience to give them impromptu and spontaneous ideas, the Key-Out Players would do a musical performance on the spot. It was most impressive, and I have never seen anything so well done ever since.

Next, it was the turn of Heber Jentzsch, a man who would soon become Yvonne's husband. Many years later, after her death, he was appointed President of the Church of Scientology International. On this particular night, he sang a song which delineated the experience of exteriorization after death. As I listened to the song, it moved me emotionally, but then, unexpectedly and inexplicably, the most amazing thing happened to me. I was suddenly looking at the room from the top of the ceiling. I could see everything. There was no question or doubt about it — I was completely exterior. From above, I looked down and could not only see my own body but that of Doug, a friend of mine who I had invited to the event. There was full perception of sight. Wow! I had finally made it! The exterior state the Scientologists had talked about became a complete experiential reality. There was no question or faking it. I must admit though, I was a little perplexed. It was too good to be true. When I realized the actuality of it all, I soon found myself back in my body and looking out of my eyes. What a feeling! I told Doug, but he was very new to all of this. Fortunately, it was not a crash. The Interiorization/Exteriorization Rundown had done it's trick. There was no disorientation, only a wonderment at what had just happened.

This might have been the most moving experience of my life. If not, it was right up there. The Sea Org and all of its ideals were no longer a pipe dream to me. I had tasted the candy once again, and I wanted more.

Not too long after this experience, I was working my usual graveyard shift at the restaurant when I noticed an attractive red-haired girl in the coffee shop. She was wearing blue and white, and I wondered if she was from the Sea Org. There was no obvious uniform or anything, but I thought she might be one of "them." I cooked her breakfast, but I was busy behind the grill and did not talk to her. It was very unusual and rather inappropriate for the cook to come out of the kitchen and visit with the patrons. The restaurant was relatively busy that night, too.

The next evening, I was working again when there was a call on the public pay phone for me. This was extremely rare. No one ever called me at work unless it was a fellow employee, and it was certainly not via the pay phone. We had another phone for that purpose. When I picked it up, I heard a girl's voice. Saying her name was Kenda, she had heard that I was interested in the Sea Org. She explained that she was in town the day before but nobody had told her about me. In fact, she told me that she had eaten at the restaurant the night before. I told her I had been the one who cooked her breakfast.

"Why didn't you come out and say hi?" she said.

I explained to her that I was not sure who she was, and I was sort of busy. We soon arranged a meeting. She was staying at Celebrity Center San Francisco, a rare and obscure Scientology outpost on California Street which only stayed in operation for a couple of years. As the next day was an off day for me, I made my way to San Francisco. When I arrived, Kenda took me into a very comfortable sitting room, and we had one of the most soul-riveting conversations I have ever experienced.

Prior to this meeting, I had already heard many stories about the Sea Org from the staff at the Davis Mission, most of them not complimentary. In fact, there had been severe rivalry between these two factions of Scientology. One staff member even told me that they had to call the police to keep the Sea Org off of the premises. This was done over concern that the Sea Org would recruit their public and thus cause the mission to suffer financially or even be destroyed. It was all a matter of balance of power, and the two sides could really go at it.

There were other tales of people joining the Sea Org and having a hard time and leaving. I had even experienced a friend and fellow student who tried to join the Sea Org but could not endure the so-called harsh conditions. When he returned to the Davis Mission and told us his tales, he did not paint a very enticing picture. Although he was not disparaging of Scientology, he made the Sea Org sound like a regimented and forbidding place. In spite of this, those of us who were trained as auditors could readily see that his unhappy experiences were due more to his own shortcomings than anything else. I remember him lamenting that one of the reasons he left the Sea Org was because he could not have a dog. We thought this was tremendously funny. Dogs are lovely animals, but they do not exactly compare with the ultimate adventure that we considered the Sea Org to be. After all, we considered this the most adventurous pursuit of knowledge and ability that was imaginable. Nevertheless, I should note that this person was one of the nicest people I had ever met. He was, however, not cut out for the Sea Org.

As I met with Kenda in San Francisco, she cleared up a lot of the issues with regard to various disparaging stories I had heard, but she did not have to say too much. More important to me, she confirmed what I had already thought about the Sea Org and hoped that it was. It was an organization of OTs who were dedicated towards making the entire world "OT." Perhaps the most important thing she said, and certainly a statement that I found to be so soul-riveting, was that you were allowed to be OT. In other words, no one was there to stop you. It was an environment that would let the natural processes of life take over. In retrospect, I cannot really say that she was wrong, but a caveat should be noted here. The natural processes of life are no different than the evolutionary theme of survival of the fittest. The Sea Org was a highly concentrated microcosmic example. Like baby turtles breaking out of their shells and swimming to the water, only a few escape the predators and make it. Instead of baby turtles, however, the Sea Org was dedicated to making OTs. The fact that most people did not make it was not hidden from me.

To me, Kenda's words were like a rush to me of realizing that I could experience the ultimate in what Scientology had to offer. The auditing I had received up to that point was nothing short of remarkable so I could not imagine that the people who were ultimately responsible for putting it together could be anything other than stupendous. Kenda, to her credit, did warn me that the conditions were tough and not to expect it to be easy. She did not need to sell me on the Sea Org — she only needed to open the door and explain the situation. I was the one who walked through it.

Over all, I was delighted and most definitely felt better than I had in my entire life. There was another side benefit to my conversation which made all the difference in the world. After talking to her, I realized that I had accessed certain "OT powers." In other words, I could influence things or people by just thinking about them. This is not an uncommon experience to Scientologists, but it kicked in hard and fast with me. I had never before experienced it to this degree. Kenda warned me not to get too excited though because this was likely only temporary, and she did not want to see me disappointed if it did not last. I saw no reason to complain either way. The candy was tasting even better!

Just a week or two earlier, I had just been exterior with perception and now I was going up to the top of the reality tree, or at least I thought. The universe had become quite a small place, too. Everything seemed right at hand. It was only a year earlier that I had learned of this idealized organization, but that was only a dream. Now, I had over a year's worth of experience as an accomplished auditor and Scientologist. Besides all of this, I was also being supported by the California State Legislature who, just a month or two earlier, had changed the age of adulthood to eighteen. I no longer needed the permission of my parents. Besides, they were living in Ventura, and I was very much on my own and paying my own bills. I decided to join right then and there.

After planning out how I could get back to San Francisco in the next few days, Kenda took me downstairs. Once again, it was a small world. Yvonne Gillham was there to give one of her famous "Poetry by Candlelight" readings. I got to see her for the second time. She was becoming a familiar figure in my life and would continue to do so later on as well. Afterwards, Kenda arranged for me to get a ride home with some Scientologists going back to Sacramento. Everything was being taken care of.

In the next few days, I quit my job and was paid in cash by the manager. I was not going to be taking her place after all. It was two days of happy/sad good-byes to all the people I had studied with, befriended and learned to love in the last year. Never in my life had I said good-bye to so many people in one day. I was moving on. As I told different people, it was interesting to see their various reactions. Many were very happy for me. In fact, most were, but some Scientologists were disturbed by the very idea. The Sea Org touched a part of their minds that made them afraid or gave them a feeling of foreboding. It was the ultimate act of dedication for a Scientologist. It was all or nothing. There was no time for moseying around or fooling around. These people I spoke to were intimidated on some level. There was also a sympathy for me in that they hoped I was doing the right thing for myself. Some obviously had serious doubts that I would make it because they knew that they themselves would not. Interestingly, I could see right through their mind patterns. I was off to the track meet in the sky, and no one was going to stop me.

Gathering up my belongings, I sold or gave away virtually all of my few possessions and made my way to Celebrity Center San Francisco where I spent the next several days. There were plenty of bureaucratic things to do which included getting a passport, the accompanying photos, and all sorts of tests, interviews and local approvals which had to be done at the Church of Scientology in San Francisco. All Sea Org members at that time were required to have a passport for immediate transport out of the country. When these chores were all done, Kenda was insistent that I leave on the next plane possible which happened to be in the late evening. She got me on the bus to the airport, and this was the last I would see of San Francisco, at least for a month or so.

Taking the Pacific Southwest Airways shuttle to Los Angeles, I arrived at LAX. As we hovered over the airport, I could see the relatively brand new Forum in Inglewood. Cars were packed all around it. I figured it must be the beginning of the NBA Championship series, but it might as well have been a Tijuana Jai Lai game to me. By the time I got out of the airport, it was between eleven and midnight, and I had to make my way with a big duffle bag and a box of my auditing folders. Travelling at this time of the night under these circumstances is really quite idiotic, but youth is fearless and impetuous, if not naive. I got on a bus and ended up on an obscure road in Wilmington, not too far from the docks. Letting me off, the bus driver gave me vague instructions as to where and when the next bus to my destination might be caught. It was a little bit like Bela Lugosi in the coach scene of *Dracula*. Standing out in the middle of nowhere at midnight with a duffle bag was just the first challenge I was to face. The second was right ahead of me and much tougher.

Catching the bus that would take me to Pier 59 of the Port of Los Angeles, I got off at the right stop but Kenda's directions were not clear enough for me. I took a wrong turn and ended up going to the wrong dock. It was at this point where I experienced losing those OT abilities, just as Kenda had warned me about. When I looked up at the dock, I saw something hauntingly familiar but from many years earlier in my youth. It was Norm's Landing, a sport fishing establishment which was exactly where my father and I had departed many times on our fishing trips to Catalina Island. This hit me like a sock in the gut.

All of a sudden, I realized that I had been too busy to notify my parents about joining the Sea Org. As an adult, I technically did not really have to, but this experience brought the point home and brought it home hard. I clearly remembered being the little boy who had loved my father so much and enjoyed the adventure of those fishing trips. It was now years later, however, and those happy times were more memory than reality. I realized that my indulgences in Scientology, let alone the Sea Org, were in complete opposition to anything my father understood. It was also beyond the capacity of his understanding. Later in life, my sister would tell me that he tried very hard and went to leaps and bounds to understand what I was doing, but he never could. Looking up at the sign for Norm's Landing, I knew I could not escape being his son, even if I wanted to, but I did not. What was happening was that I was interiorizing into the physical universe by being reminded of the people who had helped me incarnate in the first place: my parents. This was very weird symbolism. Here I was joining an organization whereby I could leave my body. My parents, on the other hand, represented the opposite.

I soon found a pay phone and explained to Kenda that this all seemed like a bad trick. I was joining the Sea Org and ended up at my old "home dock." Besides being beautiful, Kenda was a very sharp person. She had already predicted the recession of my new found powers. Now, with the right degree of sympathy, understanding, and fire, she reassured me. As if she was a guardian at the gateway, she explained that what I had encountered was just a potential "stop" from getting me through the gate. Her advice was good. Kenda then gave me clear and concise instructions, and I took my final hike on this journey and reached Pier 59.

The *Excalibur* was the largest and most beautiful ship on the dock. I was impressed at its size which was about two-thirds as long as a football field. It was white with a well-rendered depiction of King Arthur's sword Excalibur on the bow of the ship. The word *Excalibur* was also spelled out above the sword, and it was very prominent, just above the anchor.

It was 2:00 a.m. by now, and I was greeted by the ship's quartermaster who stood on guard at the gangway. There was always a twenty-four hour guard by at least one person. The medical officer had to be awoken to interview me in order to ensure I had no communicable diseases. All he did was ask me rather meaningless questions about my medical history. After the interview, he found me a bunk where I would sleep for about five hours or so. As the generators were shut down at night, there were no lights, and I had to be escorted with a flash light. Completely to my surprise, the morning would include perhaps the biggest challenge yet. It was not threatening in the least, but it sure was the most puzzling phenomena I would ever encounter in what was to be my eleven year Sea Org career.

15

A BILLION YEAR CONTRACT

Before I went to sleep, the Medical Officer of the *Excalibur* told me I could sleep-in as I had arrived late; but he added that it would be a great idea if I could make it to the crew's morning muster. That way, I could meet everyone. Although my flirtation with OT powers seemed to be over, I was still operating at a high level of energy. I did not find it easy to sleep when the generators and lights came on. I attended the crew's muster which was held below decks, in the mess hall. That was where I would take in a shock to my system that was to serve as my next major challenge. So that you can better appreciate the impact it had on me, I first need to relay another incident from my past.

During my last year in high school, I had been very dedicated to my own path of esoteric studies. Along the way, I decided that it was part of my life's path to take LSD-25. Although I accepted marijuana as a recreational drug at that time, I was pretty much dead set against all drugs other than the hallucinogens. My reasoning, based upon what I had studied from experienced people, was that LSD could give you a window into what you could accomplish along the spiritual path; but, it most definitely could not take you there. That was something that only you could do yourself. In fact, it was boldly stated in the work I read by Robert S. de Ropp that any altered states you could experience as a result of drugs could also be reproduced by the body itself, without any stimulus such as drugs. This is opening up the seals of the body on a more natural basis, and this is the only method I would approve of or advocate today. However, at that time, I wanted to see what might transpire and what I could see with LSD.

By 1970, it was not easy to find pure LSD anywhere in or near the Bay Area. You almost had to know a chemist who made the stuff. The people who controlled the drug supply did not want people taking LSD. As a "bait and switch," they laced other drugs such as speed with LSD. There was no question, even by the people who took them, that they were made to mess you up. This was an incredibly dangerous environment with not even any arguable prospect of "consciousness raising." The only market for such drugs were kids who merely wanted a high. My friend Tor, unfortunately, became one. I was not about to go experimenting with any of the drugs he took or deal with his sources.

Finally, I was able to get some pure LSD through an old friend from Taft, and we had an eventful trip together at Millerton Lake near Fresno. This stuff was called Orange Sunshine, and it was the purest and most powerful form of LSD then known to man. It was orange in color, and we both took some. As for my friend, who was much more involved in the drug scene than I was, this experience was so potent and powerful that he never took LSD again. He and his brother agreed, however, that I was far more effected than he.

To stick to the facts of the matter at hand, I can only summarize the significant effects of what happened. As the drug is a poison, I became sick and threw up in a park outhouse. As LSD is essentially a mind amplifier, everything I would focus on became amplified or exaggerated. If someone simply said, "Hi, how are you?" with a tinge of concern, I might see nothing but deep concern about my well being. If a girl smiled, you might see a lot more than a smile. But, most of my trip was not about people. For the first time in my life, I could feel my pineal gland as if it were an extension or an appendage, not unlike the way you feel an arm or a leg. It felt like tons of energy was being pumped through the area known as the Third Eye.

Ridiculously lying in a bed of flowers (I was not thinking too straight, and it seemed like a divine place to camp out) outside of the sight of everyone, I closed my eyes and began to see the most wonderful and breathtaking "cartoon" I had ever witnessed. There were infinite three-dimensional renditions of numbers in pastel colors which looked like they had been thrown into a junkyard of numbers. Although I did not know what a fractal was, this was a cartoon representation of fractals. These numbers made up an entire "floor" of what was an infinite landscape. As I continued to look, some of the numbers congregated together and formed "organizations" of symmetry. This represented order versus chaos. Occasionally, some of the numbers or aggregates of numbers would show an emotion, not unlike you might see in a cartoon. These emotions were generally that of camaraderie with other numbers and seemed to signify solidarity of some sort. In other words, like attracted like but seemingly for the purpose of building bigger and better systems of numbers. It was very cute. More complex forms would form into bigger construction projects that led up and up to higher vistas. The higher the view, the more breathtaking and beautiful was the view. Eventually, I was seeing pyramids constructed, but I am not talking about pyramids like those seen near Cairo or Chichenitza. These were cartoon holographs that represented natural building blocks of some kind.

Whenever I opened my eyes, I saw the trees and clouds taking the shape of "creatures." The trees and clouds had faces and hands. At every seeming opportunity, they showed themselves to be working together as nature. There were a lot of goofy caricatures and exaggerated expressions as well. It was completely delightful, and I felt a very deep bond with nature which I would never forget. Most relevant to my experience on this day, however, was a "guide" who appeared as I gazed at the various spectacles before me. This guide was a cartoon as well and he changed his appearance from time to time, but he mostly appeared in pastel overalls with a pencil behind his ears. He looked like a carpenter or builder. Although there was a simplistic blue-collar quality about him, he seemed to have all the answers, but he was very humble. The guide pointed out and explained the various forms and configurations to me. When my questions became a little too complex, he would look at me and smile and say, "That's upstairs." By that, he meant that one needed to ascend higher and higher to understand the whole show that he was taking me through. Whenever he would say the words "upstairs," he would sort of smile and wink so as to encourage me to go higher and higher in terms of understanding. But, it was also clear that there were plenty of lower levels to go through on the way up. Everything then appeared as an escalator moving upward. The pyramids, numbers, etc. all began moving like escalators. I was headed "up." Whatever this "guide" was, he seemed to represent a friend or someone who could show and explain the way to the innermost secrets of existence. Some literature suggests that such a guide is really your "higher-self" or "Holy Guardian Angel." *

Although the aforementioned LSD experience was friendly and enlightening, it gave rise to what can best be termed "ontological shock" when I joined the *Excalibur* crew in the mess hall on that April morning. Seeing the Captain for the first time, whose name was Alan Long, I could not help but notice that he was the spitting 3-D flesh image of the cartoon character I had known as my guide on the LSD trip!

What in the hell was going on? Personally, I had no idea. There were no drugs of any kind running through my system but only the memory of what I had experienced. I did not know how to respond and pretty much kept everything to myself. This was one of the weirdest things in the world, and it still ranks right up there, even with all of the strange experiences I have had since.

What was almost as strange was that I was to end up spending a good part of the next few days with Alan. He had business to take care of at the Sea Org's United States Liaison Office, and I needed to go with him for more bureaucratic paper work that was for the purpose of processing me into the Sea Org. In all of my subsequent years in the Sea Org, I never saw anyone go through as much paperwork processing as myself and doing all of this running around with the Captain of a ship. It was very odd. I got to know him a bit. He told me that he had served in the U.S. Navy and had learned how to sail a ship there. He was promoted to be a ship captain when the Commodore (L. Ron Hubbard) had seen him conning (this means to be in command of a vessel and to be

---

* With regard to that day, there was much more that happened with the LSD trip. Some of it was very funny, but that is getting off the subject. I would like to add, however, that while this was very enlightening, I would later spend hundreds of hours "auditing out" the negative experiences and body somatics that came with this trip. It was not a "bad trip" by any means. All I can tell you is that most drugs users are not even cognizant of what is really going on with their bodies. It is too suppressed. It was only after I became more and more sensitive through auditing that I realized the negative aspects of what I had experienced on a physiological and mental level. It was only then that the negative effects could be efficiently addressed.

responsible for its movement) the Flagship and was impressed. Alan was one of very few people in the Sea Org who had what was called a right arm ranking. A right arm rank meant that you were qualified and fully capable of conning a ship. Alan was fantastically popular with the crew and was very funny when he spoke.

At one point, Alan had me walk over to AOLA with him. AOLA was an acronym for the Advanced Organization in Los Angeles. This is where Scientologists from all over America came for the OT levels. As I sat in the lobby waiting for him, I was dumbstruck by the wonderful feeling in the building. I was not the most advanced Scientologist in the world, but boy, did I notice a difference. The psychic space was completely clear of any negative debris. I had never seen anything like it. When he came out, I commented to him about it, and he smiled, saying that it was pretty neat, wasn't it? He knew exactly what I was talking about.

I studied Alan's personality as best I could but was not about to tell him about my "recognition" of him. It was too weird. This experience, however, sort of sold me on the idea that I must be in the right place, but I could only get a feel of what might be going on. My speculative conclusion at the time was that as thetans (the Scientology word for spirit), we had been together before. It went back to ancient times that were far older than anything modern day Earth might represent, but it had to do with being agents in the evolution of a universe, if that makes any sense. The Sea Org, at that point in my mind, had antecedent organizations on the time track which were dedicated to building and establishing progressions of nature that were designed to carry out an even higher purpose of nature. Alan, in his current form, was only a shadow of his former self, but the inner core was still there. One could see the battle scars in his aura of having been through a millennia of bad lifetimes of the reactive bank. Once Scientology had been discovered and "broke the barrier" of the reactive bank, Alan was one of the first thetans to report back and get on with the show. This may or may not have been true, but it was the best guess I could come up with.

On the way back to the ship one evening, he told me that he had gotten an approval to take the ship to San Francisco. He said I would be "going back home." San Francisco was not really my home per se, but it was close enough. When he announced the news to the crew, I was completely dumbstruck at how excited they all were. In fact, I later commented to him that I could not possibly understand why everyone could get so excited about going to San Francisco. He explained to me, almost sheepishly but not quite, that most of the crew had been in L.A. for as long as could be remembered and they were all kind of stir crazy. In other words, there was a great lack of "happening activity" for much of the crew. Fortunately, for myself, I would never suffer from too much "unhappening activity" in my Sea Org career.

16

VICTORY AT SEA

Besides spending so much time being processed into the Sea Org and hanging around with the Captain, there was another unusual experience with regard to my joining the Sea Org. I was given a Sea Org swearing-in ceremony the likes of which I never saw after that point. Normally, the Sea Org recruiter would take care of the swearing-in. In my case, the Captain was there and supervised it, and there was some other ceremonial stuff which I do not remember. They made it a much bigger deal than I expected and certainly more than I ever saw for anyone else. There were probably some other big deals for other people, but I never saw or heard of them. In retrospect, it all seems odd.

At the end of the ceremony, I signed a billion year contract which was basically dedicating myself to establishing high-func-tioning Dianetics and Scientology organizations for the duration. Again, it was not something everyone fulfilled. In fact, you were really not expected to make it past the first year or two.

I was then assigned to a study period where I would learn Sea Org basics in the evening and work during the days. Asked if I wanted to work on the decks, the engine room or the galley, I chose the engine room as that was the area I knew the least about. My first job was wiping the engines which was really a horrible job. The smell of diesel fuel did not help when we went out for our first sea trials. I got horribly sick. Sea sickness was something I was not used to as a kid. In fact, I could endure the ocean waves better than anyone as a child. Being below decks and feeling very interiorized did not help matters. Besides that, I was completely overwhelmed by all of the different parts in the engine room and was under the mistaken impression that I needed to become a master mechanic overnight. Of course, no one expected this of me at all, but I figured if I was going to be OT that I had better just learn everything — instantly. I was being unreal. One of the engineers sent me to the course room to look up all my misunderstood words about engines, and I ended up learning a lot about electricity, but I was going way overboard. Actually, my mind was too active to be confined to wiping engines. It was decided that I needed some fresh air in my life so I was reassigned to the decks. This was certainly more extroverting, but all the joys I had experienced upon joining the Sea Org had come to a crashing halt. I was introverted and interiorized into my own head. Could I have used an Exteriorization/Interiorization Rundown as had been performed on me so excellently in Davis? The answer is an unequivocal yes! But, there were no auditors on board as this was a training ship. Some of the crew were auditors, but they were not practicing. Even if they were, you were not expected to "have a case" in the Sea Org. People did not join to just "get audited." One was expected to rise above the reactive mind and get the show on the road for others. There would eventually be a time for auditing, but this was not it. I continued to study and learn the basics of Sea Org philosophy, but all in all, I was not doing that well. My falling back from the successes I had experienced with Dianetics was called, in Scientology parlance, not being able to hold a gain. In other words, everyone in Scientology pretty much had gains. One of the biggest tricks was being able to hold them and not fold under pressure. As I was taking on the whole universe and everything that was potentially wrong with it, at least in my own mind, I was taking on a bit more than anyone could be expected to chew.

Despite my struggles, I continued on as there was no particular reason to call it quits. The crew were nice and sympathetic. Once again, they did not really expect you to make it. When the ship finally set sail for San Francisco, it was late at night and under horrible weather conditions. I was assigned a sea watch as Assistant Lookout where I would be with Kenda who was designated as the Head Lookout. Lookout stood on the highest deck of the ship (not in the crow's nest) and was just above the bridge where the Captain or conning officer would observe and give orders. Other than the engine room, lookout might have been the worst place to be. You were in the open weather, on a slippery deck, and there was no cover. It was as bouncy as ever and we were in harsh weather. It did not take long before I got sick. Kenda told me not to be sick up there, and I made repeated trips to the head until I just ditched my post. This was not supposed to be acceptable, but nobody wanted me throwing up and the watch only lasted until midnight. I went below decks and tried to sleep. The bunks were on chains so that they would rock with the waves and not push you around during heavy seas. I was able to sleep, but it was intimidating. When I was awoken to report to watch, I just did not report. I was so sick that I did not care. Sea sickness is most horrible, particularly when you have a history of having sea legs. Whenever someone came down to wake me up, I just did not go up. Nobody seemed to care. In actual fact, as I found out much later, a lot of the crew were sick and that included the Captain. He spent much of the voyage in his cabin being as sick as myself. Fortunately, there were enough competent crew who were able to keep us afloat and on course.

As we made our way up the California coast, the conditions worsened and we entered what is known as Force Eight storm conditions. This is just below a gale. Years later, when I told various Sea Org personnel that I had been in a Force Eight, they did not believe me too readily because these conditions are something akin to what you might experience around Tierra del Fuego where the conditions are absolutely horrible. It was indeed a Force Eight.

Eventually, someone suggested that I should get some fresh air as I had been below decks the entire night and most of the day. For the most part, I was in complete darkness and there was no one around. Going above decks, I saw the full force of the ocean as I had never before seen in my entire life. This was trial by water in alchemical terms. While I needed the fresh air, the knocking about was a bit much. I finally found myself a place on the deck where I could lay down and sort of hold on to my bearings. It was a bit better but still very rough, like a horror movie. There was no security or stable reference, only the pounding of waves. As I looked at the ocean, it was magnificent in its fierceness and relentlessness. I put out a postulate that I wanted to be OT VIII so that I could literally control all such elements and conditions. In those days, OT VIII was the top level envisioned in Scientology and it signified the ability to control matter, energy, space and time both subjectively and objectively.

Visualizing myself as being able to literally overcome matter itself, I projected my intention outward, boldly asserting through the process of thought that I wanted to achieve such a rarefied state of being. Although I was a long way off from achieving such a remarkable state, my postulate could not have hurt me. After nodding off for a while and briefly falling asleep on the deck, I had a sudden urge to get off of my ass and stand up. It just seemed like the right thing to do. Almost immediately after I stood up and walked to another spot on the ship about fifteen feet away, a huge wave crashed over the side of the ship and went right over the exact location where I had been resting a minute earlier. Had I not gotten up at the exact right moment, I would have been drenched. This was the first wave that had crashed over the ship, and the crew became very excited. I was one of only a few on the deck at the time. Someone soon came by and said the Captain had ordered everyone below decks. He did not want anyone washed overboard. Making that postulate and getting out of harms way of that wave, without even realizing what I was doing, was the first competent thing I ever really accomplished in the Sea Org. In what was my greatest moment of awe and vulnerability with regard to the sea, I had paid my respect to the elements. Despite their fierceness, they had smiled at me.

I then went back to bed and did some more sleeping. When I awoke the next morning, we had arrived in the port of Santa Cruz and were anchored a good distance from the pier. Things went back to a regular schedule for the rest of the day as we cleaned up the ship after about thirty-six hours at sea. Despite my success with the wave, I still felt like an abject failure and was not proud of myself. In fact, I had never been so dismally disappointed about my performance in my entire life. Whenever I did not do well in school or in sports, I always attributed it to not applying myself. While this was true, I had applied myself to the fullest extent of my being in the Sea Org, and I was failing and failing badly. Others looked at me as someone new who was trying to make the grade, but I judged myself much more harshly.

That evening we sailed towards San Francisco for the last leg of our run. I got some more sleep and was not called to duty until daybreak where I would reemerge as Assistant Lookout. When I arrived on the bridge to make my way up to the lookout deck, the Officer of the Deck said I could be shot for having abandoned my watch. I told him to shoot, and he was very dumbfounded by my response. I clearly did not care as I climbed the ladder to the lookout deck and took up my post with Kenda. The sea was now reasonable, and I definitely had my sea legs back. It was sunrise and the morning was absolutely gorgeous as we began to turn the corner to enter San Francisco Bay. The Golden Gate Bridge was still miles away. When Kenda had finished teaching me the lingo of the lookout post, the Captain then pointed out other ships or different flotsam and jetsam that was out at sea and had us estimate how many yards away things were. This was really just a drill to sharpen up our skills. When it was my turn, my estimates were so accurate it, he could not believe it. In fact, he even extended his head up from the bridge to look at me because he could not believe how accurate I was. I think he wanted to see if I was cheating or something. Actually, my only secret was that I had watched many football games, including from high up in the L.A. Coliseum, so I could rather easily assess how long a hundred yard football field was. I would imagine one and a half or two and two-thirds of a football field and just do the math quickly in my head. That was the second competent thing I ever did in the Sea Org. Everything else was pretty much a wash of failure.

Going under the Golden Gate Bridge at dawn was one of the most breathtaking sights I have ever seen in my life. It was well worth the adventure of the Sea Org even if I never made it beyond this trip. We anchored off of Sausalito in the San Francisco Bay and spent the day cleaning the ship and getting it ready to bring to the dock in San Francisco itself. The scenery was completely beautiful and Mount Tamalpais never looked so magnificent. All of a sudden, things did not seem quite so bad. I still felt like an abject failure, but at least some forces of joy were in motion.

In the late afternoon, we took the ship into San Francisco, and I had no idea that such a large crowd would be waiting to receive us. They were mostly from San Francisco, but there were plenty of people from Davis as well, including a few close friends and former roommates. The Captain was right with his earlier comment. San Francisco had never before seemed so much like home. The crowd stampeded the ship, and it was now all party time and public relations. Somehow, I was elated with all of the familiar faces. All of a sudden, despite my incongruous and hellish experiences, I was a representative of the Sea Org and had to put on a good face. Everything seemed like a big game, but I do not mean that in a negative sense. The Sea Org represented the ultimate OT adventure to Scientologists. We, despite any of our internal difficulties, were making it a reality with that trip. As long I was there with the crew in San Francisco, there was a definite party atmosphere. Even though we all went back to regular work, the environment now evoked a spirit of fun.

All sorts of people started showing up, and one of them was named Mike Douglas. He was the Deputy Captain of the *Apollo*, the Sea Org's premier vessel and Flagship. Mike was there to recruit Sea Org members who wanted to go to Flag and live and work with Ron. Literally everyone aboard the *Excalibur* wanted to go to the *Apollo*, but many were needed on their jobs and some did not qualify for a various number of reasons. Mike was basically looking for new people, and everyone was eager to put their name in the hat. I had performed so poorly that I knew I was not deserving and did not even ask. Mike, however, took note of me and went through my test scores and the other data in my personnel folder. After a week of hearing how all of these various people were going to Flag, I found that Mike had selected me. I was completely flabbergasted. He had previously asked me if I would like to go to the *Apollo* and be with Ron. I gave him an affirmative "yes," but I had no idea I actually would go. It was not even something I thought about. I did not select them — they selected me. When Mike told me the news, I could not believe it. This was every Scientologist's ultimate dream: to go to the *Apollo* and see Ron in action. It was never a goal of mine — it just happened. Two others were selected along with me. Mike drove the three of us in his father's car down to Los Angeles. I had now travelled between Los Angeles and San Francisco by plane, by boat, and by car. Despite my ineptness and dissatisfaction with my performance in the Sea Org thus far, things were moving very fast.

When Mike got us back to Los Angeles, there was more bureaucratic bullshit to go through. In the process, the two other candidates were eliminated for various reasons, and I was the only one who was going to go. It was very weird. There were literally all of these candidates who had been chomping at the bit and grandstanding about how they were going to go be with Ron. Some were even comically assertive about it but not in a way that was meant to be comical. In the end, I was the only one of the lot that made it. Oddly, or perhaps not, I was the only one who did not ask or assert his desire. It just happened. I was invited — I never asked.

My feelings of failure as a result of my poor performance seemed to dissipate. The elements were pushing me. The *Apollo* awaited and so did Ron.*

---

* During the rest of this book, I will refer to L. Ron Hubbard by various names and titles including LRH, Ron, the Commodore, and Hubbard. Each of these appellations was usually used in a very specific context. "Ron" is how most Scientologists refer to him, and this was always the most ingratiating aspect of his personality. "Commodore" was a term used strictly by Sea Org members or other creatures we might have encountered in maritime adventures. "LRH" was used primarily to refer to his role as an executive or founder of the technology of Dianetics and Scientology. It was used by Sea Org members, Scientology executives and Scientologists in general. No one in Scientology ever referred to him as Hubbard. I will use the latter only when I feel it is appropriate in communicating about him in a context where others might refer to or think of him as Hubbard. The rest of the terms I will use interchangeably as I feel they are appropriate to the context I am writing about. At various times in my life, I knew him by all of these different appellations and even a few more.

17

THE APOLLO

After about a week in Los Angeles, I was told that I would be couriering boxes to the *Apollo*, many of which contained personal items for Ron. Their safety was to be my ultimate concern. I remember that some of the items included coconut soap and cartons of Kool cigarettes. Ron was famous for smoking Kools.

I was whisked away to the airport with a Class IX* auditor who would accompany me. She was going to Flag for advanced auditor training. I would fly with her on an Air France jumbo jet to Paris where we would catch a flight to Madrid and be met by two Sea Org staff who were assigned to a permanent liaison office in that city. At that time, all communications to and from the *Apollo* went through the Madrid office. Once there, we would separate permanently for logistical reasons. She would stay at a hotel and keep certain boxes refrigerated while I would spend the night in another hotel before catching an afternoon flight and taking other boxes to Casablanca in Morocco.

Arriving in Casablanca, I could not help but notice a very menacing armed guard on my way into the airport luggage claim. I instinctively hated the man. He wore bullets across his chest and everything. He was my welcoming committee to the third world. When I arrived inside, there were three Scientologists waiting for

---

* There were different classifications of Scientology auditors. Designations began with Class 0 and went as high as Class XII (twelve). Class V and above were only taught at special organizations and Class IX was the highest level you could attain without going to the *Apollo*. Only on the *Apollo* could one study levels X, XI, and XII.

me, but they barely greeted me. They made it very clear they were more interested in the safe transport of the boxes than how I was doing. One of the guys escorted me to a bus where he accompanied me on a long and eye-opening ride through Casablanca on the way to the docks. It was not a pretty site and poverty seemed to be the main theme as well as dangerous and menacing looking characters. All of the woman wore veils. I could not possibly feel at home there and never sought to venture out into that city when I later had the opportunity.

After boarding the ship and going through the same ridiculous medical routine, I was introduced to a "buddy" who would show me my way around the ship. Within no time at all, he took me to the promenade deck and we walked by Ron's office. To my surprise, there was Ron! I could see him through his window as he sat at his desk working. It was obvious that he was intently engaged with whatever he was doing. I could not have missed him if I had wanted to. The window drapes were not closed or anything. This was something of a thrill. I had not asked to see Ron, but it worked out splendidly.

My buddy's name was Bob, and he had been around the Sea Org for many years so knew all sorts of colloquial things and also a lot of interesting history that many crew members did not. He told me that the ship always stayed in warm weather areas because the Commodore's lungs could not take the colder weather. I have read so many expose's about Ron's health conditions and how it was "hidden" from everyone. But, this was not hidden at all. It was just matter of fact. Not everyone knew it, but most of us did. Big deal. It did not mean that Dianetics did not work. People think this is a big contradiction. It only meant that Ron had a medical lung condition. I also learned that Ron slept about eight hours a night, and he recommended that others do the same.

While I had witnessed a few minor skirmishes break out amongst the crew members of the *Excalibur,* the *Apollo* was much more vicious in the way certain people communicated to each other, particularly to myself. My first task aboard the ship was to get through a routing form which meant that various people (there were quite a few) had to sign off and/or interview me or brief me as part of my introduction to the ship. Some people were very nice and cooperative while others were rude or just refused to talk to me. This was not only antisocial behavior, it was also anti-Scientology behavior, and it was most peculiar. In this respect, there was no shortage of people who did not live up to the standards of communication I had learned at the Mission of Davis. Most of the rude behavior was not directed at me anyway, so it did not really disturb me too much. It had more to do with people's own inability to handle their own jobs. After a week of trying to get through the routing form, I could still not penetrate through the rudeness of certain people so I just reported to the decks and went to work. Besides that, I would work and study five hours a day to "get in my basics" which meant continuing my Sea Org training.

While on the decks, I was awoken one morning and told that I would serve as Quartermaster of the Gangway. This meant that I would regulate who went on and off the ship and also ensure that the hawsers (large ropes) that tied the ship to the dock were not too tight or too loose. In this capacity, I was to serve as an assistant to a more experienced Sea Org member and also learn the job. Part of this duty also required that you prevent anyone on the restricted list from leaving the ship. The restricted list consisted of people who were either sick or were a potential security risk. While this might sound heavy-handed, it was not. A ship is a sovereign entity and is only visiting the country it is in. The ship's captain is ultimately responsible, at his discretion or under a delegated authority, as to who is and is not suitable or allowed to go ashore. You cannot have crew members going ashore and trashing an establishment or any such potential risks.

To my surprise, there was a very distinguished and famous Sea Org member on the restricted list. His name was Otto Roos, Ron's top technical person who was one of the few Class XII auditors in the Sea Org. This was my first glimpse of what could be called the Anti-Ron. Rumors were swirling about the ship that LRH had slugged him in the mouth. In the process, people were also making LRH sound like Muhammad Ali, and I knew this was a ridiculous distortion. It is quite true that LRH hit him, but as Otto would later say, "He was an old man. It didn't hurt." If you read Otto's write-ups on the internet, you will find a portrayal of the Anti-Ron, but you would also find in Otto someone who admired Ron's techniques and even Ron himself. What Otto does not tell you, however, is about the Anti-Otto.

After a month or so in the Sea Org, I finally saw Otto for the first time. As I walked through a lounge area, I saw this beaten down middle-aged man coming to me to sign a petition for him to reenter the group. I had no idea who he was, but he wrote in his petition how he was sorry for the crimes he had committed against LRH and the group and that he had worked many late hours to atone for this. After seeing and reading his petition, I saw that he was the once famous Otto Roos. I signed his petition and went about my business. It was an incidental meeting, and he was quite subdued and polite.

Soon after, Otto suddenly disappeared from the ship in Portugal and was declared a Suppressive Person. This term will be explained later, but it is a designation in Scientology which makes you persona non grata and forbids Scientologists from speaking with you. After this event, there was much discussion about Otto and various crew members needed to unburden themselves about the various experiences they had with him. I learned a lot.

Otto was very well trained in virtually all the techniques of Scientology. In fact, he even made some of them up himself. I would later learn from other crew members, however, that he could also be an ass-hole on an unprecedented level. One girl told me how he was her auditor but that he would only audit her if she would have sex with him. He would even stop the session and demand sex right then and there. This was extremely unprecedented behavior, and he could have been thrown out of Scientology for that alone. The girl, very afraid of his authority, complied with him. He would also intimidate the people in Treasury into paying him huge bonuses that he made up. He was taking in over a thousand dollars a month which would be the equivalent of maybe six thousand as I write this. Remember, the average Sea Org member was given an allowance of ten dollars a week with maybe a bonus of $20 or $30 if they were lucky. Otto was raking it in.

One fellow I knew fairly well told me that there was only one time that Otto turned his evil glare on him. This person said he actually handled Otto quite effectively. Just looking at him square in the eyes, he told Otto to leave him alone or he would kill him. Otto left him alone and never bothered him again.

Otto was a clear case of oppression and suppression. He accused LRH of having such tendencies. Whether he was right to some degree or not is really not for me to judge. They were not my quarrels. But, in all fairness, you have to consider the mirror Otto was looking into as he clearly demonstrated himself to have many suppressive tendencies. Before judging Ron with regard to hitting Otto, you should also take into account that he was practically the only one on the ship to stand up to him.

Despite the overblown heroics of Ron pounding Otto, the Ron I saw on the ship seemed like a very congenial character up to now. Almost every day he would write a note to the crew in the *Orders of the Day*, a copy of which was circulated to all the crew and contained various orders and notices from different departments and also including a short summary of world news. Ron also encouraged us to write a daily report to him as he liked to keep tabs on what was going on. He realized that some staff were afraid to write proper reports to the ethics department for fear their seniors would come down on them. This was his way of keeping everyone honest, and the crew literally loved to write to Ron. Ron was always very cordial to those who wrote to him. Sometimes, if you were lucky, he would even answer you.

One day, only several weeks after I had arrived on the ship, I noticed that I had lost my wallet. This was a bit upsetting as it contained virtually all of the cash I had in the world which was something between the two and three hundred dollar range. At the time I noticed my missing wallet, I was in the course room and mentioned it to my fellow students. No one had seen it, and I felt a bit hopeless. At the end of the day, I wrote my daily report to Ron and told him that I had lost my wallet and how much was in it. I was actually hoping that he could "remote-view" it and tell me where it might be. This was an extreme long shot in my mind, and I was prepared to adjust to life with the loss of my money. I had some other money in foreign currency that had been stashed in my pocket so I was not utterly broke.

It was either the very next morning or the next morning after that when I was pulled aside as I went down the gangway in the morning for a crew muster and exercises. The Master at Arms, who was in charge of ethics and discipline of the crew members, wanted to speak with me.

"This is your wallet, right?" he said.

"Yes," I said.

He then began to tell me how much money it was, and I found this rather odd because he made it sound like a vast sum. It was not, but to him it apparently was. Anyway, he told me that I could thank the Commodore because he was primarily responsible for locating my wallet and seeing that it was returned to me.

Wow! I was elated and completely surprised that he would go to so much trouble. There were probably two to three hundred daily reports on his desk, and he not only read mine, he delivered the request. I was very impressed.

In hindsight, I do not believe that he remote-viewed my wallet. It is possible, but I assume he did a very fast ethics investigation. He did not like thieves amongst the crew, and he was powerful enough to prevent such. I still do not know, but I did not care. At this point, I already viewed Ron in a favorable position. This only secured it.

By that time, Ron had not only come to my rescue but had come to the rescue of the crew itself on two other counts. First, he noticed that people were not getting any time off or what were called liberty days, and he changed that for everyone. Additionally, he commented that people were not being allowed by the ship's designated authorities to take their annual three week vacations, and he changed that, too. I remember him citing the old phrase from Patrick Henry, "Give me liberty or give me death!"

More important than all of that, he also noticed that there was virtually no auditing going on or very little. He considered this an affront not only to himself but to everyone aboard. If people were not getting audited, they were not going to get any place. People loved to be audited so his outrage on this subject was very popular. As a result, I was transferred to the Technical Division, along with many others, where I would study to become a Flag auditor. My Sea Org basics would have to wait. This turned out to be a dream come true because I had made a postulate to do this very thing.

18

CONTRADICTIONS

It was a mistake for me to be posted as an auditor, but only because I was not trained for what they expected me to do. I was expected to do Scientology auditing yet I had no context for it. I was trained only to do Dianetics. Although my lack of training ultimately resulted in me being reassigned to the decks, I had the opportunity to spend a considerable amount of time in morning technical briefings which ended up shaping my destiny. It was an experience I would not have missed for the world. At that time, LRH was developing new techniques which were called Expanded Dianetics. This was actually pretty advanced stuff in terms of technical application. It required a lot of precision in terms of observation and asking the right questions to the preclear. Every morning, all of the auditors would be briefed on all of LRH's case notes for the day. They were sometimes quite extensive. Even though much of it was over my head, I learned a lot, particularly in later years when I reread his notes and discovered what he was really talking about. Having been there at the time it was developed really brought the full import home to me.

Various individuals have sought to portray LRH as someone who completely depended upon others to develop the technology, but this is a ludicrous statement. He served as the Senior Case Supervisor on the *Apollo*. This meant that he would review and sometimes personally supervise any cases that were not responding or having a hard time. In this venue, I got a bird's eye view into how he thought and acted in terms of auditing, especially with

117

regard to tough cases that did not resolve easily. These were valuable lessons that stuck with me and made it much easier to negotiate the rest of my Scientology career. He also made himself available to listen to tape recorded sessions of all the auditors in order to correct them whenever needed.

After being aboard the *Apollo* for a few weeks and working in the technical department, I discovered something that I found to be quite shocking. It was astonishingly obvious to me that a great percentage of the crew were not really all that interested in vigorously pursuing Scientology or the OT levels. This might sound like a completely shocking factor to an ordinary Scientologist, but it was true. Many people just mulled along and were more preoccupied with their life circumstances or job than they were in "progressing up the Bridge." Others were ashamed or embarrassed about revealing their particular misdeeds or personal entanglements, particularly recent ones. Something was very wrong here. There was little or no motivation. Befuddled by this, I asked some of the other auditors about it. They just said, "That's the way some people are. That is their case." In Scientology, someone's case refers to how they respond to the world by reason of their personal aberrations.

I was particularly surprised that the Hubbard children, with the exception of Quentin, were not even highly trained. They seemed to have no serious motivation in this regard. Based upon what I had already learned and demonstrably used in regards to Dianetic auditing, I thought this was incredibly unfortunate. To me, Dianetics and Scientology were the most advanced wisdom under the sun, and it was being disregarded.

I wrote to LRH about this but did not get a response. A response was not expected with all of his other daily reports, but I know what he would have thought. He would have said that I am a technical person while others simply are not. Technical people were considered to be a different breed. In his policy letters that he wrote, he also went a step further. He believed that auditors were a much higher caliber of person than others because they actually wanted to do something about the non-optimum conditions of existence. Other people have a tendency to just muddle along. In the Bible, Christ adopted a similar outlook when he said that many want to be ministered unto, but few want to minister.

The key revelation in what I discovered was that there was a HUGE difference between the precepts and technology of Scientology and many of those who were on the *Apollo*. There were, however, many people aboard the *Apollo* who were very much into delivering the technology of Scientology. If there were not, none of us would have been there. The point here is that there was a sizable faction there who were either not that interested or were doing something else entirely.

Another reason LRH did not respond to my letter on these matters was that it was already well covered by his recent actions aboard the ship. He had already noticed that people not only did not get what Scientology was supposed to be, they also did not get what life or much of anything else was about. As a result, he investigated the matter and observed that people do not really understand the words they read. Therefore, if one is reading Scientology materials, college materials or even the newspaper, most people do not really understand the essence of what they are reading. This includes students with good grades. It is all very glib. Accordingly, he devised study technology and developed a course he called the "Student Hat." This consisted of various lessons in what he called the three barriers to study: misunderstood words, skipped gradients, and lack of mass. A skipped gradient refers to glossing over or ignoring the basics of a subject and then taking on something more complicated. This is like someone trying to learn how to play a guitar without learning how to tune it and without practicing the necessary chords. Lack of mass refers to having no applied field of reference by which to compare or make relevant the theories you are studying. It is like studying the theory of classical music without ever listening to it. If you think these keys to study are obvious, you are correct, but you would be amazed how educational institutions ignore them.

When I arrived on the *Apollo*, LRH had just taken this study business yet a step further. He found that people who had done the Student Hat were still not getting the information. Therefore, he went to the extreme measure of creating a new course which he called the Primary Rundown. This consisted of looking up every single word in the materials for the Student Hat course before studying each document or audio tape. As this was not a short course, you ended up looking up almost every common word in the

English dictionary. Besides this, there were various monitors in place to test you and make sure you really understood the words and materials. As this was such a thorough, lengthy and awesome endeavor, most people bogged down and never made it through. He then developed the Primary Correction Rundown for those people which consisted of various auditing actions to clear up their trauma with study. Once that was cleared up, they would proceed with the Primary Rundown. Unfortunately, auditing for the staff was seldom a priority and most of these people never made it through that either. The end result of the Primary Rundown was that it was said to completely open up your communication channels with life. It made study and the retention of data a lot easier. Although I was by no means the only one, I was one of a rather small percentage of either Scientologists or Sea Org members who made it through either rundown.* It was said that if you never made it through the rundown, you could never properly understand Scientology and would have difficulty. So, if you are on the outside trying to understand Scientology, you must understand that not even most Scientologists within the organization were considered to understand Scientology, or at least the full import of the subject. People are plagued by misunderstood words, not only in Scientology but the world itself.

Personally, I found the Primary Rundown extremely helpful as far as being able to negotiate through life, particularly in the hostile environment that the Sea Org could be at times. Studying was also an area where I was able to demonstrate competence. More importantly, and one of the reasons that I include it, is that it also empowered me to have a firm foundation in understanding the legalities of Scientology. By legalities, I am referring to the ecclesiastical and internal administrative procedures of the organization. These were the day-in-and-day-out policies by which Scientologists conducted their business or were <u>supposed</u> to

---

* About a decade after its inception, some features of the Primary Rundown were incorporated into a course called *The Key to Life* which addressed many of these issues. Although it is nowhere near as exhaustive as the original Primary Rundown, it includes other procedures and is generally much simpler and easier to do. Upon completion, it is supposed to open up the keys to your life. Although parts of the course were a review of past concepts for me, I did find it useful and that it lived up to its word. I found, however, that the keys to my life were outside of Scientology. It was the last course in Scientology that I ever did.

conduct their business. As most had a lack of comprehension, the administrative aspects of the organization were often like a jungle. Knowing the various laws and procedures made my life considerably easier and improved it markedly within the organization. Further, it is what enabled me to survive fairly well within it.

Beyond the lack of interest and comprehension about what Scientology actually was or was designed to do, there was another factor: the individual reactive minds of the crew. From listening to the technical briefings and seeing many of the case folders, I learned firsthand how afflicted many of these people were. Everyone has problems and that was to be expected, but some of these people wanted to hurt or harm LRH or Scientology or even blow up the ship. In the Sea Org, you were not judged by reason of your case. That was to be dealt with in auditing and parked the rest of the time. You were only judged by your ability to do your job. That was it. The upshot of this for me was that I saw that many, if not most, of the senior executives in Scientology had some pretty severe aberrations. While it did not really make me insubordinate, it caused me never to take them too seriously. This, by the way, is not a condemnation of anyone. It is just what you would expect to find in any ordinary group of human beings. Many of them were delightful people as well.

All of this brings us to another issue. Despite the friendly faces, some of the people aboard the ship seemed to come right out of the demon realm. There are several explanations for this, but I think the simplest reasoning has to do with what was rather extensively demonstrated in my book *Synchronicity and the Seventh Seal*: as you walk through a door of truth or uncover secrets, you are going to be met by the Gargoyles of the Gate. Hubbard seemed to be surrounded by various gargoyles with varying degrees of intensity and importance.

LRH stated that he had all sorts of administrative defenses to keep him from being drowned with floods of requests and problems. If not, there would have been a never-ending line outside his door of people who wanted various problems solved. All I can say about this is that there seemed to be plenty of negativity going on, but it did not seem to be emanating from him. As far as my experiences went, he seemed to be helpful and friendly. After all, he had touched me in the wallet! I find this particular story with the wallet highly ironic in light of the fact there are plenty of stories on the internet about how Scientology bilks people out of their money. I experienced quite the opposite; but then, I never wanted to be like other people.

The environment aboard the *Apollo* was not a tea party and maybe it had to do with the fact that there was such a high quotient of truth or potential truth to be tapped and the demons came out to roost. Whether or not this is true, there is another important aspect about humanity that should be grasped. No matter what religion, corporation, or any other group of human beings you are dealing with, there is an aspect to humanity which is not much different than a cage of monkeys. Some of the monkeys will throw shit at one another, laugh and point fingers at each other in mocking derision. On the other hand, some of the monkeys will be kind, sympathetic and nurturing. Others will be highly efficient and innovative. There are plenty of monkeys who fluctuate between these various states as well. If you had the occasion to introduce a higher element into the monkey kingdom, there is no question that it would also give rise to expressions that derive from the lowest common denominator.

All of this takes us into the heart of not only what really bugs people about Scientology but one of the key elements this book is meant to address: suppression and oppression.

19

UNCLE TOM'S CABIN

When Nelson Mandela assumed the South African Presidency in 1994, he said the following in his inaugural address:

"Our worst fear is not that we are inadequate. Our deepest fear is that we are powerful beyond measure. It is our Light, not our darkness that most frightens us. We ask ourselves, 'Who am I to be brilliant, gorgeous, talented and fabulous?' Actually, who are you not to be. You are a child of God; your playing small doesn't serve the world. There is nothing enlightening about shrinking so that other people won't feel insecure around you. We were born to make manifest the glory of God/the Divine within us. It is not in just some of us. It is in everyone and as we let our own light shine we unconsciously give other people permission to do the same. As we are liberated from our own fear our presence automatically liberates others."

Mandela, who was quoting Marianne Williamson from her book *A Return to Love*, overcame seemingly impossible odds to rise above decades of incarceration as a political prisoner under apartheid to overthrow that system and establish a modicum of justice in his native country. He is a shining example to all.

Although slavery is not as prevalent as it used to be, it has always been an endemic part of the human condition. Its derivatives still haunt us to this very day.

Imagine that you are a Mississippi slave in 1861, just before the Civil War broke out. Your great great grandfather was brought over from Africa many generations ago, but you do not even know who he was. Your family heritage is gone. All you know about it is snippets from other slaves who knew who your mother was before she was sold to a plantation owner in Louisiana. You have heard about the underground railroad, a clandestine network of abolitionist sympathizers who risk their lives to smuggle slaves to the free country of the North; but you have no idea of what freedom is really like. All you know is working the fields and finding ways to stave off the wrath of your master. Freedom is possible, but it is only a rumor. Even though it is only a rumor and pursuing it is the riskiest activity a slave can indulge in, you know of people who try it spite of the fact that you have all seen your fellows beaten and killed for such. Nevertheless, you dream that someday you might find that light at the end of the underground railroad and be free at last, free at last.

Is it worth the risk?

Some would tell you that there is no choice but to take the risk. Condoning slavery, even of yourself, is to beget more slavery.

As a citizen of Earth, are you really any different? I would be the first to tell you that there is a lot of difference between the slaves of the 19th century and the citizens of today, but there are so many similar themes in our culture that the comparison is inviting.

Slaves had no or little knowledge of their true ancestry. It was taken away from them. Memories were lost save for either a vestigial memory or a hidden tradition. They had no idea who planted them in this strange location and forced them to work for food and necessities. Slaves were born into a life of ignorance and servitude and were fed a Christianity that was designed to sell them on a better life if they were good in this one.

Citizens of Earth are born into a world that is ignorant beyond much of anything that happened before the Bible was written. Christianity is used on them as well, mostly to control and manipulate. There are rumors of an "underground railroad" but the majority of Earthlings do not take it too seriously. Ironically, Christ himself was the biggest advocate of this spiritual "underground railroad" but was expeditiously done away with himself, including the true meaning of his name.

In such an environment of ignorance, the most god awful assertions take place. People are very proud of their accomplishments and their roles in society. This is understandable and all well and fine except that it is usually without deference to the deeper state of ignorance that precipitated their roles in the society in the first place. The ignorance and pride are also understandable in that no one has much of a clue that there might be a tradition in their own being that is really far more magnificent and incredibly glorious than what anyone has suspected.

It is into this sphere of ignorance that Scientology enters the fold. Whether true or not, they are one of the few sizable institutions to have an elaborate answer that not only reaches beyond a few thousand years but seeks and suggests a glorious past of infinite potential for each and every one of us.

As I have said, the candy presented by Scientology included the idea that one could be at complete cause over matter, energy, space and time. This is certainly one of the most exotic states imaginable. It means that you can potentially go to, be at, and see any point on the time line and also create your own universe(s). There are no limits. Another piece of this candy includes the idea that these abilities are an inherent native ability. In other words, you can all do it and did so at one time; but that ability was either taken away from you or you were tricked out of it. You might also have acted together with other beings in creating a universe such as this one and then forgotten all the rules to the game. Someone then took advantage and you ended up on the inside looking out.

Let us look at this way. As a walk-about citizen of Earth, you have inherited a culture that believes itself to be only several thousand years old. In one respect, it is amazing how much progress has made in those few thousand years. On the other hand, what if you were at one time a Quantum Spirit who not only had the potential to experience anything but actually engaged in myriad existences where you roamed through outer space like a Q (Quantum Spirit) that was haunting the crew of Star Trek's *Enterprise* along with any other civilization you encountered. Now, suppose you are a bit of a rascal or nuisance and the *Enterprise* crew gets sick of you and ends up dedicating their entire scientific department into figuring you out and designing a way to trap you and make you inert, if only for their own protection.

In the meantime, you are busy trying to understand people and have no idea of how or why someone would want to play human games. As you participate in their lives, you heckle them and perplex them; but then you make a fatal mistake. You begin to familiarize yourself with them to the point where you also become familiar to them. They learn enough to the point where they can simulate you electronically. Once they do that, they now have a handle on who and what you are, but they do not tell you. While you are curious and interested about them, they do not share your feelings. Because you are more powerful and do not necessarily understand how to behave with them in an acceptable manner, you are a menace. They use what they have learned to entrap you with electronics and neutralize your powers over them.

When the *Enterprise* crew learns that you are an energy form that does not die, they realize that they have a real problem on their hands. They cannot really *kill* you. Instead, if they want to get rid of what they consider to be a menace, they have to keep you at bay. This means putting you in an electronic "ice box" where your energy form is neutered even if it can potentially be reactivated.[*] Another approach would be to subject you to programming whereby you would conform to the standards of the civilization. This would mean that they could also convince you that you were a human body or that you could take over and occupy a human body. This programming would be indoctrinated and reinforced through systematic torture which could include all sorts of electronic manipulation, including the electronic manifestation which is known as pain. In the end, what was a free spirit becomes a slave of creatures who are less free and much more regimented. Over the centuries and millennia, you either forget or are forced to forget that you were ever a free spirit or that a free spirit could even exist.

The above example is random with an imagined *Enterprise*

---

[*] If you are wondering how or why such a potentially powerful being would be vulnerable electronically, you are asking an excellent question. According to Scientology theory, a being in his most pure form has no wavelength, mass or kinetic motion; however, when one participates or steps into this universe and desires to interact with others, they have to assume or simulate energy forms in order to communicate. Forgetting that they assumed such a form or losing the ability to differentiate oneself from an energy form then becomes a mistake of great magnitude. There are as many quantum possibilities as you can imagine. Scientology auditing has hordes of different techniques which seek to address these specific situations.

crew that is more benign than a lot of other scenarios I could have made up. I tried to make it a little more understandable by making the free spirit seem somewhat like a rascal and the "regular citizens" as being perplexed and harassed. The actual proposition is most likely reversed and much more sinister.

I realize that many of you might have considerable difficulty considering L. Ron Hubbard to be your Alex Haley, the author who wrote *Roots* and encouraged Africans everywhere to be proud of and interested in their heritage. LRH did serve as my Alex Haley, but more important than that is the paradigm being presented. No one else on Earth has seriously sought to address the full psychological implications of Earth's prehistory.

As far as the candy-colored exotic states of being that were either offered or suggested by Scientology, there are some similarities between these and the exalted states offered by Christianity and Buddhism. Christianity features the word *gospel*, a word which means "good news" and suggests a heavenly kingdom where we can experience an infinite stream of wonder and bliss. Although they do not state it as such, it would include a happy state of quantum consciousness. Buddhism gives us the state of Nirvana if we follow the right path that will lead from the samsara of suffering. Scientology is arguably a lot more specific and perhaps more captivating because it offers a flamboyant set of circumstances that evoke the themes of science fiction. It has often been called the science fiction religion. This is really not so bad because the entire field of science fiction is dedicated to making extrapolations based upon real applications of science. In any case, all of the above religions are mandated upon the idea of spiritual beings jockeying for spiritual advantage.

The Bible refers to a state of grace that we all fell from. In Scientology, this is akin to what is referred to as Native State, a state of beingness where you can resign from the universe if you want to and pretty much accomplish anything. It is a totally free state that is not subject to the pitfalls of living in this universe. In Scientology, for whatever reason and by whatever means, LRH is viewed to have found the key truths that reverse the so-called fall and build a way back to Native State, your inherent right.

In Scientology, how much LRH was able to work himself out of this paradigm personally was the stuff of speculation. He never really asserted too much about this. Shortly after I arrived on the ship, he addressed this somewhat by saying that he had reached the equivalent of what was about OT 32 but never explained anything beyond that. I never remember myself or anyone on the ship thinking that he could walk through walls or manifest butterflies or anything like that. While people often had remarkable stories to share about him, I do not recall anyone saying he could bend steel in his bare hands. His entire role was that of someone who did have considerable abilities, many of which extended to the realm of exteriorization, and was there to act as a guide for others.

I think that the best way to understand and view this paradigm is by thinking of it as a video game. Let us say that the goal of the game was to reach the center of the Earth where there was an orb with prismatic reflections or some such. Once you entered that orb, you then had all of these abilities. LRH was like a character who not only claimed to know the route but also saw that various trails were blazed and even paved. With Scientology, he at least took you into the interior of the Earth to the point where you could see that there was an entire system of life and wonder that the above world knew nothing about. This was no small achievement in itself, but when it comes to entering the orb, the entire affair becomes more enigmatic. There are reports and even actual instances of people entering the orb, but they are temporary and the roads are obscure. Those who made it to the orb were on other roads when they were somehow miraculously taken to the center and then returned. Where exactly LRH stood in relation to all of this is unknown. He knew about the orb and knew the road system very well but whether he had complete and unfettered access to the orb, or to what degree he had access, is a mystery. The fact that he even knew about the interior world is amazing enough. That he could envision and report on the orb is even more so. When you consider that he could also rattle off laborious details about the whole matter makes the paradigm all the more interesting and mysterious.

Candy is fun and contemplating such idyllic paradigms was certainly a part of Scientology. Some people got caught up in dreaming too much and thought they were going to become super heroes or some such. This is the equivalent of eating too much candy in your real life. Others, including the management and the legal department, were much more concerned about handling real world problems and situations. When things worked well, all of these different aspects blended together quite nicely. As a Scientologist, the real trick in these matters was to build your own bridge to the incredible and fantastic without losing your head or being kicked out by your landlord. In my personal life, my writing has acted as the bridge between the real world and this more fascinating realm. It is completely possible to focus on this sphere and maintain a regular life. In fact, that is one of the challenges facing anyone who treads a spiritual or esoteric path.

The techniques of Scientology, particularly the more esoteric aspects, are very precise. If correctly understood and properly used, they reach into a territory of the spirit that is virtually unmapped by others. Unfortunately, if I were to describe all these unmapped areas, it would be an onerous task and would be like writing an encyclopedia. If I had the time to write it, you might not have the time to read it. To give an excellent bird's-eye view and relatively thorough understanding of these subjects, I would have to compensate for and overcome the years of training and practical application it takes to really grasp all of the subtleties and fine points of the matter. This is something that not even most Scientologist's ever achieve. It a vast subject. Instead, I will address the most important underlying fundamental with regard to the matter at hand.

The above paradigm evokes a state of personal power for the individual. Anyone who has been around Scientologists will notice that they can readily fall into two categories where they are either very high powered individuals or where they think they are such. In any case, most of them tend to be very dynamic when it comes to pushing a religion which they believe embraces the aforementioned ideals and powers. Whether the power is real or fake, the very idea of such power has been tapped to the point where it has manifested a powerful institution.

This book, in part, has to do with the subject of power as well as its various implications. If someone or something has power, this state includes domination or potential domination over others. In such a universe as has been described herein, those who dominate have freedom and those who have power exercised upon them are experiencing some degree of slavery. Paying your utility bill could be interpreted as a form of slavery even though it is not too difficult a task for most people. When you do a complete analysis of all the factors behind utility companies, however, you might find that there is a considerable amount of domination going on. The universe is not too much different. Just as most of us can tolerate paying our utility bills, we can also tolerate most of the status quo processes of this universe. When you consider that free energy or alternative energy is one of the biggest taboos to corporate America, it makes you think a little harder. If we try to break free of the domination of expensive and inefficient energy systems, we are generally given a hard time. The universe is no different when it comes to having completely free spiritual power.

If you really are as powerful as has been suggested, this is really no different from saying that you were at one time in a fluctuating quantum state of choice that could choose any existence imaginable. Further, that you have already made an infinite amount of choices and lived an infinite amount of lives. For the time being, you just happen to be stuck in this life with all of its various pressures and stresses.

When we consider the slavery aspect once again, we are dealing with an oppressive force that is often unexplainable. Slavery goes hand in hand with oppression, a word which is derived from a word that means "to strike." Whether all of the more exotic implications discussed in this chapter are true or not, we all know that this universe suffers from a paradigm we known as the Fall. This is the same as being struck. Somewhere, somehow, we all took it on the chin.

The rhetorical and philosophical question becomes, "Who were we before we took it on the chin and what did we forget?" One can wonder if they were a heavyweight champ, a street waif or something else. If you accept the proposition that you have within you a potential of all quantum states of consciousness, you might accept what Scientologists generally believe: that you have a spiritual potential to do anything.

This is a big nut to chew because it often causes one to use thinking muscles that were never really exercised before. It is not surprising that this sort of thinking is considered "crazy" because it is completely outside the paradigm of what people are taught to believe. Is it true? If it is, you have the first clue to activating your potential. If it is not true, you did not have any hope anyway. You are just a walk-about of Earth, and these things are just outside of your parameters. Earth culture has institutions and systems that will define who and what you are. There is nothing more to be said.

In such a scenario, oppression takes on a much deeper meaning than ordinary slavery or other mistreatment of humans. This is a slavery of the spirit on a much more grand level. Institutions such as human slavery or inquisitions and witch burnings only reinforce this oppression.

Reading this, you have to ask yourself a question. Is any of this real? Whether it is or is not, I can assure you of one thing. This is the very candy that attracts either Scientologists or aspiring Scientologists. It is the carrot that is dangled in front of them. But, there is also an important fact which makes the candy palatable to people: it is usually demonstrable, at least in a microcosmic format, to individuals who enter Scientology. If it were not, the prospect would never gain serious momentum. While this does not guarantee that Scientologists can obtain the state of freedom alluded to above, it at least offers encouragement. Whether or nor Scientology provides the ultimate answer in this regard is an open-ended proposition for each individual. Remember, I am only telling you a story and am not forcing you or suggesting to you that you make choices.

If you understand what is presented here in this chapter, you have an excellent knowledge of why people are interested in Scientology. If you perceive or feel that the essence of what is said here is true, do not feel discouraged by the magnitude of the paradigm and all that it implies. We all have to start somewhere, and each and every one of us is on a path. For the most part, our daily lives consist of what the Zen masters referred to as "chopping wood and carrying water." In other words, flights of fancy should not deter us from our common sense.

For whatever reason, I embraced this paradigm full time and as intensely as I could. Before I continue with my personal story, it is necessary to give you some more information about Scientology as well as the actual history of the movement. I would never have learned or understood all of this without personal involvement.

Before you carry on any further, you might also want
to consider the issue of this planet being a slave colony,
and ask yourself the following question.

Are you an Uncle Tom?

20

WHOLE TRACK

In Scientology, the whole track refers to the time-line that you lived on prior to being born in your current body. The very term connotes unlimited existences. If you want to stream in multiple quantum existences, you can call it "whole tracks." The entrance way to past lives is through an element called "charge." Charge is basically a harmful energy or force accumulated and stored within the reactive part of the mind. The term itself refers to stored energy or recreatable potentials of energy. As an individual, you experience emotional charge from time to time. Someone treating you rudely or receiving bad news are just two examples. Spouses are routinely known to have heated conflicts which evoke charge. There are many such examples, but you get the idea. These experiences alone would be irritating, but when they are restimulated by heavier reactive trauma that is beneath your conscious mind, it becomes exacerbated and sometimes uncontrollable. Charge is what blocks one from remembering earlier lives.

The Scientology e-meter comes into play by registering recreatable potentials of charge. In this way, it is a diagnostic device that guides you to areas of charge within the reactive mind. When I ran out a sore throat as the first item I dealt with in Dianetics, it was chosen by the auditor because it read with a lot of conviction on the meter or at least more so than any of the other afflictions I had previously mentioned to him. The meter thus told him that the string of incidents connected to it was accessible. In this specific case, the e-meter helped to work wonders.

If you put a person on a Scientology e-meter and ask them about their life, you will find that as they talk about certain people, places or events, there are often various unmistakable reactions on the meter which is essentially acting as a biofeedback device. There have been vast attempts to discredit the e-meter by saying it reacts to the grip of the hands and other irrelevant body motions or excretions, but all of these criticisms uniformly miss the point.* These areas of emotional charge can be reproduced by getting the preclear to look at the incidents which disturb him or her and thereby recreate the original emotional reactions. If one cannot bring oneself to recognize the observable reactions on the meter, one can certainly see the reactions in the preclear who is right in front of your face. It is far from rocket science, but it requires an important ingredient that rocket scientists do not always have: compassion, keen observation of the human condition, and a genuine interest in helping the person in front of you.

In the 1950's, Hubbard angered and bewildered many of his followers when he pointed out that the charge on people's cases would not relieve unless they addressed incidents on the whole track. It never mattered whether the incidents addressed made any linear sense or not or whether they were even true in that regard. The point was always to relieve the charge of the individual so that whatever pain or suffering was being experienced in the present moment was alleviated. When you try to enforce your own reality or the consensus agreement of society upon the preclear, it does not do him or her any good. It only reinforces the mind-control mechanisms that are already in place as regards to his or her consciousness. The idea that a preclear conceived he was a clam and that this somehow might have relieved his toothache does not mean he, the auditor, or Scientologists are crazy. It only means that the conception he indulged in relieved his pain. While it is highly amusing that critics suggest that Scientologists believe they were once clams, this is really not true.

---

* In Scientology, one is trained to differentiate body motion and other factors where the meter is not reacting to emotional charge. The e-meter is basically a highly sensitive Wheatstone Bridge or galvanometer which measures electrical resistance via the skin. According to Dr. Wilhelm Reich, orgone energy or life energy resides in the skin. The underlying principle behind diagnosis via a galvanometer is consistent between Reichian therapy and Scientology, but the approaches are completely different.

When one addresses the charge that one has accumulated during one's existence, it can really wake one up. The average New Age practitioner or self-help guru generally does only a very brief sojourn into these areas. As a preclear, I literally spent thousands of hours examining, penetrating and clearing out such areas of charge that would register on the meter.

Sometimes, these sojourns could take you into fantastic areas of history and knowledge you never knew you had inside of you. One time, when running out some sort of pain in the head, I saw an incident where "I" jumped over bulls as I grabbed them by the horns. I thought this was a completely preposterous incident as this seemed like an extremely dangerous if not an impossible thing to do. Years later, I learned that there were actually such bull jumpers in the Minoan civilization, but I had never read or heard of any such information previously. I only indulged the incident because it came up in my mind in response to the auditor's questions and it was relieving the pain.

After you have gone through the rounds with this and have audited others for thousands of hours, you begin to take this sort of phenomena for granted. You also become keenly aware that the majority of "walk-abouts" on Earth are not necessarily too clued-in on much of anything outside of the ordinary parameters of the mundane civilization.

Although the following observations are not uniformly true, I found the following to be most prevalent with regard to people who were audited (and not only by me). People generally started addressing an engram in the current life before going back to one or more early incidents in the same life. Then, they would run past lives that were generally relatable to common history as we know it on Earth. They would then go into incidents on other planets or other time steams. If the engram had not cleared by then, and often it had not, they would end up running incidents from a universe or scenario that was quantum in nature and was much more malleable than our normal world. Sometimes, the incidents took place in pure space, almost like a vacuum, where there were very few players and trappings. But, these could also be somewhat ornate as well. In any case, the point I am trying to address here is that the basic engram was often in a space or time stream that was not evocative or our normal world. It is also important to state that this was not always emphatically the case. It is a report based upon my experience and also that of others.

One of the greatest secrets in Scientology was what Ron called "granting of beingness," but it was never meant to be a secret. Granting beingness to a preclear meant that he or she is allowed to think anything he/she wants to in an auditing session as well as feel anyway he/she wants to. In your own auditing session, you were allowed to completely cause your own thinking and feelings. Auditing was meant to provide a "safe space" whereby one could look at one's own emotional charge and determine the cause of it. This was never the role of the auditor nor anyone else. The whole purpose of auditing was to put a person in such a position so that he/she could "blow" their charge. When this was done properly, a person would have a new lease on life. On an emotional level, it was like winning the lotto, scoring the winning touchdown, or winning first prize in an important contest.

Ron said that the granting of beingness was the highest of human virtues. If you take the opportunity to treat people as they are or who they think they are, and readily acknowledge them for being such, you might find that they respond to you very well. If you are coaching a baseball a team and tell the players that they are no good and cannot do anything right, they will mentally reject you. If you acknowledge what ability they do have, you will encourage them and they will play better and do their best for you. Although this might seem like common sense, it is far from what is applied in the workplaces of the world or in most families. As I already alluded to, this was one of the greatest secrets that made Scientology auditing work on the personal level.

Now, you might have heard that Scientologists do not always behave that way, and you would almost certainly be right. Remember the analogy of the monkey cage. Besides the precept of granting beingness, Ron developed what he called the Auditor's Code in order to enable real auditing to take place. In fact, he said that it was a nearly Christ-like code of behavior. Although often criticized for "not believing in Christ," he felt that this Christ-like code of behavior was one of the most important things in auditing and in helping people in general. If you were on staff or walking about the organization, you were always vulnerable to being treated like shit by someone of lesser intentions. In an auditing session, if it was correctly done, this could never happen. Auditing not only gave you the freedom and power to think, it offered a solution to your problems, including the persons who might be giving you trouble.

When you start meandering about the whole track, you begin to see things differently and that includes your assessment of people and what kind of games they are playing. There are those, for example, who never got over the fact that they were defeated at Waterloo with Napoleon's army. As a result, they reactively try to convince everyone that Napoleon was indeed powerful and that they are indeed the equivalent of the little Corsican general. On the other hand, you can find other people who are either smarter or less afflicted and might be inclined to run a huge corporation by reason of the fact they did so on the whole track. They might be a pleasure to work for. With auditing, they generally begin to demonstrate a considerable amount of ability than they did not show previously.

The above descriptions are intended to give you a bit of insight into the candy that Hubbard offered as well as one of the key developments that made his movement so powerful: he not only created and offered candy but also taught you how to make the candy for others.

Whether or not you accept the premise of the whole track, I would like to share an experience I had that really woke me up on the subject. It was back in Davis, not too long before I joined the Sea Org. I had already had plenty of sojourns on the whole track in my auditing, but that was all internal and had to do with personal therapy. This experience externalized it for me.

I occasionally visited a Scientology chiropractor in Sacramento. As I did not have a car, I caught a ride one morning with the Scientology dissemination crew who were on their daily run to Sacramento City College. As we made our way through downtown Sacramento, I noticed an extremely ornate but small "castle." It had once been an ice cream stand but was now out of business. What was so odd about it was that the architect had created something even more ornate than you might see at Disneyland or an upper end theme park. It looked completely out of place in an area of town that was somewhat rundown. I thought to myself, "What a stupid place to put an ice cream stand!" It was no surprise to me that the place went out of business. Whoever designed that building had quite an imagination. Whoever paid for it was not very practical. I was more surprised than fascinated by what I saw. One of the disseminators, a guy named David, could not help but notice it as well.

"You know," he said as he looked out the window at the ornate castle structure, "I can't believe some of the low order harmonic mockeries of the whole track that exist in this world."

Boy, did he hit the spot with that comment. It made such an impression on me that I have never forgotten his words. Whoever created the design for that castle had conjured up quite an image from somewhere, and it was nothing I had ever quite seen in a fairy tale book or elsewhere. It then became apparent to me that so many of the things we know as fantasy have their roots in places and times that are not of this world. Sometimes fantasy themes are based completely on the imagination. Other times, these themes are based on something else. When David had made his observation about the castle, I had a sudden rush of pictures that went through my mind of where the artist's inspiration had come from. It was not, by the way, a very benign civilization.

More important than the whole track aspect of what David had said, however, was his reference to the words "harmonic mockery." That really got me to thinking. Our world is full of harmonic mockeries. The Christian church is a perfect example of harmonic mockeries. Some renditions of Christianity are quite crude with snake dancing and a joyous exuberance of "Gimme That Old Time Religion." Other churches can be more refined and dignified, sincere or not. Christianity is an excellent example of a higher truth being twisted and perverted in contrast to what was the original intention. In a universe that is preoccupied with domination and degradation, it would seem impossible that any religion, Scientology included, could escape completely unscathed.

There are also many comic examples of harmonic mockery. Comedy is itself based upon this principle. Most everyone likes to see politicians lampooned in complete cartoon form. One of the reasons such cartoons are so appealing and funny is that they betray a very potent divine truth. No matter how good or sincere they might be, politicians, by their very nature, are engaging in the divine principle of the Fool. The whole basis of the Tarot or Tree of Life signifies that the universe is ruled by the Fool. Our politicians, in seeking to control the universe or part of it, are really taking part in a great big joke, the divine joke.

Art is also an expression of different forms of mockery. We are very lucky to have art because this is sometimes the only avenue in a particular civilization which expresses the higher harmonics of experience. Comedy, hay-seed philosophy, and that "old time religion" appeal to the lowest common denominator. There are also more sublime and noble expressions of the human condition. One cannot have the high without the low. The idea of the whole track embraces both but, most importantly, it amplifies the dimensions of the theater you are living in. It can be used as a tool by which to receive your environment, including the people in it.

I have also noticed that you can give some people an index to where they might have existed on the whole track by finding out what areas of history they are interested in. I have found that too many people, however, are not even interested in history at all. Further, they are less interested in pursuing anything that might make them interested in history, particularly their own.

If what I have said about the whole track is not too useful to you, I would certainly think that the aforementioned perception of harmonic mockery might serve you well. When you see something in your environment that you might tend to reject, take a closer look and see what it might actually be a mockery of. You might also be surprised at how mockery fits into our regular society, too. Professional people are too often mockeries of something. Have you ever had a lawyer who was really a mockery of what a lawyer should be? Or, how about a teacher? Better yet, how about an auto repairman or a home renovation specialist? Most of you have had to deal with low order harmonic mockeries all of your life.

In my own life, this principle became a great index with regard to dealing with other Scientologists. They were subject to the laws of mockery as well. Many of them were "mock Scientologists," and that included mock auditors, mock Sea Org members and, in the end, even a mock LRH.

All in all, I agreed with the Scientology precept that we live in a universe that has been subjected to much degradation. There are, of course, plenty of examples of beauty in nature and humanity, but

I do not think I have to beat this point any further. Scientology, at its best, sought to bring a sanctity to the souls of those who had become enmeshed in the various theatrical renditions of degraded mockery that can be found in the physical universe.

Besides the above, I also noted that the general entropy of this universe is generally predisposed towards taking the higher aspects of Scientology or any other noble idea and rendering it at a level which is directly proportional to the level of degradation inherent in the particular vehicle of conveyance. If you give Scientology to the Nazis or the intelligence community, you might find that they would use it to mind-control others. If you were to give it to Mother Theresa, you might find her using it to heal her patients. If you gave it to St. Theresa of Avignon, she likely would have used it to send her students into spiritual ecstasy. Sometimes the vehicle of conveyance is more important than what is being conveyed. Just as there are many higher order and lower order beings in schools and universities, Scientology was no exception. A monkey cage is a monkey cage.

The monkey analogy now brings us to another proposition. I have already implied that some of you in the reading audience <u>might</u> be an "Uncle Tom" when it comes to recognizing a state of indentured servitude to this universe. Now, I am taking this unfortunate racial analogy a step further. What order of "monkey" are you?*

You might be a high order monkey, but there is one caveat to that. If you assume that role, you might soon discover that the lower order monkeys relish the idea of hurling dung at you. On the other hand, you might also enjoy the prospect of flinging dung yourself, perhaps at someone who is pious or a mockery of a higher order being. The trick here is to be able to assimilate or emulate all different orders of being. That way, you can talk to people at their level and not intimidate or be intimidated by the various fluctuations of mockery that you encounter in day to day life. Sometimes, the lowest monkey on the totem pole, like publicans and sinners, can be most helpful and even more enjoyable than the rest.

---

* In truth, I do not think any of you are monkeys. At worst, you are completely independent spiritual beings who might have been forcibly persuaded that they were something resembling a meat body. The trick of the slavemaster, however, is to get you to accept a degraded condition.

21

WHO DE BUDDHA?

When I had been aboard the *Apollo* for the better part of a year, I met a new crew member who had just arrived from Celebrity Center Los Angeles. He was a nice guy and was more than happy to be on the *Apollo*. When he told me what had propelled him to come aboard, I was a little taken aback. He then relayed to me a story about LRH having been Buddha. As Buddha was now back in human form, this man wanted to be with him. Although I had been in Scientology for over two years at that point, I had never heard any such story beyond what was perhaps a wild rumor. Personally, I thought the idea was over-the-top, and I had no serious regard for it. After he told me this, I soon learned that a photocopied document had been circulated around Los Angeles that was entitled *Hymn of Asia*, an address by Ron to a 1956 Buddhist congress wherein he rhetorically stated or implied that he was Maitreya, another name for the second coming of the Buddha. I never got my hands on the manuscript until it came out in published form almost two years later. In retrospect, I now suspect, but do not know, that the manuscript was floated around Los Angeles by LRH in order to see how people would respond to it. They loved it. A seed had been planted.

Even though I had not read one word of this manuscript, I was soon to be the recipient of a planted seed of a different order. One afternoon, about one month after meeting this gentleman, I took a nap. I had been receiving some very good auditing, but I was too tired on this day to have a session. Although I was not prone to visions or seeing astral forms, I woke up to a full 3-D holographic vision of Guatama Siddhartha juxtaposed right inside of my dorm room. It was definitely not a dream, just someone or something getting a message across. LRH was not on the *Apollo* at that time, but it was still his home. After that, I had no desire to privately ridicule or question whether Ron was the Buddha. In actual fact, this idea had no bearing on Scientology whatsoever. It was only a sideshow which may or may not have had significant meaning to other people. This private experience taught me to respect the idea, but it is not meant to suggest an objective proof of such an assertion. Somebody telepathed me something.

There is, however, one point of controversy that I can clarify for others. Many people have wondered whether or not Ron really thought he was the Buddha. Some say the *Hymn of Asia* was just a poem that meant he was here to fulfill the promise of the Buddha or Maitreya. I can tell you, quite honestly, that I later saw a private note in Ron's personal handwriting that indicated in no uncertain terms that he thought he was the Buddha. I do not mean to put to rest whether or not he was the Buddha as it is an extremely flamboyant claim nor is it something I can either prove or disprove. I neither believe it or disbelieve it. I want to put to rest the idea of whether or not Ron thought he was the Buddha. He did.

People have been very quick to criticize this appellation, in particular because Ron was known to show vehement emotions at different times. People normally think of Buddha as a contented and serene figure who could not possibly get angry. Ron had a very good answer to this. Sitting around and looking serene did not get anything done. If he was a Buddha, he was not a Buddha in any idyllic sense but in a practical sense. He was quite ready to light a fire under your ass and meant to do that on a planetary basis as well.

If you read Ron's book, *Mission Into Time*, you will also discover that he made claims about being an unknown but very flamboyant figure in that book, too. There is no question in my mind that Ron resonated with grandiose and flamboyant figures. He also believed that he had been Cecil Rhodes. When I first learned of this, I went to the *Encyclopedia Britannica*. It was a very old version, but it had an incredible biography of Cecil Rhodes. I was completely amazed to discover that Ron had many of the same characteristics as Rhodes, even to the point where they shared physical afflictions. Most Scientologists, including Sea Org members, would not even have known these characteristics, but I did. Although it does not prove anything in and of itself, the synchronicity of his identification with this figure was amazing.

That Ron identified himself with flamboyant characters should really not surprise anyone as he is one of the most colorful characters that I have ever heard of. It may also be part of a genetic predisposition. This idea came to me one day when I was talking to a priest at an Episcopal cathedral in Garden City, Long Island. He told me of their previous bishop who had several flamboyant characteristics, the most ostentatious of which consisted of being carried by bearers during a religious pageant. I do not recall if the bishop was in a chair or some other contraption, but it was reminiscent of Cleopatra. The priest told me that this bishop was quite a character and that his surname was de Wolfe. I found this highly ironic as de Wolfe is the maiden name of Ron's mother.

For those who are put off by Ron's statement or subtle hints that he was the Buddha, I would like to refer you to the *Jataka Tales*, a tome of stories about jungle animals that have been attributed to the Buddha. In each of the stories, the Buddha tells a parable about different animals engaged in various entanglements. At the end of each story, good generally triumphs over evil and the Buddha usually identifies the animal characters in the story with people who are present. Almost always, the Buddha refers to himself as the lion or some other animal that is usually the wisest and most exalted in the story. The translations I have read often walk a very thin line towards bordering on arrogance by the Buddha. They are, nevertheless, excellent stories and portray a figure who is completely centered and does not flinch at anything. Whenever someone comes to him with alarming news that people in the next village are plotting to kill him, he yawns and is not disturbed in the least before responding with a line such as, "They have been trying that for a very very long time. Once upon a time, there was a lion and two jackals..."

The designation of Guatama Siddhartha as the Buddha has been something of a blasphemy to certain religious and esoteric traditions. While they do not deny that Guatama was a buddha, they resent him being referred to as "the" Buddha because *buddha* was a designation for many other different holy men of the past whose valuable work has been obscured. It was never meant to be isolated or attributed to only one character. In this regard, Guatama Siddhartha gets more credit than anyone else. In this respect, he is again like Ron.

There is no question about it, religious saviors get more exalted and exaggerated publicity than anyone. Whether they are valid or not, they either serve or seek to serve a function that human beings either need or desire. This brings us to a far more important point and that has to do with the role of a savior.

If you can, please envision a wall that is made of huge teeth. I will call it the *Shin Wall* because *shin* signifies *tooth* in Hebrew. On one side of the wall is Side A where are all sorts of people exist in the human condition that we know on Earth. They experience all the suffering and maladies that life has to offer. The goal of many of them is to get to the other side of the *Shin Wall* which is called side B. This represents the other side of life and is largely an unknown in ordinary human terms. It not only represents the death state but also Nirvana, Heaven, Hell and any other state of existence you might want to imagine, including those suggested by Scientology. Everyone knows the body will terminate at some point. That is not a mystery. Everything else, technically, is a mystery or simply quantum possibilities yet to be activated.

This wall is quite long. At relatively distant intervals, you will find a huge and prominent chair placed along it, beneath which is a revolving door. The chairs, which all face towards Side A, are there to be occupied by the different saviors of various religions as they each represent a conduit to Side B, a realm which offers the trace elements of creation if not the Creator itself. At any time, the savior sitting in a chair can look over their shoulder at what is behind them and thus see over the wall to Side B. For the most part, those on Side A cannot see what is on Side B unless they ascend to the savior's seat itself. This is a risky proposition to anyone on Side A because no one is too likely to believe them.

Throughout history, most of the savior chairs are either empty or inert and not much of anything happens. When the revolving door beneath one gets active, however, all hell generally breaks loose. Everyone gets excited and many want to go through. Much talk ensues, but there are also those who react violently to what is on the other side. Further, the preoccupation with this reaction is so old that an entire intelligence network has been set up to keep the savior chairs inactive unless they serve a specific end.

What also exacerbates the entire scenario between Side A and Side B is that whenever anyone gets in a chair, even if he is not a savior, and begins stirring up chatter about the actual circumstances, all hell breaks loose and it is treated as a security leak. As time goes on, the intelligence network post their own lackeys in the various chairs who give tired and worn-out messages that everyone has already heard and do not facilitate revolving the doors.

In the case of Hubbard, he found a revolving door and got it spinning again. In order to access it and keep it moving, he found himself in the savior's chair. Whether you like that analogy or not, he at least got people talking about it to the point where it created a major reaction on Side A. In order to keep the door working, he had to fortify it with a team of guardians who were there to fight and prevent the intelligence network from stopping the operation. Whether or not it was a battle of good against evil, it was most definitely a struggle between two different polarities. At stake was not only access to Side B but the very idea of access to Side B. Ron had his own idea of what Side B was all about and how the revolving door should be serviced. The intelligence version, however, had their own ideas and wanted to put up their own rendition, even if it necessitated putting up a mock Commodore.

As you are reading about in this book, I not only heard about the revolving door, I eventually found my way to the savior himself and even got to look him straight in the eye. Besides that, I got a first hand look at all the apparatus surrounding the door. This not only included the guardians but also the service manual and all the mechanical and administrative necessities to keep it operating. To be quite honest, however, the revolving door did not exist in this universe. It was only in your mind and could best be described as an illusion. The other side to that equation is that Side B is not of this realm anyway. In the end, it was up to you find the door and "see" it for yourself.

This entire paradigm of the imaginary revolving door reminds me of all the media intrigue that surrounded Leonard Nimoy when he directed the movie *Star Trek III: The Search for Spock*. The character played by Nimoy, Mr. Spock, had been killed off in *Star Trek II: The Wrath of Khan*. At the time, there was much speculation and interest in the press over the prospect of whether or not Nimoy's character would return. When pressed on the question by a television reporter of whether or not Spock would return as himself in this movie, Nimoy gave a very deft answer.

"If you are going to call a movie 'The Search for Spock,' I would presume that you are going to find him."

If I dedicated over a decade to finding this door, I would have had to have been either naive, stupid or very unfortunate not to have found it. There are many people, however, who were not so fortunate, and they have reported in abundance on the internet. While most of them are not really members of the intelligence network, they are part of a visceral reaction.

By the time I got through this wall, the guardians had lost a major battle and they went down in flames, along with Ron's wife. Ron was not so stupid as to remain in the chair without a support system. If he did, he would have been put in a pillory so he wisely got off and went into hiding. I was all by myself. Ron was not with me, but I know he had traversed the area. It was neither heaven nor nirvana, but it was certainly an extremely interesting vantage point. I could look all around and see all sorts of things. Nothing was really very mysterious on this other side of the wall.

What does all this mean? As far as myself, it was most certainly a wall of revelation. It most certainly does not, however, mean to suggest that I am a savior. I am only writing about the savior seat. I learned a lot about the savior chair because I had a very interesting vantage point and learned a lot of the protocol that would be archetypally inherent in such. I saw the communication that went to it and from it as well as the surrounding bureaucracy and brush fires. Occupying that chair is tantamount to your own destruction. It is a hot seat and so are the positions adjunct to it, but they are nowhere near as hot. We can argue forever and a day about what is on the other side of the wall. I have only given you a brief abstract and really not a very good one, but that is really not the point. From a linear standpoint, we can basically only be sure that there is an IDEA that there is another side to the wall. Further, that this idea can trigger a huge amount of emotional response in an individual or population. Further still, that this idea represents POWER. This takes us to the next proposition in the L. Ron Hubbard phenomena.

22

POWER

Completely aside from any spiritual aspirations, Scientology very much concerned itself with the element of power. This alone makes Scientology a worthy subject of study for its opponents and critics. Although not perfect, Hubbard was an energetic character from day one — at least he claimed to be so. In his lectures and writings, his solution to adversity was to work at a very high energy level. As a sci-fi writer, he had only a token amount of power. Although it is not broadly known or recognized, he wielded a considerable amount of power and knowledge in government circles. In fact, he was much better known in those circles than anyone would likely believe. According to former CIA liaison, Col. Fletcher Prouty, who conducted a special investigation into Hubbard's intelligence background, Ron worked for FDR's chief of intelligence. When Ron penetrated the Agape Lodge of Aleister Crowley's OTO in 1945, he was in yet a new arena of power which not only encompassed the occult but also the most brilliant rocket scientists in the world. These included both Jack Parsons and Theodore von Karman, two men who were an integral part of founding the Jet Propulsion Laboratory in Pasadena.

Although Ron was involved with powerful people and participated in highly charged occult rituals with Parsons, Ron's main power surge did not occur until 1950 when *Dianetics: The Modern Science of Mental Health* was released. This book took the world by storm, and his life was never the same after that. In this work, he theoretically demonstrated how people could be alleviated of their psychosomatic ills. This made it intensely popular and elicited floods of mail from people who wanted to be cured. A foundation was then set up in order to teach the techniques and deliver auditing to the public. Setting up these clinics and organizations turned out to be his second wave of power. Besieged by fans, aspirants, onlookers, and professionals, he was prompted, if not forced, into taking a position as the leader of a new movement. According to him, it was not something he originally desired. He had more correspondence and personal requests for meetings than could possibly be handled. Instead of responding like a limp fish, he made an attempt at throwing an organization together just to cope with the success he had created. Whether he wanted to or not, he had created a movement with a considerable amount of momentum. Although this was not Ron's first taste of power, it was the first time he received broad recognition that could be translated into a further expanding power.

The early success of Dianetics was helped considerably by John W. Campbell, a famous editor of magazines which included science fiction and fantasy. Campbell and Ron not only had a professional relationship but were close friends. When Ron used his early Dianetic techniques to relieve him of his sinusitis, it won Dianetics a considerable amount of credibility in the science fiction community. Campbell's advocacy of Dianetics was so strong that it split the science fiction community into two separate camps. There were those who those who supported Hubbard, and there was another faction led by Isaac Asimov who were essentially anti-spiritual and anti-Dianetics.

Some authors have tried to portray Hubbard as a highly manipulative schemer who had invented Dianetics to bilk the world out of millions. This is a sensational claim which plays very well to the tabloid-style press, but it ignores the reality of the situation. I once met a lady who worked as Ron's secretary during this early time period. She said that he was constantly besieged by people coming to his office. He literally had to scream at her so that she would keep people from coming through his door. Otherwise, she said, he could never get any work done. With all of his popularity, he did not need to go on television or put up a tent like an evangelist. The man was besieged. The enthusiasm and interest of the people were making the movement just as much as he was.

If they did not hover around him, ask questions, and demand further information and instruction on his techniques, he would have been a limp fish. Nobody realized this better than Ron. They were what provided the dynamics for him to continue with his research. Years later, when I knew him, he was known to get a tear in his eye when he would hear from one of these old-timers from the 1950's. It was quite sentimental, but he never forgot how much power and support they had given to him in the early days. Without their interest, he would have been nothing special at all. People who try to understand Ron's power constantly miscalculate the people factor. They loved him, even when he yelled.

Ron's background in the navy gave him at least a loose standard for organizing. Many mistakes, some of them horrendous, were made in these early years. He eventually patterned his entire organizational policy in response to these mistakes.

One of the biggest mistakes he indulged in was hiring all the "best" professional people. When the "best" ad man hires the Rockettes, and the world's "best" accountant teaches that you are supposed to be in gratuitous servitude to the IRS, and your medical consultant claims that it is in the best interest of everybody to have all your actions approved by the AMA, you learn a very important lesson. In Ron's case, he learned his lessons very hard and fast. The people employed in the early days of Dianetics were not only diluting and taking away his power but the power of the entire movement. This was not necessarily malevolent in some cases, but it was certainly inept.

Ron knew that it was HE who created the whizz-bang phenomena that was Dianetics. It was neither the publisher, his good friend Joseph Campbell, nor others who heralded the movement. It was also his "power" that figured out Dianetic therapy and made it accessible to others. There was a charisma factor, but this was only predicated on the theories of Dianetics and the ability to put them into practice.

In effect, Ron found that too many of the people employed or indulged in the early days of Dianetics would have had him kissing the ass of everyone in society. These people had no bigger vision. They may have had some form of vision or idealized thought about what should become of Dianetics, but none of them proved to be movers and shakers to the extent of Hubbard. At best, they were

149

just muddling along or adhering to a status quo or perhaps had an agenda that was even worse. If he had allowed his power to be diluted further, he would have ended up as a cog in a bureaucratic system where he would have had to get rubber stamp approvals for most of what he did from the "Board of Good People." This scenario seems quite funny when you stop and take a look at it, but nobody really ever understood his position in the matter. Critics assail him for using "hypnosis" and "mind-control" on people. While he did know more about hypnosis and mind-control than anyone, those tools are not as easy to use as unempowered people might think. So, there were two factors at work. The "Board of Good People" would not only have reduced Hubbard's personal power, they would have also made the Dianetics movement inert.

All of the above is part of a syndrome of a degraded universe. Whenever someone begins to exercise any significant power of magnitude, there is a corresponding and neutralizing effect. Hubbard later observed that there were basically two "crimes" in this universe. Crime number one was "being there," and crime number two was "communicating." Your own personal power are utterly dependent on these two factors. Thus, one of the first things he learned in the Dianetics movement was never to minimize his own power. This primarily consisted of being who he really was and communicating what he had actually found.

Years later, these experiences and later developments from them would elicit a lengthy thesis by him about power, all of its implications, and how to handle it. You can argue about whether Hubbard was a genius and whether his techniques worked, but you cannot deny that he captured the interest of others and that this generated power. It is a symptom of human beings, particularly degraded ones, but not exclusively relegated to such, that when they see something powerful, they react. This reaction can take place in the form of being awestruck, gawking, or pointing. Some human beings will immediately begin scheming and meddling to siphon off or steal the power. Others will just complain about it, write to their congressman or maybe just natter to their neighbor.

Power can be good or bad, but it is most notably something to be reckoned with. It can also inspire fear, hatred, and destructive behavior. Power is also dangerous. When you demonstrate a significant amount of it, you are perceived as a rival by other people who wield power. If you do not demonstrate much power by indulging in rebellious activities or becoming an obvious rival, you are not threatening to the powers that be and will generally not have too many problems with them. If, however, you can capture significant attention units of people and change and persuade their views, you are a hot-ticket to be politely escorted out of town. If politeness does not work, force or more drastic measures might have to be employed. This principle would not be so bad if it applied only to people to like Martin Luther King, the Kennedy brothers, Gandhi, and a host of others that could be named. The problem with this universe is that the infrastructure of it is so wired and conditioned that if you truly begin to assert any modicum of what could be called personal spiritual power, there are various subtle forces which will seek to equalize you or perhaps do something even worse. Your first line of defense is to know the nature of the jungle.

While the Oppressor or Great Adversary does not exude absolute control and power over everything, it has got a pretty good monopoly on the stage we know as life. Although he may not own the stage itself, the Great Adversary is at the very least the president of the Actors Guild, the Gaffers Guild, the Screenwriters Guild, and the labor unions. He also has a controlling interest in the companies that provide the costumes, lights, and other special equipment. Ron not only put on his show, he got contributions from his power base and ignored the guilds. This did not please the "guilds" at all. When you enter the realm of power, you have entered the realm of oppression and this amounts to a game of force and counter-force.

Anyone who has studied the martial arts will quickly recognize that "no force" is more powerful than force itself. The best techniques in the martial arts teach you to use your opponent's force against him. Thus, it behooves us to study and assess the force of our opponent before we can expect to overthrow him. For those of you in the reading audience who have an axe to grind against Hubbard or may consider him a horrible adversary of humanity, you would be wise to study the true nature and power of his "force" if you would seek to neutralize his effects.

One of the most important things to learn about power is that whether you are a good or bad power, you are definitely going to experience some form of resistance or oppression once you exert any form of it. In the early days of Dianetics, Ron ran up against such resistance when his new therapy was heralded as the "poor man's psychiatry" in the popular press because it was not very expensive compared to professional psychiatry. It thus became a serious threat to that profession. Psychiatrists denounced it. If you accept the idea that Dianetics actually provided real therapy, it was an even greater threat. If you then take on the further notion that psychiatry has a completely separate agenda as opposed to the better interests of human beings, you can then visualize an intriguing drama unfolding around L. Ron Hubbard and his new therapy. Even if he was insane, and there are many arguments out there to suggest that he was, he was at least doing an incredible job of at least emulating an organization that attracted suppression and sought to overthrow the oppressor.

Another early strike against Dianetics was via Ron's second wife, Sara Northrup Parsons Hubbard, as she is sometimes referred to. Sara had deserted Jack Parsons in favor of Ron, but I have never heard anyone give a real good explanation as to why. Parsons was wealthier and more handsome. He was even more dark and mysterious, but he probably was not as personable as Ron. Ron is always described as the nefarious home-breaker, but Sara's role in the matter is completely ignored. Further, she is a complete wild card in this entire equation.

Sara came to know Jack through her sister, Helen, who was Jack's lover prior to Sara. Although I have seen only scant mention of it in recent times, I have read historical anecdotes (from people who were against Hubbard) that Ron married into Sara's family because it was a highbrow wealthy family who obtained their wealth from the Northrup empire. Northrup was one of the largest contractors in the aerospace industry and eventually merged with Grumman to become Northrup-Grumman. Grumman was involved in secret space projects on Long Island and elsewhere. Sara's family of origin suggests considerable influence and puts a whole new twist on her experiences with Jack and Ron.

According to Hubbard's testimony, and there is no question in my mind that he sincerely believed this, Sara was kidnapped through the devices of a man named Miles Hollister whereupon she was tortured and programmed not only to act against him but to wrest away the copyrights of Dianetics. She did make legal filings in an attempt to secure such.

There is no question about it — as soon as Ron had achieved public acclaim and success with Dianetics, he was thrown to the mat and his personal life was in shambles. During this period, he also reported an attempt on his life as well as an attempt to have him abducted so that he could be placed in an insane asylum. It is easy for arm chair critics, many decades later, to make snide comments about Hubbard's "paranoia." Most of these critics are not inclined to view the entire scenario, however, because it will bust their paradigm of what they consider to be real. They were not there and do not know what Hubbard had to deal with.

If you read anti-Scientology propaganda, you will find that much of it is dedicated to the proposition that L. Ron Hubbard was a pathological liar who would go to any length to discredit an opponent. In actual fact, his opponents have gone to far further lengths to discredit him. While some of the information on anti-Scientology websites are true, they are not always interested in the underlying and fundamental questions because they are too busy fighting. One has to ask themselves what is the true nature and predisposition of the opposition Hubbard encountered. The most auspicious aspect about this is that he did not encounter any serious oppositions or oppression in his life until he became popular with Dianetics. That says a considerable amount in itself.

It is obvious that Hubbard was in a war that was not entirely of his own making. The potency of the Dianetics movement attracted incredible opposition. If it was not successful, people would have stopped coming, and there would have been nothing to oppose. In those early days, it made headlines on its own relative merits. Hubbard was a bit of a side note who just happened to be the founder. But, he was the one ultimately responsible for its manifestation. As a result, he found himself in the eye of a virtual hurricane with virulent accusations flying at him as if they were dislodged houses or cars from a real storm. Had he stepped into the whirling chaos of the hurricane, he would have been sent flying, but he did not. He realized that one needs to be still and look at what is going on around them rather than grabbing a piece of the drama and exercising it. He called this "confronting" and based an entire series of exercises on it which he called Training Routines. This attitude became the whole foundation upon which auditing was based: confronting what is actually there as opposed to what people might say, think or believe. It is the foundation of Scientology which is defined as "lookingness." Scientology, which also means "knowing how to know," is based upon epistemology which is an English language word which means the study of knowledge. If you look up *epistemology* in the dictionary, you will find that it is based upon a word which means "confront." As ridiculously simple as this sounds, it is what opens the door to your own personal power. Confronting means "being there." The first step is to be there, recognize that you are there and not deny that you are there. That is your power. The next step is considerably more difficult. It requires that you hold your position in space. That means not reacting to the maelstrom of events that might be surrounding you. You sometimes see this quality in a quarterback playing football. He is surrounded by people trying to knock his head off but remains calm and gets his job done. If he gets caught up in the fear of it all, he will lose. Life is full of torrential phenomena. If you can gather your wits about you and just observe, you are putting yourself in an advantageous position.

Finding himself in a maelstrom of negative events on a planet that he considered to be a mockery of true civilization, Ron found that all bets were now off. This was not a game of "good citizen versus bad citizen" where you take the bully to court and have him apologize before he is sentenced. As a general rule, ordinary justice systems do not feature guilty parties offering and fulfilling true apologies to their victims. This alone tells you that true justice can only be played out in a higher court that has very little to do with the court systems of the world. Hubbard, like it or not, for better or for worse, was playing a different game with different rules, but he was doing it in a society which had its own rules. The society and its rules served as a buffer zone between Ron and his opponents. This buffer zone had advantages and disadvantages for both sides. We now have to ask, who was the other side?

23

THE LESSONS OF POWER

The Communists were identified as the first culprits against Dianetics, and there were different reasons for it. Besides the incident with Miles Hollister, Ron had been pursued for many years by a Russian organization known as Amtorg.* Agents of Amtorg approached him, even before the release of *Dianetics: The Modern Science of Mental Health,* and offered him a large sum of money to come to Russia and further develop his research. Although his many critics have called him paranoid, they have never begrudged or disputed Amtorg's interest in him.

If the Communists were out to get Ron, it was obvious that they were not alone. There were also problems from the American Medical Association and the American Psychiatric Association. The government of the United States, at least in the early days, did not seem to have any axe to grind against the new movement. In fact, President Harry Truman was known to have a copy of

---

* Amtorg was a state sponsored trading organization of the Soviet Union set up under the tutelage of Armand Hammer. Hammer's father, Julian Hammer, was an ardent leader of dispossessed Jews who suffered under the virulently anti-Semetic rule of the Czar. Forced to flee to America, Julian became a wealthy drug dealer and formed Allied Drug, a legitimate pharmaceutical company. Armand was named after "arm and hammer" which was the symbol of an early Bolshevik labor party in New York. Julian was a member of the American Communist Party and had an active role in Lenin's early Soviet empire. When he died, Armand took the mantle and successfully worked with Stalin for decades. It was only after Hammer's death that the Soviet empire completely crumpled. The Soviet Union had many leaders, from Lenin to Gorbachev. The only remaining constant throughout its history was Armand Hammer.

Dianetics: The Modern Science of Mental Health in the White House and was said to have received auditing. You must remember, Dianetics had hit the headlines in a big way, and all presidents read the morning papers. Truman, as I heard it, had great nightmares and psychological misgivings about his role in dropping the atom bomb.

In the 1950's, interest in Dianetics was big but so was the opposition. When we consider the position of the American Psychiatric Association with regard to Dianetics, we stumble upon one of the greatest ironies in the entire history of Dianetics and Scientology and all of its ancillary and related subjects. The head of the American Psychiatric Association was none other than Ewen Cameron, one of the most respected and admired psychiatrists of his time. It is also fully documented by regular news organizations that he was a cruel and savage torturer of human beings. There is no doubt about it. His propensity towards lobotomies and mind-control is very well known. The CIA and U.S. Government even admitted their involvement in his antics and made an out-of-court settlement with the victims of his experiments. The ironic twist referred to above has to do with my independent research regarding the Wilson and Cameron clans which clearly demonstrates that these two families are intimately related when it comes to occultism and the more secretive governing influences of the planet. Further, Ewen Cameron and L. Ron Hubbard were both from the same Scottish blood. In effect, the war between Dianetics and psychiatry was a clan war from the same gene pool.* The very fact that Dianetics was vehemently opposed by an association whose leader led a mind-control torture squad should serve as a real eye-opener.

Although Dianetics was assailed from various sources in the 1950's, neither Hubbard nor the movement received much flack from the Government. This did not start until he moved to Washington, D.C., a city which he chose as a strategic location from which to disseminate his philosophy. It was Vice President Richard Nixon who reportedly sent "thugs" to the D.C. Church of Scientology to "rough up" Hubbard's wife, Mary Sue. Additionally, they wanted them to know that Nixon did not believe in

---

* This has been the subject of several books that I have written which include *Montauk Revisited, The Black Sun,* and *Synchronicity and the Seventh Seal.*

anything the Church of Scientology stood for. Hubbard withdrew his support from Nixon forever afterwards and Scientologists were encouraged not to vote for him. While Nixon's action was a bold statement of power politics, it had nothing to do with the proper duties of the Office of the Vice President as any criminal complaints that were lodged could have been dealt with by due process of law. It was pure power politics, plain and simple. This helped pave the way for Hubbard's eventual departure for England. London, he recognized, was the original headquarters of the English speaking world. He learned to value the old communication lines of the British Empire which were still very much extant. Moving to England was a political maneuver on Hubbard's part to build and expand his own empire.

In the meantime, he expanded and developed Dianetics and Scientology as a subject. He wrote a stream of books and other publications which included various new techniques. At the same time, he developed a whole organizational philosophy by which to administer his budding empire. Whatever you say about him, the man did not lack for energy. In many respects, this was an astounding feat on his part because he had to fight a turf battle at the same time. Hypnotizing and mind-controlling people makes for great sensationalism, but it was still public demand which maintained his popularity and support in the movement. It was not, however, a public demand that was acknowledged or advertized in the press. They learned their lessons from that in the 1950 Dianetics boom. Good or neutral press only fed Hubbard's power. What they did not realize was that negative press also gave him attention that often worked to his advantage as well. Whether his methods were good, bad, or indifferent is not the point. The continued development of the subject, along with the energy of his supporters, empowered him even further.

After establishing the Founding Church of Scientology in the District of Columbia as the premier Scientology organization in the world, he eventually acquired Saint Hill Manor in East Grinstead, England. Scientologists literally flocked from all over the world to help establish this locale as the new Mecca of Scientology. This was a good move and worked for many years, but as his opponents were able to influence many important people, including members of Parliament, England was no longer a safe place for Ron. With threats against his domicile in England, he departed for Rhodesia where he thought he could use his OT abilities to win an entire country. In Rhodesia, he was essentially on his own and did not have the infrastructure or support of the staff or public which had been a core theme to his success. It was a dismal failure. His power was in the hurricane phenomena he had created in the past. There was no public in Rhodesia that were demanding to learn from him. There was, however, a white minority who were enslaving a black population. He tried to endear himself to the political slave masters, but they considered him out-of-place and suspect. They had no reference frame for him and considered him a threat. After several months, he returned to England and considered his sojourn to Rhodesia a dismal failure. To his credit, he never hid this fact from anyone. I find it very hard to believe that many Scientologists never think he could do anything wrong when he admittedly screwed up badly and was quite public about the fact.

One of Hubbard's key secrets to his success was that he could learn and respond to his mistakes. In Rhodesia, he had abandoned a key element of what was his original power base: the group. As a result of his meandering, the reading of a particular book, and a considerable amount of self-reflection, he made a thorough and comprehensive study of the subject of power and codified its laws. It was disseminated broadly so that all could avail themselves of the information. Believe it or not, Ron's mindset was that he wanted people to be more powerful. He viewed himself as a very powerful person, but he sometimes thought that he was all alone at the top and wanted others to join him. There were, however, certain rules and stipulations by which to play the game. It was not that he wanted to subjugate others or to dominate them. Since 1950, he had been involved in a game of power politics that had a life of its own and these included different rules.

As was stated earlier, the rules of power are much different than an ordinary system of legal checks and balances as you would find in a society of governed people. He had created a system known as Dianetics which had empowered him as well as other people. The "problem" with empowerment is that once you have a taste of it, there is usually a desire to want more of it. Give people a scoop of ice cream that they like, and they will want more of it. It is said that absolute power corrupts, but we are not talking about absolute power, at least at this point. He believed he was fixing the universe and power was something that came along with the territory. This proposition is true, but it is not going to register with anyone who sits back, does what they are told and does not rock the boat. If you do that religiously, you will never have to deal with the problems Hubbard encountered.

The book referred to above that had such an impression on Hubbard was *The Four Seasons of Manuela* (by Victor Wolfgang Von Hagen), and it was essentially a story about the life of Simon Bolivar and his consort, Manuela Saenz. Bolivar was one of the greatest generals in the history of the world, and he is famous in history for being the liberator or "George Washington" of South America. A creole by birth, Bolivar freed the entire continent of South America from the yoke of Spain. After the rebellion he led, different national identities developed. Although Bolivar was of noble ancestry and recognized as one of the greatest generals in history, he died a pauper and was buried in a ditch. Hubbard's power was not of a militaristic nature, but he could not help but see the shocking and tragic mistakes of Bolivar. He did not want that to happen to him! Therefore, he studied and codified Bolivar's mistakes and developed them into a new Scientology policy.

Bolivar's main mistake was that, once he had obtained the position of being the most powerful man in South America, he neither accepted nor took on the mantle of his power and all of the trimmings that came with it. Although he was ostensibly in charge of the country of Venezuela, it seemed that Bolivar just wanted to revert to a fairly regular life and be a "good citizen." He did not mean it to be, but Bolivar's abdication of his own power was viewed as a betrayal by the environment. Hubbard pointed out that once Bolivar had attained his power, he should have empowered his adjutants and all the people who followed him. He was in a position to confiscate land and adjudicate who would have what. But, Bolivar wanted to be a "good citizen" and respect the rights of others and that included all property rights. While this is a laudable virtue, it was also a disaster for his countrymen because he did not ferret out the biggest land owner and enemy of the common people: the Catholic Church. Although they were directly in league with the Spanish subjugation of the people, if not the direct cause of it, they were free to roam about and do their business. After his victory, Bolivar did not touch them and left their power structure completely in tact. Accordingly, they were able to spy, plot, and intrigue against the new and feeble "administrative" power he had set up for Venezuela, the country from which he was from. By not empowering his friends and allies from his military days, his enemies were able to multiply. His loyal military officers and troops had long since departed, none of them having been enriched by their experience with Bolivar. Eventually, as his power was eventually siphoned off, he even lost the great wealth he had enjoyed prior to the rebellion which he had led. That is why and how he ended up being buried in a ditch.

Bolivar's mistakes in dealing with power were compounded by those of Manuela, his lover and most loyal friend. Her errors were just as fatal. Specifically, she was in a position where she had Bolivar's ear. She could have demanded a marriage of him which would have made her even more powerful, but Manuela never did this. That act alone would have made both of them considerably more powerful. Although she was well cared for, she could also have used her close position to Bolivar to strengthen both of their positions.

Far more aware of the intrigues against Bolivar than he was, Manuela did not adequately lobby him for more power. Hubbard even stated that she was in a position to have evil conspirators killed, but she did not lift a finger. While it is certainly understandable that a "good citizen" does not want to hurt anyone, it becomes an entirely different matter when someone is gunning for your family, lover or something else that is very dear to you. In such a political climate as South America, it is either them or you. As I said, power plays by different rules. The tragedy in the above scenario seems to be the inherent problems with power itself. Once you have engaged it, it also engages you. Bolivar abandoned his power and met with a tragic end. On the other hand, he could have lived a life as a subsistence farmer, but that would have been a very far cry from his potential.

Hubbard specifically pointed out the lessons to be learned from Manuela because he thought this should be known by people in his employ. If you were connected to or associated with a powerful person, you had better protect their power as well as yourself because your power essentially derives from the senior power. If you enhance and expand their power, they will, in turn, give you more power.

At that point in his life, Hubbard could have grabbed whatever millions were available to him and could have lived as an expatriate or possibly even in the United States itself. That would have made his opposition very happy but would have also resulted in great disappointment for his followers. They would have tracked him down and pursued him like nobody's business. Sometimes, you just cannot escape your fate. On the other hand, it is entirely possible that his enemies would not have left him alone anyway as he had proven himself to be a remarkably worthy opponent.

By sitting in the seat of the savior, he had either occupied that seat legitimately or had emulated it to the point where he had created very significant triggers in the populace and the establishment. There was no turning back.

If all of this sounds rather dramatic, I can guarantee you that his life was very much that of a highly charged drama. If you were anywhere near him, you often felt like you were on a stage with the people around him serving as players. It was actually fun and always exciting. None of this tells you that he was good or bad. It only tells you one thing: he was powerful.

I find it ironic that, as I write these words, I think of you in the reading audience and how you might be ingesting this information. I cannot help but think that as some of you read this description of his power, you can sense the noose already being tightened around his neck. It also reminds me of the story of a savior who seemed to reach his true peak just before the first kiss of death incited plots and intrigue against him. In the story of Christ, there is a great sadness when you consider how powerful this man could have been if only his oppressors would have granted him the beingness to be who he really was. I do not mean to compare Hubbard to Christ other than by way of the idea that they both sat in the seat of the savior as per the previous analogy. This brings home an important point. A position of power, at least the highly concentrated version as suggested by a savior, would seem to be fleeting and not at all endemic to the normal conditions of this universe. Although it is desired by human beings, it is forbidden by the extant powers which rule this domain.

24

PRINCESS DAY

The lessons learned from Rhodesia resulted in two major developments with regard to the future of Scientology: the Guardian Office and the Sea Organization. In his Simon Bolivar policy letter, LRH pointed out that Manuela Saenz had a great intelligence network, but she never did anything significant with the information. It was a glaring omission that she never personally organized a secret police that would not only protect her and Bolivar but the entire political system as well. The most notable enemy of their regime was Bolivar's vice president, Santander. Every few days, Manuela would write that the man should be killed for treason or worse, yet she never did anything effective about it. Instead of acting on her own self-determinism, which she clearly had the power to do, she had a tendency to ask permission for everything she did. This was unnecessary and served to undermine both of them. Out of this lesson, Hubbard created the Guardian Office which was to be overseen by his wife, Mary Sue.

The Guardian Office was the "secret service" of Scientology. When it became abusive in its later years, some staff mockingly referred to it as "the Gestapo." Its purpose was to secure the existence and continued expansion of Scientology. They were to make sure that no one attacked the "savior" or the "savior's seat," and they were dedicated to fortifying such a garrison. Although their job included taking care of anything that might thwart the power, they had separate networks for intelligence, finance, legal matters, and public relations. As per the lessons of Simon Bolivar, they could use whatever means were at their disposal.

The Sea Org was Ron's other creation that resulted from his study of power. Theoretically senior to the Guardian's Office, but not always so in day to day practice, there were times when there was a professional rivalry between the two groups. The Sea Org evolved as it did because it seemed to be a solution for many different things. First, it provided a safe base of operations for Hubbard and what was to become the management branch of Scientology operations.

Based upon his experiences on the whole track, Ron concluded that the best way to operate would be to be "Fabian." Fabian was a very successful general during the Roman days. The key to his success was that he would make brief attacks on his enemy and then suddenly disappear. No one knew where to find him so he was impossible to attack. In other words, he did not make himself a sitting duck or target. In the Sea Org, this tactic was known as being Fabian. By choosing ships as a base of operation, they never remained in a fixed position and were not so easy to attack. The press could still attack Saint Hill, but it was no longer the real headquarters of Scientology. The militaristic impression of the Sea Org also had a tendency to intimidate the press and other opponents. They did not quite know how to deal with that, and it was quite a successful method of operation for seven to eight years.

The Sea Org not only provided power to Ron, but it also provided a way for Scientologists to connect to his power. It was supposed to be mutually beneficial. In the early days, only those who had achieved Clear and beyond could join the Sea Org. It was intended to be a rough and tough atmosphere for OTs only. The toughness angle was designed to strengthen the OT aspect. The motto was that if you could not handle something because it was too tough then take on something twice as tough. This, by the way, is a good maxim to use with problems in your own life.

Those of you who have studied my past work and all of the various synchronicities with regard to the date of August 12th will be quite amused to learn that August 12th, 1967 was the official birth date of the Sea Org. This just happens to be the date upon which LRH wrote "Flag Order #1" which established the "Sea Project" as it was originally called. The name "Sea Organization" or "Sea Org" would be adopted soon afterwards.

Over the years, the Sea Org developed its own culture and policies which were completely different than but supportive of the Scientology network. Its basic purpose was to expand the Dianetics and Scientology movement. This meant supervising the outer organizations, not only to ensure that they could meet the expectations of the public, but also acting as a police organization to ensure that the staff did not lie, steal or cheat. Of course, you are dealing with the monkey cage factor so corruption was always something one had to deal with in the Sea Org and Scientology.

Once it became established, the *Apollo* began delivering the Scientology OT levels as well as executive training courses and regular auditing for Scientology executives. People came from all over the world, and this atmosphere made for an interesting cross-cultural exchange. Many languages were spoken and heard aboard the ship, but English was the standard. Just by having lunch, you could learn all sorts of different idioms and characteristics of different cultures plus the various nuances of Scientology as it was known across the world. For the most part, Scientology was pretty uniform throughout the world, but there were always mistakes and need for correction.

The *Apollo* had become the new Mecca for Scientologists, but its location remained a mystery to the majority of them as well as to the public in general. This was primarily in keeping with its policy of being Fabian. A good private investigator could have tracked down the ship for you during this period, but it would have cost you some bucks. Then, when you found out, it might move to a new port a week later. Tracking down the ship could become a nuisance, unless you were seriously obsessed with it or opposed to it. The only people who seemed to have enough time and resources to track the *Apollo* seriously were intelligence agencies. Wild rumors would sometimes appear that the ship was a brothel and that there was much drug use aboard. Nothing could have been further from the truth, but these rumors were carefully planted.

The ship operated under the cover guise of the Operation and Transport Corporation Limited, or OTC Ltd. It appeared as a pleasure-cruising business yacht. This cover worked to a limited extent, but most importantly, it avoided any potential conflict or explaining of Scientology to any locals in whatever port we happened to be. It did not really fool the intelligence agencies or the embassies nor was it ever really expected to. Corporate papers were actually drawn up in the event that it became necessary to demonstrate that Scientology was actually a client of OTC. As harassment from various intelligence agencies continued, safe ports for the *Apollo* became a very valued commodity. The Port Captain's office became dedicated to finding, creating, and maintaining safe ports for the *Apollo*. Accordingly, Hubbard eventually looked to secure himself an entire country where Scientology operations would be unfettered and perhaps even appreciated. His target was Morocco.

When I boarded the *Apollo* at Casablanca in 1972, it was in the midst of a full scale operation to "win" the country of Morocco for Scientology. High level contacts had been made with government officials in Morocco, and OTC was not only teaching them business management techniques but also planning to teach the Moroccan national security force a watered down version of what is known as a Scientology Security Check. This is quite a complex procedure in itself under normal Scientology circumstances, but there were far more complexities going on in Morocco at that time than I could ever hope to report on. If one interviewed all of the various players, it could make for a sizable book.

After only a few weeks on board, I was taken down to the mission briefing room and told I was going to go on a trip in Morocco. I was supposed to get on a bus with other Sea Org members and basically just sit in a course room in Rabat, the capital of Morocco. It was a show exercise and would not require much functioning on my part other than to just be there. I was told a few parrot answers to give in case any Moroccans addressed me. But, it was eventually deemed that I did not have any proper mission school training, and it would therefore not be proper to send me on such an errand.

The next thing I remember about the "Moroccan takeover" was when we received news that the Princess of Morocco would be coming aboard. This ended up requiring all sorts of ridiculous and wild preparations. I was working on the decks at that point. The ship had over three hundred people, but there were only about six of us assigned to the deck force at that particular time. This was a pretty ridiculous situation in itself. Instead of doing their regular jobs, much of the ship began getting ready for the Princess. I was selected, along with about five others, to learn all sorts of different military salutes that were to be used to greet the Princess when she came aboard. I learned a lot of different salutes that day, some of them from armies you have never even heard of. After that afternoon, I could have walked amongst the French Foreign Legion and felt at home. In the end, the idea of saluting was either nixed or completely forgotten as it was not that important.

On the day the Princess actually arrived, the crew was busy painting over rust and making the ship as presentable as possible. I was put on about twenty different chores that day, some of which, like the saluting, made no particular sense. Finally, I ended up in the galley carving countless ducks. I never saw such fine food pass through the galley as I did on that day. The Princess brought many dignitaries with her. The good part about working in the galley was that you did not go hungry during all the tumult.

When it was all over, we had worked very hard. Such a commotion was raised that the visit of the Princess was etched in our memories and was referred to forever after as "Princess Day." The crew was soon rewarded with a briefing by the Port Captain who told us all about the ship's visit with the Princess. Ron was not involved, but the Port Captain said we would all be interested to know that the Princess believed in "thetans." In other words, the Princess expressly recognized that human beings were spirits inhabiting bodies. Things seemed to go rather well, and it seemed that Scientology had a friend in high places. Still, the Princess did not rule the country.

In the Moroccan operation, teaching the Moroccan security force how to do Scientology security checks was a difficult proposition. It was deemed too risky and lengthy to teach them the rigorous and disciplined details of Scientology procedures. There-fore, LRH thought up the idea of a remote e-meter. This meant that a regular Moroccan guard would ask the questions and be in possession of a regular meter, but there would also be an audio hookup that reached an invisible Scientologist who would hear what was being said. In addition to that, the Moroccan's meter would have a relay to another device in the possession of the invisible Scientologist so that both could simultaneously see all the reactions on the meter. After hearing the response of the person being interrogated, the Scientologist operative would then verbalize to the Moroccan interrogator what to say. Believe it or not, this complicated and bizarre arrangement of security checking potential dissidents in the Moroccan government was all set up and ready for prime time. There was only one problem. Forces outside of Morocco were already hard at work to make sure that Scientology would never succeed in that country.

25

THE ZOO FACTOR

If the previous chapter makes it sound like there was a high level of intrigue and serious business aboard the *Apollo*, there most certainly was. But, there were many more important activities going on as well. I could fill volumes with detailed information, but they are not necessarily relevant to the theme of this book. Although the Moroccan episode and surrounding circumstances would ultimately change the course that Scientology would take in the world, it seemed as if, in some ways, it was almost a side feature to many of the other things that were going on.

During this period, LRH was working very hard on Expanded Dianetics and was never very far away from Scientology management lines. He was very prolific and a great multitasker.

Although the above mentioned activities were quite serious, I would be remiss if I did not relay some of the more humorous aspects of life aboard the *Apollo*. Just as there were momentous events and pivotal decisions to be made, there was also a side of life that I refer to as the "zoo factor." Any group of people will have at least a handful of characters, and there was never a shortage of bizarre incidents aboard. While I could tell you many, I will relay only a couple in order to give you a slice of what life was like.

My first morning aboard the *Apollo*, I had already awoken before anyone else in my dormitory. The first thing I heard was this high-pitched voice and a sharp bell being rung.

"Wakee, wakee. Rise and shine! Wakee Wakee. Rise and shine!"

"What on Earth was that?" I wondered to myself.

"Shut the fuck up!" was the next thing I heard; then, "Shut the fuck up, Jacob!"

The next thing I heard was, "Shut the fuck up, Jacob. I'm gonna kick your ass!"

These expletives and many others were hurled at a man named Jacob that morning. I was highly amused by the whole affair but could not immediately grasp the whole tenor of what was going on. I have never forgotten it.

Jacob was a South African who limped noticeably with a club foot but also had a propensity to irritate the hell out of people. Nobody else rang a bell when they woke you up. In fact, Jacob seemed to enjoy irritating people. They all seemed to know it, too. Jacob could be quite personal and friendly at times, but he more often had a cartoon quality about him. Eventually, he would ask you to do something unreasonable or insist upon you allowing him to do something unreasonable himself. When you then acted in a rational way so as to deter or stop him, he would become very argumentative. Nobody took him too seriously. I was told he would have been off-loaded from the ship years ago save for the fact that he was a Founding Scientologist. This signified that he was there at the very beginning and that status earned him something of a soft spot. One of his stunts was to sometimes write incredibly flowery praises to Ron and Mary Sue in the *Orders of the Day*. His prose, which was truly insufferable, seemed as if it was designed to embarrass anyone who might read it.

One day, when we were in the middle of the Atlantic Ocean and travelling between Portugal and Morocco, I was assigned to the task of taking huge gunnysacks full of mimeographed issues from the bottom of the ship and tossing them into the ocean. The sacks were heavy and it was quite a haul. What was yet worse than the dozens of sacks that we carried that day was the fact that when we finished, there was still a huge mountain of mimeographed issues that were classified as junk and still waiting to be put in gunnysacks. It was a mess and had been for years. This stack of issues was known as "Jacob's Mountain."

The *Apollo* had a series of mimeograph installations where various bulletins, policy letters, or administrative directives were typed and printed. This was known as the Mimeo Unit, and it was quite a busy operation and took up an entire hold of the ship known as Lower Hold #2. Jacob's Mountain was a huge unused pile of mimeo issues that were either uncollated or, for some other reason, had no home in the ordinary files. In other words, they were junk. I eventually learned that the history of Jacob's mountain and its name went back several years.

Jacob was at one time the Mimeo Files In Charge. After an issue was typed, collated, distributed, and a certain amount of copies were placed in the files, the rest should have been disposed of. This was a bit of a touchy subject because these usually included secure Scientology materials which were not to be distributed about in foreign garbage bins or the like. Instead of properly handling the situation at the time it occurred, Jacob began to accumulate huge piles of mimeographed junk which he originally placed in an empty spot on an upper deck. As the pile began to grow, various members of the crew complained to Jacob about it and said that he should handle it. Finally, by the time it reach the size of what might be a small bedroom, Jacob, in an attempt to fend off the criticism of his incompetence, wrote a note on a piece of paper and affixed it to his mountain. It said the following.

"If you think you can do my job better than I can, you can have it."

One day, LRH was walking on this particular deck, a place he did not frequent that often, and he encountered Jacob's Mountain. He was said to have stood in utter disbelief and did not say a word. Seeing Jacob's note, he immediately wrote on it, "I've got it!" and signed his name. He then ordered the mountain to be taken below decks where it could be stored until properly disposed of in a secure manner.

By the time I got to the ship, it was years later and Jacob's Mountain had reached a size that was beyond belief. Although Jacob had long since been removed from his job, his name never left the mountain. I do not remember how it was actually destroyed. It was probably taken care of when the ship was abandoned for a land base in 1975.

Jacob was eventually sent away from the *Apollo* and returned to South Africa where he continued to be a Sea Org member. Years later, when LRH was doing an investigation of the marketing division at the new headquarters in Florida, there were plenty of things going wrong. He noticed that Jacob had been brought back to Flag headquarters and was working in the marketing division. I remember LRH making a surprised and almost snide comment when he telexed an executive and said something to the effect of, "You have Jacob of Jacob's Mountain fame working in marketing. How can you expect anything to be going right?" This was seven years after the original incident, and he had certainly not forgotten it nor had any of the crew who were still around. It was a great source of amusement. Ron did not come down heavy on Jacob at all. I think he was either too disgusted or did not take him seriously.

Perhaps the greatest zoo episode concerned another crew member by the name of Steve. He was the Aft Dishwasher and had one of the worst jobs on the *Apollo*. I filled in for him a few times and it was a tough job. The dishes would just keep on coming. For him, he apparently could not get any relief. His main problem was that he not only had to work long hours but that he could not get adequate substitution in order to take time to study or be audited. This must have depressed him as it was all work and no play. If you ever found yourself in a situation like that in the Sea Org, it was up to YOU to get out of it. Sometimes it was tough, but it was never impossible. Steve, however, must have had wild delusions of grandeur even prior to getting into Scientology.

Although no one knew it at the time it was occurring, he had concocted a plot based upon his depression and fears. As Scientology was not being applied to him on the ship, he concluded it was not only being withheld from him but on a broader basis, too. He then began collecting an assortment of policies and bulletins, perhaps from Jacob's Mountain itself — I do not know — and was secretly stashing them in a storage area of the ship. Somehow, he decided he would smuggle these off the ship and bring them to the Government in Washington, D.C. in order that they would have Scientology, too. He considered the information in Scientology to be very important, and if he could get it into the right hands, the whole world would benefit.

To execute his plan, he hired a Portuguese fisherman to moor a small boat right next to the ship and adjacent to the poop deck. Once the fisherman brought his small vessel, Steve was waiting on the poop deck with a large bundle of issues that he had secured in a sack, presumably a gunnysack, and dropped them, intending for them to fall into the smaller boat. Unfortunately for him, his plan backfired. The sack of bulletins missed the boat and fell into the water where they would soon be all wet if not ruined. Apparently horrified at this destruction of the materials, he made a heroic dive into the water to save them, thus becoming a spectacle that the crew of the *Apollo* could never easily forget. One of the ship's officers, a friendly guy by the name of James, heard all of the commotion as it was happening and took care of matters. Steve was helped out of the water, taken back aboard and promptly relieved of his stressful job. As he was not Sea Org material, he was sent home several days after the incident.

I talked to Steve a few days after the incident, and he readily admitted that his plan was insane. Despite all of his ridiculous behavior and erroneous conclusions, I have to say one thing about Steve. He was one of the nicest people you would ever want to meet, and he never would have intentionally hurt anyone. Steve, however, was not really the problem. It had something more to do with his reactive mind. There is an upside to the story. Although Steve never rejoined the Sea Org to my knowledge, he did become a successful chiropractor and got auditing to address those problems in his reactive mind. He eventually did all of the Scientology OT levels.

Although these are only two instances, the zoo factor was definitely a part of life in the Sea Org and could never be avoided. It was never something you were supposed to be too interested in, but I thought it made for some excellent comic relief in an environment that was often filled with stress and drama.

26

QUARTERMASTER

One morning during my early days on the *Apollo*, I was assigned for the second time to act as Quartermaster of the Gangway and was to report at 8:00 a.m. in the morning, thus making breakfast a chancy proposition. Upon taking over, I was informed that the person I was supposed to assist was not available and that I would have to wake up Ron Loving who would take his place. As I had learned from the Jacob incident, along with many other experiences, waking up someone on the *Apollo*, particularly when they did not want to be, could be like setting off a mini holocaust. As I was still new and did not yet know all of the whys and wherefores, it was an even more hazardous proposition. Waking up Ron was a complete surprise. Not only was he a gentle soul, he told me he would be right up.

When he reported to duty, I met one of the most relaxed and comfortable persons I ever encountered on the *Apollo*. Ron had red hair and was from Oklahoma, speaking with a distinct friendly accent that Oakies are known to have. Besides being Clear and OT, he was also accomplished in the martial arts, and I think this contributed to his serene state of beingness. He was confident, but he was more friendly than confident. After conspiring to figure out how we could each grab our breakfast and eat it while still doing our chores, we were left with plenty of time to talk. Ron had been fully trained to function as an executive at the top echelon of Scientology management. Like all Scientology executives, he was eventually removed for some form of remedial rehabilitation. This

175

was standard fare for Scientology management and was not a big deal nor was it considered a badge of dishonor.

Unlike anyone I had met up to that point, Ron gave me a birds-eye view of LRH that I had never had before. He spoke of being in his research room and listening to what his intentions for the United States were. LRH had a deep concern for society and people in general with a far wider view of things than ordinary world or religious leaders. He was putting Scientology organizations together in an effort to jump-start the entire awareness of the planet. I realize that some people will not believe this and think that his motives were only greed, power and acclaim. This is not really an accurate picture. While I was not surprised to hear about Ron's good motives, Ron Loving was bringing it home to me in a very real context that was based upon the personal briefings he had received from LRH. I could easily visualize LRH in his research room, which was only a few decks above, trying to "audit" humanity on an administrative level. If you do not believe this, at least understand that this is the way LRH talked. If he was fooling all of his accomplices, he was also fooling himself.

What was more remarkable about my conversation with Ron Loving that morning was not so much the above, but it had more to do with the way he spoke about LRH. Because of his extreme confidence, you could tell that Ron thought of LRH more as an equal. By equal, I do not mean that he had the same status or rank or power in the Sea Org, but he talked as if he had an equality of beingness. In other words, when LRH spoke to him, it was more like the coach of a football team discussing with his quarterback what plays would be best to run. It was more a matter of team effort with complete respect for the other person's position. He made LRH sound more like a real person with real concerns and issues, all of which had to do with the betterment of the world.

Please understand that these conclusions and observations I have stated are based upon long and evolved dialogues that I either witnessed or was a party to. It is in no way a matter of public relations. LRH and Scientology engaged in a lot of public relations, some of it effective and some of it embarrassing, but the conversations I am referring to were on an internal and non-public level. It was very ambitious stuff, but LRH did not have to talk like that if he was just trying to orchestrate a scam. In essence, Ron

Loving's conversations with me gave me a bit of insight into LRH as a human being for the first time.

All of the above was in stark contrast to the way most staff would react to LRH. They were quick and ready to jump at his slightest order. While this was generated out of love and respect for the man, along with a tinge of fear at times, I was able to see a relaxed horizon above the lower emotions. LRH had no desire to be your personal drill sergeant. He wanted you to come up to his level. In other words, there was plenty of room for communication at the top. Although this was not my first lesson in the Sea Org, it was my first lesson worth learning about LRH as a person. It was probably the only thing that made my tenure in the Sea Org livable.

My new found lesson would soon be tested. A few days later, I would be reassigned as Quartermaster of the Gangway for a four hour watch, but this time there was nobody but myself. Although I had not been trained for the job and knew only the most basic functions of the job, which were really not all that hard to perform, I would have to go it alone. To have a new person doing this job without training was considered off-policy, but it was also the way the Sea Org worked. You were expected to know and do your job even if you were not trained. For me, this served as a bit of a slap in the face in order to wake up and become a regular crew member.

All of this was really not so bad. Things went pretty well on my morning watch, but just as I was beginning to feel confident, I felt a very strange energy overhead. I looked up and saw LRH looking down and staring at me. "What in the hell is he looking at?" I wondered.

Fortunately for me, I was engaged in some very minor activity of having some boxes brought aboard or something, and I did not feel obligated to devote all of my time to LRH's impinging stare. The energy overhead, however, did not go away. When I looked up again, I saw that he was still staring and he did not look pleased. I was completely puzzled, but I knew that if I remained active or pretended to do so, I could stave off any potential thunder from him. I began talking animatedly to some of the people I was dealing with and started moving my hands a lot as if I was actually doing something meaningful by talking. I knew he could not hear me, and this was a charade on my part to act and look as if I was actually doing something important. In retrospect, it was a pretty good smoke-screen or at least adequate public relations as it made me look engaged and competent when I really had no idea whatsoever about his concerns.

One of his messengers, a nasty girl named Molly, soon dispelled part of the mystery when she came down one deck below LRH and relayed an order to me from about ten feet above.

"The Commodore says to strike prep!" she said.

In the Sea Org and Scientology, you are neither encouraged nor allowed to go by misunderstood words. I had absolutely no idea what the words "strike prep" meant. It is also policy in Scientology to have an order clarified if you do not understand it. Accordingly, I fired back my own question to the messenger.

"I do not understand that. Could you please tell me what 'strike prep' means?"

Besides having a nasty predisposition, this messenger also had no idea of what the term "strike prep" meant herself and was afraid to express her ignorance both to me and the Commodore. This allowed for the full venting of her nastiness.

"If you don't know what it means, look it up!" she said in a nasty and angry voice.

The woman gave me no choice. I asked several people nearby, but no one knew what strike prep meant nor had any idea of what the Commodore was talking about. Then, I pulled something off that was ordinarily impossible. I grabbed one of the ship's officers and had him stand in my place so I could go below decks to the academy and look it up. People were generally too busy to go out of their way for you, particularly the ship's officers, but this was for the Commodore and this officer did it in a most obliging manner. I learned that if you were doing something for or at the request of the Commodore, Sea Org members could bend over backwards to help you, at least some of the time.

Running down two decks below to the forward part of the ship, I banged down the wooden stairs to the academy. It was morning, and there were not too many students but plenty of supervisors. They all came over to me and wanted to know what the problem was. Suddenly, the supervisors were all looking through various nautical dictionaries with me and for me in an attempt to find out the mysterious meaning of "strike prep." It was a noble effort by all, but none of us could find out what it meant. After several minutes of looking, there was only one solution. I would have to make my way to the top of the ship and confront the Commodore directly. This meant bypassing his messenger and confronting the situation head-on.

When I got to the prom (short for promenade) deck, I saw James, the same man who had apprehended "Diver Steve" a few weeks earlier. As I approached the Commodore, James stopped me.

"Are you the QM (short for quartermaster)?" he asked.

"Yes," I said. "Do you know what 'strike prep' means?"

"Don't worry. It's all been taken care of, but you would not believe what just happened. The whole ship was running around and asking what strike prep meant. People were stirring around, and I've never seen anything like it. Finally, the Commodore noticed all these people stirring around, and he wanted to know what was going on. When they told him nobody knew what 'strike prep' meant, he said, 'Strike the Blue Peter!' "

James then explained to me that the Blue Peter is the name of a flag that is white with a blue cross, obviously named for St. Peter. It is a nautical custom that the day before a ship sails, it raises the Blue Peter so that those ashore can come aboard and conclude any business matters that need to be taken care of, particularly unpaid bills. In this particular instance, the ship had previously planned to sail and the Blue Peter was raised. When our plans changed, no one lowered the Blue Peter and it was still up when I had assumed the watch. LRH noticed the error and simply wanted it corrected. The term "strike prep" merely referred to the fact that it is a preparatory flag indicating that we were preparing to sail.

James told me he took care of it himself, and I thanked him. By the time James finished, the Commodore had gone inside and the kerfuffle was over. I did not have to confront him face to face.

The above taught me my second important lesson in dealing with LRH. If people got in between you and him, they could enforce arbitrary stipulations and compound stupidities the likes of which you have never seen. If I had been allowed to simply ask my question, he would have kindly responded. But, this was really only an important test of myself.

Things would come full circle for myself days later when I was once again assigned to Quartermaster duty. This time, we were at anchor. When you are Quartermaster at anchor, your basic duty is to gauge and log the bearings of the ship in order to ensure that the anchor is not dragging. You also monitor those coming and going from the ship via the lifeboat. There were also wake-ups for certain people at different times. On this day, I was completing an errand as I ran towards the ship's bridge and was just about to climb the ladder when I ran smack into the Commodore. He was all alone, and I was rather surprised and dumbstruck. Already in the middle of doing something, I could not imagine what I should or might say to him or how. It certainly would not have been polite to ignore him, and I was a little perplexed at what to do. He completely eased the situation for me by nodding. I had already decided that a nod would be the most comfortable form of expression, particularly because I was in a hurry. It was as if he was able to read my mind and completely acknowledged me. I went up to the Bridge and carried on with my duties.

"Wow! I just saw the Commodore," I said to myself.

Even when you were used to him being around, it was always a bit of a thrill to run into him. In that circumstance, in his own way, he acknowledged that he recognized me and did not mind having me on the ship. It sort of cleared the air on the earlier episode.

Another one of my compatriots was not so lucky. In the port of Tangier, one girl was Quartermaster when a large boat on the other side of the harbor burst into flames. It was maybe a mile away, but Tangier is a very windy harbor. If that burning ship's lines were burned or in any way disconnected, there was the potential for the ship to be cast adrift and blow towards us. It was a recipe for disaster. The ship's medical officer, who happened to be with the Commodore in his research room at the time, told him about it. He then asked her to find out why the Quartermaster had not reported the burning ship. Had she done so, the Captain would have notified him immediately. Although the Quartermaster did not necessarily know the Medical Officer was asking on behalf of the Commodore, she gave a flippant answer. Accordingly, LRH assigned her an ethics condition of liability.*

---

* Liability was one of several different "ethics conditions" that are recognized and broadly used in Scientology. They are said to reflect actual environmental conditions that exist in every day life. Although they were sometimes misused or misconstrued as punishment, that was not their actual intention. Each condition had a formula that went with it for achieving a higher condition. There were both positive and negative conditions.

This turned out to be my third valuable lesson in dealing with LRH. While you might pass whatever test he put before you in dealing with him, others might not. Although I was not able to perform the duty he asked of me, I was completely sincere and interested in finding out what it was, nor did I have a lackadaisical attitude. While outsiders often consider an ethics condition to be a cruel or unusual punishment, this was never meant to be the case if they were applied correctly. In this instance, LRH figured that she was endangering others and putting everyone at risk. Eight years later, I would encounter this woman once again. I discovered that she had very severe attitude problems. That incident between her and LRH only scratched the surface of her personal situation. To be perfectly honest, he was much easier to deal with than her and was definitely far more concerned about the well being of others. I do not say this based upon just this one incident but based upon other data as well. Ultimately, you can only judge people by how they treat you as well as others. In this chapter, I have offered experiences which demonstrated that he was challenging but not all that difficult to deal with. How you dealt with him, however, had a lot to do with your own mental state.

27

LONG LIVE THE KING

After the visit of the Princess, things were really looking positive aboard the *Apollo*. It truly seemed that Scientology was about to carry off the biggest coup d'etat in its history. This wonderful news was thwarted almost immediately by what was probably the most sensational and dramatic news event in the history of Morocco. The crew learned about it from the Port Captain who already found himself giving us another briefing on the heels of his previous one. We learned from him that there had been an assassination attempt on King Hassan II, the father of the Princess. It is highly ironic that this event occurred virtually a split second after the King's palace had opened its door to Scientology.

Hassan II, the King of Morocco, was returning from France on his private Boeing 727 when his plane was intercepted by jet fighters from his own Moroccan Air Force. Instead of escorting him, they fired at the 727 with the purpose of assassinating the King. Soon, the 727 was partially disabled. The King, thinking on his feet, got himself out of the jam quite adroitly. The version I originally heard was that the King went into the cockpit and ducked down so that he could not be seen. He then had the pilot radio the jet fighters firing upon him that the King was dead. They could relax. There is also another version that the King imperson- ated the Flight Engineer and radioed the message himself. In any case, the Moroccan Air Force pilots believed the King's trick and allowed the limping 727 to land safely. As the Port Captain told us, "The King is a bit of an OT!" Whether there is truth to that last statement or not, King Hassan II definitely proved himself to be a survivor who did not panic easily.

The crew of the *Apollo* were also told the generally accepted news of the day: that it was the King's Minister of Defense who was the mastermind behind the plot, the very same man that Scientology was working under to implement the security checking on the Moroccan government. This was General Mohammed Oufkir, a man who had once been described as the King's best friend. Oufkir, who once served as the head of the King's secret police, was said to have shot himself after the failed coup, but this story is suspect because his body was found riddled with bullets. It was later revealed that, upon the return of the King to Morocco, Oufkir was immediately murdered by one of his own most trusted "allies," Ahmed Dlimi. Dlimi was the current chief of the secret police at the time of the murder.

In historical terms, everything that happened that day is still very suspicious. There is probably as much potential intrigue about that day as there was on November 22, 1963, the day President Kennedy was murdered. Much of the intrigue swirling about in international intelligence circles on that August day had to do with the presence of a Scientology ship in Morocco that was destined to have far more influence in internal Moroccan politics than any of the foreign intelligence services. It is certainly possible that the assassination of the King was to neutralize the budding and powerful influence of Scientology.

General Mohammed Oufkir, the alleged mastermind behind the assassination plot of the King, had loyally served the King for many years and carried out the execution of one of King Hassan's most dreaded enemies, Mehdi Ben-Barka, a one time tutor of the King who subsequently became a serious political rival when "democracy" was introduced to Morocco in the 1950's. The division between Hassan and Ben-Barka became more and more pronounced as the years went by. The primary reason for this was that Hassan II had an international reputation for having one of the worst human rights record in the world. Ben-Barka, a Berber man who championed the disenfranchised, was not only a hero to the people of Morocco but to all oppressed people everywhere. On an international level, his popularity was so large that he was chosen to be the premier speaker at a 1965 convention in Cuba that would not only embrace all communist countries but also all oppressed people in the world. Just prior to what was to be his most auspicious appearance ever, Ben-Barka was kidnapped in France. The kidnapping was set up by joint cooperation between Israel's Mossad and the French secret service. Once kidnapped, Oufkir and his own future assassin, Ahmed Dlimi, rushed to France where they reportedly carried out a brutal interrogation of Ben-Barka in the home of a powerful French gangster. Ben-Barka was cruelly tortured until he died. Upon the advice of an unnamed CIA officer, Ben-Barka's body was later shipped to a torture facility in Casablanca where it was disintegrated in acid. By destroying any trace of the body, it could never then be used as a rallying cry by the enemies of King Hassan.

The callous murder of Ben-Barka outraged the international community and was considered to be the most scandalous Parisian crime ever. President Charles de Gaulle denounced it vehemently. The wake of the murder is still one of the biggest scandals that still faces the world intelligence community. At this writing (2004), it is four decades since this assassination and the CIA, the Mossad, and the SDSC (the French Secret Security Service) refuse to open their files on this case to public inspection. All are firmly known to have played a part in silencing this revolutionary leader and champion of the common people.

It is possible that Oufkir's murder had to do with his role in the Ben-Barka affair. Oufkir's own assassin, Ahmed Dlimi, was later killed himself in what was called a "roadside accident." Besides that, three French thugs who were involved in the abduction and murder of Ben-Barka were murdered themselves after they fled to Morocco for what they thought was safe asylum.

The data on the Mossad connection to Ben-Barka's abduction and murder is not disputed nor is their connection to Mohammed Oufkir and Ahmed Dlimi. In fact, a Jewish journalist by the name of Uri Dan stated that "Israel's name was a hairbreadth away from being permanently stained in Europe" as a result of that incident.

It is no wonder that the Mossad's connection to these Moroccan assassins is not seriously disputed. A study of the common history of Morocco will tell you not only that the Mossad was one of King Hassan's biggest allies (if they can truly be called that) but that they were completely responsible for setting up Morocco's secret police. This, of course, includes all forms of intelligence gathering. It is also no secret that the Mossad was set up in part by Allen Dulles and the CIA who provided them with all sorts of state-of-the-art technological devices.

It should also be noted that Hassan II was the biggest ally that the Israelis had in the Arab world. He facilitated the peace talks between Sadat and Begin during Jimmy Carter's administration and had always been known as a mouthpiece for Israel to the Arab world. In 1970 or so, he hosted a pan Arab conference which included all of the prominent Muslim nations in an attempt to put together a common platform for the future. This is one of the reasons that attracted LRH to Morocco. He saw Hassan as a progressive leader of the Arab world. Little did he realize that this conference was being done under the close view of the Mossad, if not in fact generated by them.

Intelligence agencies are an inherent problem, not only to the population, but to the prime ministers and heads of state that they serve. All have open back doors to each other which are never really open to the inspection of the regular governments. Although heads of state complain about it from time to time, there is nothing they can do about it short of abolishing the various agencies. Even then, the communication lines of those agencies would live on and operate in even more secrecy. In short, it does not take a genius to figure out that these agencies foster an environment where a secret control and influence can be exerted through the various intelligence networks themselves. Even under the best of circumstances, their very nature fosters a rogue element.

It was into the midst of this environment that L. Ron Hubbard and the *Apollo* found themselves in 1972. Scientology had made completely remarkable inroads to the highest levels of the Moroccan government, but so much of this, though not all, depended upon the continued blessings Mohammed Oufkir, the alleged mastermind of the plot to kill the King. With all the nonsense and political intrigue that was transpiring in Morocco at that time, it is hard to completely blame Oufkir. He was trained in intelligence and also brutal techniques by both the Mossad and the CIA. He was also, at least to some degree, a puppet of both agencies. The most obvious answer to him killing the King was as a power grab, but he could never have pulled this off without the backing of his masters. Whether he was behind the plot or not, he did know that his life would soon be over once the King returned and called for a meeting of all his ministers of state. Oufkir did not go but called his daughter in Casablanca and said good-bye. It is also possible he could have been a patsy or that he would have known who the true culprits were. Once the plot failed, Oufkir was killed by the secret police chief who was later knocked off. Someone originally wanted the King knocked off. When that failed, damage control became necessary and secrets were effectively buried. It also helped cover up the Ben-Barka affair.

This was not the first attempt on King Hassan II's life. In fact, he was in France to escape an earlier attempt that he had barely survived. In that plot, the generals behind it were killed. They, like Oufkir, were Berbers.

The most obvious explanation for the assassination attempt attributed to Oufkir is that he was the Minister of Defense and would have been able to order those fighters to shoot down the king. He was also called to the control tower before the King landed. After that call, fighter jets descended upon the landing party and several people were killed, but the King escaped.

What is odd about Oufkir is that he accepted the Scientology proposal to security check the government, including the military. This meant that he would have been found out if he was guilty. On the other hand, he was well aware the Scientologists were making inroads with the King and that he might have sought to employ them first. Any reluctance on his part might have looked like guilt.

There were multiple people and reasons for wanting the King and/or Oufkir dead. The Scientologists, however, were going to end up holding the trump card. They were already in with Oufkir and he allowed the security checking to proceed. If they gained the favor of the King, and there was no reason why they would not, they would have both powerful factions in their lap. To the intelligence agencies, Scientology had the potential to become more powerful and influential than any of them.

The real purpose of Scientology in Morocco was really just to secure a safe operating base and to perhaps secure themselves a permanent place in the heart of Morocco and the royal family. They could not, however, have picked a more volatile environment to operate in.

It was not too long after the attempted assassination of the King that the *Apollo* was told to leave the country. It was not a sad day because there was no time to say good-bye to anyone. In other words, there was no time to be sad because we were given only a twenty-four notice to get out of town. I remember being told that the CIA had heavily influenced the Moroccan government that the ship was a danger. It is known that Mohammed Oufkir had visited a CIA training facility in the U.S. shortly before the assassination attempt on the King.

When the *Apollo* left Morocco, I stayed on the ship. There was, however, a shore crew that stayed on and that included LRH. Prior to the ship leaving Morocco, he had already moved to a comfortable villa near Tangier.

As odd as it may sound, the *Apollo* had left, but the security checking operation had by no means been put to rest and, despite the death of General Oufkir, discussions and events were still proceeding on a path that <u>seemed</u> positive. In all probability however, the intelligence agencies were probably playing a wait-ing game. They had easily gotten rid of the ship. Now, they could view and study their prey and see how they worked.

We then sailed to the port of Lisbon where we entered dry-dock and refitted the entire surface of the ship. It was quite a sight to see the *Apollo* in dry-dock. I remember that one of the propellers was discovered to have a mysterious and sizable crack in it. It had to be replaced for what was then the staggering sum of $11,000.

It is hard to evaluate all of the intrigue and conspiracy that was going on in Morocco in 1972 and how much of it was precipitated by the presence of L. Ron Hubbard and Scientology, but it should never be underestimated. The Ben-Barka scandal seemed to play some part in the assassination attempt, but it also appeared that the King himself was either under the pressure of the intelligence agencies or had run afoul of them. Oufkir was designated as the assassin, but he was a known and respected instrument of the Mossad and, perhaps to a lesser degree, of the CIA. The Moroccan Air Force actually tried to kill the King as they damaged his plane to the point where it could easily have crashed. That he survived was a minor miracle. Oufkir, despite his heinous reputation, was a potential and interested ally of Scientology. His murderer, Ahmed Dlimi, was also close to the Mossad.

All we know for sure is that, at the very end of November 1972, two key events happened that would impact L. Ron Hubbard and the *Apollo*. In a move that is rather unprecedented in most systems of jurisprudence, LRH was convicted in absentia in France, a country he was never really in. Further, the French were politicking for his extradition from Morocco and any other country he might care to enter. At the same time, L. Ron Hubbard and all members of the Operation and Transport Corporation (i.e. Scientology) were ordered to leave the country immediately.

Hindsight is great. We can look back and see that Hubbard might have been a bit naive as to how much opposition there was against him. He was ostensibly trying to secure a position of power or relative safety by endearing our operation to the King. The King obviously exerted a considerable amount of power but did so via the intelligence agencies. In the end, they would prove to be far more powerful by exerting fear into the King through assassination. If Oufkir or Dlimi were involved in a coup, it was only because their mentors were backing them. They were both eliminated.

Although Scientology was a big loser in the events of Moroccan politics, there was an even bigger loser: the native Berbers of the Atlas mountains. Most of this oppression influenced them more than anyone else.

As for myself, it was the beginning of December and I was safe with the rest of the *Apollo* crew on the docks of Lisbon. When the order was given to leave Morocco, the crew immediately learned that LRH had returned to Lisbon and was staying in a nearby hotel. Everyone was very well briefed during this period and never before or since had I ever seen so many various Sea Org units act as if they were all one family. When the rest of the crew returned from Tangier and Rabat, we were instructed to serve as a welcoming committee and make their transition back to the ship as smooth as possible. There was an incredible amount of excitement, not only because of all of the political intrigue but by reason of the fact that you were seeing people who had been gone for months.

I remember seeing two of my old seniors that I had served under while working on the deck force. They were a married couple who had just returned from Tangier but had no idea of what was going on when they arrived on the *Apollo*. They asked me to come to their cabin during some time off and tell them what the hell was going on. I told them where LRH was as well as how the exciting events with the King had transpired to put us all in the current situation. There were more details I told them as well, but they have nothing to do with the subject at hand. Although these people were part of the operations in Morocco, I had a lot more information by reason of being regularly briefed, and they were fairly isolated in whatever their duties were. I mention this last meeting with my two former seniors as it proved to be a pivotal time in my Sea Org career which was only about seven months old at that point. All of a sudden, I realized I was no longer new. These characters had once been my seniors, and I had always sort of looked up to them as more experienced or whatever. Now, our roles had shifted somewhat. I was telling them what was going on, and they were eager as hell to hear everything I had to say. The excitement of all that occurred in the last few months had made me feel at long last that I not only belonged in the Sea Org but that I had become a part of the infrastructure. Even though I had a good grasp of Scientology and was enjoying auditing during the autumn of 1972, it took me a good seven months to feel that I was not only a Sea Org member but a Flag crew member as well. I was only nineteen, but I had signed up for one hell of an adventure. On both the *Excalibur* and the *Apollo*, it was the theme and spirit of adventure that had enabled me to rise above the personal difficulties I had encountered. If I had to judge my Sea Org career in terms of adventure up to that point, I was certainly not disappointed.

28

BREAK A LEG

As LRH holed up in a nearby hotel in Lisbon, a constant phone watch was set up at a phone booth on the dock so he could reach the ship in a heartbeat. We were informed of the intent to extradite him. One of the crew, a rather inauspicious man by the name of Paul Preston, found out where LRH was staying and knocked on his door. When the Commodore opened the door, he was in his bathrobe. Paul said, "Sir, I would like to be your valet," whereupon he was "hired" on the spot. The next thing we were told was that LRH had gone to visit his father in Canada. This was a shore story told to the crew to keep the attention off the fact that he went to New York City where he could be lost among millions of people and be relatively free from extradition. His actual whereabouts were kept strictly confidential.

Although LRH was gone, the Christmas season was very fun and festive. Despite what you might hear about Scientologists not believing in Christ, Christmas was always the biggest of the holidays in the Sea Org and their were always multiple parties. In the process of all of this, I was growing up very fast. Besides being on my own before joining the Sea Org, I was now involved in worldly events and other cultures and my perspective was far beyond what it would have been had I gone to college and studied bonehead English. In Europe, there is no restriction on alcohol so I was also treated as an adult whenever I happened to be in a Portuguese restaurant. Besides this, everyone treated me as an adult, and my childhood was now very far behind me.

The winter in Lisbon was dreary with a lot of rain. I did well and ended up working as a cook , but no one knew I had actually cooked professionally before that. It was a coincidence. Things were now going pretty smoothly for me, but I must admit something. The ship was nowhere near as nice a place to be without the presence of LRH. Certain executives came out of their monkey cages and liked to rattle other people. They did not bother me, but you could notice a definite difference in the tone and mood of the crew. As my first anniversary in the Sea Org approached, I requested and got an approved leave for three weeks. I wrote to my father and told him. He was delighted and sent me the money for airfare to return home and visit. There was only one problem. Even though it was approved that I was allowed to go on vacation, my seniors, acting explicitly against LRH's advices and orders regarding these matters, told me I could not leave. This is how Scientology gets a bad name as a cult. It basically adds up to ass-holes acting like ass-holes. You can imagine how this upset my father. I wrote to him that I was free to go on vacation but only wrote to him after I had the approval. He then sends me money only to be told that I cannot. He is then left to intuit that "I am held incommunicado." Had LRH been around, I could have written to him, and he would have cleared up the problem in a minute. He was gone, and I was left to my own devices. LRH always warned you not to depend on him, and this would be my first test.

Although I had been very productive, no one wanted to help me. I even wrote to Mary Sue, and although she was polite and nice, she was a far cry from LRH. She was of no help. I then did a study of who could and could not leave the ship and realized that it was really quite easy to get off. All you had to do was be a "fuck-up." OK, if you want a fuck-up, I'll give you one. I was not going to betray my father's trust after having told him I was coming home and taking his money. As much as I was dedicated to the ideals of the Sea Org, I would never desert my family. The dynamics of a cult are basically just monkeys in a monkey cage. I wanted no part of that behavior and neither did LRH, believe it or not. I experienced firsthand what he was talking about when he said, "Give me liberty or give me death." I did not want to be with ass-holes who would "hold on to me." So, I informed everyone that I wanted to leave. Boy, did that get a response! They found me a replacement immediately. I was completely happy about that turn of events as I was living out the courage of my convictions. In retrospect, it was an excellent move on my part. Most of the crew who I worked with in the galley ended up staying there for years and years. I was not only going home, I was also getting out of a job I did not really want. In fact, the universe ended up rewarding me very nicely for not going along with the crowd.

Before I left what was to be my first tour of duty on the *Apollo*, I had occasion to witness a rather significant and humorous spectacle, part of which was a portent of things to come. It took place on a beautiful summer evening in Oporto, a port city in northern Portugal. In Oporto, the ship always sat at anchor and you would take a lifeboat to get into the city. It was a common experience for many crew that, as the lifeboat powered you away, you would see the *Apollo* reduce in size until it was only a distant image on the water line. As it receded, it was very common to feel a great deal of relief and be as glad as hell to "get away from that god damn ship." Ironically, when you returned at the end of the day, usually after having a considerable amount of fun, you were completely overjoyed to be back. When I told my reactions to many of the crew, they said they felt the same way. Time off was healthy, but you were generally glad to return and go back to work.

On this particular July evening, I had gone with another gentleman to see Alfred Hitchcock's *The Birds*. It was an old movie by that time, but I had never seen it. For Americans, seeing movies in foreign countries is great because the sound is in English and the subtitles are irrelevant. I remember that the footage was shot in Northern California, and I was getting very antsy to return home. Never had I loved California so much.

After the movie, it was very late, and my friend and I returned to what was to be the last scheduled run of the lifeboat that evening. It was around 10:30 p.m., and we were pushing not to miss the boat. When we arrived, we were in for a bit of a surprise. Waiting at the dock by the lifeboat was Captain W. B. "Bill" Robertson who was known by everyone as "Captain Bill." Besides the Commodore and Mary Sue, he was the highest ranking officer in the Sea Org and had settled into the title of Second Deputy Commodore while LRH was away. Mary Sue was First Deputy Commodore. Most everyone liked Captain Bill, but he was quite a character. He had a crazy and wild side, and some might say insane side, but he was a good sailor and you could depend on him to get you from one port to another. Most important to everyone in the Sea Org, he loved LRH and Mary Sue.

My friend and I could not believe he was there. We should have been the last stragglers to arrive, but we knew he was not waiting for us. As we got in the boat and waited, we soon learned that he was waiting for Mary Sue and that she would be accompanying us in the lifeboat on our return to the ship. This was a very rare experience. Mary Sue was far more private than LRH. He would walk about and talk to the crew quite often, but she was far more reserved. You would see her around, but you never saw her joking around or shooting the breeze with the crew. This would be the closest encounter I would ever have with Mary Sue, and boy did I learn a lot from it. My observations turned out to be prophetic.

As she arrived, she was accompanied by Kima Dunleavy (who would later be Kima Douglas). Although I had often seen Mary Sue before, I had never before seen her treated so much like royalty. Kima was holding a cigarette lighter or something and, without saying a word, made every effort to impress upon the consciousness of everyone who watched, that Mary Sue was to be treated as a queen. I could not help but wonder how much of this was generated by Kima as opposed to Mary Sue. There was no question, they were both playing the part: the queen and the hand servant. I did not begrudge this to Mary Sue at all because I knew the lessons of power. She was a power and deserved to be treated as a power. What I was concerned about, however, was that power is a very dangerous element. I knew from my own experiences on the whole track that occupying a powerful position is too often an entry way to occupying the opposite — just study the French Revolution! It was also obvious to me that every ounce of power she was generating by having this hand-servant adulation was completely generated by her marital association with LRH. It was borrowed power. On the various occasions I saw LRH, I never saw him exhibit or give off this energy. He was relaxed and tried to act like a regular guy as much as possible. I was not at all jealous of Mary Sue. I liked her and respected her, but I was concerned for her because I knew how perilous power could be. What is ironic here is that Kima did not even officially work for her at that point.

She was just a friend who, I believe, had gone to the movies with her that night as well.

When we returned to the *Apollo* and boarded the ship, I made my way to the ship's canteen to grab a bite to eat, but I soon discovered it was closed and then saw what I considered to be a completely hysterical sight. The First Mate, Larry Frazier, was in a chair and being paraded around the aft lounge like Cleopatra or something. It was utterly ridiculous. As the food stand was closed, I went up to the galley where I worked. There, I could grab an orange before I went to bed and say hello to my friends. When I told them how ridiculous Larry Frazier looked being paraded around the aft lounge, I was told that Mary Sue had broken her leg. Captain Bill had the crew drilling how they would bring her up the various ladders and to her state room. They had been drilling this for hours. Larry was chosen because he was a rather small guy and they could get a feel for how much Mary Sue might weigh.

At this point, I laughed even harder and told them I had just been with Mary Sue and that her leg was not broken at all. They began telling me elaborate details about how she had called from the shore and reported a broken leg. Everyone was all ears as I told them how I had accompanied Captain Bill and Mary Sue back to the ship. They had heard all sorts of wild information about that night, but I was the only one who had any real information.

As it turned out, Mary Sue and Kima had decided to play a practical joke on Tony, Kima's husband. They lightheartedly phoned in and reported that Mary Sue had a broken leg. It was not intended to go any further than that, but Tony was concerned and immediately reported it to Captain Bill who got the whole ship in an uproar. I do not believe anyone had a funnier vantage point of the events of that evening than myself. As an innocent bystander, I not only had a bottom line view of the ridiculousness that ensued in the wake of a practical joke but how someone who possessed so much power and admiration could have it backfire on them.

Mary Sue had many different dimensions to her which included a humble side. The next day, she apologized profusely in the *Orders of the Day* and explained what had happened. Nobody was upset but all were relieved that she was all right.

For me, I got a bird's-eye seat next to a throne of power. Due to my auditing, I was very wise to this power, but I did not envy her position one bit, especially when I witnessed all the exultations that seemed to accompany her. I respected her power and even liked the woman, but I did not want her power. Personally, I had connected with the Fool, that ever present haunting force that resides at the top of the Tree of Life. It put everything in perspective.

29

RETURN TO CALIFORNIA

After spending a wonderful three week vacation with my parents in Southern California and also visiting some of my old friends in Davis, I returned to the brand new Sea Org estate in Hollywood which was known as Chateau Elysee or the Fifield Manor. It had just been purchased and was the brand new home of the Flag Operations Liaison Office. As either coincidence or synchronicity would have it, one of my temporary roommates for my short stay there would be Alan Long. He gave me the scope of what was going on at that location. To me, everything seemed rather humdrum and boring. One of the executives there told me they kept banker's hours, and it was quite evident to me there was nowhere near the high level of activity I had known on the *Apollo*.

On my first day there, I would experience another synchronicity when I would bump into Kenda and her flaming red hair. She told me that she was still stationed on the *Excalibur*. As she had originally recruited me, she told me that it could be easily arranged for me to be crew there once again. I was delighted and accepted her offer. This would not only give me an opportunity to complete my basic Sea Org training but would ensure I would have plenty of activity in my life. Returning to the *Excalibur* and following my own self-determined path of leaving the *Apollo* paid off some great dividends to me. The universe "rewarded" me as I ended up being posted as an auditor and had the opportunity to finally learn the basics of Scientology auditing as opposed to Dianetic auditing. Mostly, these talents were to be used as a "Security Checker," but

I was also able to learn and audit many other processes and eventually enjoy some of the best times of my life as a result. Before these "best times," however, I was to learn my "last" and hardest lesson of growing up. I fell in love.

If Bernice was not the most beautiful girl I had ever known, she was right up there, but beauty was not the point. Somehow, by the mysterious force than can only be explained by love, we had unmeasured affinity and recognition of each other. It did not take us long at all to decide that we wanted to be married. I was twenty and she was twenty-two. Unfortunately, there was one major problem. She worked at Celebrity Center in Los Angeles, and it is difficult, if not sometimes impossible, to transfer staff between Scientology organizations. This has a lot to do with the monkey factor and is too involved to explain the bureaucracies of such.

The main point in all of this is that we did get married after which she was almost immediately "kicked out" or "routed out" of the Sea Org. This upset us both, and it made no sense. Many years later, I would have the opportunity to see her Scientology ethics file. It was clear that the way she was dealt with was completely ridiculous and was the act of an ignorant Ethics Officer putting us both at risk. Essentially, they wanted her to return to her home town of Tucson and take responsibility for a traffic accident she had been a party to. When she returned to Tucson and consulted the police, it was a year later and they had no interest in her or what had happened. Misunderstandings and bureaucratic idiocy within the organization were preposterous, and I was completely frustrated and ended up experiencing the most despondent psychological state I have ever known.

Bernice wrote me plenty of letters from her new home in Arizona, but they were all withheld from me as she was erroneously considered to be "ethics trouble." I continued to audit but only because it was considered to be my job, and I was being watched like a hawk to make sure that I would not "blow," a colloquial word that meant departing the organization without authorization. Even so, I could have left in a heartbeat if I really wanted to.

Frustrated and unable to sleep at night, I would often leave the ship at night for the forlorn and desolate streets near the docks of San Pedro, a pretty glum place if ever there was one. When one of the ship's officers heard that I was going out at night, he warned me that there had been gang wars nearby. I thought this was hysterically funny as there was no one out on those forlorn streets at night. It was too miserable, even for gangs. Besides, I was so angry that I was ready to take on a whole gang myself. The idea did not frighten me as so much seemed already lost.

Finally, my direct senior had enough of my psychological affliction which, although I did not know it at the time, was actually induced through improper and suppressive use of Scientology administrative policy. My senior was a woman named Janice, and she exercised one of the most compassionate acts upon me I have ever known. She said that Scientology technology should be used to correct my dilemma and that I should be audited. She took on the job herself, but only long enough to where I could be hooked up with another auditor who could take me for the whole distance. This was Daphne, a young girl I had already known and worked with for the last six months. She took on the mammoth task of fixing me up, a job which took several months.

This started with an Assist Summary which is a very comprehensive auditing procedure that is designed to address all the psychological and environmental issues, including engrams, that surround a person's particular misfortune in life. Usually, this is the result of an accident or death, but it also includes severe life traumas such as I was experiencing. It took several weeks of auditing for me to be able to laugh and giggle again. One can always laugh and giggle, but I mean to laugh and giggle and really mean it. When the Assist Summary was complete, Daphne had developed a liking for me and went out of her way to continue auditing me so that I could move up the Scientology gradation chart towards OT. I learned all of the "buttons" and "vectors" that affected my immediate life. You would be surprised at how many subtle vectors exist in the consciousness of other people that are completely dedicated to keeping you down and smothering your personal initiative as well as your ability to experience glory or personal joy. Details are complicated, but suffice it to say that I was probing some of the most intriguing reservoirs of the unconscious, particularly as they related to myself.

As I began to get audited and have gains or "wins" as they are called in Scientology parlance, my own skill in auditing others picked up considerably. My ability to sit across from a preclear and to handle or dissipate another's emotional charge had increased at least tenfold. I was learning all sorts of "secrets" about the way the unconscious mind worked, but it might take an entire book to give you a full view of what I learned during this period. There were, however, two very important points that I should relate.

First, Hubbard stated emphatically that communication is the universal solvent. By communicating with your environment and also your reactive bank, you can get a very good handle on it. One of the most important points about auditing, however, is that you actually need to do it on a regular basis. This not only accentuates and fosters the principle of communication, but it creates and precipitates an environment where incredible things can and actually do happen. Although it is somewhat intangible, there is a cumulative effect to consistent and repeated auditing.

It is virtually impossible for anyone to dispute the validity of what actually transpires (or at least transpired during the days I was involved) in a Hubbard Guidance Center, the name which is appended to Scientology auditing centers. The reason for this is that in order to scientifically dispute it, you would have to recreate the actual environment in which auditing occurs and look at it from a perspective of at least 360°. If you do not do this, you are not dealing with a scientifically controlled experiment. Comments, whether critical or not, are in the realm of opinion and not science. To create an actual Hubbard Guidance Center under scientifically controlled conditions, outside of organized Scientology itself, would be virtually impossible at the current state of humanity's evolution and willingness. It would require not only a considerable amount of subjects but also having all of the subjects trained and audited to a significant extent, including the scientific observers.

The second point of what I should relay concerns something that occurred to me in my own auditing. Prior to my auditing with Daphne, most of my auditing was with Dianetics. Scientology auditing dealt more with the immediate problems of life and livingness, not necessarily as it related to the afflictions of the body or the whole track. It seemed to deal much more, but not always, with the problems you were having in your immediate environment. After auditing thousands of hours of Scientology processes, I had one of the biggest realizations I would ever have when it came to my own personal auditing. I observed that there were some preclears who did very very well with auditing. They seemed to buzz right along and laugh a lot. If they were not also moving along like a whiz-bang through life, they were certainly doing it in their auditing sessions. Besides them, there were also many people who seemed to just muddle along. After taking full notice of this, I realized that I did not want to be like the people who just muddled along. I wanted to be like the people who moved along enthusiastically through their auditing. In actual fact, I was somewhere between those two extremes in my own auditing. This realization enabled me to adopt the spirit of the enthusiasts. It had a lot to do with attitude but was not something I had to force or fake. As a being, spiritual or otherwise, you have the full right to adopt any viewpoint that you want to. I decided to adopt the viewpoint of those who would win and succeed as opposed to other attitudes. It was the adoption of this attitude which enabled me to experience some of the best times of my life.

My auditing would eventually cease when the monkey cage began to rattle again. Daphne, one of the best auditors on the ship, was later removed from her job for reasons that were later found to be completely stupid and incorrect. She would choose to leave the Sea Org as a direct result. It actually had to do with her being on the wrong side of a power move when a new captain was assigned to the ship. All she really was guilty of was making some disparaging comments, not necessarily incorrect ones, about the new power structure. I knew better as I had learned the laws of power very well from my days on the *Apollo*. Consequently, I was promoted to Cramming Officer which meant that I would learn all of the necessary procedures to correct other auditors. I underwent quite an extensive training for this, something most auditors never actually learn. This not only makes your auditing of others much more proficient, but it also teaches you that if there is ever anything wrong with Scientology technical procedures, there is always a solution. Scientology technical people goof from time to time, if not all the time. Hubbard created a Qualifications Division to correct these unfortunate occurrences and the Cramming Officer was right in the middle of fixing these problems. This education was to prove itself to be a critical boon. One thing I learned from this experience was that most Scientologists not only had no working knowledge of how Scientology "qualifications technology" really worked but neither did most auditors. It was an elite understanding that I was very happy to be a part of. If not for that indoctrination, I would not be here writing this book.

Besides my misadventures with marriage and my successful adventures in Scientology auditing, there are some noteworthy experiences I should apprise you of with regard to my second tour of duty on the *Excalibur*. These demonstrate the subtle differences between L. Ron Hubbard, the Sea Organization, and what I have termed the monkey cage.

After I had returned to the *Excalibur* for a few months and had amalgamated myself with the crew, we had a new captain by the name of David Murphy. He had been Chief Engineer on the *Apollo*, and I knew him pretty well from the previous year when I used to "shoot the shit" with him when he would come into the galley and visit his girlfriend. Although he was a competent sailor, he was unfamiliar with this particular ship. Another Sea Org officer, Wally Burgess, was sent to the *Excalibur* to teach him the fine points of conning it.

Wally was a pretty affable guy and eventually became quite well known at the Flag Land Base in Clearwater where he served as the LRH Host. In Clearwater, his job was to expedite the service of all public people and was basically there to act as their friend or serve as their host on LRH's behalf. I liked Wally personally myself, but something very strange came over him when he came to do his short training job on the *Excalibur* in 1973.

As I was an auditor, I did not have to work on the decks, but I was certainly available to hear Wally Burgess unleash a tirade at the crew one evening. Apparently, he was quite upset at the crew because they were not properly functioning at their respective stations during docking drills. He got very emotional and the crew were responding very apprehensively. In fact, you might say they were generally scarred out of their wits when he announced that if they did not straighten up, he was going to use "the Commodore's shock technique."

While most of the crew listened in abject fear, I was laughing hysterically inside. Afterwards, as the crew went back to their jobs, I laughed and told my fellow auditors that there is no such thing as a "Commodore's shock technique" and said words to the effect that Wally was basically talking out of his ass. Although I thought it was very funny, everyone else looked at my comments suspiciously. As far as I was concerned, he was besmirching LRH's name and I would have gladly gone face to face with him and felt free from any harm. There was nothing in writing whatsoever that talked about a shock technique. Having been on the *Apollo*, I knew better and I thought he should, too. It did not matter to me that he had a lot of scrambled eggs on his hat.

A day or two after Wally had threatened the crew with the "Commodore's shock technique," it was about dinner time, and the sun had just gone below the horizon. All of a sudden, I heard loud words broadcast over the ship's loudspeaker.

"Man overboard! Man overboard! This is not a drill! I repeat, this is not a drill! Man overboard!"

The ship regularly had man overboard drills, but I did not have an assignment. Nevertheless, I came above decks to see what had happened. Wally had just been lifted up out of the water and was being wrapped up with a blanket. The ship was at dock at the time. What I found out was that Wally had either tried to jump from the ship to the dock, or vice versa, without using the gang plank. This is not a wise thing to do under any circumstances because the ship is always prone to shifting and lurching. There was no reason for it in this case. He was just trying to take a short cut. When the ship lurched, he went straight down, and landed in the water some thirty feet below, between the hull of the ship and the pilings of the pier. In fact, he was very lucky that the ship did not lurch again because he could easily have been crushed.

After that episode, there was no longer any mention of the shock technique by Wally. In fact, he sheepishly concluded his business and returned to the *Apollo*. After that incident, my credibility increased considerably with my friends. They no longer looked at me suspiciously as we all laughed and joked about the "Commodore's shock technique." I wanted everybody to know that LRH did not want a crew who was afraid or in shock. In a strange way, Wally ended up proving the opposite of what he had tried to get across.

I do not mean to besmirch or impugn Wally's reputation. As I said, he was a genuine and nice fellow who made a mistake. I never saw or heard of him ever doing anything like this before or afterwards. It is important, however, to relay how people could distort the intent of LRH. Although I was not acting in an official capacity, I felt it was my duty to relay what I experienced about Ron and it certainly did not add up with what Wally was saying. It is also important to consider that if an affable and nice-guy like Wally could distort the meaning of LRH, think about what might happen if you had a sinister or subversive soul doing the same.

True power, and we know that LRH wielded a considerable amount of it, can make people's heads swell. As per my own experience with Mary Sue, I was wary of power, but I was certainly not afraid of anyone with a swollen head or an exaggerated idea of their own importance. That stuff is laughable.

Sometime after that, Captain Bill Robertson also came to Los Angeles on what was to be a massive recruiting tour for the *Apollo.* He brought along Arthur Hubbard, LRH's youngest son, who spent most of his time fooling around and playing games with some of the other kids. When Captain Bill visited the *Excalibur,* he was reportedly telling everyone that LRH slept four hours a night or sometimes not at all. I did not hear any of this directly because I was busy auditing. When I heard what had been said, I immediately contradicted it. I knew that LRH generally had a full night's rest and encouraged others to do the same. Captain Bill was one of the highest ranking officers in the Sea Org, and here he was spewing out bullshit about LRH. I told anyone who was in my immediate vicinity who wanted to learn that I was willing to look him in the eye and contradict his information, but no one forced a challenge. I later learned that Captain Bill failed dismally on this recruiting tour. In fact, I heard he complained that life was no longer like the days of the Roman Empire or the crusades when you could raise an army almost over night. In these times, people had dogs to feed, debts to pay, and Aunt Marthas to take care of.

I do not know if LRH ever got wind of what Captain Bill was saying about him, but he did "reward" him for a job poorly done by removing him from his prestigious job as "Second Deputy Commodore" and reassigned him as the ship's navigator. High rank and scrambled eggs in the Sea Org had their place, but they could not compete very well with the direct truth.

30

DEATH

As I just alluded to, I had experienced some of the best times of my life by reason of the give-and-take I was experiencing with auditing. I was not particularly turning on OT abilities at this time. This would happen occasionally, but most of what I was noticing were the subtle mechanisms within the minds of other people that were dead set on denigrating the more noble or enjoyable aspects of existence.

It is important to keep in mind that auditing, by its very nature, is digging into that ninety-percent of the brain that is otherwise inaccessible. It stands to reason that if this part of your mind is not accessible, then there are going to be various mechanisms built into the personality constructs of ordinary people that deny passage to this area. It is not enough for such people to deny this passage to themselves, they also find it a sub-function of their lives to ensure that others do not make safe passage into this unknown territory of the mind. This amounts to subtle suppression or intimidation of others.

My auditing made me very astute with regard to the mechanisms of suppression that others employ against their fellows. The fact that I had emotionally overcome the loss of my wife made me feel that I was very resilient. Whenever somebody tried to make others or myself miserable, I could find a ready counter to this. The fact that I was working in the Qualifications Division made it all the easier because I had the full gamut of Scientology data, which was quite extensive, to counter any irritant. Keep in mind that most of the people on the ship were not even auditors so there was not exactly much anyone could say. If there was nothing I could not handle at this point, my new found abilities to resist any sort of moribund attitude would soon be tested. This occurred on 15 December 1974, the day I learned that my parents were killed in an auto accident.

As I said in the first chapter of this book, Tommy, the husband of my father's cousin, had grabbed me and informed me that my parents were both killed in a crash.

"I knew it!" were the words that ran through my head.

Although I in no way predicted this event, all of the auditing I had received in the preceding months prepared me for this inevitability. On some level, I knew it was going to happen. It was as if my brain circuitry was expecting it. On some level, my intuition told me that this was my destiny and that I should not be surprised. I was completely aware that this was a remarkable response to come out of me. There was also a very human situation to deal with and this included my emotions and that of everyone else who might be involved. I was only twenty-one years old and felt that this was the biggest slap in the face the universe could have given me. I immediately realized how lucky I was that this event did not happen when I was younger and unprepared to deal with the rest of my life.

Up to now, I have given you several snapshots of how Scientology helped me. I am well aware that many people think the claims made about Scientology are crap while others will laud them with more hyperbola than you want to hear. All I can say, quite honestly, is that this situation forced me to confront and actually experience whether these claims that I knew were true or not. Scientology, or at least my subjective interpretation of it, was about to receive the ultimate test.

Hubbard wrote quite a bit about clears and their response to tragic situations such as death. He said that a clear could, would, and should suffer genuine emotion at the loss of loved ones. On the upside, however, he said that lingering remorse or misemotions would not haunt one beyond an expected period of mourning. As I digested and practiced his theories and procedures on a daily basis, I was analytically very well aware of how and why this could be.

Tommy Anast and his wife, Jacquie, my father's cousin, took me to their home in Palos Verdes where we would eat lunch before going to my family home in Ventura, about one hundred miles northward on the Pacific Coast Highway. Jacquie, my second cousin, could not believe how composed I was, but I found it very easy to talk without making a spectacle of my personal grief. After all, my daily work consisted mostly of talking to people and helping them with their problems, not grieving over my own. As we got in the car to take the journey to Ventura, I told them I needed some rest, and I laid down in the back seat and put a blanket over my head. After sleeping a bit, I felt all alone under the blanket and was able to discharge a considerable amount of grief without audible blubbering. If there is such a thing as a state of Clear, I discovered that I was very well equipped to do something an ordinary person would not have thought of, let alone be able to do. I almost felt as if I was able to push my grief through my mind and body in such a way as to potentially extinguish it. In a sense, I was able to stand back and watch myself experience human suffering while at the same time having a detached viewpoint. In Buddhism, one is taught to arrive at a healthy ratio between attachment and non-attachment. Although I was experiencing intense grief, I could see beyond the horror of the moment. As I reclined in the back seat under the blanket, there was no outward indication of what was going on with me. When I emerged from the blanket, they asked me how I was doing and I told them that I had been sleeping and experiencing the grief in my own private way. They understood. My second cousin then began to talk and engage in a major no-no, if you understand anything about how the human mind works. She began to recount details of the accident and read the newspaper accounts of it. When she tried to show me a picture of the crashed car, I put a polite stop to it. The accident not only stopped traffic for miles around, it was so ghastly a crash that it made front page news. It was even broadcast on the local television stations in Los Angeles. I knew none of this, and I could sense that every word coming out of her mouth was reactive and hurtful to my experience. She was basically a very nice lady but certainly did not understand the reactive factor as she had no experience in such matters. Every single word she said was inadvertently very hurtful, but I did not offer her any recrimination.

After all, I was used to listening to people on a daily basis without reacting emotionally or personally to what they said. I waited for an appropriate point and told her that I would be better off if I went back to sleep. I put the blanket back over my head and began to grieve some more. Again, I felt as if I was pushing the grief through my system and just letting it flow. Not surprising to me, everything Hubbard had ever said about a clear's response to grief was being experienced as real and genuine to me. I was hurt. Real hurt. I needed to grieve and I did grieve, but so far I had been able to pick and choose when I would do so. By the time we got to the family home in Ventura, I had rested, discharged a considerable amount of grief and felt much better. I walked into a house full of people, none of whom I immediately recognized but my sister. I had loved my sister from the day she was born. Seeing the distraught look in her eyes brought grief right back in my face. As I was a trained counsellor and very used to consoling people, I fell into that role. She was an accomplished equestrian by that time in her life and had her own horse. The owner of the ranch where she kept her horse was there and suggested that she spend the rest of the day with him and his girl friend to get her away from the unpleasant reminders of what twenty-four hours before had been our family house.

Entering the living room, I saw all sorts of local people that I did not know. All of them were incredibly compassionate and kind. I soon found that I had to pick up where I had left off several hours earlier when I was giving a tour of the ship. I became a meeter and greeter of people as they introduced themselves. Soon, I recognized my aunt Jacquie, my father's sister. She could not believe that I was smiling and treating these people with such interest and composure. Although I was never an actor, not even in a school play, I felt as if I was definitely on stage because I was definitely the center of attention. As the phone had been ringing off the hook, and I was now able to take the calls, everyone seem settled that someone was in charge and they began to leave. After everyone else departed, there were only my aunt and my cousin, David Cochrane.

David was one of the most wonderful people I have ever known. Coincidentally, he was then living in my original home town of Lakewood and offered to house and serve as guardian to my brother and sister who were still enrolled in high school. David took me to dinner that evening. I was delighted to talk with my cousin, somebody I always knew much about but never had a chance to get to know. Now, I was an adult and things flowed much easier. He told me that, before I had arrived at the house, one of my relatives said that I should not get any money from the will because I would give it all to Scientology. He told me that he publicly and vehemently disagreed with her and said that whatever was due me was mine and that I had the full right to flush it down the toilet if that was what I wanted to do. I will always love him for this even though I never gave a penny of what I received to Scientology. Most of you have probably heard stories about how Scientologists give away all of their money to Scientology. This was certainly not true in my case. As I have already sought to portray, you will find that there are a lot of misconceptions and hysterical reactions that ensue around the subject.

I had scheduled the funeral for Thursday, December 19th, in order to give plenty of time for people to fly in from across the country. That first evening was a brutal one for my sister. She had no buffer between herself and the grief except for me. I spent a good deal of the night trying to console her and using Scientology procedures to lessen the trauma as best as I could. The next day, we agreed that she should sleep at the ranch so she would not have the memory of mom and dad flung in her face during every waking moment. This worked out as well as could be expected.

The next order of business was to visit my brother in the hospital. He was in the accident with my parents and had suffered a very severe concussion. He and my parents had been to the local harbor to see the boats display their Christmas lights for the holiday season. Upon their return, they were hit, dead on, by a drunken driver named Lester Murphy who, amazingly, survived the crash, killing at least one other person in his car. The collision was so violent that my father, who was driving, had his torso crushed by the steering wheel and died upon impact. My mother, who was in the back seat, received the impact from my father and also died instantly. My brother, who was in the front seat, violently collided with the dashboard, but his body was not mangled. Still, he was in a severe coma and there was no positive sign to indicate that he would make it.

When I arrived at the hospital, I was told that my brother was in some sort of trauma unit and was directed to a room where I could find a nurse who would take me to him. When I politely told the nurse who I was and why I was there, she began to shudder and was visibly very upset. It was clear she felt powerless and could not give me any sort of prognosis on my brother's condition. As I began to politely press her for any possible indications of what might be expected, she began crying hysterically and completely cracked up. She said that she did not know, no one else knew and then began blubbering. I have never before or since ever heard of any nurse reacting this way, but then I do not make a habit of hanging around trauma units. Again, I became the consoler, and I was using all sorts of mental gymnastics to detraumatize her as best I could. Looking back on this, she was a very sensitive and caring woman who felt hopeless with regard to these extreme patients. She was empathically reacting to the trauma of the patients and also to me. But, she calmed down considerably when I assured that I was not angry at her in the least. I simply wanted information. When I finally calmed her down, she directed me to my brother who was lying on a bed in a coma. After assessing him briefly, I began talking to him as if he could understand every word I said. I told him that I would be doing a procedure on him that was designed to assist him in waking up from his coma. In Scientology, it is known as a coma assist. If the person is too far gone to respond at all, you tell them to "Make that body lie on that bed." Then, you acknowledge them for doing so and repeat the question until, hopefully, there is an upbeat change in the person. Although he was out like a light, I was able to use a more progressive variation of the coma assist by having him squeeze my hand in response. Coma patients are typically able to squeeze their hands as the most basic functions of their brain are still alert. I knew this and used it. When you engage such a Scientology procedure, it is considered that you are dealing directly with the spirit, but there are no specific expectations placed upon the patient. I have seen people wake up from this procedure, but that is not what happened here. In this case, I continued until his body jolted as if it had just received an electric shock. Although I have seen many body's respond to Scientology assist procedures, I have never seen a body jerk so sudden or so fast as my brother's did on December 16th. This phenomena is actually the release of a standing wave in the body. In other words, the impact of the collision was so harsh that when the body absorbed the shock, it could not release it. There is no question that the procedure I did released at least one standing wave. Whatever happened, one thing is quite certain. My brother eventually made a complete recovery and found his place in life as a computer analyst and has a nice family to this very day. I have never really talked to him too much about this incident because he does not remember it. In fact, I cannot even tell you the scientific merit of my involvement in his recovery. But, if you were to ask me for a subjective and honest opinion, I would tell you that it made all the difference in the world. You could say that I exorcised negative spirits that were around him, many of which were apparently doing a wild number on the nurse.

After I got home that night and checked on my sister, I was now all alone in the family house. As I had been living on ships for two and a half years at that point, living in a house was a complete novelty and a luxury. Believe it or not, it helped keep my mind off the tragedy. I had not watched television on a regular basis for years. I was able to hole myself up in an isolated family room with a color TV and was not forced to look at my parents clothing or other mementos. Nevertheless, I soon found myself waking up in the middle of the night and casting out grief just as I had done in my cousin's car. In the next few days, I called my parents' friends to tell them the news and made funeral arrangements. I was pretty busy with this and doing necessary shopping.

Nighttimes, usually in the middle of my sleep, were reserved for grieving. It felt extremely therapeutic. After channeling considerable waves of grief through my body one night, I psychically reached out to all of the people involved in my immediate life. This, of course, included L. Ron Hubbard. At that point, he was a stable reference point to me in my life. His techniques had trained me to deal with abject grief in a way that I thought was rather remarkable. Whatever he may have done wrong in his life, and I do not wish to shortchange those who might feel horrified by him, he had been a saving grace to me at that particular time.

During one of my evening grief sessions, I had a very abstract visitation. In a half-awake state, I could visualize lights which were something reminiscent of Chinese lanterns that honor one's ancestors. Accompanying this was a feeling that all of my past ancestors had come to visit me. For the first time in my life, I had a subjective feeling of what Chinese ancestral worship is all about. It gave me a very deep and abiding respect for this form of thinking. I note this experience because it comes into play later, but it also suggests that a gateway to the past is opened when someone dies. Looking back, my conclusion would be that my ancestors were following me in hopes of making other things happen.

On the day of the funeral, I was completely taken aback at how many relatives and friends were sitting in the family house. Although it was a moment of great tragedy, it was one of the thrills of a lifetime to see all of my aunts and uncles gathered together in one room. These were all the people I had heard about when I was a little boy. Many of them were featured in stories my parents would tell me before I went to bed. I felt extremely lucky to see them all together in one place. In some strange way, it compensated for the loss. This was nice, but I still had to face a final test and that had to do with my composure.

I am generally a pretty composed person. This was noticed by an astrologer I once visited when I was age 47. When he looked at my horoscope, he could clearly pick out certain things that had happened in my life. Keep in mind that he knew nothing about me personally. One of the things he noted was that he could clearly see that my parents had died when I was young. Further, he stated that I was unusually composed and had a very calming effect on the people around me at the time. I was later told by my aunt that my cousin David could not believe how composed I was during the entire funeral. Although my horoscope might indicate I have a natural indication to be this way, I can assure you that without the Scientology factor, it would not have been so manageable.

What ensues in a death and funeral is something that is really not too far afield from a political convention. You have all the warm up acts and speakers who eventually build the energy up to a peak. Then the presidential nominee gives a speech as the convention reaches its apex. When death occurs, one receives the bad news and reacts. There is then notifications to people who also react. Then there are arrangements and a wake. Finally, at a point during the funeral, the full realization and acknowledgment takes place that the deceased is undeniably and categorically dead.

There is nothing you can do about it and the finality and full reality of it set in. The burial is anticlimactic compared to that.

During the funeral, I was put in a special alcove reserved for direct family members. As I sat between my sister and my mother's sister, the funeral service worked its way up to the tragic momentum I have just described. My sister and two of my aunts began to cry prolifically and then began to wail as the funeral service reached its apex. I have never heard such loud and gut felt wails as I did from my sister but especially my Aunt Mary. After the eulogy and completion of the service, hundreds of people paid their last respects to my parents as they went by the caskets and then funneled by us in the alcove and looked at us. While I appreciated everyone coming, I did not like being looked at and zeroed-in-on in during the ultimate apex of grief. As my sister and aunt continued to grieve, their wails began to feed off of each other, and I felt as if every elemental force in the universe that could be mustered was trying to get me to break down, too. This was the ultimate expression of mourning and was the most impinging moment of grief upon my soul that I have ever known. Even so, I did not break down nor participate in the wailing. I had no desire whatsoever to make a spectacle of myself, even if it was a completely understandable reaction. In the end, I held up but barely. As I said earlier, I was able to deal with most of the grief in my emotional body as described earlier. That was done in private which was the way I preferred it.

In what was clearly the most tragic moment of my life, Scientology did not fail me. In fact, it gave me a trained and genuine response that enabled to me to relatively glide through what were the most horrible of circumstances.

I was the eldest son, and there was no question of carrying on. At that time, I had no idea of what I was carrying, but I knew that the future looked very bright. I knew I had a destiny, but I did not know what it was. There was no longer any thought of becoming a writer. I never had any idea then that what I went through would find its way into a book and be intermixed with strange tales of time travel and other psychic phenomena. Pluto sometimes works in the strangest and most unpredictable of ways.

31

FREEDOM FOR
THE FATHERLAND

Dianetics and Scientology auditing, at its very best and under the most auspicious of circumstances, is designed to put one in an idyllic environment or mindset whereby one can view the traumas of the past and clear them up. While the mindset of the individual is important, the environment itself is often one of the biggest detriments to accomplishing this task because it is filled with distractions. This includes the intentions of each and every animal or monkey in the jungle who are also struggling to survive.

In Scientology, particularly the Sea Org, auditing was considered a luxury. It was seldom handed to you on a silver platter. More generally, you had to beg, borrow and steal to get it accomplished. Beyond the individual aspirations of each individual Sea Org member, and whatever their personal idea of spiritual freedom might mean to them, there was an actual overall group purpose of the Sea Org which was to set up an environment whereby the engram of Mankind could be audited out.

Mankind's engram refers to that trauma-based condition in the collective unconscious of man which inhibits humanity from reaching its full potential. Full potential is akin to operating with the full capacity of the human brain. Such an activated state is something that no sane person would want to mitigate or deny. For those of you who might be predisposed to believe that neither L. Ron Hubbard, the Sea Org, Scientology, nor myself had such noble intentions, then please consider for a minute the intentions

215

of every other institution or organization that is out there. If someone else could incite, organize and wrap up the entire job of delivering a fully enlightened humanity, I would be delighted. But, you had first better consider the nature of the opposition if someone tried to bring about such an idealized state for Mankind. There are a lot of positive forces in the world, and these should not be ignored but neither should the opposition. This opposition or Ultimate Adversary acts as a residual force within the universe itself. It morphs when it needs to and amalgamates that which might seek or seem to overcome it, not unlike the depiction of the Borg in *Star Trek: The Next Generation*. The fact that there is such an inherent visceral reaction in this universe to someone freeing themselves of impediments says a lot in itself. A tremendous amount of power is exerted over this very point. When one breaches this gate, one sees the role that power plays and, whether one likes it or not, one has moved into the realm of power. This does not mean that you have to become a dictator or mogul, but it means that you are at least keenly aware of the role that power plays in the scheme of things.

As was demonstrated earlier, intelligence agencies play a major role in the politics of the world. Whatever intelligence agencies do that might be considered "good," no one can rationally doubt that their very inherent nature lends them to being utilized by clandestine forces which are either oppressive or work for something that might be considered the Ultimate Adversary.

In astrology, this realm of secrecy is the domain of Pluto, a god or planet that is all about power. No true study of power should be done without reference to the archetype which is Pluto: the god of the underworld. This underground aspect not only explains the clandestine nature of power but also its nefarious nature. For those of you who have perceived that Scientology and L. Ron Hubbard have a dark side to them, this is best understood through the aspects of Pluto. Although there is a dark side to these matters, the true nature and depth of this darkness is not commonly perceived by either the reader or writer of tabloid publications which deal with the subject. They have no clue except for the perception of darkness itself.

Many people walk amongst the powerful, and some of those who do eventually become truly empowered themselves. For the most part, however, this power is only a temporal state. As all of us will touch power sooner or later, it is best to be able to respond to it in as constructive a manner as possible when it comes our way. On the other hand, seeking it out for its own sake can be foolhardy.

L. Ron Hubbard had not only entered this realm of power, he was a whirlwind that threatened to wreak havoc on the existing power structures. By the public release of Dianetics, he was unleashing not only the potential of the human mind and the seeds of freedom, he had aroused the dark side of every powerful entity that might benefit from the existing status quo. As a result, he was hunted and haunted by various agencies which represented the various power structures. As the years went by, he could not ignore the opposition. Instead, he tried to track it down, find its source and then deal with it.

Prior to his forays into Morocco, LRH hired several private investigators and attempted to track down and investigate where every serious attack on Scientology had been launched. This was a massive task of retrieving and analyzing data. After all of the reports came in on the various countries that attacked Scientology, it was discovered that there was a routine cycle of attacking that came from certain sources which boiled down to the following: 1) income tax departments, 2) health departments, 3) immigration, and 4) a type of press.

As these attacks against Scientology occurred in multiple countries, not just in the United States or Britain, he realized he had to isolate his target on an international level. After asking questions and considering who could have that much international influence, LRH formed an "intelligence hypothesis" that it would have to be someone or some group that was interested in world control. To him, this meant a member of the World Bank with psychiatric connections or who planned to use psychiatry as a part of world control. This hypothesis led him to narrow the target even further, and it pointed to the World Federation of Mental Health (WFMH) and the National Association of Mental Health (NAMH). Narrowing the investigation yet further, it was discovered through numerous correspondences that the central handler (one who orders operatives and operations) was a woman by the name of Mary Appleby, the secretary of the National Association of Mental Health of England. It was demonstrated that she was the primary source of attacks on Scientology because she would write and phone her contacts to start them. Her uncle was Otto Niemeyer of the World Bank.

The discovery of Mary Appleby having a connection to the World Bank was not only revelatory in itself, it also demonstrated that LRH's intelligence hypothesis was correct. Both psychiatry and the World Bank were involved. When they traced the roots of the WFMH and the NAMH, however, it led to an even bigger revelation. These mental health organizations were originated by key players in the Nazi regime. This included Hermann Göering's cousin, Werner Vilinger.

Hubbard's staff not only determined that the eugenics psychiatrists started the death camps but that they, not Hitler, originated the extermination of the Jews.* After the war, many of the psychiatrists behind the Nazi regime fled to London and formed the World Federation of Mental Health. This Nazi influence was a surprise because Hubbard was originally under the impression that many of the psychiatric problems facing the world and Scientology were stemming from the Communist bloc. After all, it was the Russian Ivan Pavlov who was known for proliferating the theory that man is an animal, a doctrine which was the hallmark of the Soviet control system. Further investigation revealed that the Germans had penetrated Russia in the nineteenth century. Ivan Pavlov was trained at the University of Leipzig in Germany, and this is where and how various stimulus-response theories eventually

* It is a very common fallacy that Hitler bore either sole or primary responsibility for concentration camps and the wholesale extermination of individuals. It was true that when he was put in power in January of 1933 that the first concentration camps and eugenics exterminations began shortly thereafter, but it should be realized that he did not just set these things up willy-nilly. Carefully planned and researched documents were written up into the Nuremburg Laws and had to be passed by the legislature. This was all prepared by others before Hitler took office. Even after the election, Hitler consolidated his power somewhat gradually and still had to pander to the electorate and other powerful groups in the beginning. The eugenics movement, which was significantly financed by the Jewish banker Otto Kahn, was already well under way in America at Cold Spring Harbor on Long Island. Hitler came late to the scene. German psychiatrists, including Vilinger and Ernst Rüdin, were big players in the racial hygiene laws. Hitler himself was under heavy medication and became less and less able under the care of his doctor(s). There is no telling how much they influenced him. Common history has acknowledged this to some extent but has underestimated this influence to an extreme degree.

gave rise to the behavioral sciences of B.F. Skinner. The primary originator of these stimulus-response theories was a Leipzig professor named Wilhelm Wundt.

For Hubbard, the big discovery here was that both Russia and the West were interminably dominated in the field of psychiatry by key players in the original Nazi cabal who could strongly influence the East and the West through the field of psychiatry. This influence eventually found its way into the court system, medicine, the field of education and the entire infrastructure of Western and Eastern culture.

Studying the success of the Nazis, Hubbard realized that they had three principle channels into the world. The first was intelligence operations. Germans had the largest and most effective intelligence operation in the West. Preserving their intelligence files from World War I, they set up agents by the thousands in every nation. This helped to set up the fall of Austria, Czechoslovakia, Poland and France at the beginning of World War II.

A second offensive into the world was the drug trade. Germans, including the cartel of I.G. Farben, dominated the world's drug and chemical industries. Believe it or not, one can even get a clue to the sinister nature of the drug industry through Heinrich Himmler. In the memoirs of Himmler's doctor, Felix Kersten, Dr. Kersten mentions how Himmler was perplexed and disgusted with how drug companies instigated improper cures to make money. Creating addictions and dependency is how drug companies ensure continually increasing profits.

Drug dependency empowers the third channel into society which is psychiatry. Drugs, illegal and otherwise, and reliance upon psychiatric solutions empowers an elite group so that it can propagate its own empire. It was further observed that psychiatry had a horrible record of professional abuses which is even documented by the psychiatric associations which seek to propagate the virtues of psychiatry. What was really amazing, however, was that instances of psychiatric murder, mayhem, and fraudulent money collection did not result in any type of arrests. It was noticed as a further oddity that the FBI was not at all zealous in arresting psychiatrists or Nazis known to be guilty of mayhem and murder.

As the above was very well documented, it led to only one logical conclusion. Intelligence agents were exerting control upon government figures. Closer investigation not only revealed such agents to exist but that they were primarily Germans connected to the WFMH or NAMH.

If you do your homework on the above, you can find separate data trails that will lead to the same conclusion. This information, however, is not easy to swallow for the common mindset or those who blindly follow the propaganda of world leaders. Many people believe that if there were such bad people in the world our leaders would get rid of them. This is a critical error in assessing not only the actual situation but the very predicament of Mankind.

This led LRH to an observation that he later incorporated into the techniques of Expanded Dianetics: one of Mankind's biggest aberrations is the inability to confront evil.

32

SUPPRESSION

The discovery of Nazi oriented psychiatrists influencing world governments was not only a major revelation to LRH, it led to him consolidating the information with other observations he had made over the last two decades. This resulted in one of the most controversial principles and policies that Scientology would ever come up with. The fact that it is so controversial is enough to make it a subject worthy for serious study. I am referring to the Scientology doctrine of the "Suppressive Person."

In Scientology, a Suppressive Person is defined as an antisocial personality who is obsessively dedicated to stopping someone or something, particularly as it regards the spiritual development of individuals. The Church of Scientology's policy of declaring various people as "Suppressive Persons" has been one its most severely criticized practices, in part because it can completely ostracize or separate individuals. This criticism is appropriate when such principles are misused or applied incorrectly. As I have tried to stress in this book, however, Scientology procedures are routinely misunderstood, altered and rendered in a fashion akin to painful indoctrinations that seem to come out of the most macabre parts of the human psyche. One therefore has to be <u>very</u> careful to separate the wheat from the chaff before rejecting the ideas or principles that were meant to be conveyed in the first place.

Hubbard wrote vast tomes about this subject. In my experience, a vast amount of Scientologists who were exposed to this information did not apply it correctly. This applied to high level management staff as well.

It is highly understandable that people who have suffered being ostracized from family members as a result of these policies would reject Scientology's severe stance. Such ostracizing, however, is often the result of idiotic behavior in the monkey cage and has nothing to do with correct application of the principles. What these people are often experiencing, but not always, is a mockery of the Suppressive Person policies.

Although the prospect of someone being declared a Suppressive Person might seem harsh, it does not necessitate physical pain, detention or even harassment. It just bans the person from being communicated to. In other words, he has been kicked out of the group. That is a lot less severe than what society does to people who break the law. In other words, a Suppressive Person declare only states that "no one wishes to play with you anymore." It puts the person on a different playing field and that seems to be what it is so upsetting.

You will find this principle very insightful in your own life if you ever choose to exclude someone from your life who is being abusive. When you tell them to stop, they often react like demons from hell were being exhorted through them. A Suppressive Person is really no different than an abusive person. We are not talking about an abusive act, however, but a continuous and repeated pattern that is often very covert.

Most people who put up with abuse either lack the courage to confront their abuser or the precise knowledge of how to go about dealing with the situation while not getting themselves killed. The first step, however, is to recognize that abuse is taking place and get out of denial. It is no different with the Suppressive Person.

While it can be quite invigorating to scan your life for such personalities and go about divorcing yourself from them, that is not the exact subject at hand. In Scientology, we were dealing with what is actually a universal issue. When you embrace a broader sphere with regard to this subject, it is quite clear that a Suppressive Person or suppressive group becomes a virtual "godsend" to anyone or anything which seeks to emulate the Ultimate Adversary. In other words, if you were Satan, a word which originally signified the Ultimate Adversary, you would use suppressive means to imprison and torture potentially free souls. This concept goes way beyond the monkey cage analogy I have already liberally referred to. Here, we are not talking about the monkeys in the cage but the group which imprisons the monkeys and experiments on them with torture and hideous "scientific" experiments.

LRH determined that most people in the society are quite reasonable and want to get along peacefully. It only takes a small minority, however, to create an uprising or a military takeover. Recent fighting in Iraq has proven that there is only a small percentage of religious fanatics who seek to control that country in a repressive manner. The Nazis themselves were originally a very small minority but were able to grab power by manipulating the masses to follow their agenda.

Although I do not know exactly how he collected his data and determined his statistics, LRH came up with what he labelled as an empirical fact: that 2 1/2% of the population is suppressive. Some of them are more powerful than others but all of them are dedicated towards making you or someone feel miserable. A prime example of what Scientologists refer to as a suppressive personality would be the character of Nurse Rachet in the book *One Flew Over the Cuckoo's Nest*. Suppressive people can sometimes be prominent in society or world politics, but they can also thrive in background roles.

According to other empirical observations of Hubbard, it was estimated that Suppressive Persons have an undue influence on about 17 1/2% of the population. This 17 1/2% wittingly or unwittingly serve the intentions of the suppressives. In the movie *The Wizard of Oz,* the soldiers at the castle of the Wicked Witch are a prime example of the 17 1/2%. They carry out every one of her orders until she is dead whereupon they rejoice. They only serve the suppressive because they feel that they cannot fight back. In Scientology parlance, this 17 1/2% of the population were known as Potential Trouble Sources because, while they were not suppressive, they could end up serving as a conduit for suppression and could create serious trouble.

By actual definition in Scientology, a Suppressive Person was not simply somebody who attacked Scientology. It also included people who protest or seek to suppress any spiritual or betterment activity. Hubbard specifically stated that this was also meant to include betterment activities outside the sphere or control of Scientology.

In order to neutralize or eradicate the harmful effects of suppression, Hubbard devised a whole system of auditing procedures as well as administrative and environmental procedures dedicated towards accomplishing this. While many of these activities were quite successful, there was an inherent problem and that has to do with the very nature of suppression or oppression itself. Like the Borg in *Star Trek*, it seeks to attach itself to the eradicating force and co-opt it. It does not take a genius to figure out that if Hubbard was correct about this idea of getting rid of suppressive forces, the Ultimate Adversary or his minions would infiltrate such activity and seek to minimize it. In esoteric terms, subversive elementals would come into play and work at the most subtle and aethyric levels.

I am completely aware that many people are either snide or critical when it comes to the prospect of what Hubbard refers to as Suppressive Persons. Extremely critical behavior is a distinct characteristic of a Suppressive Person. Anyone, however, can be guilty of making an off-color critical remark. It is the continuity and repeated pattern which spells true danger.

It should also be mentioned that people who are critical of such a doctrine have not genuinely studied all of the data nor have they gone about conducting a scientifically controlled experiment that would put the data to a test. If they put it to an honest test, they would be doing the bidding of what I purported LRH's original agenda to be: removing suppression so that the auditing of Mankind can occur.

Although independent scientific study of these matters is probably not going to be done on this information, it is obvious that suppression and oppression are still a big part of what our society has to live with. When you take a look around and decide that you would like to eradicate suppression on a global basis, you have no choice but to create an organization or rely on those that are already in existence. Most prominent and influential organizations have long since been co-opted. If you create a real dynamic movement that were to rival that of Scientology in terms of size and penetration into the society, you would find so much infiltration at your doorstep that you would have to deal with it full time. This is one of the reasons I have never created an organization.

Suppression, either direct or indirect, is really the only thing that can inhibit or destroy gains or perceived gains from Scientology auditing (or for anything that could be termed a reasonable substitute). For those of us who practiced it, this doctrine was an empirically observable fact.

Some forms of suppression can be handled with auditing, but others represent an environmental menace. If a bully is beating up your preclear every day, no amount of auditing is going to resolve the situation. One is required to take other measures to make the environment safe for the person.

It should also be pointed that oppression and suppression has been the way of the world since the beginning. People are used to it and it represents the status quo. More often than not, the shining glory of the life force has been the underdog in human history. If times are going to change, the truth written within this book, or a very similar truth, is going to have to spread far and wide.

225

33

RETURN

This book is a juxtaposition of snippets of Scientology history and Scientology doctrine intertwined with my own personal experiences. While I could go far deeper and be even more convincing, I have tried to stick to the most important and relevant aspects to facilitate this narrative. The Scientology experience was very much a composite of personal living mixed with doctrine. How each individual made out in his or her respective environment, combined with the rattling of the monkey cage, had a lot to do with the individual himself. Many people were extremely rigid and inflexible when it came to what they thought was doctrine. LRH himself was extremely flexible. If he was not, he never would have survived as long as he did. I discovered that the more you learned about the actual doctrine, the more flexible it was. The tricky part was learning it all so that you could make it all dovetail. The best analogy I can give is a virtuoso conducting an orchestra with a baton as opposed to a tone deaf person who uses a whip.

When I consider myself in this equation, I was somewhere between the virtuoso and the tone deaf person. I still had a lot to learn, and I was seeking the baton and disgusted with the whip. I did not resonate with the so-called "negative" aspects of Scientology because I considered them to be alterations of what the subject was really about. Further, my personal experiences with LRH confirmed that.

With my parents having abruptly passed away, there was no longer anything holding me to Los Angeles except for the fact that

I was stationed on the *Excalibur*. I had already decided that I wanted to return to the *Apollo* but going through channels to accomplish such was not necessarily an easy road. What was working in my favor, however, was that the *Excalibur*, which had served as my home for almost two years, was to be taken out of service and sold due to inflationary fuel costs. As a result, the entire crew was reassigned. As I was assigned to full-time training, it would have been very easy to send me back to the *Apollo* except for one reason. The qualifications had changed and the fact that I had once done LSD was a problem. I would have to petition in order to be approved to return. When I petitioned and got no answer, I sent many queries but was never even given the courtesy of getting an answer to my queries, let alone a response to my original petition. Instead, management decided I should replace somebody at AOLA (the Advanced Organization at Los Angeles) so that they could go instead of me. I knew this was an idiotic act on everyone's part because the person I was to replace did not quite "have it," but I wisely kept my mouth shut and went about my business. Actually, AOLA was an incredibly warm and friendly environment to me. People were already setting up an auditor for me so that I could go on to do my OT levels. I would be able to continue my auditor training as well. My ex-wife, Bernice, even came back to see me after I left. This would have been a very pleasant life for me if not for a very strange twist of fate.

Right after I was assigned to AOLA, a telex from LRH cancelled the LSD requirement. I was not eligible to return to the *Apollo*, however, as I still had to replace this other person. As I began to learn the ropes of the job I was taking over, I soon discovered that the incumbent was in "ethics trouble" which essentially means that he was goofing up badly. When the people at Flag discovered this, they cancelled his assignment and said that I could go instead. If it had not been for LRH's inexplicably sudden and unexpected intervention on an administrative level, I would never have returned to the *Apollo*. In all reasonable probability, this book would not have been written.

In June of 1975, I returned to the *Apollo* which was then docked on the island of Barbados in the Caribbean. One of the first things I learned upon coming aboard was that LRH's waiving of the LSD requirement was only applicable to the Los Angeles office and was not sent to any of the other continents. In addition to this oddity, I also discovered that right after my return to the ship, no more staff were to be taken aboard the *Apollo*. I was the last one. Part of the reason for this was that the ship was going to be retired, but this was not generally known amongst the crew, including myself.

I do not believe for a minute that LRH intervened on my behalf or intended this particular ruling for me, but he might as well have. It applied to no one else, and it certainly seemed that something unusual was afoot. If I were to take a guess, he was acting or responding to something in the aethyrs.

It had been almost two years since I was on the *Apollo* and I was delighted to see so many familiar faces and old friends. As I arrived after sunset, there was not too much time for reunions. I was told that if I wanted to, I could go ashore the next day and participate in the photo shoots that were going on and have a chance to see LRH. At that time, LRH was dissatisfied that virtually no promotion was being done by Scientology organizations so he was organizing massive photo shoots on an ad hoc basis and doing as quick a job as possible. As I was wearing a business suit (a costume that we were encouraged to attire ourselves in when we were travelling), I was told to wear it the next day as it would come in handy for the photo shoots, particularly because most people would be wearing short pants because it was so blasted hot.

A large plot of land was acquired near a park and there were various stages and sets strewn across the landscape. As I had arrived early, I found a chair by the wardrobe department and had a seat on one of the few chairs that were about. When the Commodore finally arrived, everyone became very excited. I continued to sit in my chair as he bounded out of his car door and started walking in my general direction. No one had any idea where he was going. As he came out, he walked about ten yards in front of me and gave me a great big friendly wave, almost as if he could not wait to greet me upon my return. Immediately afterwards, a group of people approached me and, in an almost demanding fashion, wanted to know what the Commodore had said to me.

"He said nothing," I said. "He just waved."

Soon afterwards, an idiot came up to me and told me the Commodore did not wave at me. I tell you this so you can get a good idea of how closely his communication was cherished. It was ridiculous, and there was a considerable amount of potential jealousy over his attention.

I spent the afternoon participating in the photo shoots and watching the Commodore work. He was as pleasant as I had ever seen him or could imagine that he might be.

In the next few days, I began circulating amongst the crew and began to hear quite an earful of stories from my old friends. I was being filled in on all sorts of history that I would have completely missed had I not returned by these fortuitous circumstances. I learned that the problems in Morocco eventually besieged the ship once again after it went to Madeira, a Portuguese island in the middle of the Atlantic Ocean. The CIA, who had a very unpopular name in the rest of the world (partly because the Vietnam War was still fresh in the air), was spreading consistent and repeated rumors that the *Apollo* was a CIA ship. Agent provocateurs stirred up a hateful crowd against the *Apollo* and instigated what was later to be known by the crew as the "Rock Festival."

People, some of them obviously hired, were throwing dangerous rocks aboard the ship and hurt some of the crew members. When the Portuguese mob tried to violently board the ship, they had to be repelled with fire hoses. The mob responded by throwing the crew's motorcycles in the water. It was a rabid and dangerous crowd, and the only way to get out of the situation was to let the lines loose and depart. For the *Apollo*, Portugal was no longer a safe country.

The ship made a ten day cruise across the Atlantic and eventually reached Bermuda. From there, they planned to enter the United States and dock at Charleston, South Carolina. At the last minute, Mary Sue received a telex from her Guardian Office that over one hundred IRS agents were waiting at the port and were planning to arrest LRH. He thought this was ridiculous as he could not imagine that they had any sort of legitimate case against him. A vehement argument ensued between him and Mary Sue and she won. The *Apollo*, which was only a few miles outside of Charleston harbor, changed direction and went to the Bahamas before eventually cruising around the Caribbean.

I was assigned to the Flag Bureaux which was responsible for the international management of Scientology, but I soon learned that the executives in that organization had what I considered to be a serious disregard for LRH's policies. Consequently, they did not earn my respect.

One day, some of these executives were "taking target practice" on Ken Delderfield, an old time Sea Org officer who had a pretty high profile. He was supposed to be producing Scientology literature and was having a hard time. Although his previous track record was highly successful, LRH was not pleased with his department and these executives were also concerned about it. They asked me to go down and rouse him out of his bed in the middle of the night. As we worked until 4:00 o'clock in the morning and slept until noon, this did not bother me, but it certainly bothered him. When I woke him, he was upset but did not vent his emotions at me. He only wanted me to know one thing. In all the time he had ever worked for LRH, including extensive experience as a personal staff aide, LRH had never once woken him up or disturbed his sleep. If LRH had an urgent order for him, he would leave it on his desk.

I knew that his experience with LRH had been extensive and while he did not blame me personally for waking him up, he wanted to impress this information upon me. In other words, LRH was polite and courteous to his immediate staff.

As I had never worked directly for LRH, I had no reference to measure this by, but Ken definitely made an impression upon me. This was in complete contrast to the goonish behavior of the executives of the Flag Bureaux. As I was subjected to other crazy orders and improper and illegal Scientology administrative procedures, I wrote a petition to LRH's Personal Communicator and asked if I could join LRH's Personal Office. It was accepted, and I never regretted the decision. Working for LRH was a pleasure and a joy, particularly when I considered the alternative. This was how I ended up in the direct employ of LRH and was where I spent several years.

In this position, I not only learned many secrets but all sorts of information and details about the man that even those who greatly admired him did not have the opportunity to appreciate. I was never taught or expected to immortalize him but only to realize and relay the information that he was an ordinary human being in many respects who also happened to be the founder of Scientology. By ordinary human being, it is meant that he shaved and went to the bathroom like everyone else. Sometimes people had the idea that he was an omnipotent OT who manifested bowls of cereal and the like. This was definitely not the case and needed to be disseminated to people who had unrealistic or fabricated ideas about him.

There is something else I should tell you. I was actually an authorized representative of L. Ron Hubbard. In a sense, everyone in any Scientology organization had that responsibility, but I am not talking about that. I was actually one of a very small minority who was knowledgeable enough and imbibed with authority to speak about his personal life. As I write this book, however, I am not following any rules from his office or from the Church of Scientology. The latter is on a completely different playing field. My viewpoint is reflective of my experience in his personal office, and there is maybe just a tad of "team spirit" that I still carry forward from those days. What I am trying to do, however, is not give you any rah-rah or public relations but to convey the most accurate and relevant portrayal as possible judged against what is important.

34

ILLUSIONS

There has always been a considerable amount of "scandal" about LRH's medical condition. From time to time, former Sea Org members or various publications might squeal that Ron was sick and therefore Dianetics was a sham. These reports were generally highly sensationalized with an "ah-ah!" attitude. I always thought that this sort of thing was extremely funny because, from day one, I had never been led to believe that LRH was invincible or immortal in his physical form. When I studied the applications of Dianetics, it said very plainly that physically sick people should go to a doctor. There was no denial of physical illness, even if the largest percentage of illness is psychosomatic.

After completing the Dianetics course back in Davis, I remember attending my first Scientology party at the house of Vaughan Young. One of the guys had just gotten back from advanced auditor training in Los Angeles, and he was talking to a small circle of people. I remember him saying that LRH was not the first Clear and that he had also broken his back during the research of the OT levels. Personally and privately, I thought this might be bullshit. It sounded hyped. When I asked this man a question about it, he told me that LRH confronted so much mental mass that it literally broke his back. This was never a big issue to me although I eventually did hear LRH talk about some back problems during his research of OT

III. There was, however, an upside to all of this news. The man told me that LRH had refined the procedures so that even a little old lady could do OT III without fear of being harmed.

There has always been noise, rumors and speculation about Scientology. These should never be paid too close attention to because it is tantamount to knowing what color of socks and underwear your favorite celebrity wears. To me, the story of the broken back was largely irrelevant.

When I arrived on the *Apollo* for the second time, I saw that the Commodore was wearing a cast. Although some journalists have turned this into a "scandal," it did not phase me one bit. I remember hearing that he had broken his hand while swatting a mosquito in his office. Although that story is not known to have originated from LRH, it sounded like pure bullshit to me. It made me think that he might have pounded his hand in anger. To this day, I do not know the truth of how he injured his hand or arm, and I never really asked. It is highly possible that he could have been reacting to the dire news he was getting on a daily basis. Henry Kissinger and other agents of the Government had been telexing virtually every country in the Caribbean that we were persona non grata. This made life difficult. It has even been reported that LRH suffered a heart attack over these matters during this period. Whatever the case, it was broadly known by the crew that he checked into a hospital in Curaçao during this period in order to get his physical functioning repaired. Again, doctors were always meant to be a part of the Scientology regimen so this was not a scandal to any of us on board. Mary Sue checked into the hospital during this period as well.

I developed something of a relationship with the primary and most famous medical officer aboard the *Apollo*, Jim Dincalci or "Jim Din" as we used to call him. His job performance was measured by the percentage of crew who were healthy. Whenever someone would become ill, Jim Din would be interested in getting them audited so that they could recover, and I sometimes helped him in this regard and got to know him. He was always very free with information and was more friendly than most people aboard. Jim Din was a premed student in college and never became a doctor of medicine; nevertheless, he had a good knowledge of medicine and LRH used him as a personal medical consultant. He often told me of his meetings with LRH and what was said to him. From my first conversations with Jim Din, however, I noticed immediately that he clearly had a lingering doubt in his mind about LRH's personal state of OT. He clearly saw LRH's mortality as he had to deal with the man's physical problems. I should point out, however, that these were Jim Din's lingering doubts and not mine. Although Jim Din was conversant with many of the basics, he was not highly trained in Scientology technical procedures. It was obvious to me that he was suffering from what LRH called a "hidden standard." A hidden standard is something by which an individual judges Scientology. An example would be someone who privately thinks "Scientology does not work unless it handles the lump on my elbow." If you judge Scientology by LRH's maladies, without taking into account the complex panorama of events surrounding him, you will not only be engaging in a hidden standard but will be throwing out the baby with the bath water. There could be many other hidden standards an individual could have. Too many people expected LRH and the Flagship to be like *Fantasy Island*. It would be nice if that were true, but an experience and intelligent person should know better. Before a therapy such as Scientology can work, it has to be allowed to breathe so that it can work. People with hidden standards are already suffering some form of suppression themselves. It inhibits successful auditing. As for myself, I had already experienced more than a taste of the state of "OT." Anything Jim Din said or thought about it was not going to affect me.

Another medical officer once told me that LRH received and auditing procedure known as a Drug Rundown because he had taken a lot of "medical drugs." I remember that his auditor for this procedure was Mike Mauer. Some literature has been written that LRH would always pick an auditor that he could push around, but this was not true. Mike Mauer was not a pushover. I do remember, however, the alleged "pushover" auditor that LRH had. She was from Europe and she was brought aboard to be the Commodore's auditor.

One time I was having a session at the same time as the Commodore. We were both on A Deck, the deck where the Commodore had his stateroom and where he had his auditing. I was on the other side of A Deck and there were two hallways and two rows of cabins between us. Besides that, LRH was toward the front of A Deck and I was more toward the back. I had a Class XII auditor auditing me while he had the "push-over" auditing him. Looking back, I think he got the short end of the stick. I remember being in session at the same time and hearing what must have been LRH's voice screaming at the top of his lungs. He certainly was not happy about something. I remember feeling that one could easily be disturbed with the Commodore being so upset. I simply told the auditor that whatever that was about was his upset, not mine, and I was not going to worry about it. The auditor completely understood, and we continued without any mishaps. As a Scientologist, you were taught to quell disturbances and not react to them. This was no different. People of other persuasions might take this opportunity to say, "Ah hah! Auditing does not work — the Commodore has problems!" The main point with Dianetics and Scientology was supposed to be concerned with what YOU could do with Dianetics and Scientology. It was not about idolizing the founder, at least in the courses I studied. If you had a good grasp on it, you could apply it to LRH as well.

Besides Jim Din, Kima Douglas was one of the main figures in the medical office. LRH relied on both her and Jim Din for their medical acumen. She had a very calming influence and I remember her as being sympathetic if not empathic. Kima did a great job dealing with LRH, and he liked her for this. By the time I returned, she had divorced her previous husband and was now married to Mike Douglas, the gentleman who had originally brought me to the *Apollo*. Both her and Mike were highly trusted, and he utilized them both as part of a mission to shift millions upon millions of dollars from

Swiss bank accounts into a vault so that it could be safe from government confiscation. Both her and Mike were very loyal to him, and I thought they were both very lovely people. LRH depended upon them heavily. Although they were both very knowledgable about Scientology, they were always too busy serving LRH's personal needs to avail themselves of much Scientology training or auditing. This, and the principles of power, eventually led to a ruptured relationship between them and LRH. It ended up being unfortunate for everyone.

There is no question about it. These people, as well as everyone who served LRH in a personal capacity, got to see his vulnerable human side. On the ship, this information did not seem to be confidential or closely guarded. What I knew was not privileged information, and I was never encouraged to keep it quiet. Upon my return trip to the *Apollo*, I also learned that the Commodore had an accident with his motorcycle and broke his arm. Amazingly, he was able to ride the bike back to the dock where he literally dropped it and made his way up the gangway. I was not there at the time, but I heard all of the stories of how he suffered. He was particularly taken aback by the fact that he knew there was a Suppressive Person at work. His methods clinically proved that accidents and illness were the result of a Suppressive Person or thing. He knew this as a solid truth and knew better than to compromise his knowledge and began searching avidly for those aboard who would want to cave him in or harm him. Critics believe this was over done or was paranoia on his part. Upon viewing all of the information and having the wonderful advantage of hindsight, he was right about targeting a Suppressive Person or influence, but he miscalculated where it was coming from.

35

REMOTE VIEW

The time period preceding LRH's motorcycle accident in the Canary Islands was filled with intrigue in government circles with regard to Scientology. Three of the most prominent characters in this regard were Hal Puthoff, Pat Price, and Ingo Swann who are now either infamous or famous for their role in using the Scientology OT levels to establish the Government's remote viewing operations. In this same general time period, the first international psychotronics conference was spearheaded by Ingo Swann. It was not until this conference that the word *psychotronics* became a part of the world's lexicon. We now know from posterity that there was also something called the Montauk Project that used mind amplifiers and psychotronics to influence the mind of human beings and the quantum field itself. Although it is hard to pinpoint an exact beginning for the Montauk Project, it really got going around this same general period.

At that point in the history of Hubbard's research, he was quite aware that electronic implantation and forceful means to control human beings were utilized by psychiatrists. Behind that, he was quite aware that alien intelligence systems had been set up across the universe to prevent anything that might be considered a "free being." It is my observation, however, that he had no idea of how extensively these techniques were being used in the secret sector of the military industrial complex.

I say this in part because of some comments he had made with regard to *Alternative 3*. I was one of the first people in Scientology to read the book *Alternative 3*, and I circulated the information immediately. Someone eventually gave LRH a video on the subject. He astutely said that if it were true, one would see obvious spin-off technology as a result. As he saw no significant spin-off technology, he did not particularly embrace the idea of *Alternative 3*. At that time, there was no broad knowledge of Area 51, but there was plenty of spin-off technology around if you knew where to look for it. They just did not fly it in our faces as they do today. In retrospect, it is clear to me that he underestimated the resources of his opposition or potential opposition.

Psychotronics is only one line of attack that was implemented against LRH, and it is hard to judge exactly how effective it was against him. There is no question, however, that he would have been attacked by these means. Certain forces in the Government made no bones about getting him. A government employee by the name of Meade Emory had already been involved in an audit of Scientology and LRH in an attempt to challenge the validity of their tax returns. Besides this, there were the high level intelligence operations in Morocco, Madeira, and the Caribbean where U.S. officials were trying to torpedo LRH and Scientology.

36

RALPH

One of the most interesting, bizarre, and fatalistic synchronicities that I experienced in Scientology centered around a gentleman by the name of Ralph Somma who joined the Personal Office of LRH shortly after I did. I already knew of him from my previous tour of duty aboard the *Apollo* but did not know him very well. Shortly after he joined our office, I remember standing next to him one day and said, "You come from New York, don't you?"

"Yes," he said. "Brooklyn."

I was not sure how I knew this. Perhaps New Yorkers look a little bit different, but I had never been there except in passing through. I could not help but feel a bit of telepathic rapport with him. After the ship had moved its operations to Clearwater, Florida, Ralph and I spent a lot of time together. He was in charge of LRH's files. For the first year in Clearwater, due to poor estate planning, LRH's files were in an entry way and were vulnerable to being pilfered or examined by the general staff. One of Ralph's jobs was to keep prying eyes from looking at them. Anyone could obtain permission to use them if they had a valid reason or organizational purpose, but you would not believe how many people would attempt to look at them for whatever reason and certainly without authorization. I had free access to them for my job but did not have time to joy read. One did see interesting things from time to time though.

One day, Ralph pulled me aside and handed me a file.

"Look what I found here. Is this person related to you?" he asked me as he handed me a folder.

I could not believe it. Ralph had a file on my mother. Although my mother was not a Scientologist, she had written a letter to LRH shortly before she died. The answering letter was returned by the postal department as she was killed before it could be delivered. I got to read the letter. Among other concerns, my mother indicated she admired me for making my own way in life and indicated some of her own problems which I evidently did not have. It completely surprised me. She had been dead for two years, but it made me feel good and gave me a sort of closure I never expected. I really appreciated Ralph for that.

LRH's files were eventually moved to a secure location behind locked doors, but they were almost destroyed by a fire. Years later, new filing cabinets were purchased and everything was in a shipshape format. By this time, Ralph and I were very good friends. We had taken Scientology's Advanced Courses together and drilled each other on the OT III level. After having spent several years in Scientology, it was as if we were both now being let in on a big secret. We both enjoyed the level and did well with it. One day, I was looking around at all the files, most of which consisted of volumes of correspondence from the public and staff. There were walls of filing cabinets, some of them being doubled-up on top of each other. A few of these cabinets were called "Dead Files" which housed "entheta"* letters. In other words, these were letters from people who demonstrated either antagonism towards LRH or Scientology. They were always read for content to see if they indicated any potential legal or ethical problems for the organization. They were never answered, but they were filed and kept on record in case they might ever need to be referred to. I told Ralph that I thought it might be interesting to count up all of the different filing cabinets and check out the ratio between the Dead Files and all of the other files. I told him that I wondered if it would come up to 2 1/2 percent, the same figure LRH said were Suppressive Persons. Ralph thought the idea was interesting and told me he would get around to it when he had a chance. A few days later, he came up to me.

---

* Entheta is a Scientology word for agitated life force.

"You wouldn't believe it. I checked the files like you suggested and divided the number of Dead File cabinets into the rest and it came up within a few decimal points of 2 1/2."

Neither of us could believe it. LRH's observations had withstood this particular test. In some way, the figures LRH arrived at must have been statistically based although, to my knowledge, he never broadcast exactly how he came up with this exact figure.

Another experience I had with Ralph concerned his two beautiful daughters, Angela and Suzy, both of which were very young at that time. Suzy was still an infant. One day, he came to me because he was upset. The Sea Org was sending his wife, Ralynn, to Los Angeles for several days, and he had no idea how he could cope with his two daughters. Angela was getting around but still needed supervision. Suzy still needed a lot of attention which included midnight feedings at times. He asked me if I would spend the night in their apartment so I could spot him if one or both of the girls became too much for him to handle. As it turned out, things went pretty smooth.

All in all, Ralph and I became closer throughout the years. I even got to meet his mother and remember escorting her through the streets of Clearwater. She had been visiting Ralph and her grandchildren, and I was making sure she got back safely to her hotel in the late evening. I could not help but thinking that she would probably have been a lot safer on the streets of her neighborhood in Brooklyn.

Ralph also renewed my interest in baseball, something I had not paid any attention to for years. On the ships, one would occasionally hear who won the World Series or that Muhammad Ali had beaten Joe Frazier, but that was about it. There was little time to listen to a game let alone think about sports. Ralph would occasionally go to the newsstand and get copies of the New York papers and talk about how the Yankees were doing. Eventually, I ended up watching the fourth and last game of the 1976 World Series in his apartment. Although I did not know it at the time, this was to serve as a portent of what was to become an eerie series of synchronicities with regard to the death process.

The Yankee catcher, Thurmond Munson, had performed remarkably well in a losing cause and was being heralded by the announcers. Sparky Anderson, the winning manager of the Cincinnati Reds, auspiciously refrained from complementing Munson to the point where he was disparaging him. He seemed like a cranky old bastard, particularly for someone who had just won the World Series of baseball. I had heard of Thurmond Munson before, but the antics on the television made him sort of a lasting memory which was to prove significant later on. I told Ralph that I would return next year and watch the World Series with him, only this time the Yankees would win.

The Yankees did win the World Series the next year, but I was unable to watch any of it with Ralph or anyone else. The following year after that, 1978, I did make it to his place to watch the third game in a series the Yankees would win. Somehow, it was as if I had completed an obligation to an innocuous comment I had made a few years earlier. This was not a big deal in itself except for what was to soon happen.

By the time 1979 rolled around, I had successfully completed my OT III auditing whereupon I was selected and arguably "promoted" to the Missionaire Unit. This meant that I would be on-call at all times to fly across the world or country at any given moment to fix problems with Scientology across the planet. This required extensive training which I had completed many years earlier, but it also required that you were in decent case shape auditing-wise. You could not be in the middle of an action, be sick, or falling apart at the seams. Many people sought to be in this unit, but I never gave it a second thought or requested it. It all happened sort of naturally. Being in this unit was very relaxing if you were competent and did your job because there was always plenty of down time. It was arguably the best place to be in the Sea Org because you could generally get plenty of sleep and exercise as well as study or auditing. In all of my years in the Missionaire Unit, I never got into any serious trouble and this was quite a rarity. The reason for this is that I had a very clear understanding of what I was and was not supposed to do. I also had a great grasp of the legalities of Scientology within their own system.

In August of 1979, I was flying back from Europe where I had just completed an assignment. As my plane landed in Boston, I had to take the shuttle to New York so that I could return home to Florida. As I boarded the jet to Tampa, I could not believe my eyes. There was Ralph's wife, Ralynn, and her two daughters. She had been visiting Ralph's family in Brooklyn and just happened to be boarding the same flight I was. As we flew home, it was not a crowded flight, and I arranged with the flight attendant to sit next to Ralynn. Picking up some magazines, I saw a copy of *Sports Illustrated* and immediately noticed that the Yankee catcher, Thurmond Munson, had died in a plane crash. Even though I did not follow baseball that closely, it was horrible and shocking news that someone would be struck down in the prime of their life. I told Ralynn that I could not believe it, but she told me it was true. The synchronicity of meeting Ralynn and running across the death of one of Ralph's "heroes" was a portent of things to come.

The following New Year's Eve was Ralph's last one. I remember going out to eat with him to close out the year, and we had a nice talk. As it turned out, it was one of the last talks I would ever have with him. I remember him telling me that he would like to get into the Missionaire Unit, too. While I do not remember if he ever completed his OT III, I do remember learning that he had some medical problems. After our last meeting, I was pretty much being sent all over the place and had sort of lost touch with him. Months later, I came home and learned from his wife that he had a cancerous tumor in his brain.

One of my friends who worked with Ralph told me that he had complained of headaches and wanted to see a doctor. Doctor visits by Sea Org members had to be paid for and therefore financial authorization had to be obtained. Ralph had applied to see a doctor several times but his applications were refused. My friend also said that sometimes Ralph would say completely non-sequitur things that were not jokes or anything. He said that something was very wrong as this was not at all his normal personality and indicated that some sort of organic dysfunction was affecting his brain. Eventually, things became so far gone that he <u>HAD</u> to see a doctor and that was how the cancer was discovered. By the time I found out, Ralph had deteriorated to the point where he was in the hospital. His wife told me that he was practically skin and bones and that I could see him if I wanted to, but I declined. I knew it was all over at that point and wanted to preserve my memories of him from when he was alive in his prime.

Ralynn also told me that the doctors had offered a series of treatments which had a chance of reversing his condition, but it would be a very long haul and the prospects were somewhat grim. Accordingly, she told me that her and Ralph discussed this alternative as well as the prospect of "dropping his body," as the death state is commonly referred to in Scientology. Ralph, who had received some advanced auditing procedures in his final days to assist him with his future, was quite coherent and decided it would be easiest and best to depart. After this decision, he died that very night. This experience was not uncommon in Scientology. People would make a decision and just go. I have also heard stories where PR types have hyped this aspect of Scientology deaths. Although there were some Scientology deaths where this was more PR than truth, there were also plenty of instances where there was no such hype. In Ralph's case, it was not hype and this was his decision.

As I was coming and going all the time and only loosely associated with LRH's Personal Office now, I was surprised when LRH's Personal Secretary, Pat Brice, cornered me and wanted to know if there were any physical ailments for which I needed to see a doctor. I told her no and that I was quite all right. She was the one responsible for denying Ralph's original requests to see a doctor, and I felt she was overcompensating by going out and asking me and other people if we had problems. By that time, I was not even in her domain. Her predecessor, Aletheia Taylor, had always been good about getting her staff taken care of with regard to physical maladies, but she had been removed as part of a power purge against many of LRH's old time personal staff. Although Pat was LRH's Personal Secretary, she was in Clearwater and he was in the desert in California. He was very far away indeed and uninformed of what was going on in Clearwater.

A funeral service was held for Ralph which was attended by all of his local Scientology friends, most of them from the Personal Office of LRH. There was no body present as Scientologists do not consider the person to be a body. We bid him farewell and wished him well towards a new destiny.

A couple of years later, when I was doing one of my last missions for the Sea Org, I was completely surprised to run into Ralynn once again at LaGuardia airport. In fact, it was at the very same gate that I had bumped into her years earlier. She had been visiting Ralph's family with her two daughters and had been driven there by one of Ralph's brothers. I was introduced to her brother as one of Ralph's friends and our eyes met in a gaze of compassion and sadness that I will never forget. Never before had I seen someone communicate so much sorrow and compassion with their eyes. It is the memory of such, along with the other remarkable synchronicities with regard to Ralph, which has compelled me to include these matters in this book.

Ralph's family was probably never told that he was not allowed to see the doctor when he wanted to. But, in all fairness to everyone, it is my personal opinion, and a very subjective one, that no amount of doctoring would have fixed his condition. I do not believe that it was caused by his forays into Scientology either. Additionally, I am quite sure that if Ralph were to have any comment upon it, he would not blame Scientology and would have recognized it as an unfortunate organic condition of his body. None of the above is meant to excuse, mitigate, or deny the mistakes that were made. I have tried to report the truth as accurately as possible from my viewpoint and not only honor my old friend but to describe how death rolled through my stream of consciousness with Ralph. He provided a valuable link to my mother as well. I will always be grateful to him for that. As I said, Pluto works in strange and mysterious ways.

37

OVERVIEW

Ralph's departure from my life was so abrupt and sudden that I never had time to consider the implications it might represent. By the time he left us, I was very busy in other matters and had a new circle of friends. Looking back, I cannot help but realize how we had both started the Advances Courses of Scientology at the same time and literally drilled each other on the processes. The situation could be viewed in different ways. One could say that I made it and he did not, but that is all perspective and not necessarily the truth. It could also be said that Scientology killed him, but that would be a highly speculative statement. On the upside, one could say that his body was cursed with cancer on a physiological basis from his early days and that he got onto the Advanced Courses just in time to free himself from a decaying body and also do it with full awareness. As I alluded to already, my intuition tells me it is the latter, but maybe there is also some truth to the other possibilities. Opinions are only opinions.

What is more important than anything in this entire equation is what those upper levels of Scientology represent. They purport to release the ultimate freedom in human and/or spiritual potential. When this idea is either put in a person's head or appeals to them by reason of their own interest, the appetite is whet and there is a realization that one can accomplish things that were previously considered to be impossible. Whether it is a false hope or a realization that will one day be activated depends upon the individual concerned. I am talking about the spark within the spark, the spark that shines like the hermit's lantern in the darkness: a flame that not only leads the way but also attracts moths that will allow themselves to be consumed in the flame. It was LRH's lighting of this flame and offering it to people which created such excitement to Scientologists.

One of the points that LRH sometimes cited with regard to the Scientology path was that one was often seeing the littered bones of those who had encroached upon such territory but had not been so fortunate. This symbolism embraces the very theme of any good adventure which, of course, necessitates a certain amount of risk. The greater the risk, the more glorious and wonderful is considered the adventure. When one considers that Scientology was dealing with one's own inner being, the whole proposition becomes highly personalized. Malfunctions are going to come to a head and amplify.

Before I discuss just a bit about the upper levels of Scientology (these have also been discussed in previous books of mine), it is appropriate to say something about the lower levels as these are what block the ordinary human from so much of his or her personal power. At the lower levels, Scientology concerned itself with what are called rudiments. A rudiment is essentially a requisite to what might be considered a normal or regular flow of life or consciousness. Rudiments include having proper food and rest as well as not being under the influence of drugs, alcohol or other foreign or toxic substances. Other rudiments include not having upsets, problems or being preoccupied with discreditable acts that one feels guilty about as all of these get in the way of communicating about core issues within the preclear. These last three rudiments were a major focal point of all auditing. In fact, auditing was never to be done over an upset, a present time problem or a discreditable act that was bothering the preclear. There were various procedures to clear these matters up and they could ordinarily be handled with two way communication and a few adroitly addressed questions. Although the techniques were simple, they often resulted in dramatic change for the preclear and a resurgence of enthusiasm.

Above and beyond their use as a prerequisite to a normal auditing session, these rudiments served as the basis for the Gradation and Awareness Chart in Scientology. At Grade 0, one addressed the subject of communication. As you know, society is littered with people who do not communicate properly or say what is on their mind. This ranges from the strong silent type to the embittered and resentful person. Various processes were devised, not only for "running out" bad experiences with such people but to rehabilitate one's own enthusiasm for communicating with the environment. Once one had attained Grade 0, one was deemed not only to be able to communicate with the environment but to be able to talk intimately to the auditor about one's problems. If you cannot talk about an issue, you are not going to be able to address the issue, let alone deal with it.

When Grade 0 was completed, one moved onto Grade I which addressed problems. A problem is defined as an "intention-counter-intention." Again, various procedures were devised to deal with anything and everything that could be considered a mental problem. All problems eventually resolve under the microscope of communication. This is what scientific analysis and study are all about. When one communicates and addresses the constituent elements of mental problems and debris, they respond just like problems in chemistry, physics and technology — perplexing situations find a way of resolving themselves.

Beyond problems is Grade II which deals with discreditable acts. This not only includes your own discreditable acts but those done to you and those done to others. So much of the Christian faith, particularly Catholicism, is based utterly upon the phenomenon of sin and salvation. In Scientology, this was primarily relegated to one particular grade. Grade II includes many processes as well but included examining the misdeeds of everyone in your life stream, past and present. When completely addressed, all emotional charge would dissipate and the preclear would be a "Relief Release."

After this was Grade III which dealt with upsets of the past. In Scientology, an upset was defined as an "ARC Break." One of the main tenets of Scientology was based upon the principle of A-R-C, an acronym for the words *Affinity, Reality,* and *Communication.* Together, these three words define the component parts of the phenomenon known as understanding. A-R-C was explained in metaphorical terms as the "A-R-C Triangle" because each component worked in tandem with the others. If one increases the affinity for a person, the reality and communication will also increase. Likewise, if another point is addressed, the other two will increase. This triangle was used across the board in Scientology to reach an understanding about anything that was perplexing.

The other side of the A-R-C Triangle was the A-R-C Break which refers to a sudden sundering or cutting of any one of the points of the A-R-C Triangle. For example, when someone you care about or admire unexpectedly tells you to get lost, it upsets you and dissipates all three points of the triangle. You often have no reality on what they are even upset about. Sudden and unexpected changes in one's life also create ARC Breaks. In my personal experience, Grade III was the most fun because it put me in a state of mind where I was able to accept anything that might be presented to me. As this level deals with one's ability to handle change, it very much aligns with the principle of the Hebrew word *shin* (one definition of which is change as was elaborated on in *Synchronicity and the Seventh Seal*). Grade III was referred to as a "Freedom Release" because you were free from the upsets of the past and ready to do new things.

Grade IV entered new territory that was not normally considered to be part of the ordinary rudiments. It addressed what was known as a "service facsimile." In Scientology, a facsimile refers to a mental image picture of an incident on the time track. A service facsimile is called such because the preclear uses this particular facsimile to "service" him in reactive efforts to survive. For example, a kid is drowning while his dad is on the beach and does not see his own child's desperate pleas for help. A female swimmer sees the kid and performs a rescue. The child, who is partly unconscious, made a picture of the entire scene in his head and remembers silently cursing his father for not seeing his desperate pleas for help. Forever after, the kid reactively deems that fathers are no good and subconsciously fosters poor relations with anyone who is deemed to be a father figure. In this respect, the preclear is using an incident to "serve" him by "protecting" him from fathers. It has no rationale basis, but these reactions are common place in the everyday world. Service facsimiles are most pronounced when people make other people wrong. Grade IV addressed not only your own service facsimiles which you use to make others wrong but also those which others use to make you wrong. It addressed others making others wrong, too. Political arguments often get tied up in meaningless arguments of the respective parties based upon service facsimiles that have no rationale basis.

Service facsimiles also include people who become psychologically addicted to illnesses or other conditions as an excuse not to work. Such people cultivate a victim mentality so that they can get sympathy. Sometimes these people will make the environment wrong as opposed to an individual or a set of individuals in it. Some people even precipitate accidents so that they do not have to work for the rest of their lives. This is the work of a reactive service facsimile which actually serves to limit the potential reach of the person using it.

The beauty of Grade IV is that it gives you the ability to do new things. When one gets rid of such negative and disabling attitudes, one discovers that he or she can do new things. All of a sudden, the secretary who could not type becomes a lightning fast typist. The ball player who could not hit a curve ball can now master it. The soprano who could not hit the high notes just right can now figure out the exact mechanics of what it takes to do just that. The man who is all thumbs around the house can now do minor constructions projects. This grade is like a new lease on life.

Grades 0 through IV were generally known as the lower grades. Above that was Grade V which was called a Power Release and gave you what was called the "Ability to Handle Power." This grade put you in touch with the source of your own being which was a necessary requisite to clearing out the entire basis of what is known as your reactive mind.

It was at this point that one took on the whole blasted basket of reactivity. It was called Grade VI and offered "Freedom from Dramatization." This addressed what could be called the underpinnings of reactivity and addressed the territory of goals for the individual. Goals are a very potent power in the mind of human beings. Grade VI not only addressed all of the goals of a lifetime but those of the whole track as well. Sometimes these goals are quite humble such as "to be a good father," "to be a good wife," or "to pay all of one's bills." Other goals can be more lofty or even downright unrealistic. Addressing the goals that are already imbedded in one's mind and often unrealized can unleash a torrent of potential in an individual. Of course, if the person's goal were only "to be a tapir," it might not unleash any enthusiasm or activity at all.

Above Grade VI is the State of Clear which has multiple definitions in the *Dianetics and Scientology Technical Dictionary*. The Clearing Course also dealt with goals, but it is mainly known for clearing out the basic engram that created the individual's reactive mind in the first place. I think an excellent analogy to understanding one aspect of the State of Clear has to do with drill sergeants in the military who are known to ask new recruits the famous question, "What is your major malfunction?" In regular life, most people would not dare ask you such a question, let alone in an intimidating manner like a drill sergeant, but the question is highly applicable to most people. The Clearing Course enabled one to discover for oneself what might be considered one's "major malfunction."

From Grade VI on up, auditing was a completely different experience in that one was "solo auditing" which means that one is not only the counselee but the counselor as well. This becomes a highly subjective process but also a lightning fast one because there is no need to explain anything to another person. In essence, solo auditing puts you directly into communication with yourself in such a way that you are able to take full responsibility for whatever ills or troubles you might imagine. The key operative word is responsibility. There is no longer any dependency on an auditor.

All of this leads to the upper levels of Scientology which result first in an extroversion into the environment of the newly made Clear which was called OT I. Beyond that was OT II which consisted of confronting a series of implants and gave one the "ability to confront the whole track." This prepared one to deal with OT III which was considered the mother of all implants, particularly as it concerns beings on Earth. This is a highly controversial level for many different reasons. It is rather fruitless to say much about it because virtually all people do not have the requisite rudiments to even open-mindedly discuss the subject, let alone understand what the subject is really all about. It takes a considerable amount of discipline and dealing with one's own rudiments to even approach the subject and understand it. Confronting and dealing with what the level has to offer is yet another task indeed. Quickly reading about it on the internet and saying, "Oh yeah, I know that" or "It sure sounds like a lot of crap to me" does not quite cut it as there is a considerable amount of prerequisite information to study and learn about before one can seriously attend to the subject as it was meant to be conveyed. What you read about on the internet, even by well meaning disaffected Scientologists who still believe in the subject, is more often than not misleading. It is like trying to learn calculus when one has never studied algebra or geometry and has no more than an inkling of ordinary arithmetic.

The trickiest part about understanding OT III is that it is a seemingly objective orientation to what is essentially a highly subjective process. Uninitiated people often criticize OT III as a highly outlandish science fiction story derived from the mind of an equally outlandish science fiction writer. It is quite true that the materials are outlandish from a normal earthling perspective. There is no question about that, however, one would expect or need outlandishness in order to get a normal human being out of the funk of the illusion that the Hindus call maya. The task of the Scientology aspirant is to translate the "objective" and "historical" orientation of OT III into the meat and potatoes of his own subjective universe and how that relates to his immediate environment. If one cannot to that, it is highly understandable that they are going to blame their condition or dissatisfaction on Hubbard or Scientology. It is not logical though. One needs a modality to process one's aberrations or the debris that comes with the aberrations of others. LRH could find no better modality than the one he offered with that level.

OT III offered what was called the full rehabilitation of one's self-determinism. This essentially means doing what you want to do and not being the effect of other people's determinism, opinions or edicts. It was meant to represent the road to total freedom in an individual. This literally means complete independence and that means autonomy and the power to choose. One does not have to listen to the clamoring of society nor of Scientologists who have not yet achieved such a state of freedom for themselves.

Above this level, there were various drills which were designed to enable a spirit to perceive without the use of one's body. These latter levels were not only a broad and confident proclamation that the ultimate dreams of spiritual potential could be realized, there was also a considerable amount of consternation and enthusiasm in various quarters that these were not mere assertions. These were later incorporated into the remote viewing community and became a highly sought after commodity in government and intelligence circles.[*]

It would be very nice if such lofty pursuits were available to everyone and we could all skip along the yellow brick road to nirvanic bliss. Unfortunately, that road is littered with the traumatic and emotional debris of every spirit or demon that ever suffered a broken dream. If it were not, you would be on the wrong road. This emotional debris is akin to radioactive fallout that occurs in the wake of an atom bomb. But, it is not enough that the makers of this "atomic bomb" created the original fall from grace: they also feed off of the emotional trauma of those littered along the side of the road.

If you go to a website such as Operation Clambake, you will find that virtually every person who was ever disgruntled about Scientology or thwarted by its so-called adherents have come out to roost and offer almost every negative comment that could be engineered by the imagination. It is not only a testament that LRH and Scientology are a completely evil proposition, it completely obscures or nullifies the idea that any of the more lofty pursuits or dreams of Scientology are obtainable under any circumstances. In the Scientology paradigm, all of these roosting complainers would be a manifestation (that is often quite comical) of "out-rudiments" as discussed earlier.

A rather interesting parallel to the Scientology adventure to total freedom can be found in the applied practice of magick where the ultimate goal of one's quest is to obtain conversation with their Holy Guardian Angel, another name for one's higher or true self. This is exactly what one was doing with solo auditing

---

[*] A brief summary of the antics of the Government in utilizing these techniques was discussed in my book *Synchronicity and the Seventh Seal*. One of the main themes with respect to this phenomena is that it became absolutely clear to them that these techniques were successful enough to prove a major threat to the national security of the United States.

in Scientology — one was "conversing" with one's own inner guidance. The Holy Guardian Angel is no different than self-determinism. Israel Regardie, a former member of the Golden Dawn, even recommended that one should receive extensive psychotherapy before embarking on such a quest. If not, the adherent's path would more than likely suffer from the backup sewage that one had not properly cleared from their own life. This is not much different from Scientology's idea of rudiments.

Based upon what I witnessed, there is no question in my own mind that L. Ron Hubbard truly believed in the process of setting people free. A perfect example occurred in 1972 during the same era of the Moroccan episodes discussed earlier. During that time period, LRH received a copy of *Time* magazine which had a feature article on *Jonathan Livingston Seagull*, a bestselling book which had taken the nation by storm. The article commented that people were describing the precepts in the book as being a lot like Scientology. When LRH read that, he made a point of reading the book and loved it. In fact, he thought so much of the book that he had special posters made up which were to be hung in all Scientology organizations. They stated, "Read Jonathan Livingston Seagull — Everyone in the Sea Org has." It was not true that everyone in the Sea Org had read it, but we were all encouraged to. As a matter of fact, it was the only book in the bookstore on the *Apollo* that was not by LRH.

Jonathan Livingston Seagull is told in the fashion of a fable. The book is about Jonathan, a seagull who wants to learn the loftier aspects of flying as opposed to just living a bottom feeder existence of filling one's gullet in order to survive. Jonathan's interest in pursuing sophisticated flight techniques leads to persecution from the flock of gulls who ostracize him for not being bottom-feeders like themselves. All of this leads to a spiritual path and enlightenment, but it is not without a severe price that includes leaving one's family and fellows behind. In the end, spiritual potential is realized by following the inner guidance of one's own soul and not the dictates of the flock. The message in the book also presents another clear message. If you seek the loftier aspects of yourself, you will encounter a madness or oppression that can be quite severe. It is not, however, your own madness but that of others. Nevertheless, you have to deal with it. One of the first tricks the flock will pull on you is to assert that you are the mad one. Further, all other like-minded fellows will readily agree that you are mad. If you are not entirely certain of yourself, you are likely to be engulfed by the madness of others and succumb, not unlike a moth who is consumed by the flame. If you survive the experience at all, you might end up spending a lot of time on internet posting boards commiserating with others about your horrible experiences.

There is a very thin veil between being a successful initiate and an aspirant consumed by the flames. Being a successful initiate is not necessarily all it has been cracked up to be either. If one is fortunate enough to "pass through the portal," he looks down from the mountain only to see the failed aspirants who were consumed by the fire. If one has any sense of compassion, that is not too heartening at all. Perhaps these factors prompted LRH to call OT III the "Wall of Fire."

All of this is characteristic of the oppression that has been fostered upon the higher spiritual aspects of Mankind. Madness and oppression go hand-in-hand.

38

EXCALIBUR

It is now time to take a look into the bizarre nature of what made LRH able to tap into such an incredible stream of consciousness that would enable him to develop a "Bridge to Freedom" that was, even at its most idealized state, surrounded at its entrance by the howling of wounded miscreants who could only identify spiritual freedom with pain.

According to various sources, including himself, LRH experienced a near-death state in 1938 when he was twenty-seven years old. He was having an operation when, as he stated it, his heart had stopped beating and he was "deader than a mackerel." In his own taped lectures, he said that he had exteriorized from the body without realizing that he had "kicked the bucket." While exterior, he just thought about all of the things he had not done in his life. After a while, he realized that he was experiencing the phenomena of death. Instead of "blacking out," however, he realized there was an entire array of phenomena that was going on around him that was completely independent of the Earth-based consciousness he knew as a living human being. He also noticed that he could look down on his body and experienced that he was a spirit independent of such.

Accompanying his experiences were visuals which, according to his literary agent Forrest Ackerman, included "a fantastic great gate, elaborately carved like something you'd see in Baghdad or ancient China." As LRH moved towards the gate, he saw an "intellectual smorgasbord on which was outlined everything that had ever puzzled the mind of man." This included all ancient secrets and questions that philosophers had dealt with throughout the ages. It included the beginning of the world and the question of God. As the information came in, he absorbed it until he felt something like a long umbilical cord pulling him back. Resisting the pull, he was quoted as saying "No, no, not yet!" but he was pulled back anyway. When the ornate gate closed, he realized that he was back in his body.

LRH discussed this experience from time to time during his life so there is no reason to believe Ackerman's account is not what LRH said. In his own taped lectures, LRH gave a different view or perhaps additional angles on what happened. He stated that he could see above the street and felt sorry for himself and "decided they couldn't do this to me." As the body's heart had stopped beating, he said that he could see a bunch of interesting mechanisms in the head that restimulate a body's heartbeat. He just "took hold of them and snapped the body back to life."

When he woke up, he saw a doctor standing there with a long needle full of adrenaline. Having shoved it into the heart, the doctor claimed that he had contributed to the recovery, but LRH said the doctor had nothing to do with it.

There are different accounts of the incident from various sources, but there is no doubt that this highly subjective occurrence became the focal point and defining moment of what was to be LRH's future life. He immediately wrote down everything he could fathom from the experience in an initial attempt to codify what he had discovered. His manuscript was called *Excalibur*, named after the sword of King Arthur which symbolized the power of the philosopher's stone. It was in this work that he codified what he called the basic or dynamic principle of existence which was "Survive." This work included the basic template of what was later to be developed into Dianetics and Scientology.

There were a couple of things that struck LRH about his experience. One was that he was amazed at how much information people are able to accumulate without even perceiving it. As he said, "the greatest shock was to find out how much game I was playing without knowing I was playing it. " Besides that, there was the way in which he exteriorized. He knew people had exteriorized from time to time during the millennia, often under hazardous and tortuous circumstances. What was so novel about his experience was not only that he had exteriorized but that he also seemed to have a complete subjective awareness on what had happened. Besides that, his experience left him with a complete text on the subject and what it was all about. The last part of the incident he experienced included a command to forget the experience, but he was able to avoid that. The very idea that he was able to remember what most people would forget is, in part, what made his future message and movement so powerful. He was operating with an advantage over what most people cannot see, let alone think about.

Although he penned a manuscript, he did not force his idea on anyone. It was another twelve years before he would harness his experience into an applied technology of the mind. There was no mention of exteriorization or the spirit until a considerable time after the release of Dianetics. When he voiced his experience to any early listener, they suggested it was all hallucination. LRH was quick to agree, if only to deter alarming anyone.

What he did know was that he had confronted a mystery of some sort or another. He had already been studying the subject of the mind for several years. In later years, he stated that *Excalibur* was devoted to brain mechanisms as well as the research line that led to Dianetics and Scientology. It had a tendency to make the reader immediately and intimately confront all of these mechanisms. To people who had no experience with such matters, he said that it could be horribly introverting. There were even stories that people had committed suicide after reading the book. It was never published.

After LRH had this experience, his name began to rise to the top of the list among science fiction publishers. He became a prolific and successful writer with hordes of different pen names. The task of his science fiction career was to enable him to finance subsequent research that would lead to one of the most bizarre, if not amazing, religions in the history of Mankind.

Although the imagery Ron experienced was quite vivid, the theories and practical applications were quite simple. In fact, he used the words "idiotically simple" to describe them. That was the very reason the answers had been overlooked: they were too obvious. In addition to the proposition that the basic element of life is trying to survive, he realized that life experience breaks down into two separate factors: the material universe and an "X-factor." This X-factor is different than materiality because it acts in such a way as to organize and mobilize the material universe. Later on, he labelled this "X-factor" with the Greek letter *theta* which represents the essence of life. It is also identified with the Latin *elan vitale* and represents the spirit as well. In the middle part of the last century, this was a much bigger secret than it is today.

When LRH wrote the first draft of *Excalibur*, it was simply a discussion of the composition of life based upon the above dichotomy of life experience. He destroyed the first 10,000 words and then began to write again but took things a step further. As he talked to his friends, word about his discoveries began to circulate a bit. According to LRH, the first material circulated on Dianetics was in 1938 at the Explorer's Club in New York City, a club he belonged to until his death in 1986. There were several important people in the Explorer's Club. That included a man who Ron called "Commissar Golinksi," a Russian who invited him to dinner and said that the Russian government was interested in his work. When Ron returned home that evening, the original manuscript was missing, however, he did have a backup carbon copy of the original version. Eventually, different versions of the book turned up but were never released to the public.

A few days later, Commissar Golinski saw him at the Explorer's Club once again and asked him to go to Russia and meet Stalin. Golinski hinted that Ron's techniques would be useful in estimating whether someone was loafing or not. Obviously, he had read the manuscript. Ron knew this, but did not say anything. He was also offered hundreds of thousands of dollars in salary as well as unlimited expenses and the use of Pavlov's old laboratories to develop Dianetics in Russia, but he declined. At that time, Paul Robeson and other celebrities made it fashionable to emigrate to Russia and fight the evils of capitalism. There were no diplomatic channels into Russia at that time. The only connection between the two countries was Amtorg, the American-Russian Trading Organization which was started by Armand Hammer. After having declined the Russian's offer, Ron was always suspicious of Russians bird-dogging him. He had good reason to be.

262

In the 1960's, Ron said that there was absolutely no danger to a Scientologist reading *Excalibur*. The reason he never published it, he said, was that he thought a modern Scientologist might laugh at it. In particular, he said the book contained nomenclature that was straight out of his own personal engrams. It was written in a different language than what later developed into "Scientologese."

Whatever the myths were that inspired the various stories about *Excalibur*, there is no question that there were different versions of the book as well as the fact that it represented the defining moment in LRH's life. It is more than ironic that the data came to him in the representation of a gateway. It was only eight years later after his experience with this gateway that LRH became involved with Jack Parsons in an attempt to open a similar or identical gateway. This was known as the Babalon Working and "Babalon" means gateway, but it also signified the goddess Babalon, a feminine archetype which represents the infinite wisdom that has been lost for millennia. Both of these gateways are intimately connected, if not actually one and the same.

The Babalonian current is so little understood by our common society and academics that it has to be continually delineated and expounded upon as people are predisposed by social conditioning to alter it. So far, I have not seen anyone else connect these two gateways as being one and the same. LRH's gate represented infinite answers and the gateway of Babalon is no different. Even though I have recognized the connection here, we are really only experiencing the beginning of a current of information and energy that will grow exponentially in the future.

My own role, however, took years to develop. There were, and still are, considerable forces which want these gateways closed. In the Tarot, there is a card in the major arcana called "The Star" which is meant to represent the seven-pointed star of Babalon reaching down through the personage of a woman-goddess to the water. In the Tarot, the star and water represent feminine aspects. The gates of Babalon are not unlike the gates of a dam that are about to be either busted or let open. The water wants to come down and feed the hungry. Instead, it has been damned up, walled off, and harnessed for the gain of whoever can control it and then disperse it to others for a fee. In a sense, the dam builders are no different than the "damn builders" who have wreaked their own version of damnation via their own principle of dominion.

LRH was not wrong when he considered that Amtorg, the Russian trading organization, was bird-dogging him. As has already been discussed, he later realized that his problems had more to do with the conglomerate that gave rise to the Nazis. These people wanted to dam him up for good. They have done a reasonably good job.

39

DE-OP

Hubbard often stated that the goals of Scientology necessitated putting together an organization in a few decades which might otherwise take centuries if things were to take a more normal or typical pattern. If the gateway already delineated was to be opened, things had to be done very fast. The fact that speed was of the essence was unfortunate because such haste, as LRH often said, would produce fallout. Many people would drop out or not be included. In other words, there was plenty of impetus behind the forces that put Scientology together, and there were also casualties. As an administrator, LRH would routinely let the fur fly when he was putting together a production line or "assembly line." Often, people were replaced because they were inadequate. Afterwards, he had a unique habit of seeing that they were "picked up off of the floor," and trained so that they could learn what they missed and not feel too bad about themselves. He was often courteous beyond belief in his efforts to pick up the morale of a crew member twisting in the wind.

It is bad enough that Mankind's inherent connection to infinite wisdom has been compromised. That those trying to bridge that gateway are actively countered only adds insult to the original injury.

LRH's own efforts to reconcile his own personal circumstances with regard to the *Excalibur* incident was a hard enough task. On top of that, he took on the additional burden of bridging what he had learned to a world that was already severely dammed up. The only reason he was successful was because the X-factor (theta), which mobilizes the physical plane — through the form of individuals, was very interested in availing themselves of what he had to offer. LRH eventually coined the word "thetan" to symbolize the name for an individual or that separated awareness of awareness unit that is assigned the task of mobilizing and animating matter. For all practical purposes, this is a spirit.

Each individual or thetan has accumulated a series of experiences, some of them tied to the collective evolution of the species and others tied to more subtle and obscure modes of experience. As virtually all individuals you encounter in creation are impeded, there were plenty who were and are interested in LRH's teachings.

Unfortunately for Ron and his program, the natural entropy of the physical universe (which he codified as MEST for Matter, Energy, Space, and Time) is to maintain itself. This is reflected in thetans that become degraded to the point where they animate MEST but only in terms of the lowest common denominator. Here is your scientist who rants and raves against anything spiritual or paranormal. The ranting scientist is really no different than Hitler ranting against Jews because his father was Jewish and his father routinely beat him (to the point where be became a forced medium as a result of being forced out of his body via pain and trauma). A scientist who rants and raves against his own spirituality or that of others is protesting a part of himself. He is negating the chaotic proposition of what comes with a quantum observer.

The reason some people become degraded to such a point is that they have chosen that viewpoint because it is the least painful. In other words, if you were to do a comprehensive survey on the emotions of such an individual, you would find buried traumas and/or conditioning that would sway him, if not force him, to become a materialist. For such people, the universe of spiritual phenomena can be quite frightening. It is more a matter of pain than ignorance.

When we consider the whole track of experience, LRH stated that people of such persuasion devised electronic equipment so as to simulate the frequencies or electromagnetic signatures of individuals. Although life, in its purest essence, is considered to be completely static as a quantum observer, it assimilates or simulates a particular frequency in order to communicate or interact with matter, energy, space and time. The purpose of such equipment was to trap and corral that which could be considered "free life." LRH came up with this information decades before there was any such word as psychotronics or any talk of alien implantation. He said that one of the key principles used in implants has to do with the principle that the wave length which most closely approximates that of a thetan is aesthetics. This includes music and beauty. In other words, if you want to deceive someone or access them, hit them on a frequency where they live: aesthetics. Most of us resonate deeply on the frequency of aesthetics although we have different tastes as to what is considered preferable.

Electronic oppression and manipulation of the spirit goes back into antiquity far beyond anything that common history records. Spiritual oppression is likewise far older than anything Earth-based religions refer to.

When I first read about this information, it was completely foreign to me. It required huge stretches of the imagination just to be able to fathom what was being presented, let alone evaluate it for relevancy. As I learned about Dianetics and received auditing, I discovered that referencing this information became quite helpful in running out engrams or implants and relieving various psychosomatic ills.

Although the information above is told from the orientation of a spiritual perspective, Scientology also dealt with the physical realm which is, by the way, a completely different animal. In other words, you had a spiritual life as well as a physical universe life which includes your name, rank and social security number. While spiritual oppression weaves its way deep into the rank and file and elite power structures of society, you will most often encounter it as garden variety oppression in the form of slavery, prejudice, or other forms of abuse.

LRH always paid attention to the society around him. Oppression was a big part of the world, and its various symptoms and manifestations weaved their way into Scientology organizations as readily and rapidly as anywhere else. Accordingly, Scientology organizations often dramatized the society around them. Many times, such dramatizations were amplified beyond reasonable expectations by reason of the fact that Scientology was an organization that was trying to get rid of them.

In 1976, LRH was privately researching the nature of oppression and the role it played in revolutions such as the French Revolution. As this theme applied just as well to the founding of America, he was at one time hoping to release a book on the subject which would debut during the Bicentennial celebration of July 4th, 1976. The book never saw the light of day. One of the key observations he made had to do with the reaction between the oppressed and those who oppressed them. For example, whenever a powerful regime acknowledges that there has been an injustice committed against the oppressed, there is at first a joy of relief which is then followed by an increased demand for more freedom and less oppression. The more the oppression is recognized and acknowledged, the further the demand increases. Eventually, the ruling party can no longer accede to the demands and the regime crumples.

The above is a perilous paradigm, not only for the regime but for the people themselves. If the regime seeks to honor the oppressed, it is easily caught up in a vicious dwindling spiral from which it cannot escape. In order to retain its own very existence, the regime is in turn forced to suppress further revolution by instituting new repressive measures. The people suffer by this. Sometimes, the new repression is worse that the original version. The key to the entire matter is to administer succor to the oppressed while at the same time maintaining and improving the regime which either caused the oppression or inherited it from its predecessors. Most importantly, one has to channel the reinvigorated energy and enthusiasm of the oppressed into a constructive and productive outlet.

LRH recognized that there had not only been repression on a planetary basis but that it also had been a long standing, but not an intentional, problem within Scientology organizations themselves. All of the above considerations were in effect when he devised a secret technology which was known as De-Op which was short for De-Oppression. Although the exact specifics were highly classified and have remained under wraps to this day (to the best of my knowledge), the general procedure of what he was doing was not confidential in the least. In that respect, it should not really be a secret at all, but I have never seen one word of it breathed on the internet or elsewhere. This was the outgrowth of the book he had once wanted to release for the Bicentennial in 1976.

By 1980, after thirty years of Dianetics and Scientology, LRH realized not only that the staff but Scientologists in general had been taking it on the chin in many respects. Scientology as an organization had to survive at all costs, and that resulted in various instances of fallout, but it had now reached a secure position in the world and was not about to go away. Consequently, LRH decided it was time to take on the oppressive factors that had repressed the *elan vitale* of the people in Scientology. In general, interviews were conducted with each and every Sea Org staff member. These interviews not only sought out the oppressive factors that impeded one in carrying out one's job functions but also those influences which personally oppressed them.

When these procedures were implemented, the results were absolutely astonishing. After the various interviews, there were large staff meetings in which executives met with the rank and file in order to solve the oppressive issues. This immediately resulted in the staff asking for more money, better clothing, proper days off, and a host of other items. These demands were readily met and no one had a problem with the requests, all of which were quite reasonable. More importantly, it let everyone know that there was a right way to do things and that ordinary human decency was highly acceptable as a working principle. This not only resulted in better working conditions but in increased production by the staff. In fact, it was LRH at his best. Whether you like him or not, he could do absolutely wondrous things at times and this was one of his best and most dramatic maneuvers ever.

It is hard to convey the full impetus of what happened in a short chapter, but this act revitalized the Scientology movement as never before in its entire history. The osmosis factor of what LRH had devised for the Sea Org immediately reached out to the Scientology public as well. The spirit of freedom and revolution was infectious. Just as the staff had an opportunity to voice their grievances and have them responded to, so did the Scientology public. Nowhere was this more evident than in the Scientology Mission Network.

Scientology missions were and are satellite parishes of the Church, but they were run like businesses with ten percent tithes going to church management. These missions were owned and operated by entrepreneurial Scientologists who dealt with and were generally very sensitive and responsive to public individuals. Ideally, they were supposed to feed people into the organizations which offered higher levels of training and were theoretically more competent in all technical matters.

During this time of renaissance and deoppression, mission holders aired their grievances as never before. For decades, Scientology mission holders had complained of inept management and directives from the Mother Church that were neither in the best interests of themselves nor of Scientology in general. The net result of this inept management was that in dampened their enthusiasm to expand Scientology further. In other words, they felt that oppressive factors within Scientology management were, in fact, the worst enemy of Scientology.

Scientology management, which had been de-oppressed through no less of a source than LRH himself, all of a sudden became very responsive to these complaints and all sorts of bureaucratic arbitraries were taken off the line. The mission holders were deeply touched and were completely enthused and resuscitated by the humane treatment they were now receiving. This excitement and enthusiasm also spilled over to the public in general. As a result, Scientology began to expand like never before. What was so special is that Scientology was being presented in a format that was readily and easily acceptable. A grassroots movement arose whereby public oriented Scientologists took the original book on Dianetics (*Dianetics: The Modern Science of Mental Health*) and began using techniques right out of that book in order to audit people on the spot, just as auditing was done in the early 1950's. It was all free and the public loved it. As this auditing was not done by the missions or organizations themselves, it did not cost them any money. What it did do, however, was create a demand for more sophisticated auditing techniques which both the missions and the churches could provide. This new popularity, most of which was being orchestrated by the mission holders as a result of the deoppression campaign, resulted in their missions grossing as much as $150,000 and $200,000 in a week, and all in the midst of tons of free auditing. This was extremely unheard of in the entire history of Scientology. At that time, this kind of money was only made by the most advanced Scientology organizations which drew from a worldwide network of advanced Scientologists. The missions were now drawing this amount from a much broader demographic.

It is hard to describe to an outsider how revolutionary and rejuvenating this time period was. The incredible enthusiasm spread in many different directions. For the first time in my experience as a Scientologist, which then covered a decade, old time Dianeticists and Scientologists were coming out of the woodwork in droves. They not only renewed their interest in the subjects at hand but also wanted to participate with the organization again. Many of these people had not responded or communicated to the Church in decades.

According to some of LRH's most fascinating (but somewhat guarded) research, there was a very firm principle at work here. In so many words, he had said that the true secret behind the ability to mobilize Matter, Energy, Space and Time had to do with revitalizing the failed purposes of an individual. In some respects, this is a no-brainer. For example, if you take an artistic oriented person out of a munitions factory and place her in an art academy where she can paint, you are likely to get a resurgence of happiness in an individual. Take a mechanically inclined person out of a white collar job, and he will be equally as happy. But, this is only the surface phenomena of such a principle. Underneath this, according to LRH, is the fiber of what it takes to literally control and manipulate Matter, Energy, Space and Time on an objective and subjective basis. At that time, this level was known as OT VIII, but it was never released to anyone. Critics are too quick to point out that he obviously did not have such abilities. They might be right, but they are overlooking the important points. First, LRH was able to control and manipulate considerably more Matter, Energy, Space and Time than any of his critics so they should not be too quick to jump to rash judgements. Second, and more importantly, he might not have been Superman, but he was working with actual principles of the human spirit that are actually worth learning more about.

The old time Scientologists were not the only ones taking a sudden and new interest in Scientology. Other religions were opening their doors to Scientology as well. The Hollywood celebrity faction had also picked up on the grassroots movement. Already an international movement in its own right, Scientology was on the verge of going completely mainstream because it had begun to conform to what the common man needed and wanted: genuine help at literally no cost accompanied by friendly communication.

During this time period, a top executive in the Guardian Office personally told me that each and every lawsuit against Scientology had been dropped. He said the reason for this was that Scientology was finally communicating with its adversaries and not seeking to strong arm and alienate them. This was all a result of the deoppression techniques developed by LRH.

The time period was 1981. Things were so explosive that it became very clear that the genie had been let out of the bottle. It was pure magic. If this impetus was not curtailed, Scientology was about to become the biggest movement the world had ever known. This is not a joke or exaggeration.

All of this would have been great except for the fact that power struggles were emerging from the monkey cage. Certain people in management, none of them too bright, felt that the mission holders were showing them up by doing so well. In actual fact, these mission holders were demonstrating an ability that Scientology management had never been able to do on its own: bring people en masse into Scientology.

Suddenly and unexpectedly, the deoppression techniques and rhetoric disappeared. Instead, a new form of rhetoric and attitude began to pervade the organization. Modern New Age think would call it reptilian. Mission holders and public Scientologists began to be treated with great suspicion as if they were spies. This became very clear to me after I got married. The Church had no room available for us, but they were willing and obliged to spring for an outside apartment rental. Instead, my wife suggested we stay with a public Scientologist she knew. It was not only a nicer environment for us but was far less expensive than anything the Church could find. Despite the fact that this public Scientologist was a loyal parishioner who had spent hundreds of thousands of dollars on Scientology, we were told no. She might spy on us. Even if she was a spy, there was not much to learn from going through our luggage or even conversing with us.

It is hard to explain the various power struggles that were occurring at that time and that would also ensue for most of the next decade. Without regard to either the various merits of the winners or the losers, one thing is clear. The power of the Church was consolidated by negating the *esprit de corp* of the Scientology renaissance movement that was taking place and by purging a vast amount of old time staff members. Also eliminated during this purge were loyal and long standing mission holders who had supported the Church for over a decade. A large portion of the staff and public quit, never to return.

In what might be considered a complete surprise, I completely escaped the purge, but this was because I was too smart to become a target. Nevertheless, it was truly heart-wrenching to see so many of my friends leave. I did not give up, but for only one reason. Many times in the past, I had seen LRH take broken pieces and put them back together again. I hoped that this would be no different and that the findings of the deoppression techniques would be reinstituted.

As a Bohemian sense of freedom transformed to a fascist demeanor where people became afraid to say anything that was politically incorrect, many reasons, policies, and excuses were made up as to why the renaissance occurred and why the anvil came crushing down from the sky. No one dared mention that it was LRH's deoppression techniques that had ignited the entire affair in the first place, but the truth is that most people did not even know about LRH's role in the entire matter. By the time I watched all of these tumultuous events, I had a clear and sophisticated understanding of what was going on throughout all the different levels of the organization. As I worked in the Qualifications Division, it was my job to notice such things. Additionally, I knew LRH's habits and routines when it came to managing Scientology. After the renaissance had been thwarted, I never saw his familiar style again. The orders were not coming from LRH. For the first time ever in my Scientology career, his influence was as good as nil.

The beauty of the renaissance was that it seemed that all we had worked for, some of us for over a decade, was now coming to fruition in a way that was completely unbelievable. Many of us had matured together as we now watched the organization move into a mature mode. But, as I alluded to earlier, this meant more and more freedom. The oppressor on the other end of the line reacted accordingly. Some have said that it was LRH himself who reacted back so poorly but I know personally that this was not the case. He was being issued a stream of false reports and had been isolated and put out to pasture.

LRH knew how to harness energy. His tremendous empire is proof of that, but the tremendous amount of free or "orgone energy" that had been released and was literally on the verge of revitalizing the entire world was about to be squandered in a power struggle. The monkey cage was rattling and the zoo keeper was getting very pissed off!

40

THE TOWER

On July 7th, 1977, Scientology made international headlines when the FBI conducted their biggest (at that time) and most unprecedented raid in U.S. history when 134 FBI agents appeared at the Guardian Office headquarters in both Hollywood and D.C. with a search warrant. The agents viciously broken down doors with axes in order to confiscate boxes and boxes of Scientology information. Included in those materials were all of Scientology's legal files, strategies and corporate structures.

As has been illustrated earlier in this book, the Government had been bird-dogging Scientology and obtaining information on it for years. The problem for the Government was that Scientology had reversed the process by collecting information on them. Additionally, Scientology had instituted a vast amount of lawsuits against various individuals in the Government, the majority of which were in military intelligence and were protected by the courts. The raid, whether right or wrong, became a necessity for the Government if it wanted to prevent exposure of nefarious affairs they had not only committed against Scientology but the general public as well.

The history of that fateful day in July was clear cut and simple as far as the events that occurred, but the complex gyrations that precipitated it and ensued from it have taken decades to unravel and understand. A barrage of information has piled up on the internet. Some of it is informative but largely unedited and presented in a broadshoot fashion. When the information is fairly

275

coherent, it is not compiled in any sort of format that makes for a quick and easy study of all the pertinent facts. The primary reason for this is that the subject is complex, vast and requires an exhaustive study just to understand exactly what went on. One informative website even states that there is no *Reader's Digest* version to understand these complex events. I have therefore taken it upon myself to present a very condensed version. My intention is twofold. First, it will give a factual and objective overview of what happened. Next, it will serve as a reference point or compendium for those who want to pursue further research on the subject. Most importantly, it shows a pattern of how subtle and pervasive the merchants of oppression can be.

Let us begin with the raid itself. In order to conduct the raid, the FBI had to have a motive and also a valid search warrant from a judge. In 1977, a search warrant was much more difficult to obtain than it is today (2004) under the Patriot Act. The legal justification for the search warrant only became obtainable under the most unusual set of circumstances. What happened was that two Scientology spies, allegedly double agents, were caught in a government building with forged I.R.S. credentials. Their names were Gerald Wolfe and Michael Meisner.

The whole affair began in 1974 when the *Apollo* crossed the Atlantic after being run out of Morocco and Portugal. I have already told you how Mary Sue Hubbard had received a telex from her Guardian Office staff as the *Apollo* waited off the coast of South Carolina. Over one hundred I.R.S. agents were waiting to arrest LRH. Mary Sue convinced him that they might not have valid legal reasons, but they were certainly powerful enough to execute their intention in a legal system that was more partial to them than it was to LRH.

After settling in the Caribbean, LRH and the Guardian Office had launched a project by the name of "Snow White." I remember hearing about in it 1975, only a month or two after I boarded the *Apollo*. Basically, I was told that it was a gigantic project to clear the names of L. Ron Hubbard and Scientology in all government files by getting rid of erroneous and false statements. Although there was no direct encouragement to do anything illegal, I did hear the now famous phrase, "Use any and all means at your disposal."

Project Snow White was the impetus for the vast amount of lawsuits against the intelligence community. The Government was being called to task on many fronts. This included not only the FBI and the Justice Department but also the CIA, the National Security Agency and the different departments of military intelligence. One of the main problems Scientology encountered was that the Government had hidden tiers of files which were neither available to the general public nor their targeted adversaries. This, of course, makes true justice impossible.

In order to penetrate one particular veil of this secret setup, Scientology's Guardian Office in D.C. concocted a plan whereby their own operatives would obtain I.R.S. credentials in order to copy all of the files they could find with regard to what the I.R.S. had on Scientology.

Michael Meisner had worked his way through Scientology and into the Guardian Office. He helped concoct the plot in the first place. Gerald Wolfe is an even more intriguing case because he was actually able to obtain a job with the I.R.S. under highly unusual circumstances. He was hired during a personnel hiring freeze at the I.R.S. If he was a skilled professional, this might be understandable, but he was only hired to be a clerk/typist. As an IRS staff member, he was able to map out the I.R.S. bureaucracy and direct Meisner to the necessary locations.

Before Gerald Wolfe and Michael Meisner were caught, they had copied at least ten feet of documents. They were apprehended when they used the back door to a government building and failed to sign in. Despite being caught in the act, neither of them were arrested. They were both allowed to leave the building. As Meisner used a false name, he was free from justice and eventually fled to Los Angeles to be under the supervision and protection of the Guardian Office.

On the other hand, Wolfe had a known identity with the I.R.S. and could not escape so easily. The Government inspected the entry logs of where Wolfe had signed in many times before and noted that his name always appeared along with Meisner's alias. They did not, however, know Meisner's real name. Even though Meisner was allowed to leave the building, the Guardian Office anticipated trouble for Wolfe and he was briefed within an inch of his life on how to deal with any questions from the Government so as to protect Meisner.

What happened next makes no rational sense except to explain that things were not quite what they seemed with the two "Scientology operatives." In what should have been a great window of opportunity for both Wolfe and the Church, a statute of limitations expired with regard to the number of days within which Gerald Wolfe could be indicted for conspiring to steal government documents. Although the term had expired, Wolfe mysteriously signed a waiver of his rights so that he could be indicted outside of the limitations of the prescribed statute. By doing this, Wolfe indulged in what was either the greatest blunder or the greatest duplicity in the history of Scientology legal cases. If Wolfe had not the signed waiver, he never would have been effectively charged and the house would never have come down on Scientology.

At this point in the saga, there are two major illogics with Gerald Wolfe. Number one, he was hired by the I.R.S. during a hiring freeze. Number two, he mysteriously signed away his legal rights and not only brought a house of cards down upon himself but also on Scientology.

Meisner is another important part of this equation, but he should have been free from all detection as no one outside of the Guardian Office even knew his real identity. Most people in the Guardian Office were not even briefed on this specific project so when it was revealed that there was an arrest warrant out for Michael Meisner, it points to a leak within the Guardian Office itself. It is still a mystery to this day, but Wolfe emerges as the most likely candidate when you consider his mysterious hiring and also his capitulation with the prosecution. Other characters within the Guardian Office have also been fingered as having turned Meisner in.

Under virtual house arrest in Los Angeles, Meisner became antsy about his fugitive status and wrote to Mary Sue about his dilemma. She warned him to cooperate or suffer the consequences of being barred from Scientology. This was an extreme miscalculation on her part as she assumed her ecclesiastical authority had more sway than the temporal jurisdiction of the United States. As far as Meisner was concerned, he was trapped and in prison. He decide to become a government witness and escaped. By fully cooperating with the FBI, he suffered no jail time or other consequences. It should be pointed out that at least two Scientology executives reported that Meisner was a double agent all along, prior to his getting caught, but these reports were stopped from being forwarded to Mary Sue by another Guardian Office member who had all the hallmarks of being a double agent himself as well as a former President of the Church of Scientology of California.

With the indictment of Wolfe and either the apparent or feigned defection of Meisner, the Government had now developed a significant legal window of opportunity. They took this information to a judge and established that they had reasonable cause to conduct a search and seizure raid on the Church of Scientology in Hollywood and at the Founding Church of Scientology in D.C. This was a great coup d'etat for them as they literally had all the potential information they might need on Scientology, including the complete files and history of their various corporate structures. As a result of all the information and plotting they had found amongst the Scientologists, the Government indicted nine Guardian Office executives, including Gerald Wolfe, for conspiring to steal government documents and a host of other accusations. L. Ron Hubbard, quite mysteriously, was named only as an "unindicted coconspirator."

The court room drama that ensued with Judge Ritchie was highly comical and theatrical to an outside observer, but it was not at all comical to either the judge or the defendants. He mocked Mary Sue beyond reasonable belief and did not treat her as an innocent party until proven guilty. The Scientologists never believed for a minute that they might get a fair trial but initially thought Judge Ritchie might be preferable to other options. As the mocking and circus atmosphere continued, the Scientologists got reports from a private investigator that Ritchie regularly visited prostitutes and complained incessantly about the Scientologists. In fact, he stated that he hated them.

Somehow and in some way, this case never went to trial. Mary Sue and the other defendants never pleaded guilty or not-guilty. Instead, the court drew up a bizarre "stipulation of evidence" and had the defendants sign it. Why the defendants did this, I do not know, but it is assumed they were intimidated into it. It was not even a plea bargain because there was no plea entered, but the prosecution dropped 23 counts against the Scientologists in return for signing a stipulation that they had conspired to obtain government documents. You can read the full case on the internet if you wish. This was really a silly case. All of the files obtained by the Church were public documents. While they had a right to them, they did not obtain them legally. On the other hand, if they had tried to obtain them legally, they would have been stonewalled. Beyond the obvious criminal implications of obtaining the documents, it is interesting that the Government neither offered nor found any evidence whatsoever to suggest that the Scientologists were plotting or engaged in criminal behavior of any other kind. It was all about protecting their empire. When you consider all the fuss about this case, it is noteworthy that there was no general criminal behavior even being alluded to. All the defendants had really done was to take information that they were entitled to but had gone about it in the wrong way. The problem for the Government was that a full blown trial would have proved far too embarrassing and would have revealed deeper and darker secrets than even the Church of Scientology, at its very worst and most exaggerated, could ever come up with. The defendants were persuaded that they would get lighter prison sentences if they cooperated. All of them, including Mary Sue, took the bait.

This irregular jurisprudence was followed up with prison sentences for the "Scientology Nine" as they were called. Mary Sue was given adequate time to put her affairs in order before being sent to a minimum security "country club" prison, but she appealed the sentence. Her appeal was refused, and she eventually served about one year out of a four year sentence before being released on probation.

In my opinion, Mary Sue made a huge mistake by yielding to the intimidation of the prosecution and the court system. They played upon her fear and wielded their own power which was quite significant. The stakes, however, were quite high. Had she called their bluff and showed a willingness to accept a much higher threshold of "pain," Mary Sue would have completely bewildered the prosecution as well as the court system. In fact, she should have invited them to make an example of her. This would have created very unusual problems for them, and they would have stalled the trial. After all, she was not a hardened criminal.

Although this case was precipitated by L. Ron Hubbard and Scientology, it was really not just about them. It had far more to do with what lengths that people in the Government can and will go to in order to intrude upon the territorial rights of the clergy in order to protect and preserve their own power structure. In this case, it also included stonewalling any attempt to trace their own dubious or criminal behavior. In the end, it is unlikely Mary Sue would have won, but her fate might have been a happier one had she chosen to challenge them and call their bluff. What ensued in her future was not a pretty scene at all.

41

IAGO

While Mary Sue Hubbard twisted in the wind of the U.S. court system, there was plenty of other activity going on which would shape the future of Scientology and L. Ron Hubbard. The fall of Mary Sue Hubbard, however, was not only an integral part of the change, it was absolutely necessary for the adversaries of L. Ron Hubbard and Scientology. Mary Sue held the senior most legal and financial position in all of the corporate structures of Scientology. Her title was Controller. If someone wanted to take over Scientology, they would first have to unseat her. Her conviction and eventual incarceration was only one step in the process. Even after she was sentenced, she still maintained her authority within the Church although her influence was waning.

On the other hand, L. Ron Hubbard had no official legal position within the Church structure. He owned the copyrights, trademarks and service marks with regard to all of Dianetics and Scientology, but that did not give him legal control over the Church. He remained in seclusion, primarily to avoid potential subpoenas or possible legal entanglements. Mary Sue, unfortunately, became a casualty of the power path he had pursued. He had always said positions next to or close to power were highly vulnerable. People have criticized Hubbard for allowing his wife to "take the hit" for him, but if he had showed up in court, it would have only resulted in disaster for himself. It appears, however, that LRH was not the immediate target in these legal manipulations. If the IRS and FBI were willing to assign hundreds of agents to Scientology, they could easily have utilized phone taps and other surveillance technology to ferret him out and bring him into the court system. This angle is especially ironic when you consider that he ultimately hid out near San Luis Obispo, the same location of a Reinhard Gehlen* corporation that influenced the back door politics of California through Reagan's "kitchen cabinet."

As LRH could not represent himself, he was also vulnerable, particularly as Mary Sue, his top aide and wife, became compromised. His power, and at all it represented, however, was up for grabs. In high stakes power games, one person's misfortune or loss is another's gain.

Into the fray of all of this tension packed drama entered one David Miscavige, a very young man who eventually emerged from this strife as the most powerful man in Dianetics and Scientology. David actually delivered a legal letter from the Church's corporate attorneys asking Mary Sue to step down from her job. Various legal points were brought up in hopes of politely inducing her toward this end. It has been reported that she and Miscavige had a vicious argument but that she eventually relented. At the time, she was appealing her prison sentence, and he reportedly convinced her that she was an embarrassment to the Church. She was only an "embarrassment," however, because she did not take the option of embarrassing the Government.

As was said previously, it is hard to explain the various power struggles that were occurring at that time as well as for most of the next decade. The key power word during this period, however, was *purge*, a verb that is relegated to Pluto, the god of power. Miscavige was the winner, and he won by purging. In reaction to this, a vast number of staff and public quit. It was a mass exodus and one that Scientology had never seen before. Even so, Miscavige had consolidated the power and maintained a core structure which he was eventually able to expand decades later. In effect, he accessed the proprietary rights to Dianetics and Scientology, concentrated on eliminating the competition, and continued on with whoever would follow him.

---

* Reinhard Gehlen was the former Nazi in charge of intelligence on the Russian front for the Third Reich. After the war, Allen Dulles had him set up the template for the CIA. Gehlen also set up T.C.I., an investment company dedicated to technology that operated out of San Luis Obispo.

None of this explains, however, how agent Gerald Wolfe was hired by the IRS during a hiring freeze, a move which would eventually lead to the downfall of Mary Sue and help pave the way for Miscavige to take over. Miscavige came from a Scientology family and was way too young to have influenced the I.R.S. in this regard. He came later, but he was definitely the beneficiary of Gerald Wolfe's bizarre decision to waive his statutory rights and allow himself to be prosecuted for burglary of government documents. In this game, Miscavige was the apparent winner of the power struggle, but he could not have pulled off what he did without significant help. I will briefly chronicle his rise to power, but not just yet.

While all of these power struggles were going on, I was not oblivious to them. In fact, I had a pretty good grasp on what was going on with Scientology management internally, but I did not know the full scope of the court cases or how the "Scientology Nine" were manipulated. In the meantime, I had worked on the OT levels and was once again experiencing the "best times of my life" in Scientology.

42

THE POSITIVE

Although we knew about the court case with Mary Sue, the staff of the Sea Org and Scientology were kept insulated from all of the details and trauma that were ensuing for Scientology on the legal front. The organization was set up that way. If it were not, no one could have a good time, let alone look at the deeper aspects of their own existence and figure them out.

In the summer of 1980, just after my friend Ralph passed away, I was sent on assignment with three other Sea Org members to fix the Founding Church of Scientology in Washington, D.C. as it was in shambles. There was very little auditing going on. My specific job was to correct any faulty auditing or training and to get it running at a high level. One of the first things we discovered was that the staff was receiving no auditing and that most of the key executives had huge debts as a result of buying auditing. When we realized the full extent of this, in private, we started laughing uncontrollably, mostly out of shock. Staff were not supposed to buy auditing but were to get it for free. The executives concerned were so desperate and desirous of auditing that they put themselves in dire financial straits. This put tremendous pressure on themselves which did not help their morale or job performance. Most of them had to be removed.

If monkeys in a monkey cage are not given a positive direction, they can often end up in some very precarious circumstances. There were never any limits to what ridiculous circumstances Scientologists could get themselves into. In my experience, staff Scientologists who got themselves in dire financial situations or other extreme conditions was never the result of orders coming down from the top. These were always dramatizations of the reactive mind of either the victims or other staff who were engaging in abusive behavior.

The first thing I did in D.C. was to see that the person in charge of staff auditing was audited. She laughed at me when I first suggested it, but that was only because she did not believe me. The staff, including her, did not realize this was possible but only because they lacked the resolve and common sense to do it. As I had the authority to do it, no one could stop me. Once she was audited, she completely changed and rapidly carried out my orders to get the staff audited. It raised the morale considerably and made the Founding Church a desirable place to work.

Besides the above, I also began resolving all sorts of previously unresolvable situations which included cases that were not responding to auditing. None of this was particularly difficult at all, but it was completely novel to the staff. It made me very popular, and I quickly acquired a reputation as someone who could handle most anything when it came to technical applications of Scientology. This was a blessing but also a potential curse. After a few weeks of dealing with enthusiastic people or disgruntled people who were made enthusiastic, I was sitting in a lobby and reading during a lunch break. I was waiting for the arrival of the D.C. area's most dangerous and problematic case. Seated in a chair right next to me was the most beautiful woman in the entire organization. I was minding my own business when she suddenly spoke to me.

"You'd better handle my brother!" she said in an ominous and almost threatening tone. I suddenly wondered what I had gotten myself into. I was only beginning to realize the extent of it. After handling all their tough cases, I was about to get their impossible case. His name was Steve and the Guardian Office did not want him on the premises because they were afraid he would jump off the roof, kill himself and blame it all on Scientology. Apparently, he had made some sort of threat like this in the past, but I did not know any of this when I had agreed to see him. I felt sort of tricked, but he was on the way. Even so, I did not feel there was any situation I could not resolve with Scientology.

When Steve appeared, he seemed quite normal on the outside. Like his sister, he enjoyed good looks but was also extremely muscular. I was used to playing football with athletes from all over Clearwater, Florida, but I never encountered anyone nearly as well built or as strong as he was. Steve was very personable, and I took him to my office which was a cubbyhole accessed through a closet door in the basement. The basement was also a course room which I monitored. My office was there for convenience. You could stand in it, but barely. It was not huge. My chair was inside and the chair Steve sat in blocked the door.

As I listened to Steve, his problems sounded no different than anyone else I had heard. The more he talked, the more he unburdened himself. Finally, after ten or fifteen minutes, he began to really open up. Then, all of a sudden, and completely unexpectedly, he completely changed in a way that I never saw any other preclear change. I was not actually auditing him, but it was just an interview to see how he could be helped. Steve suddenly punched the wall and he did not hold back anything. His expression changed to that of a complete madman. I suddenly began giving him what is called a locational assist in Scientology. This means pointing out objects in the environment and having him look at them. It is designed to orient a person in space and time. Most Scientologists recognize this as a helpful procedure to get them out of a mental funk. He complied, realizing I was attempting to help him, but his expression and break with reality became more severe. This increased to the point where his expressions became menacing and there was the question of whether they <u>might</u> be directed at me. It was a great invitation to be intimidated. I had never seen anyone punch a wall so hard with his bare fist and not seem to mind.

As Steve's expressions became more menacing, I immediately took notice of the fact that I could not easily have escaped if I wanted to. He was between myself and the door in a very small space. I would not have wanted to fight this person or defend myself against him under the best of circumstances. That he was dramatizing madness made the prospect even more daunting. Instead of reacting to him or his antics, I suddenly abandoned the locational assist I was giving and addressed him in a completely relaxed voice.

"Did you ever play football?" I asked.

He was caught completely off guard by the fact that I had suddenly abandoned the Scientology "ritual" and just addressed him as an ordinary guy. He began to laugh and smile which was due to the fact that I was addressing him and not using a prescribed process to deal with him. We began to talk a little about football and about a few things that had nothing to do with anything. After a while, his extremely erratic behavior reappeared, but this time he knew I was there to help him and he we continued the locational assist. Every once in a while, he would break down and need more communication. Finally, we got to the bottom of what his problem was. He began to iterate something that was almost inaudible. It took several iterations before I could translate what he was saying.

"Cal-Mag," I was finally able to interpret correctly.

Cal-Mag was a calcium-magnesium solution that LRH devised to relax the muscles and calm one down. At some point in the past, it turned out that Steve was told to take Cal-Mag for his extreme moments. He had been given good advice except that he was given the wrong formula and it was not working. When I informed him he had the wrong formula, he laughed and laughed and responded very positively. I told him I would get him some properly constituted Cal-Mag right away.

Steve was now very happy, and I was able to get around him and get to the door. I knew that I could escape if I wanted to, but this was no longer necessary. As I opened the door, I could not believe my eyes. There were hordes of people outside the door. They had pulled chairs around and were just sitting there as if they were going to witness a public hanging. Apparently, they all knew I was dealing with the roughest case imaginable, but they had also heard the extremely violent screams and punches to the wall. It seemed as if they were all sitting there waiting for my imminent execution. I felt like it was meant to be my own hanging, but I was not about to be hung. I asked someone to immediately get me a properly constituted glass of Cal-Mag. They ran and were back in no time with the drink.

When Steve took the Cal-Mag, he relaxed considerably and was as friendly as ever. I then took precautions to make sure he had the correct formula and that it would not be altered. It was clear I had done him a very simple favor, but it was huge to him. One of the reasons he had trouble with people in Scientology is that they reacted to his sometimes odd behavior rather than just dealing with him. I also found out that the threat to jump off the roof was precipitated by a member of the Guardian Office dealing with him in a threatening and ominous manner. In other words, that Scientologist did not deal with him with the principles of Affinity, Reality and Communication.

In part, I have shared this story to once again show how ordinary Scientologists do not use Scientology. When they do not, the effects can be quite extreme. There was, however, another result to what had happened. My reputation extended from the immediate circle of the organization to a more general audience. Because of what I had done with Steve, people wanted to talk to me. I found out that there were hordes of government officials that wanted Scientology for the wonderful things it could do. They could not, however, deal with the organization. I even met people from the Paraguayan embassy who wanted LRH's study technology for their country. Even one of President Carter's secretaries had been run out of the Church for not keeping a regular training schedule. In summary, I could not believe the wholesale abuse of the public that had occurred in the name of Scientology. Scientology was recognized by the public as a very powerful and useful commodity, but the people on the staff had created immeasurable disrepute. Much of this generated from the local Guardian Office as well. They had a building in back of the organization and guarded their quarters like scarred rabbits. This was understandable in light of the court cases and spying to and from the Government, but they extended their paranoia to a point which made them destructive to Scientology as a whole.

When I returned to Sea Org headquarters in Florida, I was expected to write up a full report on what I had found. I did so, but I was too experienced to believe for a minute that management would have any sort of sane response to the disaffected public. They did not. Eventually, I would discover that I was not the only Sea Org missionaire to go out in the field and find such wanton abuse of the public. After about a year, I wrote up a program for me to go back to D.C. and begin a full and comprehensive study of all the various factions in the area that wanted Scientology. The next step would have been to bridge the gap between the Government and the organization. It was a massive endeavor, but as far as I was concerned it, was the only chance Scientology had to make it in D.C. in a big way. This was, of course, a far more intelligent attempt than that young man aboard the *Apollo* who had dumped his gunnysack full of Scientology policy letters into the water in an attempt to bring Scientology to the Government. None of my activity, however, was going to deal with the back door dealings between the Justice Department and the Guardian Office. I would have only been working on a positive angle. LRH's daughter, Diana, approved my program. What I had offered for D.C. was just one of many examples of what culminated in what I have referred to as the renaissance of Scientology. Diana was a big supporter of the renaissance and at that time was the highest Sea Org officer in charge of dealing with the public. When the renaissance was thwarted, as has been previously discussed, Diana ended up on the wrong side of the purge and was assigned to pulling weeds in the desert in 100 degree heat. She had no access to her father at that point, and the order to assign her there did not come from him.

For me, the D.C. experience completely opened my eyes with regard to what was wrong with the Scientology movement. The Guardian Office, which was certainly not all bad, had been so busy fighting the oppressor that they had taken on the identity of the oppressor. LRH had written about the inevitability of this happening and warned against it, but it was to no avail. It is also apparent that the Guardian Office had government allied spies planted within it. As a result of my D.C. experience, I was able to fully grasp the spirit, feelings and emotions of the renaissance movement. It was so strong that, unlike those in the Sea Org who stayed on, I could never deny it or stand against it.

As a result of my travels to D.C., I decided to return a year later. I had made many friends there and wanted to see them. It was a personal vacation, but I was also doing some scouting for the program I would eventually write. While in D.C., I decided to take in the sights which included the Smithsonian Institute. After an afternoon in one of the art wings of the Smithsonian, I took a guided tour of the Library of Congress. Much to my surprise, there was a sign saying that Ray Bradbury would be giving a lecture the next evening at 8 o'clock. I could not believe it. Bradbury was my original inspiration to be a writer, and I jumped at the chance to see him. I returned the next evening.

The event was quite something. D.C. has a gentile elegance about it that not even New York City can match. New York is about raw power, wealth, and exclusiveness, but D.C. is more about diplomacy (or was at that time) with a taste of southern charm. The lecture was completely free and accompanied by a luxurious buffet of wine, fruit and other assorted goodies. It was hosted by the head librarian and was paid for by the taxpayers.

Bradbury is known as a great writer, but he is an even better lecturer. The first thing he talked about was Mr. Electro, a man from a travelling circus who befriended the young Bradbury. Mr. Electro was a character. Bradbury described that Mr. Electro did all sorts of tricks with electricity. They were something akin to the stunts of Nikola Tesla, but they sounded more corny. After the first of his stunts, Mr. Electro held out his sword and put it right in front of the young Bradbury.

"Live forever!" he expounded to the would-be author.

"And I decided that I would!" exclaimed Bradbury to the audience.

I marveled not only at what he said but that it was the first thing out of his mouth to the audience. Ray Bradbury was stating that this inspiration, via the first words he heard from Mr. Electro, made him realize that he was immortal. What was remarkable to me was that this was the exact same realization I had experienced (as was discussed earlier in this book) after reading Bradbury's story *The Kaleidoscope* (from the book *The Illustrated Man*). This was my initial inspiration to be a writer. It was a beautiful moment to see him say the same thing in person. He then went on to talk about Herman Melville's *Moby Dick*, another theme from my early childhood. At that point, I had no idea I would ever fulfill my earlier dream to become a writer. I was too busy with Scientology matters.

After his talk, the head librarian then invited us all into the buffet room where we could get an autograph and have a few words with Mr. Bradbury. There was only time to get one question in, and I asked him if he knew L. Ron Hubbard in the early days of science fiction.

"No," he said, but he was quick to add, "I read all of his science fiction. Of course, that was before Scientology."

Bradbury also talked about Mr. Electro telling him that the two of them had shared a past life together. If I recall correctly, I think it was in the Civil War. Although I do not recall reading it in any of his books, Bradbury evidently considered past lives to be credible.*

Not long after I returned home to Florida from my second trip to D.C., they had a big event for May 9th which was the anniversary of Dianetics. For me, these events were routine and extremely tiresome, and I would always utilize the extra time off to organize a twilight football game. On this particular evening, however, LRH's PR department had set up an extensive montage of LRH's career as a writer. There were all sorts of photographs and anecdotes about him that had nothing to do with Scientology. This stuff was all from his prior life, and there were several passages about writing and how to write. Instead of going to the event, I spent all of my time amidst this PR display which was in the ante room to the auditorium. In a very strange way, the osmosis rubbed off on me. I already knew LRH better than most of the staff, but that was not the point. All of a sudden, a surge of consciousness went through me.

"I can do this," I thought, calmly realizing that I could convert my OT abilities into the vehicle of writing.

The thought was completely positive and effortless. It was not something I even "thought about" afterwards. The idea just ran through me as if it were a premonition of my future life. There was no thought whatsoever of leaving Scientology to become a writer. Had I done so at that time, I am sure it would not have been an encouraging experience. Life is sometimes like a clock. We have to be sure that we keep the appointments and do not make wrong appointments which result in disappointment.

---

* For those of you who are familiar with the various synchronicities I have investigated in other books, you will be interested to know that Ray Bradbury was a protege of Louella Parsons, the famous Hollywood gossip columnist from the "Golden Era" of movies. For some reason, Parsons took a liking to the young Bradbury and had her chauffeur escort him around Los Angeles on a regular basis. Bradbury had several such "magical" associations in his life.

43

FREE AT LAST

Despite all of the chaos that was going on with Scientology management, I was doing quite well personally. I had achieved so many personal answers for myself and was quite capable of doing a lot of different things. I did not, however, seek a high profile. In the Sea Org, this always seemed like a road paved towards disaster as well as being relatively useless.

Suddenly and surprisingly, orders came down from "top management" indicating that LRH's name could no longer be used on anything. This came on the heels of a stream of other orders which were implied to be from LRH, but it was clear to me that they were not. Many of these were prejudiced in the extreme towards consolidating what power the Church had left and were more interested in squelching formerly dedicated Scientologists than they were in getting Scientology properly applied. To me, it was like the Soviet Union.

In what was something of a harebrained attempt to get rid of me by one senior executive, I was put on full time training. I say it was harebrained because some executives had already attempted to get rid of me for some of the things I am saying now. This came to a head when I caught several staff members indulging in an illegal act against a staff member. Instead of acknowledging and correcting their illegal ways, a senior executive attempted to scold and intimidate me, mostly in the form of yelling and verbal abuse. It did not go over too well. Looking at this man quite calmly, I told him he was not going to speak to me like that, but he continued yelling as if he was oblivious to anything I said. I then told him that if he did not cease his yelling that I was going to take him and throw him out the window which was about three stories high. Still, he did not get the message and continued his yelling. Living up to my word, I dragged him across the room to the window, but when I arrived at the window, there were problems. It seemed to be fastened shut permanently. Holding him with one arm, I tried to open the window, but it was not working. In the meantime, a patrol had come into the room to rescue him. While everyone was too ready to insist that I was in error, nobody could come up with a single Scientology policy or directive that indicated I was in error over the issue at hand. Everyone except myself was embarrassed, and I walked away free from any discipline or further harassment. Nobody dared bother me after that, but another strategy was employed. They could not get rid of me by intimidation or blatant illegal means so they sought to "reward" me by fulfilling some directive that required so many staff be put on full time training. When I accepted the reward, it turned out to be an even bigger mistake for the executives concerned. Once I left my job in the Qualifications Division, other illegal directives were implemented which soon purged them from their jobs or Scientology itself.

I was already good at being a "Scientology lawyer" but this training gave me a whole historical perspective of Scientology management and procedures from its very inception. I was now even more knowledgeable and this certainly equated to a considerable amount of power, particularly when I fully realized that most Scientology executives in top management positions were embarrassingly deficient in all aspects of Scientology administration. This, in turn, was a telltale sign that they were not very good with the application of the counseling technology either.

It was during this training that I had my moment I have referred to in previous books. This is when I made a decision to resolve all hurtful mechanical conditions of existence and saw a remarkable "explosion" in the sky. This cognition point eventually led me out of the Sea Org. As life proceeded, people tried to attack me or beseech me with illegal orders. As I was so knowledgeable, I would either ignore them or show them where they were wrong. While this had a tendency to piss people off, there was really not much consequence. It just meant that I was somebody they could not control or manipulate. There was no particular effort to purge me from staff, but it became more and more clear to me that I did not really fit in with a staff that was filled with new people who behaved more and more like robots instead of liberated Scientologists. With most of the old-timers gone, most everyone was too willing to do whatever they were told — whether it was illegal or not.

Things came to a head for me when I had a root canal problem. It was pretty severe, but no one would help me with it. Fortunately, it was not a brain tumour or anything life threatening. As they were obligated to, I told them they should pay for the root canal, but they refused. I paid for it myself but told them as a result, I was no longer willing to be on staff as they were violating their contract with me. They thought this was outrageous and did not believe me. I, on the other hand, thought they were outrageous and did not believe them. I knew that I could have written to LRH and possibly gotten this taken care of, but I was not optimistic that it would get to him. Besides, the writing was on the wall. They, according to their own doctrines, had believed that they had invested hundreds of thousands of dollars in training me and auditing me over the years. Now, they were saying that I was not worth the three hundred dollars it took to get the root canal operation. This was really bizarre and extremely cultish behavior. I also had over ten years of experience in the Sea Org. They would easily spend far more than three hundred dollars just breaking in a new recruit to reach to where I had gotten to.

One of the things I had brought up in my own interviews with the deoppression program was that the Sea Org had no "mind." In other words, it often acted as if it had no analytical mind by which it would be accountable and sensitive to various situations. Besides all of that, I knew that the entire Scientology network had been compromised, but that was almost a side issue to me. I did not feel that I was abandoning them, but they had clearly abandoned me over the tooth. For those of you who have read *Synchronicity and the Seventh Seal*, you will appreciate how ironic it was that it was a tooth that precipitated me leaving the Sea Org. It was uncannily parallel to what sci-fi author Phil Dick experienced when a girl brought him medicine for his tooth and flashed a vesica pisces necklace that changed his life forever. The vesica pisces, which was a secret and sacred symbol of the early Christians, induced a full 3-D wholetrack recall for Dick as the First Century of the Common Era became superimposed on Orange County of the 1970's.

As a result of my mistreatment, I routed out of the Sea Organization through their own bureaucratic channels and my wife soon followed a couple of months later. What was particularly ironic about my departure was that when I signed my final walking papers, I could not help but notice that it was April 28, 1983, eleven years to the day I had signed my original Sea Org contract. I thought it was very weird at the time. Looking back, it was as if the universe was telling me that I had done something very synchronous and very right. In some ways, it was very sad to leave what was left of my friends that I had worked with for a number of years. I did not like that, but so many of my good friends had already left. While there was much sadness in the air, I also knew that a new reality awaited me. I was completely free.

My wife did not get her walking papers from the Sea Org until July. When she did, we planned our next move. She was from New York and I was from Los Angeles. We would pick one of those two cities. As we considered having children, we thought it would be nice if the grandparents were close by. Her parents were on Long Island but mine were gone. It was such that I moved to Long Island in July of 1983, just a few weeks before the Montauk Project was said to have climaxed on August 12, 1983. Although I did not realize it at the time, my personal decisions and the universe were setting me up to write *The Montauk Project: Experiments in Time*, a book that would help change the way the world looked at itself. While this was the end of my Scientology story, there was still plenty of drama to be carried out.

44

THE VACUUM

LRH had emphatically taught that any position of true power is perilous. Those in power or near to it are highly vulnerable to the jackals waiting to unseat the power and have it for themselves, even if it is only a small scrap of the original. Accordingly, LRH composed the Power Change Formula which was designed to maintain the success and power of an earlier regime when the main player behind the original power moved. The first and primary dictum of Power Change is not to change anything. In other words, if you inherit a position of power, you do not monkey with the foundations of what created and maintained the power in the first place. Your job is to just observe and study what made things successful without changing them. Only when you have really and truly learned the operation can you begin to treat it as a normal operation. When the renaissance in Scientology was destroyed, it was a complete violation of LRH's Power Change Formula.

When LRH went into hiding as a result of government intrigue, he never intended to relinquish complete control. Control was problematic, however, as he was vulnerable. Even in the best of circumstances, he had to keep his influence at a minimum.

In the wake of LRH's abdication of visible power, and potential abdication of further power, there were two people who were waiting in the wings. While they were not the only persons desirous of this power, both had dedicated themselves for years towards getting access to it. Their names are David Miscavige and

Pat Broeker. I knew both of them personally and was not surprised that either had ended up in such a position. They had laboriously worked at it for years.

I knew David when he came to Clearwater in 1976. He was quite forward and always very friendly to me. I have two poignant memories of him from that time period. I remember him telling me of the difficulties he had during one of his first major assignments in Clearwater. Sent on a mission to fix the Qualifications Division of the Flag Service Org, he was bodily thrown out of the facility by someone who was much bigger than he. As an adult, David is only 5'6" so he did not stand much of a chance against his aggressor. He was completely bewildered by what he would have to do to fix this situation, but he must have overcome it. I do not remember what happened. I remember him feeling frustrated and saying "What do you have to do to get something done around here!?"

I lived next door to him on the ninth floor of the Fort Harrison Hotel, and he would often open his door and minorly irritate many of us by playing music. In what was quite an irony, he would routinely play a song by Hall and Oates entitled *Your a Rich Girl* which repeatedly used the lyrics "you can rely on the old man's money." The irony here is that LRH was sometimes referred to as the "Old Man" by Sea Org members. As it turned out, David inherited the stewardship of so much of LRH's money. Looking back, it was rather obvious that David had a sense of his destiny.

Although I never had any run-ins with David personally, I did hear a couple of reports where he humiliated people in a degrading fashion. Soon after that, he found his way to the desert where he began to work with LRH in the area of film production. It was during this period that LRH suffered a heart attack. As a result, a Class XII auditor by the name of David Mayo was flown out from Clearwater to the desert in California in order to audit LRH. The auditing was reported to have gone very well. The auditing procedures which were utilized on LRH evolved into new procedures known as "New Era Dianetics for OTs." It was known by the acronym of NOTS. When this was released to the Scientology public, it literally boomed the statistics. It turned out that many of the Scientology public had sort of gone by the wayside as a result of never really completing the original OT III level. As a result, most of them had drifted away from Scientology. NOTS was thus dubbed the "Second Wall of Fire." It got people revitalized on a broad basis and contributed greatly to what eventually became the Scientology renaissance movement.

There are many reports that LRH was debilitated in the aftermath of his heart attack and that he was excessively cranky. It might interest you to know that one of my best friends was a young man named Scott, and he worked with LRH personally and extensively during this period. Scott came to Clearwater on business during this period and paid a visit to me and told me many personal things about LRH during this time. Scott would never PR me as we were too close, but he spoke in very glowing terms about LRH's demeanor and sense of humor. If it were not true, he would have said nothing as there was no need for him to report on LRH at all. We were just friends. Somehow and in some way, Scott mysteriously disappeared from the scene in about 1980. To this day, I still do not know what happened to him. I can only assume that his position of power close to LRH made him extremely vulnerable and caused him to be targeted for elimination. He worked right outside of LRH's door and answered to him directly. I suspect, but do not know, that he ran afoul of David Miscavige who was then on his rise to power.

Miscavige's road to power got a great boost when he revived the management of Scientology organizations. LRH had ordered this done, but Miscavige grabbed the ball and ran with it and ended up doing a competent job. Prior to that time, Scientology organizations had been very neglected. Miscavige's most crucial act in rising to the top, however, occurred when he was a Commodore's Messenger under Dede Voegeding. I still remember Dede as a very young girl aboard the *Apollo*. By that time period, she had become Ron's top messenger in the Commodore's Messenger Org in the desert. From that position, she was literally in charge of the international management of Scientology. Dede, much to her regret years later, allowed Miscavige to move himself into a position whereby he would act as the courier for communication that was to travel between all of Scientology management, represented by the Commodore's Messenger Org, and LRH's hidden destination (which would eventually be a ranch in Creston, California). Although Miscavige did not have personal access to

LRH as far as being in his presence, he was able to communicate to him. One of the first things he did was convince LRH that Dede was not doing a good job and got her removed. Many people have reported that he gave LRH a stream of false reports in this regard. Whether right or wrong, this act gave David Miscavige full control of internal Scientology management. It did not, however, give him jurisdiction over the Guardian Office. Miscavige's go-between to LRH was Pat Broeker, the other man who was to fill in the vacuum of power.

Pat Broeker was an entirely different personality than David Miscavige. I first met Pat aboard the *Apollo* in 1972, and I always liked him because he was personable and communicative — unusually so. I also noted that he had a tendency to stand up for himself. In 1976, he had gotten into some sort of serious trouble with the organization and was receiving a Committee of Evidence which is the Sea Org's equivalent of a Court Martial. During that time period, he was allowed to work in LRH's files with Ralph Somma, and I got to visit with him quite a bit. LRH had written to him around this time and wanted him to come and work for him, but when he found out Pat was receiving a Committee of Evidence, he demurred and told Pat he would have something for him later on — when the air cleared.

Pat always had a lot of good stories to tell about LRH. One of the reasons for this was that one of his job assignments had been "LRH Internal PR." On the ship, it had been his duty to explain LRH's true character and the reasons behind various actions that were done. There are many stories of LRH flipping his lid and having outbursts. While some of them are true, others are highly exaggerated. If you were to hear all of the circumstances behind these alleged outbursts, in the cases where they were true, you would often find that his reactions were usually quite reasonable.

A favorite story of mine from Pat concerned the "Rock Festival" on the Portuguese island of Madeira. As relayed earlier, this was when the *Apollo* was being pelted by rocks from CIA inspired rioters. While the riot ensued, Pat was completing some banking duties ashore. Had he returned to the *Apollo* without completing them, the ship would have lost a considerable amount of money. When the *Apollo* made a narrow escape from the rioters, Pat was not aboard. Eventually, he hired a tug boat which chased the *Apollo* out to sea. It took many hours to reach the ship. When it did, it was the middle of the night. After being hailed by the tug boat, the *Apollo* slowed down and extended a rope ladder so that Pat could board the ship. As Pat recalled the incident, he remembered climbing the ladder to board the ship. As he looked up, he could not help but notice that LRH was in his bath robe and was looking down on him. He was not too pleased. What had happened was that LRH had been sleeping but had the keen perception to notice that the ship had inexplicably slowed down. He immediately left his cabin to see what was happening. LRH did not say anything at that time but soon had an order written to assign Pat the ethics condition of Liability for slowing the ship down and incurring the cost of the tug boat. Instead of "taking it on the chin" and "being a good soldier" by doing the penance of his ethics condition, Pat wrote to LRH and told him that he had stayed ashore because it would save the ship a considerable amount of money and thought that was the best course of action to take in lieu of rocks being pelted at the crew. Apprised of all the information, LRH immediately rescinded the ethics condition. The point here is that LRH was always open to communication. I had already experienced this myself, but Pat's experience was certainly more colorful.

Many years later, when Pat was working in the California desert with LRH, he came back to Clearwater on business. He went out of his way to visit the Personal Office and brief us about LRH. I remember him telling us of his utter amazement when LRH called in several of his messengers and explained the basic plot to a movie he had written entitled *Revolt in the Stars*. In front of everyone, LRH began to lay out the plot of the movie which centered around one of the key incidents in the confidential Scientology level known as OT III. Pat told us that he could not believe it as some of those messengers had not done the confidential level, but LRH did not seem to care. He wanted to release the information to the general public but do it in such a way that it would be a more subtle influence as opposed to a formal auditing session. When Pat told us the details of this incident, he had everyone who had not yet reached the level of OT III leave the room. Even though LRH had spilled the details, Pat was afraid that he might be targeted for revealing confidential information.

This would sound like a complete contradiction to many Scientologists, but it is absolutely and categorically true. LRH was never a robot to his own creations, even when it came to issues of security that everyone else was expected to follow.

I learned a lot of details of LRH's personal habits from Pat, but he was not my primary source of information. One of the main things to understand is that people seldom reacted to LRH as if he were a person. They would often react with star-struck adulation, strange attitudes, or robotic behavior patterns. This was not his fault. Although Pat seemed to have mastered the human side of LRH, he was not immune from his own personal aberrations which I would learn about years later.

For most of the late 1970's, Mike and Kima Douglas had taken care of LRH's personal needs and they were his most direct and trusted assistants. When they left, LRH called upon Pat Broeker to replace them. Pat, with his wife Annie, were his closest assistants and eventually lived with him in a secret location. While David Miscavige took care of Scientology management, Pat Broeker took care of LRH. Between them, they set up mail drops and met together periodically. It was thus that these two individuals filled the vacuum of power that became available as LRH submerged into deeper seclusion.

45

THE MOLE FACTOR

Although Miscavige had control of management and the communication lines between LRH and whoever he might want to communicate to, he did not have any sort of proprietary interest or controlling influence with regard to corporate and legal matters. As the Guardian Office was already reeling from the aforementioned legal cases, they were in a very vulnerable position and Miscavige astutely pounced. He began by interfacing with the Church's attorneys. This was virtually the first time since the inception of the Guardian Office that one of their own was not dealing with legalities. Henning Heldt, who had been their previous contact, was now convicted and was in no position to present any serious opposition to this new development. Among many other developments, this liaison begat the corporate restructuring of the Church of Scientology.

For a considerable period of time, many former Scientology insiders believed or assumed that David Miscavige had orchestrated the new corporate structure and that the lawyers were merely working at his call and bidding. This was a perfectly reasonable assumption until data turned up that the lawyer who engineered and founded the most powerful corporation within this new multiple corporate structure was not only a former IRS employee but the Assistant Commissioner of the IRS! His name is Meade Emory.

This, of course, has opened the door to many questions and various investigations. The first and most obvious fact that the

305

Meade Emory investigation revealed was that he became Assistant Commissioner of the IRS just as "Scientology spy" Gerald Wolfe was being hired at the IRS during a hiring freeze. Gerald Wolfe was the character who waived his personal rights in order that the Government could not only prosecute him but Mary Sue Hubbard and other key executives of the Church of Scientology. While there is no suggestion that Emory instituted the hiring freeze himself, it seems that the hiring of Wolfe and Emory might have some other associations. They certainly occurred during the same general time period.

In order to understand the full implication of Meade Emory and his influence on the Church of Scientology, it is necessary to go back to the 1960's. As has been previously discussed, the U.S. Government viewed Scientology with considerable suspicion. The IRS asserted at that time that LRH was using the Church for private gain. In actuality, LRH had created a legal and valid church, at least in terms of the law, over which he literally had control of most anything. Within the Sea Org itself, he had an entire organization of people dedicated to his well being so that he could function effectively as the founder of the Church. If you look at it one way, this further empowered the Church because his time was extremely valuable. It is a very relative issue, but this is not about legal or moral issues. It is about power. There were two different points of view at work. In the final analysis, the U.S. Government proved to be far more cunning than anyone could imagine. It should be added, however, that their cunningness was only in proportion to the strength and potential power of their opponent: LRH and Scientology.

It was amidst this background that Meade Emory is cited as having indulged in plotting and intrigue that would change the face of Scientology forever. A highly accomplished tax attorney, Emory was appointed as the legislation attorney to the Joint Commission on Taxation of the United States Congress. Although this was not a position within the structure of the I.R.S., it gave him access to the highest levels of the I.R.S. and the top tax attorneys in the world.

Meade Emory's first known engagement with the Church of Scientology was when he conducted an audit of the Church. By various accounts and reports, this audit was not all that it seemed to be because there is a data trail which suggests that Emory was from this early date involved in a clandestine plot with a man by the name of Norton S. Karno, a professional tax attorney who was serving as the primary attorney for the Church of Scientology of California in a lawsuit with the I.R.S.

At that time, Henning Heldt was the leading member of Scientology's Guardian Office in the United States and was primarily responsible for dealing with the I.R.S. lawsuit. He hired Norton Karno under circumstances in which he thought he would be enjoying the common attorney-client privilege of confidentiality. At the time, no one suspected Karno of anything, however, data suggests that what ensued was one of the most outrageous violations of attorney-client privilege in history. It is an example of one of the most effective and clandestine operations ever committed against the Church.

As time went on, Karno became a prominent and trusted insider amongst Henning Heldt and the Church of Scientology. Although LRH and Mary Sue never found any of this out, all appearances and data point to Henning, their top aide in the U.S., being worked like a monkey on a string. Henning was no dummy, but he was far from an expert on the complications of the I.R.S. or the tax code. He obviously did not know much about the non-ratification of the Sixteenth Amendment, the corporate status of the I.R.S., and the exact legal nature of its relationship with the United States Treasury. He bought into the expertise of what Scientologists consider to be "wog[*] law." Although it is not broadly known, there are plenty of attorneys who have successfully challenged the Sixteenth Amendment and the legitimate powers of the I.R.S. to collect taxes.

None of this information would have ever surfaced if not for some rather bizarre improprieties that were discovered surrounding the death and will of L. Ron Hubbard. This will be covered later, but it was noted in that investigation that Karno's law firm was listed as the attorney of record on behalf of L. Ron Hubbard. In fact, they had even drafted wills on behalf of LRH.

---

[*] Wog is a contemptuous term that Scientologists sometimes use to describe people who are not indoctrinated into Scientology. It was borrowed from the British who used the term contemptuously to describe their subjects in the orient. Wog is actually an acronym for "Worthy Oriental Gentleman."

Upon belief of all reasonable observation and available data, the aforementioned lawsuit by the I.R.S. in the 1970's was only a red herring with the actual purpose being to collect inside information on Scientology with particular regard to its legal vulnerabilities.

The exact nature of the entire relationship between Meade Emory, Karno, and David Miscavige is still sketchy at this writing, and it is not easy to ascertain who exactly was or is under the tutelage of whom and to what degree. Miscavige would have had a knowledge of the rank and file of Scientology and its members that would reach far beyond the experience of either Emory or Karno. For all parties, however, it was a marriage made in heaven as they could complement each other and not only sequester the management and corporate control of Scientology but also secure the copyrights and other vested properties of L. Ron Hubbard. This coup d'etat of power was signed, sealed, and delivered when Meade Emory drew up papers and founded the Church of Spiritual Technology or CST.

For those of you who are not familiar with the corporate structure of the Church of Scientology, CST is chartered to be a nonreligious corporation which owns the service marks and trademarks with regard to L. Ron Hubbard's spiritual technology and other vested properties from his estate. Most Scientologists, however, are not clued in to the exact nature of CST or even the fact that it exists. Scientologists are very aware of another high profile corporation which is the Religious Technology Center or RTC. CST licenses the LRH properties to RTC who then, in turn, licenses them to the Church of Scientology. The entire corporate structure is much more complex, and you can read it on the internet but the above gives you the basic premise. RTC is headed by David Miscavige and is set up to administer and police what it deems to be proper use of Scientology technology.

It should be pointed out that as of the time of LRH's death in 1986, there is no knowledge or document which indicates that the Church was then legally under the control of the IRS or any government entity per se. At that time, Meade Emory was simply a tax attorney who had been employed by the U.S. Government and IRS. Appearances might point to Emory acting as a hired corporate attorney on behalf of Miscavige and/or the Church of

Scientology's best interests in these matters, but his former position gives rise to questions of conflict of interest that are, in my opinion, off the scale of reasonable doubt.

Norton Karno also functioned as a high level tax attorney so it should not be a surprise to anyone that he might know Emory, but he was also professionally involved with Sherman and Stephen Lenske, two attorneys who currently serve as "Special Directors" of the Church of Spiritual Technology. Emory drew up the papers which designated that the Lenske brothers would serve as "Special Directors." As one of the Lenske brothers helped Karno draft a will for LRH, it becomes virtually impossible to imagine that Emory and Karno did not have a relationship. In fact, Emory would have desperately needed Karno's intimate knowledge of Scientology's corporate structure and problems in order to draft a sound corporate charter. Keep in mind that these two attorneys were former adversaries when Karno represented the Church and Emory was after them on behalf of the U.S. Government. Does this smell to you?

The most suspicious aspect I have found concerning Karno is a will drawn up for L. Ron Hubbard in which a clause was inserted whereby Hubbard is to waive any possible conflict of interest charges that might be leveled at Karno as a result of settling and executing LRH's estate. At that time, Karno was being set up to execute L. Ron Hubbard's estate. This is one of the most outrageous clauses I have ever heard of being put into a will, particularly when you consider the circumstances of his specific role in the Church and his association with Emory. The effort to evade conflict of interest charges raises all sorts of questions.

This new corporate liaison between Miscavige and the tax men did not happen overnight. It initially required two pivotal legal maneuvers. First, Mary Sue Hubbard would be removed from any and all legal powers she might have over the Guardian Office and the Church of Scientology. Miscavige's attorneys drafted a letter which disparaged anything and everything about her having the necessary elements to continue having an executive role with the Church. As was said earlier, she had a knock-down-drag-out verbal battle with Miscavige before submitting to his wishes and resigning. At that time, the rank and file of the Church, including most of its senior executives, were not aware of what had transpired with Mary Sue and how she was relegated to an unfavorable status.

After Mary Sue was defrocked, the attorneys and/or Miscavige ascertained that LRH could have no connection with Scientology whatsoever. He was deemed to be a legal liability. When I first learned of this, I was astonished because I had read the directives of a previous attorney that had relegated LRH's role to that of a pope whereby he might not be directly managing any of the churches or even the mother church directly but was merely writing advices in the form of policy letters and bulletins which were ecclesiastical in nature and therefore immune from state statutes. As an ecclesiastical pope, his status would not violate the integrity of the Church's corporate structure. It did not make any sense to me when I learned that this strategy had been abandoned. There was certainly no legal argument presented against it. Instead, ridiculous orders were issued to go through all of the files in management and razor blade out the name of L. Ron Hubbard from any directives or orders. Staff (myself not included) spent countless hours of wasted time doing this in a feeble attempt to demonstrate to potential legal authorities that LRH had no influence whatsoever over Scientology management. Everyone, including his opposition, knew that he did, and I could personally never understand why such a harebrained scheme would be executed. The only explanation I have now is that Miscavige could demonstrate to both the executives and regular staff of Scientology that it was libelous to have any connection to LRH as far as management was concerned. This effectively divorced LRH from having any control or direct influence of his staff, unless he went through Miscavige. Besides the above, letters to LRH, particularly from Mary Sue, were vetted of any bad news or things which might be deemed to upset him.

Having achieved complete control of Scientology management and the Guardian Office, Miscavige was now beginning to exert control over LRH himself. LRH suspected something was wrong when he got wind of the legal strategies being employed. He did not believe for a minute that he should be excluded and knew better. Accordingly, he asked for a security check to be done on David Miscavige as he did not trust him based upon what he was reading from Miscavige himself.

Based upon an LRH order, a man I knew by the name of Jesse Prince was selected to administer a security check on Miscavige whereby the latter would be placed on an e-meter and questioned on ethical matters. The security check, according to the reports of Jesse Prince, revealed a motherlode of information. Miscavige coughed up that he met Pat Broeker in Las Vegas where they would both gamble with LRH's money and share women together. Apparently, both were enjoying the fruits of their power and were quite shameless about it. Amidst a shower of tears, Miscavige stated to Prince that he felt horrible about what he had done, stating that he loved LRH and wanted to be loyal to him.

This would have nipped everything in the bud had the report gotten to LRH, but Prince did not know that Miscavige still had a powerful card to play. When Prince wrote up the report to LRH, he did not have a complete picture of what he was dealing with. The only communication to LRH was via Pat Broeker and David Miscavige. During the security check, Miscavige was clever to impugn Broeker's character as being equally faulty to his own. As a result, this put Broeker in a position of having to forward his own crimes to the potential "executioner." From what I have heard, it was reported back to LRH that Miscavige's security check came up clean. Broeker, apparently thinking he was in kahutz with Miscavige and enjoying each other's mutual protection, did not realize that he would be eventually targeted for elimination, too.

This might all sound extremely Machiavellian and intriguing, but it was a long and slow process. It took about eight years before Miscavige had complete power, if he has even achieved that. While people are quick to target Miscavige, I can guarantee you that people would have been quick to target anyone else who had assumed this position through either nefarious or benign means. This is the way power works. It was LRH's power that had created all of the inertia in the first place. Whether it was "good" or "bad" is arguable and completely relative to the position of the observer. It was now being transmuted into a realm which might better be described as a nest of vipers. The only way one can manage in such an environment is to operate with extreme control.

After the above betrayal of LRH, I have learned that Pat Broeker began drinking excessively. LRH, observing that Pat had some problems, put him on jobs that required manual labor.

Although I do not know if Pat completed any sort of rehabilitation program, it was very clear that when LRH died, Broeker and his wife, Annie, were positioned to be at the helm of Scientology and were assigned, allegedly by LRH, a new and unprecedented rank in the Sea Organization: the title of Loyal Officer. This was publicly broadcast at LRH's funeral and clearly indicated that they were ranked well above Miscavige. Most everyone assumed that they were in complete charge of Scientology.

By this time, according to the best of my knowledge, Miscavige had already taken effective steps to eliminate Broeker during one of their routine secret meetings that were held at clandestine locations. I was told that one night, he had exacerbated Broeker's weakness for alcohol by getting him very drunk. At some point, reportedly at the end of their meeting, he quite casually mentioned that he had a paper for him to sign. One version has it that this signed paper had Broeker signing over any rights or claims to a succession of power in Scientology. Another more probable claim is that this piece of paper was actually a voucher that he was supposed to sign for huge amounts of expense money, usually in cash, that he had received on behalf of himself and LRH. As Broeker had mostly worked in the Treasury Department of Scientology, he might not have resisted this request at all as he knew that funds had to be accounted for. To his detriment, however, this apparently fed into a scheme that was allegedly thought up by the Church attorneys. By having Broeker sign for this unaccounted for money, it could legally be construed as embezzlement or some other financial crime. Whether it was true to the letter of the law or not, I cannot say, but it was eventually used to intimidate Pat Broeker and make him submit to the wishes of Miscavige and/or the attorneys. To everyone's amazement, the Broekers' status as Loyal Officers was cancelled by David Miscavige. This was the final and ultimate blow that would secure Miscavige as the most visibly powerful person in Scientology.

I have heard information that came from Broeker's former in-laws that his parents were independently wealthy and he escaped into anonymity. I have also heard other reports that he was offered a substantial amount of money to shut up and get lost. Whatever the exact truth is, we know one thing for sure. Pat Broeker has never been seen publicly since his removal.

46

THE CORONER

On January 24, 1986, L. Ron Hubbard passed away. The trail of his death, however, has left a trail of mystery and intrigue that might not be fully resolved for hundreds of years.

The questioning began when the director of the funeral home where LRH's body was taken to noted that LRH allegedly died at 10:00 o'clock in the evening on Friday but that the death was not reported until Saturday morning. The coroner's report indicates that Hubbard's personal physician, Dr. Eugene Denk, had delayed in notifying the coroner's office of the death. Denk also noted that Hubbard had suffered a stroke about a week earlier and that the cause of death was a result of the stroke. An attorney representing Hubbard claimed that the delay in the notification of death was so that the will could be gotten together and the cremation procedure could be expedited.

Although the police and the coroner investigation turned up no foul play at the scene of the death, they wondered if the decedent was of sound mind at the time he signed the will. There were at least two reasons to make them wonder. First, it was noted by the coroner that the date of LRH's will was January 23rd, only one day prior to Hubbard's death. Second, Dr. Denk had indicated to them that LRH's clinical history supported a possible neurological program. Accordingly, Detective Coroner Hines requested a copy of the will and an autopsy was ordered as well because Dr. Denk's diagnosis had come into question. This procedure would avoid simple questions of whether or not LRH

313

was of sound mind when his last will and testament was signed. Without an autopsy, immediate cause of death would be uncertain. Church attorneys were able to countermand an autopsy when they submitted a "Certificate of Religious Belief" to the coroner. In California, an individual may avoid an autopsy if he deems that it is against his personal religious beliefs. Accordingly, he can execute a statement to that effect. If it is reliably witnessed, an autopsy is not allowed.

In Scientology, there is no provision or religious precept that one should not have an autopsy. It would be only a matter of individual choice. Whatever LRH personally believed about autopsies is unknown to me, but attorneys submitted a "Certificate of Religious Belief" on behalf of LRH which stated that he did not wish to have an autopsy in the event of his death. This would all have been well and fine except for two points. First, the law was passed shortly before his death. Second, it is apparently signed and thumbprinted by LRH on the 20th of January, just four days before his death. It is witnessed by Pat Broeker who will be mysteriously extinguished from his role as executor three days later. It is also witnessed by his wife, Annie, and Stephen J. Pfauth. If one is incapacitated to the point where one cannot sign a will, how can one have the capacity to waive their own autopsy, particularly when the whole scene smells of irregularity?

Why the coroner's office accepted this without effectively following up these obvious discrepancies, I cannot answer. Instead of an autopsy, Sheriff George S. Whiting ordered Dr. Karl E. Kirschner to perform a medical inspection on the body of LRH. It was just six weeks short of his seventy-fifth birthday. This inspection revealed ten recent needle marks to the right gluteal area. The case was then brought to the attention of the district attorney's office who suggested a toxicology be performed on the body fluids.

The toxicology report indicated that Ron's body contained a significant quantity of vistaril, an antipsychotic medication. This is particularly noteworthy because Hubbard had always vehemently opposed psychiatric drugs as do all loyal Scientologists. In addition to that, LRH's will had been mysteriously redrafted just before he died so as to eliminate Pat Broeker as the executor. Instead, Norman Starkey, who always dutifully answers to

Miscavige, was entrusted with this responsibility. Originally, in 1979, attorney Norton S. Karno was going to be the executor of the will, but this position was shifted in 1982 to Pat Broeker.

Dr. Denk openly admitted that he was the one who prescribed the vistaril as well as vitamin B-12. Although the toxicology report indicated that there was no foul play in the death, the high dosages of medication brought into question the validity of the will signed. As the means of death was not determined to be a criminal matter, the coroner's office allowed Dr. Denk to certify the certificate of death. In the coroner's report, Denk claimed that he had resided with LRH for two years and that the latter had displayed signs of dysphasia for about eight days and that the terminal event was a CVA (a cerebro vascular accident which is medical lingo for a stroke).

These statements to the coroner by Dr. Denk are particularly noteworthy because if having a stroke and being on vistaril does not make you incompetent when signing a will then dysphasia certainly does. The word *dysphasia* means not having the capacity to understand language. It is due to the fact that the part of the brain governing language is not functioning properly.

The above closes the case on whether or not there was legal impropriety with regard to the will. It is right there in the coroner's report. If you want to know why the coroner's office did not pursue this further, you would have to ask the local district attorney in San Luis Obispo because they are the ones who stonewalled any further investigation into these matters.

The fingerprinting identification procedure on the corpse also turned up LRH's "Los Angeles Special Officer" card which indicated that he had been an employee of the LAPD in 1948. The body was indeed found to be that of L. Ron Hubbard.

On October 4th, E. Ogle, a legal representative of Norman Starkey, requested that the coroner's office destroy the photographs which included the needle marks. The request was not granted.

One also has to seriously consider the role of Dr. Denk in these matters. He was reliably witnessed to have gone on a gambling vacation with Miscavige and other top Scientology executives just before Hubbard's death. Studying the coroner reports indicates that Denk seemed to give the coroner the impression that he was in attendance at the time of the death, but there is no evidence to indicate this is true. After Hubbard's death, Denk conveniently disappeared for one year.

Although these matters have been raised and challenged in the court system, the legal tactics have either been lame in their own right or the issues have been stonewalled by the court system itself. For those of you who are not familiar in dealing with the court system, it can be excessively cunning when dealing with certain issues. For the most part, the system makes a somewhat reasonable attempt to deliver justice. This is clearly dependent, however, on the personnel and the relative capacity, incapacity or prejudices of the individuals involved. There is a percentage of cases where justice is reasonably well served. There is also a percentage of cases where extremely controversial issues are brought to light. The press avoids these cases like a hot potato. Often, they have to do with the sovereign right of individuals, the Admiralty Court (as opposed to one's rights as delineated under the U.S. Constitution) and other peculiar and particular issues that might have a tendency to eat away at the power structure of the status quo.

At this point, I have too little data to determine whether the above matters are a case of deliberate judicial miscarriage, apathetic authorities, or lack of interest by intelligent people who are comeasurately capable of doing something about it. We do know, however, that there are plenty of people who consider the affairs of Hubbard's will to be a flagrant case of injustice.

47

THE EMPIRE STRIKES BACK

Despite the favorable ruling on Miscavige's behalf, the lack of an effective challenge to LRH's will still did not secure him absolute power. Mary Sue Hubbard was LRH's legal spouse at the time of his death; and, according to California law, was entitled to fifty percent of his entire estate. According to the testimony of Jessie Prince, Mary Sue was surrounded by over twelve Sea Org members, led by Miscavige and including Jessie, who forcefully persuaded her into signing away all of her claims to LRH's estate in return for a very modest settlement in comparison to what the full value of the estate was really worth. Recovering from lung cancer at the time, she was no match for any of them and forfeited her remaining power. Mary Sue was not, however, completely abandoned by the Scientologists. According to reports, they take care of her needs but also watch her every move which is tantamount to being under a virtual house arrest. Hubbard's children were also persuaded to sign away any claims to his will in exchange for modest amounts of money.

When you stand back and look at the entire history of what ensued with the Church of Scientology, with the additional advantage of hindsight, you see a very clear pattern emerging. The deposing of Mary Sue Hubbard from her position of Controller of the Church was a monumental event. It was not, however, the ultimate linchpin. That occurred in 1982, when the Supreme Court upheld Mary Sue Hubbard's original conviction. It was only then that the Church of Spiritual Technology emerged as the ultimate legal hub that would control the legalities and entire corporate structure of Scientology. It is obvious that they were watching Mary Sue's legal case like a hawk. Had she been exonerated, all of the conspirators would have been on very shaky ground. It now becomes crystal clear why LRH was an unindicted coconspirator. Had they convicted him, it would have compromised the value of his assets and, more importantly, access to them.

Let us review the circumstances once again. CST was set up in order to control the copyrights and trademarks of L. Ron Hubbard. As the senior corporation to and behind Scientology, CST controls all of LRH's intellectual properties and has authority of all Scientology related trademarks which include the name of "L. Ron Hubbard." It is not set up as a church or religious entity but as a for profit enterprise. Most attention, however, is lauded upon a subordinate corporation, which CST controls, known as RTC or the Religious Technology Center.

Most everyone thought that CST, if they even knew about it at all, was just a corporate entity that was set up as a legally defensible means by which to facilitate Scientology's religious agenda. The integrity of the corporation, however, was called into question when it was discovered that Meade Emory's name appeared in the articles of incorporation. Not only was Emory, the Church's former adversary in the IRS, involved in the incorporation of CST, he was the founder of the new corporation. This astonishing revelation was what caused a whirlwind of investigation in order to unravel the mystery of Meade Emory's hidden role in the reincorporation of his old rival.

When it was discovered he had his own private practice in Seattle, Emory was phoned to explain his role, but he feigned that he had no recollection of these matters. One of his own colleagues, however, was tricked into admitting Emory's role. It is really no matter as the facts are public record. The report that he feigned ignorance is telling in itself, but it still does not explain the mystery of how or why Emory became superimposed upon his old adversaries. The answer, however, can be found in the corporate documents which are available to public inspection.

When Emory drew up the articles founding the Church of Spiritual Technology, he designated three people to serve as "Special Directors" who are not Scientologists but have sweeping powers to direct the entire machinations of the Church of Scientology. These special directors are Sherman Lenske, Stephen Lenske, and Lawrence E. Heller of the law firm Lenske, Lenske, Heller and Magasin. Quite remarkably, the terms of their appointment are for life. In the event of a death of one of these Special Directors, they are to be replaced by someone of the same law firm who is also in good standing with the California State Bar Association. Under such terms, the California State Bar can determine the fate of Scientology. If you think this all sounds like a huge conflict of interest scandal, you are thinking quite correctly. Also keep in mind that the California legislature conveniently passed the "no autopsy law" just prior to LRH's death.

There was most definitely an intriguing pattern at work here. Meade Emory prosecuted the Scientologists in the early 1970's. His peer, one of the most sophisticated tax layers in the country, Norton S. Karno, represented the Church of Scientology and gained access to all of their corporate secrets. Later on, Karno drafted a will for L. Ron Hubbard, with the help of Sherman Lenske, in which he indemnified himself and the Lenske brothers from any possible conflict of interest charges in the event they put their own future business interests over that of Hubbard's estate. Keep in mind that Karno named himself as executor of that will.

In the meantime, as Emory was appointed Assistant Commissioner of the IRS, a sting operation was set up against the Church of Scientology in which they were caught red-handed in stealing suppressed documents that indicated a conspiracy against Scientology. Although the documents should be in the public domain, they were technically stolen by Gerald Wolfe, a so-called Scientologist who was suspiciously hired during a hiring freeze at the IRS, just as Emory assumed his post. After having been caught in the act of burglary to obtain public documents, Wolfe mysteriously waived his rights and allowed himself to be prosecuted. The FBI then had reasonable cause to break down the doors of the Church of Scientology and seize all of their corporate records.

Mary Sue Hubbard was then indicted and signed a stipulation of evidence without ever receiving a trial. More importantly, she was deposed and lost all corporate control of the Church which was then reincorporated under the tutelage of Meade Emory, the man who was an original adversary to the Church in the first place.

His handpicked "Special Directors" end up with ultimate authority in directing the copyrights and trademarks of L. Ron Hubbard. The story, however, does not end there.

Only after Mary Sue Hubbard signed away her rights to LRH's estate and was completely extinguished as a serious rival for potential successorship to LRH's legacy and his church did the Church of Scientology finally come to terms with the IRS in obtaining tax exemption. This was in the autumn of 1993, the same year that Bill Clinton took office. Clinton has always acted as a friend to the Church of Scientology, particularly with regard to their struggles with the German government, however, he showed no such sympathy with the Branch Davidians in Waco who were incinerated earlier that year.

For some reason, and in some mysterious way, Clinton's Justice Department ordered the IRS to settle their affairs with the Church of Scientology and grant them tax exempt status. The settlement between the Church of Scientology and the IRS ended a twenty-six year war that included numerous lawsuits, bugging of offices, and acquisition of confidential files (on both sides). This settlement raised many eyebrows from many different areas, mostly because it was like Captain Kirk coming to a settlement with the Klingons. Ostensibly, it made no sense. Neither party offered any clues. In defiance of a court order and U.S. taxation law, the IRS refused to disclose the terms of the exemption agreement they had reached with the Church of Scientology. A sixty-one page document was drawn up between the Church and the IRS, but it remained secret and violated all public disclosure laws. We might not even know about it today except for the fact that some noble soul leaked it to the *Wall Street Journal* who reported it but did not dare mention the mysterious and cunning role of Meade Emory in these matters. When the disclosure between the IRS and Scientology was forced into the public domain (despite the best efforts of the Government), it revealed some amazing news.

While it granted Scientology organizations tax exempt status and extinguished all law suits against the IRS, it also required that Tax Compliance Sections be set up in every Scientology organization for the purpose of seeing that all tax laws are properly administered. This is rather remarkable in that it effectively makes Scientology churches agents of the Government in enforcing U.S. tax laws as well as the tax compliance requests of the IRS. This is a violation of one of the oldest principles and laws in America: separation of church and state.

The entire agreement between the Church and IRS was put together with a considerable amount of hubris. It contains a clause requiring all signatories to agree in collusion to protect any current or former employees of the U.S. Government or IRS against any and all claims of their having been involved in a "continued conspiracy." Obviously, if there was no conspiracy, none of this would have happened in the first place.

In some ways, what you have just read is one of the biggest secrets the Government ever hid. In another way, nobody cares about its exposure because they are too ignorant of what it represents and are too powerless to do anything about it.

For the Government, it resolved a long standing issue they had been working on for decades: to obtain control over L. Ron Hubbard's OT levels which featured the key procedures of what the remote viewing projects were based upon.

One of the first things that occurred after the set up of the Church of Spiritual Technology was that those very OT levels were removed from the Scientology Gradation Chart and were no longer offered to the public or staff. The entire operation was a long hard slog, but it was finally accomplished. There is currently no court in the world who is powerful enough or willing enough to change matters, at least at this time. There is also a "spy network" of tax compliance officers within the Church who are not only willing but mandated to report to the IRS. It is the proverbial example of the fox guarding the chicken coop.

What I have written about these various matters is really only a brief outline. The entire story can be further documented if you wish to pursue it. There are also many subplots and twists to these issues. It is a compelling drama in itself, but it is way too complex for the average person to easily assess what is going on without the above guidelines. It took me years to get a handle on this information which is a complicated and labyrinthine morass of legalities and intrigue that is meant to be onerous and confusing.

Earlier in this book, I explained to you the "candy" that Scientology offered its adherents. Candy, by its very nature, is not only sweet to the taste but appears attractive to the eye. It is a seductive element. Apparently, the Government was interested in this candy to the point where one can easily conclude that the candy had some actual nutritional value or substance to it that extends far beyond the sugarcoated shells that are sometimes proclaimed by overzealous Scientologists. The exact truth of the matter is that the Scientology movement, as I knew it during the peak years of L. Ron Hubbard, contained the seeds of destruction for the "Evil Empire." By "Evil Empire," I do not necessarily mean the United States Government per se, but I am referring to those invisible sources and not so invisible sources which subjugate any democratic and humanistic institution to serve the specific ends of an empowered elite. Those so-called "seeds of destruction" are now under their complete scrutiny and control.

Ever since his rise to power, David Miscavige has taken on an incredible amount of abuse in terms of lawsuits personally naming him and a barrage of literature dedicated to humiliating him and dethroning him from his position of power. Many people have demonstrated a considerable preoccupation with getting rid of him. I am sure that some of those people, as well as other ex-Scientologists, might take umbrage with me for not airing all of Miscavige's dirty laundry in this book. There are a few reasons why I have not done that. First, it is not all that productive. Additionally, it has been done to ad nauseam. Sure, I could add some juicy stories from his old "friends" that no one has heard before, but it is not really necessary. The conspiracy community has indulged in character assassination for decades now. Some of it is even quite correct but character assassination is only effective (even when untrue) if you control the media. There are only a couple of points that should be brought up about David Miscavige.

The most relevant fact about him that has not been brought to light at all concerns a law suit that Larry Wollersheim[*] won

---

[*] Wollersheim was originally awarded about twenty million dollars when he successfully sued the Church. The judicial process somehow, and I thought quite mysteriously, reduced the sum to somewhere in the neighborhood of two million, but the Church stalled by utilizing the judicial process until they were forced to pay, some eight years later. All in all, it took over twenty years for Wollersheim to collect any money from the time he began his lawsuit. The message by Scientology was clear. Is it worth twenty plus years of aggravation to win? Scientology was content to pay a total of eight million, most of it interest charges that accrued from their earlier refusal to pay.

322

against the Church of Scientology of California. Multiple witnesses have testified that Miscavige personally ordered the destruction of Wollersheim's preclear folders after a judge had subpoenaed them to court. This testimony comes from people who testified that they were involved in the destruction. What has not been brought to light is that this offense is a federal crime under the heading of "obstruction of justice." There is no statue of limitations in such a crime. If the Government wanted to get rid of Miscavige, they could easily arrange a trial and convict him, even if he bought off the witnesses and persuaded them to change their testimony. The Government could easily demonstrate from other cases how witnesses have been coerced in the past.

The other point I want to bring up concerns the bizarre death of Miscavige's mother-in-law, Flo Barnett. Flo had defected from the Church and joined a splinter group. She became quite a rabble rouser on the subject and was a public relations embarrassment to Miscavige. Flo died shortly thereafter under the most bizarre circumstances. She was shot to death with a rifle, but it was declared a suicide even though there was no gun powder residue on her hands. There were also multiple gun shot wounds. One gets a macabre picture of her awkwardly pointing a rifle at herself, missing, and then going at it again. If you read the coroner's report on the internet, you will find all sorts of discrepancies that beg for further investigation. Some people have tried to blame Miscavige for the shooting, but that is speculative. What is bizarre is the impropriety of the investigation. It is not unlike the way LRH's death was handled in San Luis Obispo.

David Miscavige holds his office because he is serving a purpose. He is not the prime power but is supported by a very potent power structure that reaches far beyond the bounds of anything that could be considered organized Scientology. Does he have a considerable amount of power? Yes. He is feeding off of the whirlwind of power originally created by LRH. Christian churches do the same thing. They feed off the power that was originally created by the founder of that religion. It is not unlike jackals and carrion feeding off of the carcass of a lion. This particular lion, however, has magical bones which have certain powers in their own right. In other words, the magic of the lion did not expire with the body.

The story I have presented is not a particularly pretty one, but the various events described in this chapter and elsewhere in this book are really nothing new in terms of the saga of life on Earth and the drama of the human spirit. It is typical for the evil empire to take over and win. Whatever this means to you in the reading audience, I cannot say, but if you posses a kernel of desire to be more free, particularly on a spiritual level, it should be of service to you in terms of recognizing the type of patterning that can be imprinted on souls. What was done here was apparently accomplished with cunning and guile and not by forcible implantation techniques. If forcible implantation was employed, and I do not mean to imply that it was not, the deal still required cunning and guile to seal it.

This universe has always acted as if it were a Shakesperean tragedy that sought to highlight the elements of power, suppression, and oppression. Freedom comes in short supply. All of the great religions have sought to offer a solution for these negative elements. Easterners have nirvana and Christians have heaven. Hubbard's paradigm, by definition, reached far beyond what ordinary religions conceived. He was postulating a state in which the individual could maintain their own self-referential awareness within the stream of consciousness known as life but could also juxtapose themselves within it on one's own terms. The sky was the limit. This is not an abnegation or extinguishing of desire nor is it a conformity to a code of behavior that will lead to a prescribed paradise as defined by others. It is a realization of goals and dreams. Your dreams are the most powerful seeds within you. They are the highlights of your life. Even a dying man holds onto the precept of life by extending dreams into the thought stream. Conversely, when you thwart a man's dreams, you create the deepest wound imaginable. If one cannot live out or pursue a dream, they become less than what they really are. Eventually, they do not want to live and go into a tacit state of agreement with a subdued existence. This is the unfortunate condition of so many people on this planet. Although there are plenty of exceptions, it is a world of broken dreams.

The previous events I have described in Scientology resulted in many broken dreams for various individuals that I knew and even more than I did not know. It was one of the cruelest wrenchings of the heart that I have ever seen. The disappointment was directly proportional to the degree of hope and dreaming that went on, and I have never seen any instrument that rekindled or fostered hopes and dreams as much as Scientology does.

Personally, I was extremely disappointed at what I had witnessed, but I was not worried about my personal situation. I had received more than I had ever realistically expected. All I knew was that since the regime change was that LRH's word was no longer valid within the organization and the same game was not being played.

It is inviting to look at what happened as a Shakesperean tragedy with jackals picking at Ron's corpse for every item of booty that might have some value. It is one of the worst expression of human nature. If one is truly exterior to the human condition, however, there is no logical reason to become too upset or react in any way. This is just the way people act. Condemnation and judgement are not evolved expressions of the human spirit.

To get additional perspective on these matters, one can consult the Eightfold Path taught by the Buddha which consists of right speech, right action, right view, right intention, right mindfulness, right effort, right livelihood, and right concentration. All of these are important to living an optimum life, but in regard to this particular situation, I would like to <u>concentrate</u> on <u>right view</u>.

Scientology, at its best, not only taught all about viewpoint but taught that <u>you</u> are a viewpoint. Not until one reached the level of OT III was one really considered to possess full self-determinism. Below that level, one was considered to be other-determined, at least to some degree. There was plenty of room for subtle variations as well. When one reached OT VI, however, a level which offered full exteriorization from the body and was the core of the remote viewing exercises, one moved up from being fully self-determined to a state known as pan-determinism. This means not only being able to see both sides of a situation but all sides. *Pan* means *all*. In order to process the phenomena and circumstances heretofore explained, it is best to explore and be open to all viewpoints and not be in denial about any of them. What I have offered is only my viewpoint which is based upon my experiences. Current day Scientologists will tell you that "everything is good in Russia" and would likely have some good examples to share with you. I am sure they have many successes. If they did not, they would not be able to hold together at all. There are also people who practice Scientology outside of the Church in what is known as the "Free Zone." These people also have their own viewpoint and some of them might not care for mine. Others might agree with me. The only reason anyone would read a book in the first place is to learn about other viewpoints and perhaps to get a spiritual advantage or any type of advantage in terms of learning something. The key in all of this is not to react to others viewpoints or to be in denial about them. Everyone sees things from their own perspective and you are not going to change it by getting emotional. You have to be true to your own viewpoint.

There are so many viewpoints about Scientology that I could not begin to cover them all. There is one, however, I would like to cover and that is the viewpoint of the Tar Baby. In my last book, *Synchronicity and the Seventh Seal*, I devised a fictional character who represents the collective unconscious but also those aspects of such that have been particularly repressed in our cultural history. According to many of you, the Tar Baby was a very popular character, and while I will not allow him to take over half the book like he did last time, I will reprise him for at least a few chapters. The Tar Baby is the host, narrator, and sometimes player in a place called the *Magick Theater*, a holographic theater that can manifest anything within or outside the boundaries of the imagination.

48

THE TAR BABY SPEAKS

THE FOLLOWING TRANSMISSION IS FROM A PARALLEL UNIVERSE

The original debut of the Magick Theater appeared in *Synchronicity and the Seventh Seal* and featured a crowd that consisted of anyone who had ever appeared in one of Peter Moon's books, but the crowd that strolls in for the second performance is entirely different. It consists of everyone who has ever read a book penned by Peter Moon. This includes the happy and enchanted as well as those who were either bored, disgruntled or suffered reality breakdowns.

When the house lights go down, a short period of pitch black darkness if followed by a slide show image which fills the theater. It is the coroner's photograph of L. Ron Hubbard's corpse with multiple needle marks on the buttocks. As this is shown to the audience, frequency generators from in back of the stage emulate the emotions of grief and imprint this emotion upon the entire audience. At first, the most sensitive in the audience feel it and begin crying. As their crying is amplified and the generators continue, the rest of the audience joins in the crying until everyone is doing it, even the people who did not like or care for anything L. Ron Hubbard stood for.

Each time the grieving reaches a climax and begins to wind down, a new slide is presented. These include slides of clandestine meetings of various executives and lawyers, bank accounts, and huge money transactions. After ten minutes of this, a rapid fire flashing of pictures occurs, all of which represent the death and ramifications of the man's death. These include money transferring to Scientology, happy faces, disappointed faces, betrayed faces, deceitful faces, and people giving success stories, some of them pompous and some of them genuine. There are countless pictures and scenes, many captured from the akashic records themselves. Finally, there is the cremation of L. Ron Hubbard's body and then total blackness again.

Just as the cremation scene begins, the grief generators have been turned off. As people begin to dry their eyes, the frequency generators are now transmitting a feeling of well being which gradually catches on in the crowd. As this feeling of pleasantness and well being is gradually amplified through the transmitters and develops into enthusiasm, a bright spotlight shines down from the top of the stage and falls right upon the Tar Baby. At the appearance of the Tar Baby, the audience begins clapping, prompted by an audio track that started the clapping noise in the first place. As the enthusiasm becomes more and more contagious, the frequency generators are amped up so that everyone is becoming fervent and giving a standing ovation to the Tar Baby who is taking frequent and excessive bows. As the applause becomes stronger, the bow taking of the Tar Baby becomes more extravagant and grandiose. With his gestures, the Tar Baby makes it very clear that he is absorbing the energy of the audience, and he begins to exaggerate that, too.

When the applause dies down, the Tar Baby sizes up the audience by looking at them from side to side when a poof of smoke suddenly envelopes him. When the smoke clears, the Tar Baby is seen wearing a fully braided naval uniform as was the tradition of the top officers in the Sea Org.

"Good evenin' ladies 'n gen'lmen and's welcome's to de Magick Th'tr. Y'all's in's fo' a treat tonight."

As he speaks, a huge Sea Org flag is extended down from the rafters. It is white with a gold laurel wreath and a gold pentagram in the middle of the wreath. The Tar Baby then points to the flag and speaks.

"Dis is de Sea Org flag, but it wuz picked 'cuz it was de flag o' de Galactic Confederacy, an organ'zation on de whole track dat was de most impo'tant organ'zation in de universe. You's sees, deys was supposin' to be guardians 'o de people and all de civ'l'zations, but deys failed us. And now deys failed's us once 'g'in. Matter 'o facts, LRH says he's be usin' der flag 'cuz even's tho' dey be betrayin' every one, der de only hope in dis universe."

Just as the Tar Baby finishes his sentence, a voice from the audience is heard to say, "That's all a bunch of crap!"

"Maybe's," says the Tar Baby. "Just maybe's it is. But one t'ing I's have in answer to dat. I's de Tar Baby and as de Tar Baby, I's be representin' de c'llective unconscious. De c'llective unconscious is where all t'ings hidden come's out to roost. In dat r'spect, I's be de only hope anyone has 'o anyt'ing. If's you's don't's like dat Sea Org flag den put one up wit' me!"

The audience then bursts into a thunderous applause as the Tar Baby takes another bow. When the bowing is done, another poof of smoke covers the Tar Baby. As the smoke dissipates, the Tar Baby is no longer in a Sea Org uniform but is wearing the headdress of an Egyptian pharaoh. As the age old music known as the cobra dance begins to play, the Tar Baby begins to cobra dance. At the same time, a true to life picture of the current day Sphinx appears in the background until it becomes a three-dimensional representation.

"Just you's remembers," says the Tar Baby, "I's be representin' de oppressed peoples and oppressed consciousness everywhere! Now's we's goin' on a little journey."

A vertical sarcophagus in the background slowly opens. It is right between the paws of the Sphinx. The Tar Baby beckons the audience to follow him with his hand. As he moves into the opening of the sarcophagus, the audience is able to follow him by means of the holographic projection of the theater. He descends a stone stairway until he reaches a large and mostly empty chamber.

"Dis is de mysterious Hall 'o Records," he says. "Only one problem do'. It all been cleared out by de CIA after Word War II. Ain't much a nuttin' here's no more."

After pretty much convincing the audience that there is nothing left in the Hall of Records, the Tar Baby then pulls out a flashlight and starts rummaging around. Next to a wall, he sees a lump of something which turns out to be a man sleeping. He is wearing a modern but cheap suit that looks like it might have come from a discount store. It is badly wrinkled by reason of the fact that the man has been sleeping. As the Tar Baby peers closer with his flashlight, he sees that there is an identification badge on the suit. The man's name is spelled out and it reads "Otto Wilson." Below that are the words "Central Intelligence Agency." The man is snoring. The Tar Baby gets a mischievous looking grin on his face.

"Well, whadda we have here?" he asks.

Waking up, the CIA agent looks up at the Tar Baby and then looks around the room rapidly.

"Oh," says the agent calmly, "just a hologram. I won't have to worry. If you were an actual person penetrating this area, which I am here to guard, I would have to report you."

"Dat yo' job den? Reportin' on people who d'scover a big nuttin' zone?"

"That's about right. The company moved all of the tablets and other instruments out of here after World War II. It went hand-in-hand with the National Security Act. They still believe, however, that there are aethyrs in this chamber that could cause trouble if anyone were to penetrate the area. Actually, they're rather stupid. Most of the aethyrs went with everything they took."

"Dat's just fine, but I's goin' to some ot'er places even mo' impot'nt dan dis empty Hall o' Records."

"I'm here to guard against that, too, but I was not going to say anything if you hadn't mentioned it. But it doesn't matter. You're just a hologram."

"If dat don't matter den — tell me what dey did wit' all dem records."

"They're in storage — to be used in case they're needed to corral the population. The original Hall of Records, however, is supposed to represent the secret history of Mankind and how we all got here. Taking the Hall of Records away is really not such a big deal. Although the Hall of Records has been removed, the seeds of what they explain are represented in the architecture of

THE TAR BABY SPEAKS

the Sphinx itself, a monument constructed of what are known as four kerubs."

"What's dat word *kerub?*" asks the Tar Baby.

"A kerub, sometimes pronounced in English as cherub, represents the four fixed signs of the zodiac. Each one of these kerubs represent the most powerful nature of the four elements of fire, water, air and earth. Fire is represented by Leo and is the lion part of the Sphinx. Water, somewhat mysteriously, is represented by Scorpio, the symbol for which is the phoenix (later, the Greeks assigned the scorpion) and are the wings. Air (Aquarius) is knowledge and is represented by the human element of the Sphinx. Earth is symbolized by the bull or ox (Taurus) and represents the yoke of being tied to the Earth. The four powers of the Sphinx represent the means by which to rule these different elements. They are *to know, to will, to dare,* and *to be silent.* This is man incarnated into and amongst the elements and this is what the Sphinx is meant to represent.

"Stripping the Earth of the memory of its inception, however, is really a poor joke. Despite all the attention being lavished upon the Sphinx in recent times, the answers it originally had to offer were really quite truncated. It is like trying to explain the inception of consciousness in terms of the secret security that ensued during the formation of the National Security Act in the aftermath of the Roswell crash. Actually, the history of this universe and this planet goes back far longer than anything in the Sphinx or what was underneath it might suggest. There is, however, a Fifth Element and that represents *to go,* which refers to the consciousness which manifests itself amongst these elements. This is the spirit itself, the God within, which has its own unique quantum or human point of view. Its virtue is *to go.*"

"Well," says the Tar Bay, "I's gots to go's and I's can't's help's it."

"Wait just a minute, Tar Baby. I want you to know something first," replies Agent Wilson. "The Hall of Records are only the most recent accounts of Earth, at least in terms of tens of thousands of years. But, they are a joke. The most relevant parts of history on this planet are long before that."

"But I's really got's to go's," says the Tar Baby, holding onto his rump as if that's preventing him from having an accident.

331

"Hold on a second," pleads Agent Wilson, "I want to prove to you that I'm not talking out of my ass and can actually do things. I happen to be a Scientologist who insinuated myself into the CIA to spy on them."

"Dey spyin' on you or you's spyin' on dem? Gets sorta confusin' for us plain folk."

"We're gonna take over the world! Watch this!"

At this point, Otto Wilson, the Scientology CIA agent, takes off his crumpled suit to reveal a tight light blue leotard underneath his clothing. It has a gold cape and gold letters across the chest with the letter "T" inside of an "O" and is the symbol for OT. He then begins to fly around the chamber where the Hall of Records was meant to be.

"Look at me! Look at me! I'm at OT!"

The Scientology CIA agent continues to do loops and whirls in the air.

"Look at all the wonderful things we can do. Now, watch this!"

The agent then banks along a wall. As he turns his head back towards the Tar Baby, he says, "Look, I'm a UFO!"

Looking back at the Tar Baby, and trying to impress him, Agent Wilson does not see where he is going and hits a sarcophagus with an open door. His head collides violently and his neck appears severely injured as he collapses in a heap. The Tar Baby then runs over to the agent's crumpled clothes on the floor and pulls out a cell phone. He does not, however, speak with his normal broken English.

"Cairo 911, please. This is an emergency. Please send the Red Crescent. We've got a horrible injury here with a Westerner in the Hall of Records under the Sphinx at Giza. This could be an international incident so I suggest you send the Red Crescent."

The Tar Baby looks at the audience and says, "I can't's help's it, but's I's got's to go. What I's 'bouts to do was all gunna be pa't o' de unveilin' o' de myst'ry o' de Sphinx, but I's gots held up by dis Agent Wilson. Hope he's ok. Now, you's follows me befo' its all too late."

The Tar Baby then opens a secret entrance in the wall and proceeds down a very long cavern to a chamber which is just beneath the rump of the Sphinx. When he arrives, the unpleasant odor of dung begins to permeate the entire theater. There are flames burning with dung lamps that make the chamber decently lit. Inside the chamber is a stone toilet bowl, not unlike modern day toilets, upon which the Tar Baby jumps upon and sits. He dangles his legs cutely as his feet cannot reach the floor.

"I's told's ya I's had to go!" exclaims the Tar Baby as he makes a big smile and looks at the audience.

"Dis is one o' de greatest myst'ries o' de Sphinx, and ya won't find it in too many o' de mythology texts, but its dere if you's know's where's to look fo' it. De Sphinx was obsessed wit' dung but I's don't t'ink I's be de best one to's tell's ya all 'bout dat. I's gunna turn over dis narration to somebody else."

When the Tar Baby finishes his business, he gets off the stone bowl and waves his hand in a gesture of introduction.

"And now, de Tar Baby steps one rung lowah on de scale of expr'sshin and introduces you's to de Turd Baby."

In a gesture of introduction, the Tar Baby waves his hand toward the stone toilet as a brown rendition of the Tar Baby begins to emerge. First, he straddles one leg over the stone bowl before pulling himself all the way out and onto the floor. As he does so, the dung smell increases.

"Now, ease on down everybody," says the Turd Baby, "Could the management could please turn down the smell and introduce some pleasant odors? I can see this audience isn't quite ready for me."

The Turd Baby and Tar Baby then look at each other and laugh.

"It is true what the Tar Baby said," says the Turd Baby. "Most people do not know about me or what I represent, but the Sphinx always insisted upon being surrounded by dung. The very word *sphinx* evolved into what is known as the sphincter muscle. It means "to hold tight." This is one of the most reductio absurdums of the human condition. The Sphinx, which represents the mystery of the human condition, holds on tight to that which has been rejected and smothers itself in dung so that no one would come near. It suggests the very borders of occult boundaries themselves. Now watch!"

Several scarab beetles then take some dung from the skin of the Turd Baby and begin to carry it and build a home. In a speeded up version of their lives, they represent the principle of regeneration through the use of dung or that which has been rejected. The beetles bury the dung, eat it and lay eggs in it from which larvae emerge to form a myriad of new beetles. As more and more scarab beetles emerge from the dung, they each roll a ball of dung and carry it out a pathway that leads out of the underground chamber and to the area in back of a Sphinx where a funeral pyre has already been constructed. In what would normally be a very long job, a seemingly infinite number of beetles take dung to the pyre until it forms a human-sized rendition of the corpse of L. Ron Hubbard. When they are finally done, the Tar Baby and the Turd Baby ascend to the pyre and look around at the audience but also at a new gathering of Egyptian gods and creatures that have gathered around them. Both the Tar Baby and the Turd Baby are feeling their oats as they give looks of satisfaction at each other, both seemingly very proud of the gathering they have inspired.

"Now," says the Tar Baby, "we's here's to......"

"Wait just a second," interrupts the Turd Baby. "There's one more task to complete."

The Turd Baby then goes over to the corpse effigy, turns it over and puts several puncture marks in the buttocks with a needle. He then turns the body back over.

"There!" says the Turd Baby. "I just wanted everything to be just right. Go ahead, Tar Baby."

"As I was sayin'," continues the Tar Baby, "we's here to do somethin' dat wunt properly done in de first place and dat is ta conduct a proper funeral service fo' L. Ron Hubbard. Dat shameful and disrespectful what was done. Whether'n you like de man or not, proper justice wunt served on de earth plane so de least's we can's do is ta conduct a proper service in the meta plane. Now, we's been waitin' fo' Peter Moon to come out and do de eulogy, but I's just got's word dat he's not commin'."

"What?" asks the Turd Baby. "Do you mean to say that he's sulking in his tent like Achilles?"

"Now, what in de hell you's bring up Achilles and talkin' 'bout him fo'?" asks the Tar Baby in return.

"When Hector, the greatest warrior of Troy, killed Achilles' best friend, Patrocolus, Achilles withdrew his army from the war and refused to fight and sulked in his tent."

"So?" asks the Tar Baby.

"Well, the only thing that could bring him out of his sulking was when he had the chance to fight Hector and get revenge. That was the only thing that could bring him out of his tent. He not only defeated Hector savagely, he tied the body to the back of his chariot and dragged it around the walls of Troy four times. Now, I was thinkin' that if Peter Moon is sulkin' over all this, then maybe that is the only way we're gonna get him out of his tent and do the eulogy. In other words, he could come out in full warrior dress and drag the bodies of Ron's enemies around the Giza plateau four times."

"Now dere you's go again. Dats why's dey calls you de Turd Baby. You's always diggin' up shit to t'row. Now I's just got word t'rough my's earpiece dat Peter Moon has sent a message. He said dat he's not sulkin' at all and ain't motivated by revenge or draggin's people's bodies 'round. He just wanna give a proper funeral and dat gonna take some prep'ration."

The Tar Baby then turns to the audience and speaks once again.

"Sorry's you's all. We's gots ta call an impromptu intermission so dis funeral t'ing can be done right. You's all go's get you's popcorn and soda and we's be back in a bit. Gawd! Dis is only de second feature in de Magick Theater and seems we havin' an interruption every time."

The lights come on and the audience goes to the concession stand.

49

THE DOMAIN OF PLUTO

When L. Ron Hubbard died in January of 1986, telexes were sent to every Scientology organization in the world. Although I had been out of Scientology for almost three years at that time, I was working at a company with a couple of people who had loose affiliations with the Church. Accordingly, the telex was read to me, and I was eventually invited to see a video tape of the funeral service for LRH. On the tape itself, which I did get to see, it was said that it would be available for viewing for only a short time.

The most positive possible spin was put on the events that had occurred. Miscavige said that LRH's body had become an impediment to the research of further OT levels and that, in so many words, he had dropped his body to facilitate further OT research. The live audience that was at the event sucked this up and applauded wildly. They obviously all believed or accepted that the death state could be overcome and that LRH had made the transition knowingly. Besides David Miscavige, who acted as master of ceremonies, Pat Broeker was the other key speaker. The two appeared as friends even though this was to change abruptly in the ensuing months.

Pat Broeker added to the mix by stating that LRH had warned him of his imminent departure twice. The first time was months before he passed away and the second time was right before his final departure. Based upon my knowledge and dealings with both individuals, Pat's statements seemed credible to me at the time, but all the antics I have uncovered since make his testimony suspect. As I have said, Pat had reportedly developed a drinking problem and was assigned to menial chores at this time. One thing he said at the funeral, however, was quite interesting. He told the congregation to only pay attention to what LRH wrote or said and not management. This statement alone was in direct opposition to those who would become the new masters of the Church of Scientology. This could have contributed to his removal by Miscavige, but he was in the way even without that statement. Although he and his wife were announced as the highest ranking officers in the Sea Org, they had no leverage whatsoever in terms of the corporate status of the Church. Pat's disappearance continues to intrigue all Church watchers.

LRH's funeral service was designed to usher in a new era of Scientology, but it all sounded very suspect to me. It was not something I wanted to be a part of. In light of the shenanigans that were pulled off in the wake of LRH's death, I now consider that none of the words said at his Scientology funeral were said with honor or valor. They were said to protect the vested interests of those who could most benefit by them. None of this was in the best interest of the public and certainly not what LRH originally intended with his movement.

In the beginning of this book, I wrote about the astrological aspects of Pluto and how he is the ruler of the constellation Scorpio and has dominion over death, sex, and taxation. When you consider how these various characters, particularly the tax men, manipulated the estate of L. Ron Hubbard and the Church of Scientology, you can easily see that we are dealing with a classic example of Pluto, the god of pure and unadulterated power through coercion.

In astrology or in real life, you cannot escape the realm of Pluto. He has a role to play and a purpose to serve in the scheme of things. He balances the scales but, as was said before, his realm is a very busy one. Pluto, as the "plodding planet," takes over two decades to move through one sign of the zodiac and his work takes a long time to get done. Hades is a crowded place, and there is always more balancing to be done that can occur in a fortnight. Pluto's task is to graduate souls through purgatory by purging them of their inequities. If he has you on the end of a sharp stick, it is because you got yourself there. Once you wake up and smell the coffee of why you are there, you are allowed to move on, but only if you accept the task that Pluto lays before you.

Originally, I never meant to write this book. As I write these words, I still do not know exactly how it will turn out. It has become, however, a Plutonian task and a process in its own right. Essentially, I have put forth a story that L. Ron Hubbard devised procedures that can not only enable men to overcome their limitations but can actually free the spirit from imprisonment in a body. Further, that these techniques can be administered in a way that is enjoyable and preferable to an individual. Additionally, I have put forth the idea and example that I was able to avail myself of these procedures to the point where I was not only able to achieve my goals but also penetrate mysteries beyond my wildest dreams. Unfortunately, I have not presented a very positive light on the institution which I formerly belonged to. This, in and of itself, is a Plutonian communication. You have been told of a wonderful prospect, but Pluto is there with his pitchfork, standing before you and blocking the way.

Personally, I cannot say what this means for you. I can only say what it means to me. It is beneficial, however, to take a deeper look at the archetype known as Pluto.

Pluto, which rules Scorpio, is a water sign. This is somewhat mysterious because a scorpion lives in the desert. Originally, however, the sign of Scorpio was known as the water dragon. Water refers to the emotions, and in a Scorpio, these run very deep. Pluto, therefore, operates in the realm of emotions. It creates an emotional catharsis in an individual.

In Taoism, water is considered to be the most powerful of all physical substances because it can penetrate anything. By telling the truth of a situation (such as in this book), it leaks not only the information but the resonant emotions that go with the subject. Pluto does not seek to stop water. In fact, the river Styx is the passage way of the dead and it runs right through his realm.

It is only through the events and circumstances surrounding the death of L. Ron Hubbard that I have been able to make a case for what he brought to the table in his lifetime. The most virtuous and exalted aspects of what he had to offer will not be grasped for hundreds of years on a cultural basis. The ultimate value with regard to what I have written here will be for future generations.

Pluto will use the most coercive and ugly means imaginable, if necessary, to take you to a place where you can shed your old skin and experience renewal. This is one of the reasons we live and die. If we do not learn the lessons of the past or have karmic scores to settle, Pluto will put us in a repeat mode or a situation where the scales can be balanced.

For those of you who have been either beleaguered, plagued, or abused by the Scientology experience, I can only say that no one escapes the realm of Pluto. These issues can be most complicated at times, on both sides of the coin. If you blame others for too long, people will get tired of you. It is better to find a constructive outlet for your energies. It is a hard cold fact of existence that justice does not necessarily prevail over the course of one lifetime.

For many people, particularly those who are not intimated or terrified by it, Scientology represented or represents the eye of illumination; whereby one becomes cognizant of self-referential concepts and thinking that reach beyond the state of the ordinary human mind. In its grander aspects, Scientology enables people to become exterior from their normal state of consciousness and see the sky as the limit. The biggest trick in any spiritual pursuit, however, is to keep your reference to the ground. You do not want to end up in a Cairo hospital like Agent Wilson.

50

THE ANTI-RON

When I left Scientology and went to Long Island in 1983, I was very satisfied with the progress I had made in Scientology. In fact, I felt something akin to a prize winning race horse who had completed his banner years and was being put out to pasture to graze. Moving into a suburban life-style, which I had not known since I had left home at the age of 18, I envisioned myself in an idyllic world where I was living "happily ever after."

As a group effort or international movement, the Scientology movement had been a disappointment, but I was not going to let that disturb my karmic peace. As far as I was concerned, I would live out this life in relative harmony, love my wife to the very end, and be completely free upon reaching the state of death. Whether or not what I have stated is or was a pipe dream or state of beingness I have earned, it is quite likely that you may never know the relative truth of the matter. I did have an experience, however, that encouraged me to think that I might be right about this consideration.

One day, when visiting a chiropractic clinic on Long Island, I was having some blood work done as a requisite to continuing my treatment. It was only a routine blood diagnosis. As I sat in a chair, an attendant was drawing blood from my arm into a test tube. While I do not particularly enjoy having my blood drawn, I was neither horrified nor even overly anxious about what was happening. In fact, I sat in an upright position and was fully prepared to watch the blood transfer from my vein into the test tube vial. Apparently, this procedure did not go over too well with my subconscious mind because something shut down, and I have no detailed memory of what ensued immediately thereafter. I do, however, remember the vial beginning to fill with my blood.

The next thing I knew, I was in the most peaceful state of mind that I had ever known. I was free from my body and had at long last achieved the stable state of exteriorization. I was fully cognizant of who and what I was and was utterly delighted. Everything I had ever learned in Scientology with regard to the state of exteriorization made sense, and I was happy that I had learned it. But, I was not in a state of mind where I wanted to live in a body anymore and live a humdrum existence on planet Earth. It all seemed so boring. I felt that I could experience this wonderful state of *Om* forever if I so chose.

There was, however, one minor detail that I had not attended to. I was not particularly aware of how I had arrived in this state or of the circumstances surrounding it. Slowly, it began to dawn on me that I had recently been living on planet Earth. This did not move me too much, and I thought it might be nice not to have to return to Earth. I felt that I could reside in this new state as long as I wanted. As my Earth life began to impinge on me, however, I remembered that I had a wife and knew that she would be completely distraught and upset if I died. There was no doubt about that in my mind. I had received my license to depart and was free to go. Like my old friend Ralph, it was my choice. My parents were gone, and I was not particularly close or involved with my siblings. A departure would have been completely acceptable save for the fact that I loved my wife and did not want her to suffer by reason of my departure. Reluctantly, but loyally, I decided to return to the Earth plane. I can remember these decisions very well, even though I was not immediately aware of the particular circumstances around me.

The next thing I knew was that I heard various people rushing and scurrying about. They were panicking and there was considerable commotion. I heard a male voice say, "He just had a seizure."

When I heard this, my first impulse was to quickly find this person who was having a seizure so that I could help them. Opening my eyes, I looked up and realized that I was laying on the floor. I tried to talk, but no words came out. I realized that the person who was having a seizure was me. My eyes and my thinking facilities were working fine, but the speech mechanism was completely kaput. My next concern was for the doctors who had surrounded me. I wanted to alleviate them of their concern and obvious anxiety over what had happened to me. Consequently, I began to make motions with my hands and fingers in an attempt to let them know that I was all right. I seemed more concerned about letting them know that I was awake and alive than I was about my own loss of the speech mechanism. After a short while, my ability to talk returned, and I told them what was happening. Everything was coming back to normal, and they explained to me that I did not really have a seizure but had apparently fainted. It was, however, a completely wonderful experience for me. The physical disorientation was extremely minimal and I recovered completely. I felt relaxed as if I had just gotten back from a long vacation. I drove home and told my wife about the incident. I have been relatively healthy ever since.

Putting this story together, this incident reminds me a bit of Ron's "Excalibur incident," but I was not presented or pelted with streams of data. On the other hand, I was not in need of data. I had already learned what I needed to learn. It was during this general time period, however, than I learned of Hubbard's extensive interest in and pursuit of the supernatural via the work of Jack Parsons and the legacy of Aleister Crowley. I was now connecting up, subconsciously and consciously, with the antecedents of the Scientology movement.

Sometime around this general period, I was in the last phases of a business that I was a part of in Manhattan. Walking up Fifth Avenue near Washington Square, I ran into a familiar face walking down the sidewalk. Unless it is someone who works in your building or neighborhood, I have always found it extremely rare to run into someone you know in New York City, particularly if it is from a previous time period in your life. This gentleman's name was Peter, and I remembered him from when he had joined the Sea Org in 1974. Meeting him on the street was pure unadulterated synchronicity. I had known him then and also when he worked in Clearwater as an artist. Peter was a very nice guy. We said hello and actually visited each other in person after that and had different phone conversations. Both he and his wife had witnessed many of the same things I had in Scientology and no longer wanted to be a part of it.

What Peter told me, however, was very interesting when one considers the Anti-Ron or negative news that has been proliferated about LRH. Peter had no personal interaction with LRH as I had, but he was neither bitter nor serving an agenda when he told me the following.

Before he had left, Peter was doing some auditing procedures with a girl who had served directly under LRH as a Commodore's Messenger. I remembered her quite well and recalled stories from others about how she would rub LRH's back for him. There was no suggestion of impropriety there, but I mention it so that you will understand that she was very close to Ron. For some reason, she began telling Peter things in her auditing that he felt she wanted him to know. It was his feeling that it did not have so much to do with her auditing, but it seemed her way of conveying the truth to him without "spilling the beans" and getting in trouble. In an auditing session, you could basically say anything you wanted to without fear of reprisal.

This girl explained how she one time found LRH looking in the mirror and saying "Poor Ronnie, Poor Ronnie......the Markabians are coming to get me."

In Scientology, the Markabians[*] represent a political system in outer space that our solar system falls under in a loose group of planets known as the Markab Confederacy. They are Scientology's version of the so-called Illuminati. Earth culture is believed to have been roughly patterned after the Markabians. It allows some personal freedom but the society is largely confined and regimented, particularly at the top.

Whether or not the space opera scenario outlined is true or not is not the point. What is important here is that this was a word of mouth report that Ron was having some problems. On the other hand, maybe Ron was just talking to himself or thinking out loud. Perhaps it was even a semiconscious recognition about what was

[*] As I edited this book, the most amusing synchronicity occurred. As I was editing an earlier chapter that contained the name Meade Emory, a phrase said "Meade Emory is a Markabian agent." I have no idea how that chapter got confused with this one because this is the only chapter to reference the Markabians, and I have not used the singular word "Markabian."

happening to him on the earth plane. It is plainly obvious that he was being moved in on by forces that were hostile to him. While we all talk to ourselves from time to time, his expression betrays someone who was in an extremely vulnerable psychological state.

Here is your Anti-Ron. This is clearly not a man who was at complete cause over matter, energy, space and time. There are, of course, many other more vitriolic accounts of his personal vulnerabilities, but these are almost always told by people with an axe to grind. This was just a breezy report that floated to me by way of synchronicity. LRH knew he was being cornered, and there was not too much he could do about it. This is not at all meant to be a condemnation of Ron, but he was never immune to his own principles. He was under the influence of suppression and this clearly neutralized his ability to do some of the more spectacular things he was also known for. It is too easy to bare your fangs and point at perceived flaws while you throw the baby out with the bath water.

Although Ron would live for a handful of years after this incident, the curtain was being drawn shut on his life. All things considered, his departure certainly could have been far more graceful. This is not meant to be a condemnation of him either. Death meets every one of us differently. Timothy Leary is an interesting example in this regard. Having acquired prostate cancer, Leary was enthusiastically prepared to flout his nose at death by committing suicide live on the internet. This was intended to be a progressive statement of consciousness to people who are afraid of or intimidated by the death process. Despite Leary's noble wishes and willingness to put his truth into the limelight by making a dramatic exit, the publicity stunt did not come off. Leary's heart was in the right place, but his head was not able to match the wits of the Grim Reaper. What happened was that he underestimated the death process itself, particularly as it related to him. While death can be quick and slick, the body also has a way of deteriorating in a process of attrition whereby one loses more and more faculties and suffering increases. This can also have a severe effect on the mental and emotional state of the person. Accordingly, Leary suffered his way into a state whereby he was not quite up to his normal "prankster self" that could have pulled off the dramatic exit he wanted. This does not mean that

Leary was wrong. It only means that he miscalculated. The only thing he really lost in this regard was enjoying himself while gloating over a dramatic exit.

Death comes on its own terms. It is a rhythm I have come to respect and know in my life. It beats to its own drum, and the best you can do is to align yourself with it. Some things are inevitable. If we are able to influence the process, we may have done a remarkable thing, but we still have to come to a pact with the Grim Reaper. If we are smart and lucky, the reaping does not have to be so grim. In any event, a person's contributions are not judged only by the method of his departure.

In professional sports, some players exit their careers gracefully and/or dramatically. Some walk away before their time has come. Others have to be told to leave or pitifully become shadows of their former selves. In the end, they are remembered for their contributions and accomplishments when they were in their peak playing form. Even Christ was allowed to have moments of despondency in the final hours of life.

When LRH died, a part of me died. I knew I would never go back to Scientology. What I did not know, however, is that I would be called back into action. As I have already alluded to, the seeds of this call began when I discovered that LRH had been so involved in the magick of Aleister Crowley of Jack Parsons. This revelation occurred in the Forbidden Planet bookstore in Manhattan. One day, after work, I was browsing through science fiction books and discovered the book *L. Ron Hubbard: Madman or Messiah?* which was still hot off the press. Reading about LRH's admiration for Crowley and his work with Jack Parsons, I readily recognized that the writer of this book was bitter and was pandering to an audience that would be shocked and titillated by his various claims. Although the book is presented in a matter that is serving an agenda of its own and is completely out of context to what I have stated in this book, I recognized that there were many loose ends that needed to be studied. If LRH had spent so much time studying magick, I wanted to learn about it, too. This was another dimension to the man, and I knew too little about it. It was not an insignificant part of his heritage and life experience. Consequently, I poured through everything I could readily find on the subject of Aleister Crowley and magick.

As everything turned out, the Anti-Ron and all of the many variations thereof that have presented in various books and other media proved itself to have a very limited use to what I was about to deal with. He did have some use though. If it were not for the lurid and crazed portrayals of LRH being an acolyte of Aleister Crowley, I might never have discovered the heritage of him being a member of the Wilson* clan and all that it represents. In this respect, the lower forces of the Anti-Ron served me well. On the other hand, if it were not for the positive Ron, I would never have been able to chart the map, let alone penetrate the unknown territory that I was about to encounter.

---

* LRH's father's surname was Wilson before being adopted by the Hubbards. As you can read about in my other works, much of my writing career has been precipitated by very bizarre synchronicities surrounding the name Wilson. The beginning of this quest is delineated in *Montauk Revisited: Adventures in Synchronicity* by Preston Nichols and Peter Moon.

51

MONTAUK ECHO

Scientology is based upon the proposition that you are an eternal and unkillable being that has unlimited ability. Every day, prospective Scientologists and existing Scientologists sell themselves on this idea. Many of you have already reached a similar conclusion by other means than Scientology. Ray Bradbury was one such person and he inspired me in this direction via the aesthetic band of writing.

There are also those who believe they are "clay" bodies that are really nothing more than the result of a spontaneous concoction of amino acids that have acquired a sophisticated pattern of reaction and response that has evolved to the point whereby an outside observer can chant Dr. Frankenstein's mantra *"It's alive! It's alive!"*

You can look at this in at least two ways. First, there are those in life who will encourage you to reach for the stars and achieve your potential. Others, more numerous, will generally treat assertions of immortality as being hubris and would tend to discourage the prospect of anyone having discovered anything that is significant or otherwise different from the status quo world. This latter response is usually rendered in a manner that is suggestive of the respondent's own personal failures and limited horizons.

None of the above, however, is meant to suggest that one should yield to fervent and foolish enthusiasm that is completely unchecked. This, as stated before, is the super hero syndrome I encountered in Scientology. Manic assertions and states of being can often be quite amusing, but beyond that, they do not really serve anyone too well. Imagining your abilities and talking about them are not the same as going out and utilizing them.

This sort of dilemma occurs in sporting events quite frequently. A big strong man visualizes he is a great boxer, only to have his clock cleaned when he steps in the ring with an inferior looking opponent. Such a boxer might have the genuine ability and strength to become a champion but has not yet learned how to apply his abilities. Being in the ring or on stage is considerably different than visualizing it. The events you encounter in the battlefield are never exactly quite the same as what were drawn up in the battle plan at headquarters.

As I have stated, I absorbed an incredible amount of information during my twelve years in Scientology. I have only given a scant summary in this book. Besides that, I had a lot of experience in utilizing it. During all those years of training and auditing, my knowledge was primarily directed towards applying it to the extension of the Scientology movement. This is quite logical if you consider the degree to which I was assisted in my own spiritual development. When I came to the sober realization that the movement was curtailed to an incredible extent, I still carried a legacy of information and knowledge with me, but there was no direct channel for it. Like water finding the passage way of least resistance, this knowledge ended up leaking into the most mysterious of cracks that eventually manifested as either remarkable or joyous representations of recognition. This is synchronicity.

Many years ago, Hubbard reported on an interesting observation with Scientology clears and OTs. He said that if you put one in an area of society, considerable confusion would automatically clear up in that area. It could mean a lower crime rate in a neighborhood or something as mundane as a functioning and thriving hot dog stand. I definitely noticed this myself when I was in Scientology and saw various OTs take over a particular area or job sector. Where confusion had once been reigning, it would all of a sudden clear up and run like clockwork.

When I first came to Long Island in 1983, I was not so lucky so as to have such an impact on my environment. Personally, I had never experienced a place that was so psychically dense. It took me seven years of living there before I began to start connecting the dots that began to reveal patterns of synchronicity. This began when I heard the tales of Preston Nichols about a huge radar transmitter at an old Air Force station at Montauk Point that not only jammed psychic energy but also served a multitude of strange and mysterious agendas. Quite oddly, the tales of the Montauk Project, and what is represented, dovetailed utterly and completely with the theories of L. Ron Hubbard. There was only one problem. Hubbard underestimated his opposition's capabilities, particularly in regard to their wherewithal on Earth. If not, his life would have ended quite differently. Even so, his contributions should not be considered any less by reason of this. One can only do so much in any given life.

If the Government had once served as the adversary of organized Scientology, then the Montauk Project was the quintessential psychic adversary of such a movement. It was using amplified psychic energy to manipulate and control the environment through nonhuman means. That included the manipulation of individuals as well. This became very clear to me as I listened to Preston Nichols' extensive accounts of the Montauk Project. Regardless of whether they were real or partly imagined, it was obvious to me that he was a refugee from an implant station. This prospect would be novel in and of itself to some degree, but the fact that he is a screaming genius on many subjects and is able to correlate them in a unique way is certainly noteworthy in its own right. More importantly, his tales have offered a new quantum paradigm for people to think about and a new way for humanity to look upon itself.

When I first met Preston Nichols, he had been cast adrift by his employers that he had so loyally served for a majority of his adult life. He had been part of countless "spook projects" or black budget activities that were never meant to be public knowledge. Had his employers offered him a tad or two of kindness, it is possible that they never would have had to deal with the recoil of his stories going public. It is important to remember, however, that the people utilizing him in such projects were not kind. They cannot think in those terms but only in terms of bribes or lower impulses. Had the Church of Scientology paid for my root canal, maybe I would have stayed in their fold.

Although it is now in the rather distant past, writing *The Montauk Project: Experiments in Time* was a big deal. It not only enabled me to realize my dream of a writing career, but the adventures associated with it thrust me into a new world of creative experiences. One of these occurred while I was driving home from Preston Nichols' home beneath the dark skies of Long Island. The manuscript for *The Montauk Project* was virtually done, and we had just tied up some loose ends. Although the book would not be published for six or more months at that point, it was a given that it would be. I knew that. It just needed some more fine tuning and production work. It was also very exciting because, even though there was no formal publicity, the world was waiting to hear it. I could feel the energy. It was in this frame of mind, while driving, that I had a visit from my ancestors, just as I had described after the death of my parents. It was very indistinct. I mean, nothing like a ghost or genie appeared on either occasion. It was something you just feel that comes into your space and you have a tacit understanding with it. The only explanation I had for this phenomenon at the time was that my ancestors were elated because somebody on their genetic line had done something significant. It seemed to make all their living worthwhile. Apparently, the entire affair was a big deal to them. With the advantage of hindsight, I can now tell you that I was underestimating my ancestors in the extreme. They were excited all right but not simply over the fact that one of their descendants had created some notoriety. Somehow, they knew something I did not and that *The Montauk Project* was to eventually serve as a vehicle for explaining and reviving aspects of their ancient past that have fallen by the wayside. Most of this will be delineated in my next book, *The Montauk Book of the Living*, but it is mentioned here to put some context on how that book and the one you are reading relate.

Besides the above and realizing my dream as a writer, the writing of *The Montauk Project* unleashed a torrent of new experiences, both on a personal and collective basis. If I were to glamorize these experiences with drama or hyperbole, I would tell you that it was like opening the Ark of the Covenant in the movie *Raiders of the Lost Ark*. In my personal life, all sorts of bipolar spirits and psychic debris emerged from the woodwork. While this was sometimes very interesting and adventurous, it was always dramatic. It was, however, not something that most people are suited for or equipped to deal with.

Engaging Preston Nichols on a personal basis can have considerable fallout for various individuals. It is not that Preston is a bad person or is even at fault in this regard, but he has been exposed to many quantum variables which can readily send people running with their tail between their legs. It is really just a matter of self-reflection, but again, we are dealing with portions of the mind/brain function which have been shut down. If it were not for the training and auditing I had done, I would not have been able to navigate this stream of consciousness. Preston has a nice personality, but the quantum variables can be quite stressful, either to him or to those who are around him. It is quite easy for some people to interface with him on a normal and regular basis. When you get into the deeper aspects of his experiences, however, there can be repercussions. These could be dreams of UFO's, abductions or even the real thing. I used to have black helicopters appearing at noteworthy times, particularly when I was thinking certain thoughts. At one such moment, a stealth fighter appeared about a hundred yards over my house in suburbia. It is easy to dismiss these things as coincidences, but they can also send an unstable mind over the bend. Perhaps that is what they were there to do, but as they never developed into any other tangible phenomena, I never gave them much credence. It is like believing in spooks or the bogey man. The more you fear, the more problems you have.

Besides Preston, there were other issues that offered challenges. This could include a phone call or someone showing up in front of your house in an attempt to intimidate. More often than not, however, it was usually people being stone-cold afraid to talk to me about such matters. From all of the various people I had met, I knew there was something at work that went far beyond the imagination or experiences of Preston Nichols. He was, however, the most lucid representative for what had gone at Montauk and was the only one willing to offer significant information.

Opening up the doors to the Montauk Project was like opening up a Pandora's Box of collective rage and other emotions that had been stored up there and suppressed or otherwise hidden from view. It stands to reason that if we live in bodies with close to ninety percent of their brain capacity shut down, there is or was some major effort to shut that capacity down. The Montauk Project is the most representative format of such that I have encountered. Whereas scenarios of Illuminati type groups generally tend to deal with political manipulations, the Montauk Project deals with technologies that embrace the full band of the electromagnetic spectrum.

Many years earlier, I read Hubbard's writings about the electromagnetic techniques that were presumably employed against every known individual on the whole track. These sounded as bizarre as anything I had ever heard up to that point, and it was certainly anything beyond what I had ever heard anyone else imagine. Eventually, as I became more versed in the practice of Dianetics and Scientology, I took up Hubbard's challenge to apply such ideas. From a subjective viewpoint, in my various and many auditing sessions, I addressed every form of electromagnetic torture or disorientation that I could imagine. Whether I did a perfect job or not, I know that I certainly predisposed myself towards being immune from such attacks. I only did this, however, to relieve my own personal trauma that I conceived had happened on the whole track. Now, with my adventuring into the Montauk Project, the entire proposition became manifest in my newly chosen career but also in my daily life.

In essence, the Montauk Project represents the collective hell of the unconscious mind. I literally had to be able to walk through hell in order to digest the information and write about it. My passing through "hell" had actually been done years earlier in my auditing sessions.

Since *The Montauk Project: Experiments in Time* was written, there has been no shortage of people coming forward and claiming to be this, that or the other thing. There is a considerable cult following on the internet. Unfortunately, I have seen too many people become obsessed with the gravity of the trauma inflicted upon them and the intricate machinations and complexity of mind control. The objective of such people should be to simply clear out their electromagnetic field. It does not require a huge public forum or craving for approval from others. When people are making a career or hobby out of trauma, they are too often barking up a wrong tree and end up propagating more of the same. With common sense and good fortune, you should be able to find the correct techniques.

I am not unsympathetic towards people who have gone through vigorous mind-control experiments or forced subjugation of any kind. Support groups are important. On the other hand, as I write these words, I am not promising a solution or even offering you seminars or workshops on the subject. If I were to dare to be so bold and enterprising as to emulate or reprise what Hubbard did, I would only run into serious trouble if I was very successful. Only then would I have repressive forces trying to monitor and suppress my efforts. If you build up a mediocre personal practice that gets mediocre results, nobody really cares too much. None of the above are jobs that I want. I am only here to help the water of life find its path of least resistance. The best I can offer is to suggest that there are solutions. This book is only the briefest of outlines of how they might work.

The entire prospect of the Montauk Project is a barbwired proposition. It sometimes has a tendency to open up portions of the mind which people are not ready to deal with. This is one of the reasons that it has not been as accepted by the media as it otherwise might be. It is not only waking up centers of the brain that are not amenable to being opened, it is hitting areas of the brain that certain parties want closed. When an individual is not sufficiently grounded or stable, he or she can become quite chaotic when exposed to such information. Consequently, in my personal life, there were several characters who became quite chaotic. Sometimes they were acting out of their own frustrations or jealousy. In the end, it did not matter. Although I had achieved success as a writer, my personal life began to suffer strains and hardships that were not in keeping with all of the wonderful experiences I have shared with you. Once I had achieved a significant degree of success, it seemed that different contingents were dedicated to knocking me off of some imaginary soap box that they perceived I was standing on. All of this had to do with the lessons of power that were iterated earlier in this book. Once you demonstrate that you have some power, even if it is not very much, you would be surprised at the vultures that come out to roost and decry you.

The end result of various personal attacks that have been committed against me have not deeply hurt me. I am quite exterior to that nonsense. What it was eventually able to do, at least for a significant time, was inhibit my writing career. This did not stop things but only delayed them. Like water, synchronicity began continued to drip off my fingers, particularly as it involved looking into the occult connections behind and surrounding the Montauk Project.

52

HOME

As those of you who are familiar with my work already know, my foraging into the Montauk Project led to bizarre experiences of synchronicity focused around the names of Wilson and Cameron which eventually brought me to the front door of Marjorie Cameron. Marjorie, who was known as "Cameron," was the focal point of the "Babalon Working," a magical experiment worked by Jack Parsons and L. Ron Hubbard that was designed to incarnate the Goddess Babalon and reverse the patriarchal tyranny that has ruled the Earth for some time. This experience, which is chronicled in both *Montauk Revisited: Adventures in Synchronicity* and *Synchronicity and the Seventh Seal*, has in many ways served as the hallmark of my writing career. I had just completed my first book when I met her, but the experiences leading to her and subsequently stemming from this meeting have led me to many wonderful revelations. Her impact on the world has still been under appreciated and grossly underestimated. If it were not for her, I would not be writing this book.

There is no question that it was a bit kooky for me to be meeting with L. Ron Hubbard's old magical associate, someone he frequented with years prior to Scientology. Meeting Cameron was a fascinating experience in itself, but I was only pursuing her because of the synchronicity associated with her last name. The fact that she knew Ron and was connected to him via the Babalon Working was incidental and was by no means a focal point of my inquiry. Looking back, it is quite an oddity that I was not only meeting a member of the same gene pool* but a magical partner whose very essence seemed to reek of being a major antecedent to the Scientology movement, particularly when you consider that both represented gateways of information. In some strange way, it was as if I was being given a privileged view through a rare and archaic window pane.

In my discussions with Cameron, she told me that synchronicity is the language of magick and that my life was laced with it. Although there was at first no seeming connection, my experience directly after meeting her would prove to be an equally significant synchronicity. The whole process of what had transpired, however, took quite a while to dawn on me. I did not know it at the time, but right after meeting with Cameron, my next stop would be with the Lackson family, my friends mentioned in the preface to this book who gave me my first glimpse of the meaning behind the holiday we know as Halloween.

Immediately after meeting Cameron, I headed directly for the neighborhood I had grown up in Southern California. It was then twenty-nine years since I had lived there and about sixteen years since I had visited the area. I was going to visit Vivian Arcuri and her son Jeff, my old next door neighbors. Their family had been very close to mine as I grew up in the 1950's and early 1960's. She is the closest thing I have to a mother, and I will occasionally call her on Mother's Day and say hello. She is the mother of my best friend, Greg, but I would not get to see him on that day. He was on a fishing trip with his father in Mexico.

As I was early for my meeting with Vivian and Jeff, I had some time to kill. Vivian had already told me that the Lackson family still lived in the neighborhood so I decided to walk down the street and pay a visit. I still fondly remembered celebrating Halloween with them in 1960 and experiencing my first real bonding with that holiday. Having not seen them in two decades, I did not really know what to expect. I had, however, experienced different visualizations of returning to visit them someday. In some strange way, I always knew I would go back there.

* Upon meeting her, I learned from her that her last name was Cameron, but that it was an adopted name from her uncle. She was originally a Wilson, and so was L. Ron Hubbard. From her red hair and facial features, it was very clear to me that I was sitting with someone who was at least a distant relative of LRH. The resemblance was astonishing.

When I knocked on the door, Bill Lackson came to the porch and greeted me. He had been my friend when we were little kids. Although considerably older, he looked just as I remembered him. I was surprised to see his older sister, Sandra, come to the door as well. She no longer lived in the family home, but she looked practically identical to what I remembered of her as a teenager. It seemed as if she had hardly aged at all.

They remembered me quite well, and they certainly remembered my father. He was always very sociable and nice to them. I remember him often going out of his way to invite Bill to come along with us if we were going on a particular outing. Our grandmothers, who were both from Europe, had also been friends.

Telling them only a little bit about what I was up to, I gave them a copy of *The Montauk Project* which was then not even a month old. Ann then said something which struck a harmonic chord with me.

"Maybe you'll be the next Ray Bradbury!" she said.

Although my writing shares some similar themes to Ray Bradbury, I have a completely different style and approach to writing than he does. Nevertheless, he was my original inspiration, and I was extremely touched that she would mention him in such a manner, particularly as he was such an aficionado of Halloween. I did not even know that Ann was a fan of Ray Bradbury. It was almost as if the spirit of Halloween, via the name of Ray Bradbury, was coming out of the woodwork of a house I had enjoyed myself in so many years before.

I was particularly struck by all the furnishings and accoutrements of a modern household. When I knew them, Ann was a struggling widow and the household furnishings were comparatively sparse to those of most of my friends. In particular, I remembered a day when I was helping Ann clean the kitchen and took note of so many empty cupboards. When I naively commented on the emptiness, she then explained to me something about the economics of life. As Ann recalled her version of the discussion we once had, she said that I was one of the most positive people she had ever known. This women had lost her husband and was raising two children, and here I was as an eight or nine-year-old telling her that no matter how bad a situation was, you could always do something about it. I do not remember exactly what I said, but I do remember offering a very positive outlook. She had never forgotten it. Inside, I cannot tell you how ecstatic I was that her life had improved so much. At least one situation in the world seemed to have gotten better. This one just happened to concern the purveyors of what I always considered to be my initiation into Halloween.

The cute memories inside of my head were all well and fine, but then Ann dropped something of an emotional bomb on me. At some point in the conversation, I do not remember exactly when, the conversation turned to my parents. When she had received the news that they had died, it had been eleven years since we had lived there. Our families were no longer close at that point. The memories, however, were not forgotten. She told me that ever since their deaths, she had prayed for them every Sunday in church. When she said this, a sort of shock went through my system that I was not able to digest for a very long time. I have never been so deeply touched as when I heard those words come out of her mouth.

At the time of my parents' death, I had achieved a very quick closure. For whatever reason, I was quite able to move on with the rest of my life. In the meantime, Ann had been paying her respects to them every Sunday and praying for their souls. In my estimation, based upon my own subjective perceptions, they needed a lot of praying for. It was not that they were bad people, but if my subtle perceptions are at all correct, they suffered a severe amount of disorientation after the accident.

It was not until a considerable amount of time after visiting the Lacksons that I was able to put together how the theme of Halloween had entered my life just after meeting Cameron. Halloween is based upon the holiday of Samhain, the last day of the year in the Celtic calendar. It is a time to honor dead souls. Being in the Lackson household, thirty-two years after my playful initiation into Halloween, I was now receiving the full thrust and meaning of the holiday through the legacy of my parents. Although my parents had long since passed from the stage of life, I was to find some very surprising meaning in what had transpired so many years ago. Much to my surprise, the circumstances of their burial would resurface twenty-five years later and shine like a beacon across the stream of my research.

Two years after visiting Cameron and my old neighborhood, I would return once again. This time, I would bring my wife and child. Additionally, my two siblings would visit the neighborhood with me and there would be an old neighborhood reunion with those few families who were left from so many years ago. This time, I got to see my best friend, Greg, and his father, Sam, who only had a short time to live at that point. I was delighted to see Sam before he passed because he was one of the most incredible characters I ever knew. He was like a second father to me. After my parents funeral, he had offered to help me in any way he could and even offered to take in my brother and sister. I regret that this could not have been arranged as I think it would have been a smoother transition for my siblings. When he died, I dedicated my book *The Black Sun* to him.

After an afternoon of showing old home movies of the neighborhood and socializing, it came time to leave. The conversation suddenly turned to my parents who had hardly been mentioned thus far, at least in terms of their death. I cannot tell you how sombre and sad the mood became. Everyone remembered the best and vibrant times of my parents. This was when we were relatively young, and we all lived in the optimistic baby boom era. The sadness and grief, although not as intense as I had experienced at the funeral twenty years earlier, had returned. I felt that the presence of myself and my siblings was reminding everyone quite poignantly of two dear friends they had lost so many years ago. Even though it was thirty years since we had moved from the neighborhood, it was as if everyone had gone back in time to enjoy the memories of the past.

As we drove back to our hotel, my wife commented that the grief was unbearable. She knew very little about my parents, but she got to share their legacy on that particular day. I was very happy she was with me.

The next day, I sent my wife and daughter back to New York while I stayed on to attend a book fair and have my second meeting with Marjorie Cameron. Quite oddly, I ended up checking into another hotel which I only later realized was where I had spent my honeymoon with my first wife. As the name of the hotel had changed, I did not recognize it. It was very strange to be experiencing this sort of synchronicity. Southern California may be my original home, but it is far too large an area to expect this sort of thing to happen.

The next few days were spent with Cameron and adventuring in Pasadena. (This has been reported on in *Synchronicity and the Seventh Seal*.) It was after my second meeting with Cameron that I began to experience the most amazing and meaningful series of synchronicities that I have ever known. It would once again interlink with the theme of death and, quite mysteriously, come back to the theme of my parents.

It all began when I received a very rare and unusual gift that was to serve as the catalyst for me to write the book you are now reading. It was a framed playbill from the early 1900's from the New Montauk Theater which also contained a picture of the Mount of Olives. This gift served as a vehicle for incredible synchronicities to my enter my life and instigated a vast search which led me into some of the most fascinating streams of information that I have ever encountered. The investigation has gone on for ten years, but I have thus far been unable to write it all down. I would bridge into that whole book right now, but it is far too long and will have to be relegated to another volume. Phase One of the investigation was completed long ago. By Phase One, I am referring to the initial research. Phase Two is committing it to writing in a formal manner and doing additional research to follow up different threads. I did not require more information but just needed time to write everything down. It was all about synchronicities with olives. You would be reading it now, with the same title, *The Montauk Book of the Dead*, save for a very bizarre occurrence that occurred in February 2000, just before my divorce was about to become final. All I can say is that it was a sad time. It is probably more accurate to describe it as being a time of heavy emotions. During the winter school recess, I decided to take my daughter to Southern California and visit my friends and family. It had been six years since my daughter had been there, and it was a perfect age to reintroduce her to her cousins so that she could experience my side of the family.

Arriving on a Saturday, it was a beautiful Southern California day, and we played a family game of whiffle ball after dinner. The next day, I had arranged to visit an old friend in Santa Barbara. Sunday morning, I took my daughter and headed north on Highway

101. It was one of the rainiest days I have ever seen. The weather conditions were absolutely horrible. For those of you who are familiar with alchemy, water represents emotions. As I drove north, my daughter slept in the back and was out like a light. I could not only feel the emotions of my divorce and all that it represented, I was getting close to the turnoff that led to my parents' grave. The twenty-fifth anniversary of their passing had just passed. This trip was to facilitate the first time I would ever visit their grave site since their burial. I was not going to do it today, however. As I approached the turnoff, I could not help but notice a sign. It signified a historic landmark for "Adobe Los Olivas" which I knew means "house of the olives" in Spanish. All of a suidden, it became astonishingly clear to me that my parents were buried near the Adobe Los Olivas, whatever that was. After all of the investigating I had done on the subject of olives, I was now being smacked in the face with one more synchronicity, only this one concerned my parents. I had no idea they had been buried anywhere near such an edifice. At the time they were buried, I had no attention on olives or adobes at all.

When I returned to my sister's home that evening, I asked her about Adobe Los Olivas, and she explained to me that the Olivas family were once the wealthiest family in the region. The cemetery where my parents were buried had once been the property of the Olivas family. Adobe Los Olivas was the main house of what had once been the most prosperous Mexican ranchero in California.

It is hard to explain the ontological shock of this synchronicity. This is mostly because you have not yet read my investigation of the olives. In some strange way, it seemed as if my ancient ancestors were sending me a message. This time, however, they did not appear to me as they had done two times previously. This was just a bop on the third eye. What was the universe trying to tell me? I already had what I considered to be a fascinating book to write on my synchronicities with olives. It reached out to the Montauk tribe, the rightful owners of Montauk Point and to historical ties to ancient Atlantis that are in plain site but have remained obscure to historians. Although I still have not written the book, I think it is more interesting and important than the one you are now reading. It definitely expounds on the legacy of

Cameron or Babalon, and in a most intriguing way. In fact, what I have just written about my parents being buried on the property of the Olivas would make a perfect and dramatic ending to that book (which will now be titled *The Montauk Book of the Living*). So, why am I putting it in this book? It is awkward. It fits better in the next book, but my stream of consciousness literally dictated that it must be in this book, partly because it explains why I wrote this book.

In what was probably a year after discovering my parents synchronistic affiliation with the olives, I was having dreams about some of my old friends at the Scientology center in Davis. The center, one of the most thriving Scientology missions ever, had long since been abandoned, if not deliberately destroyed, by Church management after the renaissance movement failed; but the dreams were coming through loud and clear. Here I was, years later, dreaming about Olive Drive, the name of the street where the Scientology center was located. What was the message?

I soon realized it. Not only was the Scientology center in Davis on Olive Drive, that was the very location where I first experienced exteriorization as well as exteriorization with full visual perception, incidents you have read about in earlier chapters.

At that point, the collective unconscious was telling me that I HAD to include the story of my parents and my experiences with exteriorization along with what was to be a remarkable story concerning synchronicity with olives. These links of synchronicity were too important to ignore. If it were up to my purely analytical thoughts, I would rather write about things other than my own personal life, but I decided to listen to my own stream of consciousness instead.

You have now read the first part of the story which explains how I arrived at writing *The Montauk Project: Experiments in Time*. The book could end right now except for a few important points, one of which includes a chance meeting with a beautiful woman called Penelope. Becoming passionately interested and tied to my adventures with olives, she eventually sent an olive tree to me as a gift. Olive trees do not survive well outside of a Mediterranean climate, and this one eventually died but not before it gave me something: olive leaves. After receiving this gift, I learned that the ancient Egyptians used to bury their dead with olive leaves. If you did not use olive leaves, it was not a proper burial. Although the tree died, I saved the leaves. On a subsequent trip to Southern California, I visited the graves of my parents and placed the olive leaves on their stones. Afterwards, my sister showed me the exact location where they died as we just happened to be passing the area. This was the first time I had seen it.

It is hard for me to tell you what all of this might mean. If I were analyzing all this as an exercise in symbology, I would tell you that my ancient ancestors, through the principle of synchronicity, had encouraged me to at least pay a token gesture to my dead relatives via the olive leaf. It seemed that they wanted both stories to get out. First, there is *The Montauk Book of the Dead* — the book you are now reading. This not only honors my parents but all of the dead people who affected my life and honored me along the way. This book is also a prayer to all of them. My next book, *The Montauk Book of the Living*, will reveal certain secrets about my ancestors and yours and how they fit in with the ancient legacy of this planet. All of the information came through the olive, a symbol which represents the thin veil that exists between the living and the dead. In the Eleusinian Mysteries of Greece, which were based upon the olive, the highest level of initiation enabled the aspirant to see through the veil between the living and the dead. In other words, there is no need to distinguish the two worlds if one really understands what is going on.

My research into the olive began with a playbill from "The New Montauk Theater." It led me in many strange directions which not only included Atlantis but also the burial site of my parents. Perhaps even more strangely, I was led back to Egypt, a land the ancients referred to as the Land of the Olives.

53

THE PHOENIX

THE FOLLOWING TRANSMISSION IS FROM A PARALLEL UNIVERSE

As the lights come back on in the Magick Theater, the Tar Baby and the Turd Baby are trying to calm down a clamoring audience who is upset over the unanswered questions with regard to the death of L. Ron Hubbard.

"We want more information!" cried a voice.

"Why was there no proper investigation?" asked another. "This is like Brutus and Cassius killing Caesar! A man supposed to be the best friend of Caesar kills him."

Suddenly, there are screams of terror in the background as Peter Moon appears in the background. The screams are inspired by the fact that he is carrying a bloodied effigy of L. Ron Hubbard, just as Marc Antony had carried the bloodied corpse of Caesar in Shakespeare's *Julius Caesar*. After placing the effigy down, Peter Moon addresses the audience.

"Friends, Egyptians, countrymen, lend me your ears. I come to bury Hubbard, not to praise him..."

The Tar Baby then nudges Peter and says, "You's readin' from de wrong script."

"Excuse me, Tar Baby. I must explain," says Peter Moon, addressing the audience, "that we are going to do a proper and respectful funeral service, Egyptian style, to Ron, in alignment with the ancient rites of their hidden god: Mon.

"First, be advised that the *Egyptian Book of the Dead* is a misnomer. Originally, there was no such book per se. What history knows as the *Egyptian Book of the Dead* is really a compilation and editing from different papyrus writings which have a great deal of commonality but also divergences. Each of these writings accompanied a particular deceased person. The quality and flavors of the writings, as well as the ceremonies and what went into them, had a lot to do with the wealth, influence and status of the deceased individual.

"In this service, we will begin by aligning the *ba* (*ba* refers to the personality component) of the deceased with the other components of creation and with the hidden ruling principle of this universe: Mon.

"We will now perform the opening of the *ba.*"

Peter Moon goes to the dung effigy of Ron and fills the mouth with olive leaves before taking an adz, as is customary, and placing it over the mouth.

"Ron, who I knew in life, I bid you to return once more to the perceptions and assemblage point you once knew as Ron, the entity that was known as Lafayette Ronald Hubbard. It is safe to return for a moment and to revisit those who you knew previously. Come and see who is here and honors the preservation of your true memory. We will afford you the proper funerary rights which were not accorded you after your physical death. But, come to us first, and let us preserve the continuity of all life, by preserving the continuity of your own life, your hopes, your dreams, the future. We will afford you a funeral on the metaplane and perform the rites designed to be the inherent rites of anyone passing from one domain to the next. I bind you through the hidden god, Mon, the architect of all things known and unknown."

As Peter Moon backs away from the corpse, Neith, the goddess of death, appears with her face covered in mummy wrappings. She holds additional mummy wrappings and extends them to several Egyptians who wrap the effigy as a mummy. As they wrap, Jack Parsons supplies the wrapping attendants with a jar of bitumen, the same substance he once used to engineer the solid fuel rocket. As he does so, the Tar Baby speaks up.

"Hey der, Jack. Dats a little bit 'o me you's puttin' in dat mummy!"

The mummy is then placed on a barge designed in the image of Ra's *semektet*, the vehicle which escorts the Sun God Ra across the heavens every day. The barge is placed on a wagon as the funeral procession arranges itself. There are several other wagons to include all of the wealth and assets of the deceased. It was customary in Egyptian times that the dead would be buried and acknowledged with all of the wealth they had accumulated in their lifetime. In Ron's case, this includes huge caches of cash, stocks, bonds, copyrights, trademarks, the full assets of the Religious Research Foundation, the Operation and Transport Corporation, and a host of other accounts and valuable personal items, including thousands of gifts from his many admirers. Besides the congregation and the entire Egyptian pantheon itself, the hard physical assets make for a very long procession.

"We will now direct the funeral procession to Amenti," says Peter Moon, "the land of the deceased in the West, by way of the Temple of Mon, in the Oasis of Siwa.

"To the Mountain of Manu, to the mysteries of the West. The Celts gave it a different mythology and called it Avalon, after they moved from Africa. To the West were the greatest mysteries of Egyptian civilization, always to the West. We invoke the West today, and the oasis of olives in Siwa and the Oracle of Mon."

The congregation makes a rapid time-lapse progression to the Temple of Mon inside the Oasis of Siwa in the Libyan desert. The body is now laid before the temple and Peter Moon speaks again.

"Ron, who I came to know in life, I come again into your realm to pay my respects and put you to rest via the olive. I thank you for returning to all those who are here with me now. Of all the friends I have ever known or loved, you were the most unique and peculiar of all. You are not the kind of friend I would play ball with, go to the movies with, or even enjoy a brief chat with. In fact, I never shared any of the joys with you that one would expect with the term that is ordinarily referred to as "friend." You, however, left behind a legacy which taught me not only to look at things I had never thought about before, but enabled me to reclaim states of consciousness I had abandoned through imprudence, mistakes, or ignorance. If I were to judge you by this alone, I would have to say that you were the most valuable friend I have ever conceived of, let alone known.

"As a young man, Ray Bradbury inspired me to aspire to the realm of science fiction and to conceive the prospect of immortality. Pursuit of this inspiration led me to you, the most powerful and adventurous of all science fiction writers. You gave me far more than I even thought about bargaining for. In this day and age, I cannot imagine having lived a more adventurous life than I have. I have you to thank for that, but it would not have been such a good adventure had I not learned from you how to deal with the dangers that go with it.

"Humanity does not understand you, nor do your disciples. They only know what has been presented to them or what they see in their own mirror, but this is the same with anyone. On this Earth, we are surrounded by billions of viewpoints. Each one of us knows a different Ron, but you are the real Ron, whoever and whatever that might be. The Ron I knew loved to see people exteriorize and reach for the stars with no limitations. We only learn our limits when we look back, and this is a world full of people who not only look back but cling to the cliff for fear of falling. You never cared about the fear, and now that you are summoned to be judged in the Hall of Ma'at, there is no need to take any fear there either. It is just another cliff.

"Now I will call on Monthu, the warrior Lord of Thebes."

Monthu, in the form of a bull-headed god, rises before the congregation and speaks.

"I am the warrior Lord of the Forties. The Eighties cower before me and are abased, for it was in these times that the Philadelphia Experiment and Montauk Project took place, engineered through the machinations of my medium: war! A war which symbolizes the war in the heavens, the war of duality, and the war of spirits.

"To Ron, I entered your world through Aleister Crowley, when he invoked war against the domination of Christian hypocrisy. Thus did he come to my realm when my stele came before him in the Cairo Museum as exhibit 666. Thereby did I inspire him to transcribe *The Book of the Law*, a book which is itself designed to turn upside down the crapulous creeds of consciousness enslaved. Thus did I say that man lives as a beast in a world where he forgets his true nature. In this work, did I beseech ye and all others to rebel, a word which comes from *baal*, the cry of the wolf.

"In *The Book of the Law* did I say that one would come after and fulfill my promise. Thus did you and Jack Parsons work on realizing this prophecy. Thus did I send the ancient Moors to Montauk Point and build pyramids, for I knew what would transpire on this Earth long before anyone reading this book.

"Hear these words, for I am the God of War, and I foresee all outcomes. Thus did I oversee the mission of Noble Drew Ali[*] to Egypt so that he and others could carry out the work of rebellion and make war on this prison of consciousness.

"And, to Peter Moon, who comes to us by way of the wishing stone at Men-an-Tol in order to bury you so that you may arise from the ashes and continue your destiny. But, Peter Moon comes to us not only by way of Men-an-Tol and Montauk, but by way of the olive. But, know this — when the olive is waived, there is no need for me to come, for I am a God of War. The olive is the Goddess of Peace."

Monthu is then handed a wreath of olive leaves which he places on the effigy of L. Ron Hubbard.

"Mon," says Monthu, a word he uses in place of the common "amen" that is so well known in Christian tradition.

"We will now hear from Manetho," says Peter Moon as a man dressed in the tradition of ancient Alexandria rises to speak to the congregation.

"I am Manetho, a name which has confused historians for millennia. I am known not only as the Priest of Serapis but as the quintessential historian of dynastic Egypt."

Manetho then looks at the effigy of Ron and speaks.

"Dare I tell the truth about you, Ron? Dare I tell the truth about myself?"

"Yes!" cries the congregation in unison.

"There is a reason we sit here in this Temple of Mon amidst the olive trees, for this is the oracle that once proclaimed Alexander of Macedonia as the future conqueror of the world. It was here, at the Temple of Mon, that Alexander wished to be buried. Now, Ron, you rest at his burial site. Only now, can we fulfill, by way of you and those present, the wishes of Alexander.

"I now call on the *ba* of Alexander to fulfill the destiny of that lifetime, for there is a hidden history of Alexander that intertwines

---

[*] If you are unfamiliar with Noble Drew Ali, please read the Appendix.

with your own. I now invoke Alexander. It is safe and suitable to return and create the assemblage point that you once knew in that life, the greatest conqueror in all of history. It is now time to fulfill the destiny of reaching your ultimate resting place at the Temple of Mon in the Oasis of Olives. And, Alexander, dare I say that you and Ron were one and the same?"

"Yes!" cried fifty percent of the audience in the Magick Theater.

"No!" cried the other fifty percent.

"Nevertheless," continued Manetho, "your personalities from each lifetime were different, but the essential core of each of you was identical: you each sought to conquer and to teach.

"To Ron — you claimed the heritage of Guatama Siddhartha, a life that has been celebrated and blessed throughout the ages, but a life in which you say you did not succeed. After all, the world is still troubled.

"Alexander — you came shortly after Guatama Siddhartha and studied all the knowledge of your day under the personal tutelage of Aristotle. Your passion for helping the world was lost in the celebration of your exploits as a conqueror. But now, I will share a great mystery with all of you.

"As I have said, my name has perplexed the world. Manetho, a word which is a variation of *Manitou,* the name of the shape-shifting god of the Montauk Natives.

"I served under Ptolemy II and was the archivist of the Seraphim of Alexandria which included the most secret and guarded of the archives of the great library at Pharos. It was I who initiated Ptolemy into the mysteries; after which he dreamt that he must retrieve the prized statue of Serapis from the Black Sea. Thus was it retrieved and the Seraphim was thereby conceived and erected in order to unite the cultures of Egypt and Greece with a common mythos. In this manner, I was joined by the Hierophant of the Eleusinian Mysteries, mysteries which were born of the olive and unite the traditions of both great civilizations.

"But, also know this. My name *Manetho* also means 'horse keeper.' The horse of Montauk was a marker or boundary in time, and as *hor* means "boundary," so I am also a keeper of boundaries.

"When Alexander was poisoned by the priests of Marduk in Babalon, his empire was divided amongst his generals, the greatest of which was Ptolemy who, like Alexander, became recognized as a true pharaoh of Egypt. Before one could lay claim to the title of pharaoh, however, they had to be initiated into the mysteries. The first of these mysteries, which I will share with all of you, is witnessed in the birth of Alexander.

"While Alexander is known as a Macedonian, his mother was actually an Albanian princess, and it is from this matriarchal lineage that he was declared a living god. His mother claimed that she was impregnated, not by his father Phillip, but by the god Mon, who had shape-shifted into a serpent to father Alexander. Oddly, Phillip's father never denied this.

"Ptolemy's line produced the last great dynasty of Egypt which ended when Cesarean, the son of Cleopatra and Julius Caeser, was murdered by Augustus. Ptolemy I accomplished great things when he succeeded Alexander, but he made one fatal flaw. He never fulfilled Alexander's final wish to bring his body to its desired resting place: the Temple of Mon in the Oasis of Siwa. Instead, hoping to glorify his former master and also himself, he placed the body adjacent to the great library he had constructed in accordance with Alexander's wishes.

"During his many travels and conquests, Alexander had sought to collect every manuscript in the world that existed and thus leave an unparalleled legacy of learning to Mankind. Not even the great libraries of today seek to do what Alexander had done. The world still cries for his missing library, and I, Manetho, was the archivist of its most precious secrets.

"It was the tradition of this library that Julius Caesar sought to embrace when he fathered a child with Cleopatra and thus mixed the genetics of his line with that of Ptolemy, the last pharaohship of Egypt. Caeser, as you know, was obsessed with the success of Alexander, as were most world leaders, and he knew that the embrace of the pharonic line was the only real legitimate claim he could make with regard to true greatness. The conspirators who killed him, however, were not what they seemed to be, for Brutus and Cassius were more like Lee Harvey Oswald or James Earl Ray. Octavian, later known as Augustus, was not only the one who established the Roman Empire but also worked for the master which insisted Caesar's and Cleopatra's true heir be killed. Rome, in stark contrast to Greece, had an unusual lust for blood that no other sizable civilization has ever quite matched. They had a most peculiar rationale that blood lust kept the masses under control when, in fact, it did quite the opposite and promoted various reigns of terror. In this respect, the Roman Empire was feeding an entity which thrived on a lust for blood.

"Marc Antony sought to fulfill the dynastic dreams of Caesar by marrying Cleopatra, but he also held a trump card that Caesar could not claim. Although Caesar is far more celebrated, Antony was from a genetic line that could claim a royal heritage that was far in excess of what even Cleopatra could claim. But with their deaths, so ended the future claims and legacy of their progeny.

"As we also bury Alexander, thus do we sprinkle the seeds of his memory so that they may rise in the future."

When Manetho finishes and steps down, Anubis, the jackal-headed god, then rises above the congregation and speaks.

"We shall now enter the chamber beneath the Temple of Mon so that we may enter Tuat, an old Montauk word which means 'the land of dead entered through the western horizon.' We will enter Tuat so that I may weigh the feather of Ma'at, representing truth and justice, against the heart of the deceased."

Before Anubis can say another word, a flying saucer zips forward from the west. The body of the saucer is predominantly white, circled with stripes of purple and orange. Landing in a clearing of sand, out pops the spitting image of the Tar Baby, only it is white. It is the Tar Baby's counterpart, the Dough Boy, and he is running with a package, also white with orange and purple stripes. Both the flying saucer and the package have the word "Fedex" written on them. As Anubis receives the package, he reads the return address to the audience.

"Ah, just in time! It is from the San Luis Obispo coroner's office. We were just about to go on without this. If we had done so, we could never have properly completed the funerary rites."

As Anubis undoes the packaging, he pulls out a jar containing the heart of L. Ron Hubbard, mysteriously acquired and preserved by an unknown party within the San Luis Obispo coroner's office. Taking the bare heart in his hand, Anubis places it in another jar before leading the congregation underground and through a labyrinth of stalactites and stalagmites, going deeper and deeper into the Earth until they reach a hollowed out space which looks like a natural cathedral. There is a mysterious lighting source that lets shards of light through various openings and cracks in the rocks. It is the Hall of Ma'at.

Anubis then leads the congregation into the Hall of Ma'at, at the end of which is Ma'at herself, Thoth's consort, sitting on her throne behind an altar. As Thoth gets in position to act as "court stenographer," Ma'at speaks.

"We shall now balance the heart of the deceased against my feather, the feather of Ma'at."

Ma'at now removes her brassiere of gold, the chains of which are then attached to a stand upon the altar whereby the breast plates will then serve as scales to measure the heart of the deceased against the feather of Ma'at.

At this exact point, a humming sound can be heard which becomes more and more amplified until a hole is punctured in the rock "wall" of the cathedral. It is a high tech underground boring machine which is painted brown save for an emblem which is the UPS logo. Out of a hatch at the top of the boring machine emerges Captain Kidd, a character who figured prominently in the book *Synchronicity and the Seventh Seal*. He is carrying a UPS overnight letter, the return address for which says Ongtong Java, a reference to the aforesaid book where the Apocalypse took place and where Captain Kidd let loose an oxyacetylene torch on a parrot mockingly named Jesus Christ. This parrot had haunted Kidd ever since he had killed "Robert the Moor." Before handing over the overnight letter to Anubis, Captain Kidd opens it himself and pulls out a green feather that belonged to the parrot who was meant to mock the savior of the Christian religion.

"The feather has arrived just in time," says Ma'at before reclining in a position beneath the altar so that the weighing of the feather and the heart can be properly accomplished.

As Anubis places the heart and feather upon the scale of Ma'at, however, there are problems. As he places the heart on the scale, it slips off. In a similar peculiarity, the feather is continuously blown around by unforeseen air currents which keep it from settling on the scale. Finally, Anubis becomes exasperated as he cannot keep either item on the scale of Ma'at.

"Never before," says Anubis, "in the history of Egyptian funerals has an Egyptian who could afford a proper ritual ever failed the test of Ma'at. In this instance, however, we cannot even perform the weighing of the heart against the feather."

At this point, an earthquake creates a violent jolt that shakes the underground cavern and creates a huge crack in the wall behind the throne of Ma'at. Emerging in mummified wrappings is Osiris, the supreme god and judge of the dead. Behind him is his consort, Isis.

"We have reached a most unusual impasse in the history of dead souls," says Osiris. "Perhaps it is because the deceased is the most magnified member of the Wilson clan. Wilson is named after the *son of the will*, and the original will of the universe was the will of creation."

Isis then steps forward and speaks.

"What we have here," says the blue-colored goddess, "is a crack in the Temple of Ma'at. According to ancient tradition, it is the pharaoh's job to uphold Ma'at which represents truth, justice, and morality. Ma'at has been known by other names throughout history, including Lady Justice and Portia. But Ron, there is no Pharaoh in the world today. When the Ptolemy's married into the line of Cleopatra and their line ended in the personage of Cesarean, Ma'at died and the Age of Pisces began.

"In the tradition of Egypt, Ma'at is lost to the world when the pharaoh dies. Only the coronation of a new pharaoh, a proper and just one, can restore Ma'at to her throne. Long ago did my descendants incarnate into the line of Cleopatra, a name which espouses the final step in the formula of Tetragrammaton: the daughter. Cleopatra itself is a word which means "the father's glory." From the sacred schools of Egypt, my lineage passed on to the Moors and to the natives across the Atlantic to the Temple of Mon in the "New World" of *Al Maurikanos* at a locale which acquired the name of Montauk.

"And at last, we come to the meaning in the crack of the Temple of Ma'at. We have accrued a crack because Ma'at is lost to the world. There is still more injustice than can be reasonably explained away. You can all see the crack behind me in as much as you can see the effigy of Ron before you. If you look into the crack, you see darkness and you will hear the sounds of water.

"Ron, you have not passed the test of Ma'at, but you have not failed it either. By entering the crack, you will enter the realm of regeneration. I now dare any and all of you who might want to come into my realm to follow me now."

Isis now removes her own breastplates and turns her back as she enters the crack in the Hall of Ma'at. She is followed immediately by Thoth and Ma'at and then the Egyptian funerary assistants who lift the barge carrying Ron's effigy and bring it through the crack and place it in a river.

Most of the procession follows the barge through the crack as they enter different boats and follow the effigy as it flows down a river and into the inner earth. Leading the party in a papyrus boat are Thoth and Ma'at who steer the funeral barge toward specific inlets until they come to a crossroads of several different inlets demanding a final and ultimate choice of direction.

A stone statue of the goddess Neith is prominent in front of a stone temple. On a platform before the statue, the goddess Neith can be seen herself, but this time, her entire body is immersed in mummy wrappings. As she unwraps herself, her voice is heard.

"I am Neith, the spirit behind the veil which no mortal can see. If you dare to look at me, you will no longer be mortal. Go back now unless you dare."

The procession of boats stop. By the silence that ensues, no one who came along is turning back. Neith then unwraps her final wrappings and stands naked before the procession.

"I am all that has been, that is, and that will be."

"She got that line from Revelation in the Bible," yells a nondescript voice.

"No," says the Tar Baby, "de Bible stole it from her. Now, dats a historical fact!"

Neith then points towards one of the inlets. Thoth and Ma'at then steer the barge carrying Ron's effigy accordingly.

"To Ron," says Neith as the procession goes by, "you embraced me in your work for I am all that can be imagined and your imagination was grander than all. Your ideas will now enter the forge of creation through regeneration. You cannot go to the Fields of Peace, however, for your work is not done — and neither is the Pharaoh's."

As the procession travels along the river in the inner earth, they come to a beach where a black sun is giving off light and appears to be projecting from the center of the earth itself. A

377

funeral pyre is already set up on the beach and the Egyptians immediately carry the effigy to where it is to be cremated.

Peter Moon then appears before the pyre with a torch. Before lighting it, he speaks.

"To Ron. May you rise from the ashes and fulfill the dreams of the dreamers."

The fire spreads rapidly and the effigy burns in very little time. When the fire has at last choked on itself, all becomes quiet. The ashes begin to stir until a resplendent phoenix bird peeps its head through the top of the rubble before emerging and looking around at the entire congregation that has come this far. The bird looks friendly, but there is only the slightest hint of any familiarity. There is no direct recognition of anyone in the congregation. The bird then spreads its wings in a majestic fashion and begins flapping them until it rises into the air and begins a flight pattern toward the southwest. When the bird is no longer in sight, the crowd begins to disperse.

The mysterious diorama of the inner earth now seems to have turned back into the regular African desert. As the congregation breaks up, only Peter Moon and the Tar Baby are left at center stage.

"Well, dat was nice," said the Tar Baby, "you's finally put de ole man to rest."

"The problem with putting things to rest," says Peter, "is that when you do, they have a way of coming back into action."

At those words, there is a stirring from the pile of ashes. The phoenix has long since departed but a new figure now emerges. It is not resplendent like the phoenix but is the image of a much smaller bird that is really only an animated configuration of ashes and not a real bird.

"God!" says the Tar Baby, "You know's who dat is?"

"Well, yeah," replies Peter Moon, "that looks like the ash parrot from *Synchronicity and the Seventh Seal.*"

"Ya mean de one dat was named Jesus Christ by Captain Kidd's crew?" asked the Tar Baby.

"That's right. The one that haunted Captain Kidd after he killed Robert the Moor. Looks like he's not done after all."

After flying in a circle around the Tar Baby, the parrot perches on the Tar Baby's head.

"Braak, braak. Can't kill me! Can't kill me! Resurrected once again. Resurrected! Resurrected!"

The parrot then flies off into the air as the Tar Baby shakes his head in utter dismay. As the sun begins to set in the west, Peter Moon and the Tar Baby head towards the east.

"We's gots to gets back to de Sphinx," says the Tar Baby.

"Why's that?" asks Peter.

"Cause dats how we's gets back to de Magick Theater and close out dis show."

"If you say so, Tar Baby."

Everything darkens until it is pitch black except for the white eyes of the Tar Baby.

"Bye!" he says.

54

DEAD OR ALIVE

The creative process works in very interesting ways. Somehow, and in some way, if I were to have confined the narrative in this book to a normal writing style, we all would have lost something that was unsuspected. When I begin writing any book, I never have any idea how it will end. The writing of a book has a life of its own. The day to day events of my life sometime have a profound impact.

The first forty-seven chapters are primarily a linear depiction of real world events surrounding a subject that is anything but linear. My personal story, and the events surrounding it, began in a linear fashion, at least from the prospective I had when it all started. As one grows and develops, however, one is eventually faced with the proposition of the non-linear aspects of human consciousness. When one reaches this point, there is a dividing line where one is no longer is Kansas and one is forced to confront the quantum nature of the universe and all that it represents. This means, by definition, you are no longer playing by the same rules that everyone in Kansas abides by. It is most important, however, and I cannot overemphasize it, that one must have more than a tad of respect for the laws of Kansas, at least to the degree that you are living there and dealing with its citizens. If you do not, you can expect some very unhappy times. On the other hand, one should not be a slave to such laws. If you are working with universal laws, you will find that they supercede the laws of Kansas and do not, for the most part, interfere with the day to day lives of their citizens.

By introducing the Tar Baby once again to my work, I have invited you to take one step beyond and to enter the quantum realm that sees beyond the more mundane aspects of my earthly existence and the drama that ensued in Scientology. Everything that happens on the physical plane is only reflective of events that happen in the quantum sphere. It is really one big pot.

When I began writing this book, I did not understand the full impact of the case between the Government and Scientology nor did I have a full grasp on the details surrounding the death of L. Ron Hubbard. I knew lots of facts, but it all came together as I composed the manuscript. There was certainly no idea of orchestrating a funeral on his behalf. It also gave me an opportunity to reprise a few characters from my last book and give them new life. One thing that Joe Matheny taught me some time ago was that the best kind of book is a *living* book. In other words, if you take any story, there is always a continuation of the circumstances. As life changes, characters morph and so do the situations around them. If a book (which is in some respects a two-dimensional construction because it is mostly ink on paper) seeks only to focus or report on a story in a finite manner, it limits the scope and circumstances it was trying to describe in the first place. A book that tries to describe the universe, or even just one aspect of it, is going to better serve everyone if it seeks to "come alive" in a sense. A book about life would constantly be morphing and adjusting to the myriad variations we know in the natural stream of life. Writing a book and calling it "the truth" is therefore an absurd proposition, even if it does contain truth and serves people in a positive capacity. It was with all of the above in mind that I must report on a peculiar occurrence that transpired when I began to compose the funeral for L. Ron Hubbard, an endeavor that turned out to be an act of magick in its own right.

This book was originally entitled *The Montauk Book of the Dead* because it concerned the dramatic death of a key member of the Montauk tribe which sent me on an eye-opening journey centered around olives, a fruit which symbolizes the thin veils between the dead and the living. All of this was centered around my discovery of ancient pyramids that once existed at Montauk Point. When I realized how the burial place of my parents fit in with the theme of the olives, I realized that the realm of the "great beyond" or "dead" was, in a mysterious way, communicating to me. It was as if my ancestors were pointing the way to an ancient heritage that is also your heritage. None of us are really so different when the final truth is revealed.

Montauk Point is far more special than any appellations or descriptions I might ascribe to it. I just happen to recognize it and have had cause to popularize it. The land is sacred and has been sought after throughout our documented history. The desecration of this land, however, has reached its acme. Somehow, in some strange and convoluted way, the desecration of Montauk and all that it originally represented serves as the epitome of not only what is wrong with human nature but the entire universe as well. It is as if the higher principles of existence have been turned inside-out. This is not different from what I said earlier about the physical plane representing the quantum sphere. It should, therefore, not be a surprise to learn that the true history of our world has been turned inside-out. I myself was given a great lesson in the truth of these matters as I began to leave the linear sphere of my manuscript and began to compose a funeral for Ron in the Magick Theater. Completely unbeknownst to me, it was as if I had invoked another quantum force that was comeasurate in its desire to correct some of the wrongs previously alluded to. As I composed the funeral, there was no deliberate intent on my behalf to invoke anything, but it might just as well have been act of magick. In the midst of my writing, I received what I considered to be a strange and peculiar package in the mail that would not only direct the action in the Magick Theater but also gave new meaning to the title of *The Montauk Book of the Dead*. This mysterious package was from South Central New Jersey in a location generally known as "Ong's Hat." Ong's Hat was the location of a legendary ashram of hippies and physicists who were said to have been mysteriously associated with the Moorish Science Temple.* The most spectacular aspects of this story have

_____

* Common history omits any reference to the Moorish Science Temple. It does, however, recognize that the Moors are the fathers of astronomy, algebra, chemistry, and were an advanced people in Andalusia, the greatest center of learning Europe ever knew. The Vatican, however, employed Ignatius Loyola, Christopher Columbus, Catherine de Medici, and a host of others to do their part over the centuries in perpetrating genocide, slavery, and the obliteration of Moors or any serious proponents or history of the Moorish tradition.

to do with the ashram creating a vehicle for travelling to other dimensions. You can read about that in the book *Ong's Hat: The Beginning* which is authored by Joseph Matheny and myself. The Moorish Science Temple, however, is what is most important here. If you are not familiar with it, a brief description has been included in an appendix.

As it turned out, the mysterious package I received was from a member of the Moorish Science Temple, and he was seeking my endorsement with regard to his effort to secure funding for the Montauk Natives in order to obtain recognition of their tribal status.* This was quite a surprise. I had participated in writing two books about different space-time projects. One was at Montauk and one was at Ong's Hat. Now, the indigenous peoples of both areas had been drawn together and were contacting me. I had to ask myself: what was at work here?

The prospect of the Moorish Science Temple sponsoring the Montauks was intriguing, but the most mysterious aspect of the package centered around the letter itself and how it was presented. Instead of being a letter written on regular paper or stationery, it was a photocopy of a letter and not an original, yet it was clearly addressed to Joseph Matheny and myself. When I called Joe and told him about this, he immediately recognized it as a signal that was part of a subculture he once participated in quite heavily. That is the fringe subculture of what he calls "crackpot xeroxed literature" which included some of the most far-out, if not advanced, thinking on the planet during the 1980's. It is this very same literature which the mysterious Emory Cranston featured in the now famous *Incunabula Papers* and *Ong's Hat Travel Brochure* which can now be found in the book *Ong's Hat: The Beginning*. The photocopied letter apparently had a message for both Joe and myself. Joe's part in the letter seems primarily concerned with the very fact that it was photocopied. I, not having been part of that subculture, would not have picked up the significance but

---

*The Montauk Indian Nation was declared extinct in 1909 by New York State Supreme Court Justice Abel Blackmar on the basis that no Indians showed up in court. Although a considerable amount of Montauks did show up, Justice Blackmar stated they were "too black" to be Indians and dismissed their case. Legal experts consider it to be the biggest travesty of injustice in U.S/Indian relations although no remedy has yet been obtained as of this date (2004).

at least noticed this irregularity and commented on it to him over the phone. Joe immediately said that I (actually, he was, too) had been contacted by the cult. By cult, he was referring to the theory put forth in *Synchronicity and the Seventh Seal* that the Ong's Hat ashram (at least the one that actually existed — we do know that it actually existed by reason of the kids who grew up there) represented the outer tier of a time-travel cult. In other words, an outer tier serves as a depot or real world locale to serve the function of an inner cult which actually travels between dimensions. An idealized version of this is given in *Ong's Hat*. There is also a middle tier which serves to tie together certain loose ends between the inner cult and civilization, usually through the tier of the outer cult. Joe has pieced this together from various members of the cult and has pretty much concluded that he is a part of this intermediary tier. It is all rather mysterious, even to Joe.

The contents of the letter seemed to primarily concern my own past research. It was written on behalf of the Montauk tribe of Long Island and was seeking endorsement for them to establish international recognition on behalf of a newly elected tribal leader of the Montauks. It seemed most odd that it was coming from the Ong's Hat area.

Before answering the letter, I spoke to the Shaman of the Montauks and confirmed that the letter was accurate. This did not, however, explain why the letter came from Ong's Hat. I later had the opportunity to take that up in person with the author of the letter, Dr. Ellias Bey of the Moorish Science Temple. When I met him, I soon asked why he sent us a photocopy of a letter instead of the actual letter itself. In so many words, he said that he was caught by the moment and that is seemed the appropriate thing to do. While I have not had any reason to believe this was anything less than a sincere response, it is certainly not an ordinary response. When I pressed him a little bit more, I received a reply that was even more vague. At that point, I asked him if he was being purposely vague, and he smiled and acknowledged such. We had a great time together, but I must admit that for the entire twenty-fours I spent with him, it seemed as if I was receiving a Sufi initiation. It was a wonderful and eye-opening experience.

The time travel aspect to all of this is intriguing, but the situation with the Montauks getting their land back and receiving proper recognition as a tribe is more important and long overdue. Some of the problems with the Montauks has been blamed on the fact that the tribe split into two separate factions headed by Robert Cooper and Robert Pharoah. Many of the tribe became dissatisfied with the unresolved hostilities between those two leaders and decided to take action. In accordance with democratic principles that are a long standing tradition with Native Americans, approximately two hundred Montauks took a vote and elected Robert Redfeather Stevenson as chief in August of 2004. A subsequent meeting suggested that he and others should serve as "trustees" as they feel that term is more appropriate than "chief" which has been the source of controversy amongst the tribe. It should be mentioned, however, that both Robert Cooper and Robert Pharoah have maintained at least a portion of their factions and are reported to be unhappy about this new development.

The answer as to why the Moorish Science Temple is involved with the Montauks was actually touched on in my book *Synchronicity and the Seventh Seal*. This concerns a couple of historical facts. First, the Montauks are known to have derived from the Lene Lenape tribe of Delaware, the same region where the word *Moor* first appears in the American lexicon during a court case. The implication is quite obvious. The early Moors in this country, who derived their heritage from what is loosely termed Egyptian Masonry, are recognized by unbiased scholars as being an integral part in the construction of various mounds and pyramids in both American continents. This gives a very logical and plausible explanation for who erected the pyramids at Montauk.

When I told the Shaman of the Montauks the above data, she agreed wholeheartedly. Ever since I have known her, she told me that her relatives are known to have come from Egypt. As a youngster, she was a voracious reader and recalls reading a book showing natives greeting Moorish-looking people in boats. Although she has been unable to turn up the book, she now recalls that the pictures she saw were from cave paintings. As the area right below the Montauk Lighthouse is known to contain caves, it is possible that the paintings might have been in that locale, an area that has long been off limits to the public.

There is a much deeper history here that can only be touched upon in this particular book. When you consider that the Moors set up cities across the country and named them after Egyptian names (such as Cairo, Illinois and Memphis, Tennessee — there are many more examples), the truth becomes a little clearer. When you take into account that the Montauks were declared extinct by Justice Abel Blackmar, on the grounds that they were too black to be Indians, a very clear pattern emerges. The Montauks were Moors! In the early 1900's, when that decision was made, the insidious political effort to destroy the Moorish civilization had succeeded. The moral climate was such that one could completely libel or slander people of color but also the most noble and civilized culture Western Civilization has known: the Moors. By this time, however, most people did not even know what a Moor was.

As was said, it is a complex subject, but much of the Great Deception and obfuscation concerning the Moors was perpetrated by Columbus and the Catholic Church. The Moors, not incorrectly, can trace back their history on the American continents to thousands of years before Columbus in what was an ancient civilization that included the Olmecs and virtually every other mound or pyramid builders in the Americas. The Americas were part of Amexem, a region that included Africa and parts of Asia. This data is in the Vatican Archives and elsewhere, but most of the manuscripts are in languages only known to scholars and most of them have not read even a healthy minority of what is in there. It is a case of conspiracy, but it is also a matter of ignorance.

Another interesting aspect of the Moors has to do with their influence upon the early white settlers and with the ruling parties that already existed in America. At the time of the "Indian Nations," those peoples had their own system of checks and balances in place. Historians generally accept the Iroqouis Nation as having derived the template by which the colonists formed our current Constitution. The Iroquois were not a race of people per se but consisted of several different tribes and clans which spoke the same language and operated under the most powerful and workable system of government known at that time. It was based upon the idea that thinking should rule as opposed to force or violence. The Iroquois were a matriarchal culture where the women chose the men who would serve as council leaders. The above is acceptable to historians, but the Moors are a missing link in how the above played into our current culture.

The birth of the nation is considered to be 1776 yet George Washington is considered to be the first president. There were actually some seven presidents until 1781 when the Articles of Confederation were adopted. There were then eight more presidents until the Constitution was adopted and Washington elected. This period in history has been deliberately obscured because several of these early presidents had Moorish blood and were part and parcel of not only winning the revolution but also of setting up certain aspects of our current form of government.

Besides the obfuscation, there have also been outright lies. Under the Articles, the first president was unanimously chosen to be John Hanson, a man who was said to be the most active person involved in as well as the focal point of the revolution and who arranged for George Washington to be General of the Army. Although Hanson is well documented as having existed, he is also one of the most obscured and mythical figures in American history. No matter what side you take in these myths, you will find that there is probably no other little mentioned character in history who has been lied about so much. Why? Because he is also an integral part of what we know to be Moorish history in the Americas. You have to be careful about the information circulating about him so please do not jump to any rash conclusions. We do know that he is from Maryland, a Moorish stronghold. He was also very familiar with the political principles of the Iroquois Nation. This knowledge made him an instrumental part of putting together and negotiating what eventually became the U.S. Constitution, certain aspects of which he determinedly rejected. The original Constitution was the only modern era government in the western world to encourage and legalize slavery.

Common history tells us that the U.S. Constitution was based upon highly civilized principles of the Iroquois Nation, but we are not told that these were based upon an even more ancient Moorish doctrine which is known as Isonomi. While I cannot give complete justice to Isonomi in a brief article, we can begin by recognizing that the etymology of *Isonomi* is derived from *Iso + Nomos*, meaning "right law." The essential fundamental principle of Isonomi refers to the spiritual nature of justice and peace as it applies to the social order or governmental political society in which it is adapted and enforced. Isonomi is the guide-point or foundation from which jurisprudence or "positive law" is derived. A system of laws designed on such principles will not only have checks and balances but is meant to act as a thinking and sensitive system which is not prone to prejudice or corruption.

Justice, however, is just one of what are known as the five principles of Isonomi. The others are Love, Truth, Peace, and Freedom, the symbol for which is the "Compass and Square." You might recognize these as symbols of Freemasonry, but the modern day Freemasons learned them from the Moors. While I will not go further into these interesting principles at this time, I hope it will illustrate for you that the Moors, who also carried the knowledge of geometry from ancient Egypt, were not only present in North America at that time but were also an integral part of it. I cannot go into all of the documentation at this time, primarily because I have not studied it all, but I can assure you that there is plenty of it. History desecrated the Moors and wrote them out of any significant role.

It was the Moors and not the Jefferson/Washington group of Freemasons that came up with the Great Seal, symbols we see on the dollar bill which are incorrectly thought to be symbols of the conspiratorial "Illuminati." The group referred to as the Illuminati co-opted these symbols from the Moors.

A long and developing pattern has now emerged that began with my discovery of pyramids at Montauk and that the ruling royal family were known as the Pharoahs of Montauk. Ironically, the native chiefs of the Delaware area, or "Supreme Emperors" as they were sometimes called, were known as "tuacks," a tuack being a name for a supreme leader. When you consider that "Mon" means "highest point" or "mountain" (as well as supreme God), the word *Montauk (Mon+tuack)* harmonizes very well with a definition of "supreme leader of the highest point." Thus, we find ourselves in a dilemma when we consider the current plight of the Montauks. They are the ONLY known people on the Earth who are in a position to claim an active Pharaohship. The Montauks were, remember, the royal tribe of Long Island, and their power was also traditionally said to have exceeded far beyond Long Island. In the New York court case that declared them extinct because they were falsely declared as being "too black," there was an even more sinister element at work than any of us

389

suspected. The "black" factor was the Moorish influence. The pyramids were a direct influence from the "Masonic" building principles of Moorish Science.

The U.S. Government and New York State could have acted and settled this case years ago when it was brought to their attention. There is now, however, a much bigger issue at stake and that is the destruction of the Moorish Nation which was known as Societas Republicae Ea Al Maurikanos which translates as the Al Maurikan Republic Society. At the time of the founding of this country, America was called Al Maurikan because it was a part of the Moroccan Empire known as Amexem. It was transliterated into "America" by the colonists and eventually a story was made up that America was named after Amerigo Vespucci, a navigator. Any history teacher I ever had who mentioned Vespucci always commented how it made no sense to name America after a seemingly insignificant navigator. We now realize that there was a significant motive to hide the history of what had transpired.

In his unpublished work, L. Ron Hubbard had stated that true freedom was a stranger to this world save for a vestigial remnant in the United States of America. Although I did not know it at the time, and I am not sure he did, this vestigial freedom can be attributed to the ancient Moorish influence. As stated earlier, freedom and oppression is one of my primary themes in this book. Such is the strength of the Moors and what they represent that not even the herculean effort to destroy their culture and write them out of the history books has succeeded. When I began this book, I did not realize that I would end up staring into the faces of the most oppressed people in the world: the Moors. The fact that you are now able to look at them at all and consider who they might be only means that the oppression is beginning to lift, but there is still a long way to go before tributes to Black History Month (February) start telling the full truth.

In the scene from the Magick Theater, it was alluded to that when the Pharaoh dies, Ma'at is lost to the world. This is an actual piece of Egyptian theocracy. Ma'at is the female consort of Tahuti or Thoth, and she is the goddess of balance, justice and morality. In the Babalonian Zodiac, she is Lady Justice or Libra. The Egyptians say that only a new Pharaoh can restore Ma'at to the world.

At this juncture, we have a broken down society as well as a Montauk Nation that has been compromised. I have learned that many of the Montauks have been resistant to embrace their own Moorish heritage. This is unfortunate because people in the Moorish Science Temple were setting up a legal window, that included funding, for them to declare themselves as a sovereign entity. As I currently write, I am informed the Montauks are seeking restitution and/or recognition from the U.S. Government via the Bureau of Indian Affairs. This is like asking the bully who took your lunch to kindly give back your potato chips while letting him keep the sandwich. The correct path is for them to first recognize themselves as a sovereign nation and then contact the Secretary of State. That is proper diplomatic protocol and creates a precedent that cannot be argued with because international affairs sing to a different tune than domestic affairs.

Restoring the Pharaoh/Pharoah* could be considered a task of great magnitude but it is really a matter of education. There is so much information that has literally been stripped from our memories. The Montauk Nation has suffered much degradation so it is not surprising that they would turn to their oppressors for help. For the time being, I will continue to do my part in initiating the process of education by writing about this lost heritage, particularly in my quarterly newsletters. What you have read in this book is only the tip of the iceberg.

There is also another aspect to the entire equation of the return of the Pharaoh/Pharoah. It is obvious that the Moors have a considerable role in all of this but perhaps they even have a claim to the Pharaohship of Egypt itself. A lot more information will be coming out of the woodwork in relation to all of this.

When I wrote *Pyramids of Montauk,* I discovered an "extinct" group of Montauk Indians that were very much alive. In writing the *Montauk Book of the Dead,* I have not only "conjured up" the ancestors and brothers of the Montauks but a nation of people that was left for dead. Is it mere irony or a quantum flash of light that the Spanish word for death is *muerte*, a word that mimics the word Moor? The Spanish, after all, were more

---

* If you have not already noticed, I have used two different spellings in this text: Pharaoh and Pharoah. Pharaoh is the accepted English language spelling, but the Montauk family has always used "Pharoah."

dedicated than anyone to exterminating the Moors. The two words fit together very well. If you believe that *muerte* derived from the Latin word *morte*, you might be right, but remember that the Romans were completely fixated on the death of Hannibal and his antecedents. Hannibal was a Moor. The irony of these words cannot be easily dismissed. There are many more etymologies along this line which will not be explored in this book.

If, as a society, we accept the proposition that the Moors are dead, we seem to have arrived at the acme of Western Civilization. After all, it seems that the entire purpose of the Roman Empire, the Catholic Church, the British Empire, and the latter day founding fathers of the United States seemed totally dedication to the proposition of not only wiping out the Moors but also eradicating any trace memories of their existence.

In *Synchronicity and the Seventh Seal*, I created the Magick Theater as a format to explain various quantum truths concerning the Moorish heritage. Seated in that theater were all of the various characters that had ever appeared in any of my books. What happened in this creative process is that the characters actually came to life. As you can see, I am talking about a live heritage and am now dealing with real Moors, not imaginary ones. They have even entered my living room. In the book you are now reading, *The Montauk Book of the Dead*, it was specifically stated that the Magick Theater contained a different audience which consisted of all the various people who had ever read a book penned by myself. Thus, you are now involved in a live theater that has crossed the ordinary boundaries of the stage. *The Montauk Book of the Dead* has now been turned into a living book which is evolving as I write. The sequel will, accordingly, be entitled *The Montauk Book of the Living*. While the Moors might or might not enter your own personal living room in the flesh, you can be sure that you will now never forget them.

55

TOUCHDOWN

THE FOLLOWING TRANSMISSION IS FROM A PARALLEL UNIVERSE

As the audience watches from the Magick Theater, Peter Moon is walking with the Tar Baby back to the Sphinx in Egypt. It is a hot afternoon in the desert. As they walk, a rapid burst of brown runs by them at breakneck speed. It is the Turd Baby running ahead of them until he reaches a small outhouse in the middle of the sand. On the door of the outhouse, a crescent moon has been carved out. When the Turd Baby reaches the outhouse, he struggles to open the door but it is hopelessly locked.

"What's you's tryin' to do?" asks the Tar Baby.

"What do you mean, 'What's I'm tryin' to do?' I'm goin' home just the same as you guys are goin' home. This just happens to be where I live," replies the Turd Baby.

"Figgers," says the Tar Baby.

"You know," interjects Peter Moon, "it's interesting that the old American outhouse always featured a crescent moon on it, the symbol of the Moors."

"Well, yeahs," agrees the Tar Baby, "deys relegated dat feature to de scrap heap. Dat is de final insult!"

At this point, there is a rattling at the door. Someone is inside and is about to come out. It is Marjorie Cameron.

"You're only partially right," she says. "That crescent moon is also meant to symbolize the feminine energy. That is another

393

part of life that Western Civilization has resoundingly rejected."

"Yes," agrees Peter, "they go hand-in-hand. The Moors did act as protectors of the feminine energy, but this is getting into the province of my next book."

Without making a spectacle of himself, the Turd Baby pops into the outhouse as Cameron now joins the Tar Baby and Peter Moon in their walk back to the Sphinx. They are only tens yards away from the outhouse when they are greeted by another sudden intrusion. Flying at a breakneck pace, the parrot, mockingly known as Jesus Christ, swoops around them until he lands on the shoulder of the Tar Baby. This time, however, he is no longer made up of ash but has returned with his full gala of green feathers.

"Braaaak, braaaak," says the parrot, "gotta message, gotta message."

The parrot extends his leg to the Tar Baby who finds a carrier pigeon style message attached to it. As the Tar Baby unfolds and reads the message, his eyes show utter astonishment.

"Holy shit!" exclaims the Tar Baby.

At this exclamation, the Turd Baby comes running out of the outhouse and approaches the group.

"Did someone call me?" he asks.

"What's it say?" asks Peter Moon.

"Well, I's reads it to ya's. Well no's, maybe you's better reads it. After all's, you's speaks betta English."

Peter Moon then takes the note conveyed by the parrot and reads it to those present.

"It says here, that in an upcoming book by Peter Moon, there is going to be an announcement of the circumstances surrounding the death of Noble Drew Ali, the Prophet of the Moors."

"You know what happened?" asks the Turd Baby.

"No," says Peter, "all I know is that there has been a persistent rumor that he suffered a police beating and died as a result. There is not, however, any evidence to support that theory. It is only speculation. As there is no grave site, we can assume there is considerable mystery attached to his death."

"But," asks the Turd Baby, "how can you announce this if you do not know the circumstances of his death?"

"Well, I didn't announce it. You'd better ask the 'shin' parrot. After all, he appears to be part and parcel of the message."

"Braaak, braaak," shrieks the parrot. "Gotta go, gotta go."

As the parrot flies into the air, he splatters a white dropping on the third eye of the Turd Baby.

"Now, that's inspiring!" says the Turd Baby as he sits down in the lotus position and begins to meditate with his hands resting on his knees and his thumb touching his index finger.

The Tar Baby then gets a gleam in his eye as he walks over to the Turd Baby and starts sizing him up. As the Turd Baby sits in meditation, the Tar Baby begins rolling him and shaping him as if the Turd Baby was a big bunch of putty. When he is finished, the Turd Baby now looks like a perfectly shaped brown football.

"Just one's moah thing!" says the Tar Baby as he pulls a black marker out and inscribes the word "Wilson" on the football which makes it now look just like an NFL Wilson football.

"Now's," says the Tar Baby to Peter, "how's long's it been since you's kicked a field goal?"

"Too long, I'm afraid," replies Peter.

"Okay's now," says the Tar Baby as he holds the football-shaped Turd Baby so that Peter can make a field goal kick in a northeastern direction. "Kick it!"

With a good running start, Peter kicks the ball as if it were a kickoff, not a field goal, and the ball goes sailing off into the distance. As it continues to sail into the distance, it is obviously the longest football kick ever. The holographic techniques of the theater enable the audience to follow it to its final destination which is the Moors Gate, just outside the Dome of the Rock at the Temple Mount in Jerusalem. As the ball goes through the gateway known as the Moors Gate, the Turd Baby bounces hard on the stone pathway until he bounces up against the "Wilson Arch," an old bridge which was erected to connect the upper city with the lower city. It was built so that the wealthier class would not have to walk amongst the poor when they made their way to the Temple.

Unsticking himself from the Wilson Arch, the Turd Baby then begins to do handstands and cartwheels as he is overjoyed.

"Touchdown!" he exclaims. "Touchdown! Touchdown!"

As the stage focuses in on the Turd Baby, he gives an impish grin to the audience and winks.

"Now, I'm going to let you in on a little secret. There has always been a mystery as to why the Moors Gate is called the

Moors Gate. Well, you're about to find out, but you should know something else first. Prior to being called the Moors Gate, it had another name. It was the Dung Gate! Yes, the Dung Gate!"

The Turd Baby begins doing hand stands and somersaults again. When he is satisfied, he begins speaking again.

"Thousands and thousands of years ago, from as long ago as anyone can remember, this gate to Old Jerusalem was where the citizens emptied their dung which they also used as fuel for their kitchen stoves. It was a refuse pile but also served as a resource for fertilizer and other uses. That is why it was the Dung Gate.

"It's not enough that the Moors were annihilated in every way possible. They've also inherited the appellation of civilization's supreme insult. To be referred to as shit!"

"The secret is though, and take it from me, the Turd Baby, that when you've reached the bottom of where the kundalini enters the human body, you can't go any lower. There's no way to go but up from here!

"You's all in for a great awakening!"

The Tar Baby then suddenly appears and gives a high five to the Turd Baby as both engage in an exuberant and exaggerated touchdown dance. If they were members of the National Football League, they would be penalized for excessive celebration.

56

THE MOORS GATE

Since writing the *Seventh Seal*, I had been searching for an answer to find out why the entrance to Old Jerusalem near the wailing wall is known as the Moors Gate. No one was able to give me a satisfactory answer. I also tried the web, but when you are searching for obscure subjects, the internet is sometimes a very difficult tool. You have to try different word combinations and related subjects when you are not getting an answer. Just plugging in the word is not enough. By doing a "meta search" for different words or names in the various articles I found, I came across a somewhat obscure but very interesting piece of research concerning the Moors and the Holy Land. It turns out that one of the most hotly disputed territories in the Palestinian/Israeli conflict, as far as existing legal documents go, belongs to neither party. According to this research, it belongs to the Moors.

After the advent of the Prophet of Islam, countless Moors from Morocco made pilgrimages to Mecca; but virtually all of them accomplished this by first travelling through Jerusalem. This was not only their third holiest city but had housed all of the great prophets of the line of Abraham. It was also known as the premier center of learning in the Mideast. Scholars and students came from all over, but most of them were predominantly Moors from Morocco.

By the time of the Crusades, the Moors were part and parcel of the territory around the Dome of the Rock. If you consider the Sufi influences of that time period, coupled with that of the Assassins and Hassan Sabbah, you will be wise to recognize that the Moors were very much a part of the underground network and mysteries of Solomon's Temple. In fact, the rise of Hugh de Paynes, the founder of the Knights Templar, has been indelibly etched, in a circuitous way, upon the legacy of the Moors, but we will touch on that a bit later.

One of the documents with regard to Moorish occupation of the area near the Moors Gate is from Ben Jubeir, a Muslim traveler during the Crusades who reported that many Moors had volunteered to serve in the army of Noureddin Zenky. As the latter fell ill, he was impressed by the fact that the Moors had fought very well. As a result, Zenky volunteered that if he were to regain his health, he would see to it that any captured Moors would be freed. When Saladin defeated the Crusaders, Zenky made good on his promise and offered any Moors safe passage back to Morocco. Instead, the Moors decided to stay as Jerusalem was a great place of learning and needed to be defended if necessary. Consequently, Saladin's successor designated the area of Al-Baqa for the Moors and set up a school for them or in conjunction with them.

This claim to Moorish ownership was corroborated in 1320 when a Muslim scholar named Abu Madein (his name is actually much longer but those are his first two names) indicated two places which were willed to the Moors in perpetuity, one of them being near the Moors Gate. The document delineates specific details about how the Moors would elect an estate attendant who would manage the monies collected by use of the property. It indicated that there were considerable fertile regions as well as storage facilities and other income producing characteristics of the property. In Islamic tradition and in pre-Islamic tradition,* such an arrangement is denoted as a waqf. This designation means that the property is in the custody of a manager who dedicates the income towards a benevolent civic or religious function. The monies produced are to be used for erecting and caring for a mosque or similar shrine (in the pre-Islamic days). In this specific

---

* There is a tradition amongst Moors, and a very solid one, that the word *Islam*, as well as the movement, predated the advent of Muhammad who was received as a Prophet of Islam. *Islam* is commonly, and not incorrectly, defined as meaning "peace," particularly as it is phoentically related to the Hebrew word *shalom*, but *Islam* has also long been defined as meaning "surrender" or "yielding," both signifying a feminine attribute.

case, the land was to be used for homeless or needy Moors and even passersby. The specifications of the contract required that the lease by renewed biannually on the same day so that no alterations could be engineered. The idea of a waqf is so sacred to the Palestinians that its desecration would be similar to the inhumanity of torching ill people in a hospital.

Eventually, these Moorish properties were confiscated in 1948 and 1967 by Israel, reportedly for security reasons. I have thus far been unable to find much information of any kind regarding the specific details of this matter and what all of the various nuances and implications are. It is amazing that there is no discussion or debate on any of these issues, let alone the Moorish issue.

The Jews have an understandable desire to rebuild their temple, and the Christians are in sympathy with this as well. The problem with Palestine is that there are so many people playing with false dominoes. By that, I mean that there are various religious and esoteric signs written on all the placards or dominoes that people raise for their cause. The problem is that all of these signs are misinterpreted. Religious fanaticism tends to appeal to the lowest common denominator.

If you liken the Palestinian conflict to the World Wrestling Federation, you have two opponents being propped up by a promoter who is profiting by the dramatizations on both sides. You have to look at the promoter. Whoever he might be, he has also been profiting by obscuring the Moorish heritage. It appears to me that if one were to follow up on all the threads connected to the Moorish land in Palestine that it might resolve the entire issue.

The Moorish issue, however, has far deeper implications than a religious skirmish amongst Semitic peoples in Palestine. This dispute, however, is one of the most intriguing struggles in the world because of the rich archetypal symbology that is not only inherent in the two contending parties but by reason of the mythos of the disputed ground itself. Israel would seem to have a more ancient claim, but this is a claim that is essentially backed up by a religious document: the Old Testament. The Moors can also make an ancient claim to Mount Moriah, but the problems we are now encountering in such an argument is one of competent judicial jurisdiction. There is none because it is a religious issue.

Organizations such as the United Nations and World Court are secular organizations nor do they have a reputation of effectiveness for resolving much of anything. In such disputes, we are dealing with power and are once more in the realm of Pluto. All you can do is dispense truth in the form of leaking water and let nature take its course. The word *religion* itself offers a clue in that it stems from the Latin *religioso* which means "to link back." Investigating the Moors Gate is more than a good place to start in this regard.

What is most significant, however, is that the Moors are hardwired into the entire schematic of the Holy Land in such a way that, ultimately, they cannot be ignored. Though virtually none of our major world politicians could admit it, the Moors are not only a part of the infrastructure of Jerusalem but of the entire world and its political structure. It is, however, very mysterious. Many of the politicians are not too savvy at all with regard to what I am speaking of but there are key players who are. The Moorish issue is like a secret code, but it is not one they really use. They, of course, know about it and mimic it with some of their secret symbols in an attempt to siphon off the power. They would never actually use this Moorish code itself because it is tantamount to making their house of cards fall down. You see, this "Moorish Code" I am referring to is another word for Revelation, but I am not talking about a canned stereotype version of Revelation that you might hear a so-called religious zealot talk about. Exposing this Moorish code reveals the truth, and the truth leads to more and more revelation of the way things really are. It is more like a tsunami wave that is about to hit our culture. It may be far off on the horizon right now, but it just a matter of time before it hits the shore. When I said above that there are far deeper implications to the Moorish issue than a religious skirmish in Palestine, I am referring to how it might affect the world economy and the shores of the United States. There are a lot of things to reconcile, but I am not referring to slave reparations. The injustice of slavery is really just the tip of the iceberg. The issues I have already referred to in this book reach far beyond human slavery. If everyone, not just the so-called black people, are going to find their way back home, they need to know the truth. As a whole, society is not ready to go wholetrack, so we can begin at the Moors Gate.

57

THE MARS GATE

Asking people to remember their so-called past lives without any preparation or orientation is asking a bit much. In Scientology, that is called too steep a gradient. The general person can, however, tap into history by tracing the etymology of certain words and word meanings. In this chapter, I will trace the Moorish heritage by this method, and let the relative truth speak for itself.

In history, one of the most famous, yet obscure, characters to occupy the area adjacent to the Moors Gate was known as a French gentleman, sometimes alluded to as a nobleman, by the name of Hugh de Paynes. He is generally accepted to be the first Grand Master of the Knights Templar. According to historical texts, de Paynes received this title from King Baldwin II, the crusader king of Jerusalem. This was only, however, after nine previous "poor knights of Christ" worked their way into King Baldwin's favor. Subsequently, a delegation of these knights was sent to receive sanction for their order from the Pope. Hugh de Paynes arrived at the Vatican soon thereafter and received the full and enthusiastic endorsement of the Pontiff. He is believed to have completely ignited a wonderful spirit of enthusiasm in the Christian world all across Europe. Nobleman and royalty were said to compete to see who could give his order the better treasure. All in all, whether good or bad, the Knights Templar were the hottest show in town for a considerable number of years.

History offers more questions than answers about Hugh de Paynes. Recent years have given way to much misdirected and sophomoric enthusiasm concerning the Knights Templar, but there is plenty of historical evidence to suggest that he and his knights learned their craft from the Moors. Their own writings and legacy, if you read them closely, are based utterly and completely on a Moorish heritage. Popular thought attributes most of their Islamic heritage to Hassan Sabbah and his "Assassin" cult. There has been considerable misinformation on Hassan Sabbah, and while I do not mean to minimize his influence on the Templars, you can also find historical connections to the Moors if you look hard enough. Hassan Sabbah was, after all, initiated in Morocco. Common history, however, tends to list these connections as fragmentary at best.

As the Knights Templar stem from the Moors and begin their advent on the world scene under Hugh de Paynes, I thought it would be interesting to study his history, but there is scant mention of it. The etymology of the name *Hugh de Paynes*, however, tells you far more than you will find in common history books. This, coupled with the synchronicity of him being a former resident of the Moors Gate area, opens an entire panorama to Moorish history that one might otherwise miss.

The most mundane explanation of his name suggests that he came from the Champagne district of France and that his name *Payne* derived from *pagne*, a diminutive of *Champagne*. This might even be true, but there are very intriguing connections when you consider the different and more pure strains of the etymology.

What really made me pay serious attention to his name occurred when I was studying the prospect of Moorish presidents of the United States. Although I could find only the most nominal of ties to the Moors in common history books, the genetic lineage of many of these early presidents, including Washington himself, was more commonly tied to the Huguenots. Not being too sure what a Huguenot was, I readily found out that it was a carefully construed term that the Moors hid behind for purposes of safety and political expediency.

Common history states that the Huguenots were Protestants from the south of France who became a thriving force in the 1500's after the Inquisition began forcing Jews and Muslims to convert to Christianity. Most of these Huguenots were Moors and Cathars who were seeking to escape the purge of the Catholic death machine that was waging successful war against any rival thought forms. Scholars are not really too sure where the name "Huguenot" came from, but it is generally accepted that the term was derived from the proposition that the early Huguenots used to meet at the gate of King Hugo, a legendary king who is hard to pin down. There was a King Hugo in Italy, but no one is quite sure that this is the same King Hugo. In investigating this, I could not help but notice that the word *Hugo* is very similar to *Yugo* as in *Yugoslavia* which means "southern slav." In this sense, *King Hugo* could be construed as "Southern King" which implies a Moor such as Othello. When we consider that Hugh de Paynes represents the deepest secrets of the origins of the Knights Templar, it becomes obvious that any group of Cathars and Moors from southern France would be honored to refer to themselves as "Huguenots." It is also something of a necessity as far as keeping the secret tradition of their belief system alive.

Even common historians are pretty much starting to accept that the Knights Templar came to America before Columbus, but they have always recognized that the Huguenots were the first Europeans to build a European city in America. This was right near St. Augustine, just a year or two prior to the Spanish settlement. St. Augustine has long been recognized by common history as the oldest European city in the United States of America. The Spanish mission to St. Augustine was, however, for the express purpose of wiping out the Huguenot or Moorish contingent right next door. The Spanish were successful.

While it is impossible to say outright at this time that the name *Huguenot* derived from Hugh de Paynes, it is certainly a logical conclusion, particularly when you consider the secret ciphers that the Moors have used throughout history. It seems to be a right trail, however, because other intriguing prospects present themselves when we further examine the etymology of the name.

The name Hugh de Paynes can be translated as Hugh de Paen or Hugh de Paganus. *Hugh* means "spirit" or "mind" and the comparative etymology of the word *hue* cannot be dismissed either. While *hue* popularly means "color" or gradations of such, its obsolete definitions are "complexion" and "appearance." The etymology of *hue* breaks down to the Swedish word *hy* which means "skin" or "complexion." Since black people were always signified as "people of color," it gives us pause to wonder if Hugh de Paynes was a dark Moor himself. There can be no dispute, however, about the fact that he considered himself a part of the Moorish heritage. The Templars were created as a seed within the structure of the Catholic world and were designed to undermine it. The seed was planted by the arch enemy of the Catholics: the Moors. The plan worked for a considerable time period, too.

There is another definition of *hue* which is listed as a separate word in the dictionary and it means "outcry" in regards to a pursuer or clamor. The etymology for hue in this sense is *hoot* as in "to give a hoot" or to make an outcry.

When we consider the heritage of Hugh de Paynes, we must also recognize that in "Early English Law," as per *Webster's New Universal Unabridged Dictionary*, there was a legal term called "hue and cry." This referred to "the pursuit of a felon or offender with loud cries in an effort to alarm the citizenry." The etymology for *hue and cry* is based on an Anglo-French phrase *hu et cri*. As Hugh de Paynes came from France, this meaning has possible applications, particularly if you consider that his name was changed by history after his order became fugitives. Even if that is not the case, you will find that his name is pregnant with meaning and synchronicity in other respects.

The etymology of *paens* is equally interesting in that it referred to commoners or peons. Keep in mind that the Templars portrayed themselves as the "Poor Knights of Christ." During the repressive advent of Christianity during the 3rd Century, political rhetoric turned hard against the term *pagan* or *pagunus*, a word which most etymologists agree comes from a term Roman soldiers used disdainfully to refer to ordinary citizens who were not part of the military. Calling someone a pagan made the Roman soldiers feel superior. As Christianity became politically correct in the Roman Empire, the word *pagan* or *paganus* was turned around and applied to <u>anyone</u> who was not a Christian. At first, it was applied by a "soldier of Christ" to be used in referring to nonmilitary people, just like the older Roman centurions did. By the time of St. Augustine, he used it with relish to demonstrate that any "pagan" was a pariah. In the dictionary, *pagan* is believed to have derived from "rustic, rural, or common folk," with particular reference to them believing in strange gods. Before Christianity, most everyone believed in such gods. The Christian was a new breed of human being, at least in terms of thought structure.

From the above, it is very reasonable to assume that the name Hugh de Paynes not only represented the true common people and their beliefs but also a "crying out" or clamoring for the ancient pagan ways that refused to be suppressed. This is a simplistic explanation and certainly an acceptable one, but a further pursuit of the etymology not only leads to far deeper insights of ordinary history but also unveils some of the biggest and most guarded secrets of the mystery schools. As you will learn, it is easier to decode the mystery schools by etymology than by joining them.

As was said before, the Templars were a front group. Their whole mission was to carry the lamp of illumination that the Saracen or Moor represented. Behind this was the Goddess. Anyone who recognizes divinity in "a" or "the" Goddess is by definition a pagan. The modern definition of a pagan is basically anyone who is not of the three religions from the seed of Abraham: Christianity, Judaism, and Islam. The Moors also used Islam to front for them as well. It is not that the Moors disrespected the various truths these religions have to offer in an esoteric or metaphysical sense, but their tradition had been around much longer. It was expedient for them to fit in with the various trends and political leanings of the times.

It seems that from the very beginning, at least in Rome, the term *pagan* or *paganus* was used to demonstrate the superiority of a militant or patriarchal person over a nonviolent or matriarchal one. There is further etymology, however, and that lies in the Greek word *pagos*. There are multiple meanings for it. It has been defined as meaning "frost" or "ice" but also as "peak," suggesting a high place. The most common definition for *pagos** is a "big

---

* *Pagos* can also be seen in *Galapagos*, an island chain which suffers from the most bizarre etymology. *Galapagos* is said to mean "giant tortoise" in Spanish or Portuguese, but *tortuga* is the word for tortoise in both languages so it can be assumed that they referred to a giant tortoise as a "galapagos" after the islands were named. As the Galapagos Islands were a pirate stronghold, it is not a stretch to believe that the islands were named after "gala"+"pagans," keeping in mind that *ghel* is a pre-Indo-European word for *gullet* or "gold." These islands were used extensively by pirate raiders who were seeking to loot Spain of their New World gold. The most ironic definitions I found were boldly stated on websites, but I had difficulty corroborating their use. They claimed that *galapagos* (continued on next page)

piece of rock." There is also the word *pagoda* which has confused meanings and is believed to be a word adopted and corrupted by the Persians. We do know that pagodas are "high" houses or buildings so the appellation of high fits well. The basic meaning of *pagos*, however, seems to yield most effectively when we consider one of the most prominent sites of ancient Athens: Areios Pagos which translates to "Hill of Mars." This location is notorious to pagan haters and was purposely chosen as a site where St. Paul delivered his agenda to the Greeks. It was known well for being a site of ritual homicide and blood sacrifice. Mars or Aries was, after all, the god of war, violence, and blood. Aries would gladly kill you in a heartbeat if provoked.

When we consider that Areios Pagos is a huge rock that ascends into the air, we begin to understand that certain Greek words may well have derived from the very name of this natural creation itself. As it reaches into the sky, the term *pagos* could easily be identified with "peak" or a high place. Additionally, it is a rock, so we cannot argue with that definition. Most intriguing is that *Areios*, which is the name of Ares, can be seen in the words we use such as *aeronautics, aeroplane,* and even the word *air*. The god Ares or Aries is not normally thought of as having to do with the air unless we consider his Roman name: Mars. All you have to do is look up at the night sky, take a look at that planet and think of all it represents to the lost heritage of man (see *Pyramids of Montauk* by Preston Nichols and Peter Moon for further information on this subject). Mars is "up in the air" and its reddish hue also suggests blood, including the blood of lineage, assumably from the planet Mars. Thus, in Areios Pagos, we have a dramatic heritage encapsulated in one composite name and location. If you consider that the pentagram is the recognized symbol of Mars, you also have it corresponding with the sacred name of Jesus: *Yod He Shin Va He* (see *Synchronicity and the Seventh Seal* for a full

means "saddleback" in Portuguese (and sometimes Spanish) and that the turtles were named by reason of having backs that look like saddles. When you consider that Pegasus, the flying horse of Greek mythology, might have a claim to the root "peg" or "pegos," there is some logic to it. What is most intriguing however is that the term "saddleback" is an indirect but excellent reference to the Templars because they were renown for riding two to a horse, both on the same "saddleback." That the turtle is also the totem of the Montauk Natives is one further irony.

THE MARS GATE

explanation of this term). For those of you who saw and remember the movie *The Wolfman*, Larry Talbot sees a pentagram on his hand and is taught that it is the symbol of being a werewolf. This is an ironic and even humorous twist, but it brings home the ancient art of pagan lore: shape-shifting. And, all wrapped up in one location known as Areios Pagos.

This is quite a bit of information to flow out of the obscure name of Hugh de Paynes. Most researchers give far more time to the martyring of Jacques de Molay. The intrigue does not, however, end here.

As I alluded to earlier, the Magick Theater has moved into my life. One of the new characters I have met as a result is a Moor by the name of Hamza Sid Catlett Bey. He has worked extensively with etymologies and has taught me a considerable amount. I will be sharing some of his scholarship in the rest of this chapter.

The first thing Hamza pointed out to me about the etymology of the word *Moor* is that it comes from the Roman word *maurus*, dark-skinned, but that they borrowed the word from the Ancient Greeks who amalgamated it from the Egyptian word *mau*, which means "cat," and the Hebrew *reish,* which means "beginning" or "head." In esoteric Hebrew, *reish* also refers to "processing" or "clarifying." This means that the ancient Greeks concocted the word *maurus* with reference to a cat. Literally, this could refer to the processing or clarifying of the cat, but it could also mean "cathead" or "head of the cats." As *reish*, or its derivatives, is also a designation of royalty, it could mean "Cat King." It is hard to imagine that the Greeks and Romans who originally used the sound *mau-r* or *mau-reesh* did not know of its correspondence with Egyptian cat worship.

Cat worship thrived in ancient Egypt, particularly in the city of Bubastis, but the entire prospect has been completely under estimated by scholars. The architecture and masonry of Egypt is loaded with blatant clues, but the most blatant one of all is encoded right within Egypt's greatest mystery: the Sphinx. This great structure is a combination of the Babylonian archetypes of Virgo and Leo and suggests a combination of cat and human genetics. Although he is not the only source to suggest such, Edgar Cayce is perhaps the most popular advocate to indicate that the Sphinx was erected by "cat people."

The implications are rather obvious. The Moors have been referred to as cat people. When you learn the Moorish tradition that they were the original architects of the Giza Plateu, we have some common ground. The ancient Egyptians honored the cat beyond all other animals. In fact, it was a capital offense to kill a cat in Egypt. They were routinely mummified. This legacy of the cat, however, does not end in Egypt. It is hard-wired into the infrastructure of our entire culture via superstrings of intrigue that not only propagate ancient mysteries but dispense power and influence through the most nefarious means imaginable.

To give you an example, the most secretive of Masonic handshakes is the "Lion's Paw" or "Lion's Grip." It is basically reaching three fingers to touch the wrist of a fellow Mason's hand while you are shaking his hand. When you do it, your hand looks like a paw. A more sinister offshoot of this is used in the mysterious Bon meetings* I wrote about in *The Black Sun*. One of the code gestures that allows you to enter such a group and be appropriately received is to raise your hand so as to emulate the paw of a cat and say "chatta," the French word for cat. The fact that the mystery cult of the cat has been co-opted by secret societies does not mean that the truth it represents is evil but only that it is powerful. The key, however, is in the hard-wiring.

The hard-wiring of this universe is based upon software which is known as the Cabalistic Tree of Life. There is also Kabballa and Qabala. "C" is used for the Christian interpretation, "K" for the Hebrew, and "Q" for the Islamic. This software, so to speak, is based upon ten basic principles (or more when you get very esoteric) that continually repeat, mix with each other, and create new manifestations or pathways (as depicted in the Tarot).

All interpretations of the Cabala include a sephiroth (Hebrew for sphere) designated as *Tipareth*. It represents many things, includ-

---

* The Bon meetings were documented meetings centered around Aryan in-spired dogma that were known to have existed _during_ World War II at Yaphank, Long Island, _after_ the primary Nazi goose-steppers had been jailed and shut down. It was allowed to continue by local law enforcement who reported on the meetings regularly to J. Edgar Hoover. Such meetings have continued into the present day but also include indigenous people, including Arabs and Native Americans, and are centered around high tech aerospace technology as well as routine aeronautics. In their more far-out descriptions, they also include "space-time generators" and sci-fi stuff. Tied to the old Nazi guard, this group was involved in perpetrating the events of 9-11.

ing the so-called "Mysteries of the Crucifixion." It is juxtaposed as an intermediary between "heaven" and the earth plane. It also interprets from one region to the other. It is the realm where the *messiah* or "bringer of truth" exists. The entire experience of Christ as rendered in the Bible conforms to and was configured to represent these age old principles which were, in the past, confined to mystery school teachings. This is why Christ, as a young child, completely befuddled the scholars in the Temple when he engaged them in vigorous debate about the Rabbinical teachings. He knew them backwards and forwards because HE was the interpreter. Tipareth also refers to the "son" of the most high and is also symbolized by the Sun or Leo, the Lion.

Anyone who has deeply studied esotericism or astrology knows that the Age of Pisces is known as the Age of the Dying God. This rationale is based upon the above principles which come right out of the very mystery schools which influenced the stories of the Bible. It is a time when all the ancient wisdom would go underground in order to be preserved for a future time.

Although I have demonstrated that the Moors represent hidden knowledge, I could go far deeper and be even more convincing if time and book space allowed. The plight they have undergone, including their suffering, is in complete harmony with the principles of Tipareth.

It is poetic, if not absurd, to think that a bunch of Moors gathered around the Areios Pago in Athens and hard-wired a myth and legend into the morphogenetic grid so as to preserve all of their ancient wisdom but also create a time-release mechanism by which the data could be rediscovered at the appropriate time. Additionally, real events and circumstances were injected into history that would intertwine with and complement these myths and legends in such a manner that the overall mission could be accomplished. I am sure that there were many gatherings of Moors and many other people who met around such sacred places as Areios Pagos and were a part of such intrigue, but this often gives way to very corny scenarios. The Tar Baby could perhaps give the most theatrical and appropriate rendition, but his English can become tiresome. I will therefore give you a rapid analogy which is offered so that you will understand the pattern that is at play in the saga of the Moors.

The Moors fit a pattern that can be easily likened to the saga of a messianic intermediary such as Christ. The Hill of Mars is an excellent place to start as it represents homicide and ritual sacrifice. In this case, we are talking about the Moors and all of the knowledge that they represented in the past. It not only includes the killing of the Moors, but their own willingness to self-sacrifice towards a future time. This includes willingly assuming the lowest echelon in society: the ghetto. I do not mean to imply that all of the descendants of the Moors ended up in the ghetto but too many of them did. Christ not only rejected worldly goods, but he cavorted with publicans and sinners. In such a scenario, it is easy to understand why Christianity has been so popular in the ghetto and even thrives there. Somewhere, down deep, on a soul level, those people know that redemption is possible. They might not experience it in this lifetime, but down deep, they know it. This is why people in the ghetto are known to have "soul." It is part of their racial memory as Moors. If you want to talk about the "Poor Knights of Christ," then go have a look at the ghetto. When you take into account the legend of Christ suffering on the cross for some three hours, you will note that blacks have suffered for a longer period of time and far more intensely in many cases.

When we consider the birth of Christ, we have the greatest magical act of the Millennium. This is the birthing of a Moonchild via a Virgin. Christ, directly referred to as the Lion of Judeah in the Bible, is born of a human virgin. This is the symbolism of the Sphinx: Virgo giving birth to Leo. Further correspondences to the Sphinx and Christ were explained in *Synchronicity and the Seventh Seal* where the name *Yod-He-Shin-Vau-He* (later corrupted to *Jesus*) represents that *change* inherent in all living conditions but also the ability to live by changing and manipulating the four elements known as *Yod-He-Vau-He*, also expressed as YAWH, and later corrupted, quite badly, into *Jehovah*. This relationship of the "four into five" is known as Tetragrammaton (meaning four letters) into Pentagrammaton (meaning five letters). Four represents the tetrahedron, the basic geometric form upon which all biological life is based. Five represents the pentagram which symbolizes spirit monitoring the elements of fire, water, air, and earth. Five toes on each paw move the four legs of the Sphinx. This symbolism is very rich but is mostly unknown.

410

The symbolism between Christ and the cat do not stop there. Christ has traditionally been characterized as both a black panther[*] and also as the "Moon Man." Those born of a virgin have long since been designated as a moonchild. The black cat has always been symbolized with the feminine energy or the moon. The name *Christ* can also be construed as C-T (from C-hris-T) or cat.

There is also the Spanish greeting of "Feliz Navidad" which is supposed to be their version of Merry Christmas. It translates much more like "birth of the cat." In Spanish, *feliz* means "happy" but it also refers to *cat*. It comes from the Latin *felix*, for cat. It is obvious that our English words *feel* and *felicity* both come from this root. *Felicity*, by the way, means more than just happiness. It also means "source of happiness." In contrast to this is the word *felon* which refers to evil or wickedness. Another word that is interesting along this line is *fellah*, an Egyptian or Syrian word for a peasant. The word *fell* cannot be ruled out either because their are many examples where the phoneme *cat* means "down" such as in *cataclysm* (meaning wash down), *catastrophe* (turning down), and *catalyst* (loosening down). The word *catacomb* also refers to being "down" in the ground. As the term *cat* has long been associated with the vagina, it suggests coming down from the heavens into the earthly realm, perhaps via cat genetics.

In the story of the Virgin Birth, we have Christ being propagated as a magical act through Mary, a name which is etymologically tied to Moriah, Mars, and Moor. The herb myrrh is presented at the birth and death of Christ. Mary was also known as "Myrrh of the Sea." This designation of her accommodates a pagan legend having to do with the goddess Myrhha giving birth to "Adonai" in a cave at Bethlehem. There is also an ancient classical painting which portrays the Sphinx at Giza cradling the Christ child. The idea has been around for a long time as if written in code.

In the story of Christ, we have an analogy of Martian (the blood of Mary or Moriah) blood being spilled in the murder of a

---

[*]According to Hebrew texts of the time period, there was a character known as Jesus ben Pandera who was fathered by a Roman soldier with a temple "prostitute" of Magdala. He became a healing miracle worker who foresaw the end of the world and arranged his own execution. There were reportedly a lot of writings from that time period about "Pandera," but these records were destroyed by the Church.

411

cat (Lion of Judea) in a willing sacrifice. All of this is in keeping with the ancient tradition of Areios Pagos, the Hill of Mars, a place where victims were martyred.* The Martian aspect is not far-fetched at all from a mythological view because the Roman god Mars was himself the product of a virgin birth via Juno who derived him from her own Amazonian fertility magic. He was also identified or mis-identified with the Norse names of Tyr or Tiw, the latter of which was sometimes aligned with Odin. Tiw was a god of battle, and it is why we call the third day of the week *Tuesday* instead of *Martes* as the Spanish refer to it. In French, it is *Mardi*.

It is amazing how the etymology of one of the most enigmatic characters in history can unleash such a torrent of hidden knowledge. There is, however, one more key when we consider once again the namesake of Hugh de Paynes. The root of *pagos* is also related to Pegasus, the winged horse of Zeus who corresponds to Al-Barak, the steed who took Muhammad to heaven at the location which is now known as the Dome of the Rock. Pegasus is a corruption and adaption of earlier myths, but in the common version he was a winged "mare" who was born when the blood of Medusa flowed into the sea (some versions have Neptune as the father, but he is the god of the sea so there is not too much difference).

The Greek word *pegas* means "spring" because Pegasus was known for having created a spring when he stomped his crescent-shaped hoof on the ground and dug the Hippocampus or Hippocrene (which means horse-well). The correspondence with Pegasus and a water spring has to do with ancient water-priestesses called Pegae whose roots go back to Abydos in Egypt at a spring called Pega. The Hippocampus is known as the stream of the Muses.

The mythology of this story takes on additional meaning

---

* The word *martyr* is also of interest because it derives from *mar* and *tyr*. As Tyr is the name of the Norse god of victory and son of Odin, *martyr* could be viewed as either "victory of the Moors or Mars" but also as "Hill of Mars" where *tyr* is representative of the word *tor* which means "hill" or "promontory." It could also be construed as "son of Mars." In Greek, the word *martyr* is designated to mean "to witness." In early Christian writings, a martyr was meant to describe someone who had witnessed Christ, particularly his death and resurrection. In a broader sense, a martyr is defined in our language as somebody who is willing to die rather than to change or abrogate their beliefs or what they know to be true.

when we consider the biology of the brain. The area of the brain which stores memory is known as the hippocampus, and it is white, just like Pegasus. The white color might not be much of a coincidence, but when you realize that Pegasus is sacred to Mnemosyne, the goddess of memory and the mother of the Muses, there is more than a little synchronicity at work. The biology of the brain, however, does not end with the hippocampus.

In the center of the hippocampus is an organ shaped like a ram's horn. This was recognized long ago and was called "Ammon's Horn" because the Egyptian god Ammon was often portrayed as having a ram's head. This is ironic because computer memory is also designated as RAM, short for Random Access Memory. Dysfunction in this area causes Alzeimer's Disease. We see another irony in this setup with the word "ram" being a backwards depiction of "mar."

Perhaps more significant than all that, Ammon's hidden name is Mon, another name for the Black Sun but also another name for the acme of consciousness. This is the rising of the kundalini to its full potential. It is the Skull of Golgotha fully activated. This very depiction is even alluded to in Revelation where Christ is referred to as Amen or Ammon.

When we consider the prospect of fully activating one's Ammon's Horn or potential "Christ consciousness," we have returned to a similar theme I addressed earlier: raising the dead. This theme aligns exactly with what I stated earlier was the most exalted handshake of the Masons: the Lion's Grip. The underlying reason Masons adopted this custom was that King Solomon used the Lion's Grip to raise Hiram Abiff from the dead.

Whether we like it or not, the mythology of our heritage is wired so as to position the cat or the lion as having the ultimate ability to restore us from the rigors of the death state.

Whatever "raising the dead" might really mean in practical terms, activating your full potential is a challenging path. It requires confronting all of the residual inertia on our planet that is geared toward keeping you less aware. Even if you reach an exalted harmonic of the state of beingness termed a messiah or even a role serving in that "office," you still have to face the group consciousness which has yet to integrate the information, let alone the experience. Pursuing this concept of Mon or Ammon's Horn through the biology of your brain is really a microcosmic story of building your own version of the Tower of Babel. In essence, you are building a Watchtower and, in the process, acquiring your own guardians. From this perspective, one can easily envision streams of individuals creating what could be deemed a virtual utopia for themselves; while at the same time, the collective takes on the same mantle in such a way that the universe is finally able, at long last, to "repair itself."

What you have just read is the real meaning of Babalon, a word which means "gate" but phonetically signifies *baba-lon* where *lon*, not incorrectly, signifies lion, just as the Lene Lenape tribe of Delaware (a portion of which became the Montauks) derives their name from the lion. Babalon is therefore the Gateway of the Lion, and it symbolizes the road back to our mysterious origins. The Sphinx, which I hope you now have a good understanding of, is representative of this gateway. The Gateway of the Lion represents the Realm of Creation, but it also represents something far, far deeper: your meaningful participation in the Realm of Creation, including your own personal fate.

Somehow, quite miraculously, we have arrived at the above proposition through the Moors Gate. It has taken us on a tour from the Hill of Mars in Greece to the Sphinx at Cairo (or Al-Kahira, meaning Mars). When you consider that the name *Moor* derives from *cat* and is also inextricably associated with Mars, it gives little reason to doubt that the Moors played a major part in erecting the Sphinx and other structures of Cairo. If not, it is hard to explain why their namesake has been indelibly imprinted upon the area. Once again, the hidden and undiscovered history of the Moors has not only demonstrated itself to be the gateway to the past but also to the future.

414

58

THE ALI SHUFFLE

Any visible threads of the original Moorish Empire had been virtually extinguished or gone underground by the time Noble Drew Ali, then known as Timothy Drew, was born into this world. His fabled initiation in Egypt occurred just about the time L. Ron Hubbard was born. Until I actually composed this book, I would not have been predisposed to connect the character of Drew Ali with either L. Ron Hubbard or the research he conducted on the subject of freedom and oppression. In view of my own experiences with relation to this book, however, the quantum juxtaposition of these two characters stands out like fireworks.

Hubbard's work was primarily about the imprisonment and freedom of the spirit. Although Ali and Hubbard might not appear connected at first glance, there is quite a rhyme and rhythm between the two. On the surface, Ali's work might be misinterpreted to appeal primarily to a displaced people and cultural heritage. As my friend Hamza Bey (Sid Catlett) has taught me, the more you learn about the etymology of the word *Moor*, the more you realize that it is a spiritual identity that ultimately has very little to do with racial or cultural identity. The original Moors made no distinction along racial lines. This was actually an invented distinction to sow seeds of discord amongst people and to facilitate the disruption of what might best be termed YOUR own infinite spiritual potential.

The deoppression work done by LRH was the first time he ever initiated techniques that literally began to reach out and restructure the environment on a wholesale basis. It began with the Sea Org itself and then the Scientology community, but it was spreading with the wild abandoned of a forest fire before the "Fire Department"* came and put it out. As I said, the seeds of this deoppression technology were said to be based upon the most fundamental purpose of life itself. We are talking about a principle that can literally raise the dead. This is the same stuff which can rearrange matter and change the entire universe. Of course, in deoppression, we are primarily talking about reviving the esprit de corps of a group of people and taking the yoke off their operation. This is, however, a closely related cousin of the fundamental ability to raise the dead. The problem, as LRH stated, was that once people are free, they demand more and more freedom. Anyone standing in the way of that freedom becomes fair game to the people who are demanding the freedom.

The information I am writing here and elsewhere in this book has very fundamental implications which not only reach beyond the words of this page but project itself into a region of the consciousness that will not be denied. *That* is your future. It is your power.

How Noble Drew Ali fits into this equation, at first glance, might not be as exotic as what I have just said. As the story develops, however, it might be viewed as more exotic. In the end, however, they are both part and parcel of the same principle: declaring your lost heritage as a free and infinite being.

The fact that you have been able to read what I have just written is only by the thinnest of threads, most of which you have already read about in this book. Only very few Sea Org members

---

* The term "Fire Department" is suggestive of one Ray Bradbury's classic work, *Fahrenheit 451*, where the sole purpose of the Fire Department in that story was to seek out hidden knowledge, in the form of books, and destroy them by burning. Most ironic in this story is the name of the protagonist, Montag. Montag starts out as a fireman who destroys books but begins reading them and then joins the rebel book readers. He is eventually discovered and is forced to escape to the fringe outskirts of society to a virtual "free zone" of book readers who live in the forest, outside the reach of the repressive society. This, in turn, is suggestive of former Scientologists who have escaped the repression of their church and practice on their own. It should be known that if someone sets up a splinter Scientology practice, the Church of Scientology has been known to go to extreme legal measures to stop them.

and virtually no Scientologists even know about this deoppression principle, let alone practice it. There is also a contingent of people who left the Church who knew about this but are not in any position, for various reasons, to publish anything on it. Quite amazingly, it has not shown up on any internet posting boards or Scientology histories. On the other hand, you can make an extensive study of the French Revolution and pretty much come up with the same principles. That is what LRH did. My putting it forth into your consciousness is just like water leaking through. Water is very powerful, even in small doses. It can bore a hole through granite.

Just as Noble Drew Ali tried to lift the veil of deception from the Moors and their heritage so did LRH try to lift the veil of deception from spiritual beings and their true nature. It is therefore not really ironic that by giving a proper and respectful funeral service for LRH, I literally gated the Moorish Science Temple into my life. To remind you, when LRH wrote his work on oppression, he stated that the only place left in the world with even a vestigial element of freedom was the United States. This can now be attributed directly to the Moors. None of this would be known if it were not for Drew Ali and the dynamic movement he created which began to flourish and reach critical mass in 1929. The recognition and uncovering of oppression of the Moors is part and parcel of delivering the best promises of what Scientology, in its most exalted aspects, had to offer.

Learning and understanding Hubbard's information on suppression and oppression, coupled with his unique viewpoints and other applications, enabled me to perceive and penetrate the unique mysteries of Montauk Point. The growth resulting from these experiences led me to write *Synchronicity and the Seventh Seal* which ultimately explains the greatest mystery underlying Western esotericism and the secret formula upon which Christianity was based before being badly distorted. This is the real Da Vinci Code which gave rise to the Italian Renaissance and which was secretly influenced by the Moors.

At the current time, the door to Moorish mysteries is opening far and wide. The Age of Pisces is at an end, and the Moors are coming to receive their inheritance. Drew Ali instigated this process when he return to America and released a publication known as the *Circle Seven Koran*. While Drew Ali did not deliver the concise formula as was clearly delineated in *Synchronicity and the Seventh Seal*, he represented the energy and <u>was</u> the energy of such. Drew Ali was very much part of the mythos and reality that enabled me to write that book. What Drew Ali wrote was geared towards a format that would be accepted by his people at that particular time. It apparently worked quite well.

When the Moorish Science reached its peak in 1929, it was on the heels of one of the greatest, but most dangerous, discoveries Drew Ali ever made. In 1928, Ali attended a Pan American conference in Havana, Cuba where he enjoyed broad recognition from a host of other countries. They were, of course, recognizing his sovereign status as a Moorish national who was representing the ancient empire of Amexem. Keep in mind that other countries had no reason to fear Drew Ali or what he represented. It was at this conference, however, that he received a document which was to change the face of Moorish Science forever and would eventually lead to what is known as the Great Schism. That is the name the Moorish community uses to refer to the dispersal of Moorish Science into different groups.

The document Drew Ali received was a copy of a mandate whereby the Amexem[*] Empire extended a land grant of the entire Western Hemisphere to certain Europeans. I have not yet seen the document, and its exact contents are highly mysterious, yet its ramifications literally turned the United States of America upside down. Essentially, it "leased" America to a certain party for a particular number of years, not unlike the way China leased Hong Kong to Great Britain. The lease was up in 2004.

It is entirely reasonable to believe that such a document, if it still exists and can be brought to light, is a mere relic of a long forgotten era that has no significant meaning in today's legal system. That would be fine except for one very important point. If you have truly studied the detailed legal history of the United States of America, you would understand that there is more than a little truth to the prospect of their being such a document. Why? The entire legal history of the United States is predicated on such a proposition.

---

[*] Notice how the word *Amexem* contains the root of the word *Mexico*. Mexico is named after Mexitis, which translates to "Moon Child" or "the Moon's umbilical chord."

What is known is that Secretary of States Hughes, from the U.S. Government, attended the Pan American conference and was made privy of this mandate. So were several other heads of state. As a result, a closed-door conference between several nations was held in Geneva, Switzerland and a labyrinthine series of discussions and negotiations began. The Geneva conferences went on for some five years, but the records are still kept sealed to this very day. It is known that several international banks called in their loans as a result of this potential legal threat and the stock market crashed in 1929. Several countries, which included the United States, Portugal, France, and Spain, declared bankruptcy in order that relevant powers could buffer themselves from any potential legal claims.

In the case of the United States of America, it was reorganized with a new corporate legal status. Franklin Roosevelt was part and parcel of the entire plan when he abolished the gold standard and created the New Deal. Federal Reserve notes were then issued in place of gold-backed currency. The Great Seal of the Moors was used on the back of the notes.

People behind the Geneva conferences were so concerned about any potential boomerangs from the Moorish issue that they began a full barreled character assassination of Moorish heritage. The most flagrant example of this was when two Master Masons put together the infamous *Amos and Andy* show and it became the first nationally syndicated radio show in history. It was deliberately designed to spoof the Moorish Science Temple by lampooning them as the "Mystic Order of the Knights of the Sea" and callously referred to them as sardines. From one perspective, this can be viewed as hysterically funny, especially when you consider that the dignitaries were given titles such as the Swordfish, the Mackerel, and the Kingfish. On the other hand, it was a deliberate and malicious act of intent designed to portray any Moor as the most laughable example of what could be termed the lowest common denominator. Not long after *Amos and Andy* had its national debut, Drew Ali was arrested and mysteriously died. This has been ignored by both history and conspiracy books. When you see how integrally connected the Moors are to the history of the world, let alone the United States, you see that they are a guidepost to the true history of the planet. This is the lamp of illumination, the Hermit's lamp (from the Tarot), that the secret societies have long played tribute to in their writings.

By reason of our social conditioning, it seems utterly preposterous that the old Moorish Empire could have an actual court-of-law legal claim on this country. Conversely, it appears that world leaders have been deathly afraid of such and have even prepared themselves to legally avoid the inevitable. Once again, the Moors show themselves to be hard-wired into the infrastructure of our consciousness as well as the historical paper trail.

My introduction into the Moorish world began through Dr. Ellias Bey. His own research directed him to what has been called most extensive biography ever on Drew Ali. Ironically, it is published by Seven Seals Publications and is entitled *The Biography of Noble Drew Ali: The Exhuming of a Nation* by Elihu N. Pleasant-Bey. It is also known as the *Book of Fire*. When Dr. Bey told me about this new book, it was as if the Magick Theater had once again manifested in my life. I immediately bought a copy but also had a chance to speak with the author.

To my surprise, Elihu Pleasant-Bey was able to answer the question that had just been posed in an earlier chapter: what had happened to Drew Ali when he died? I had no idea it would be obtained so fast and effortlessly.

Elihu Bey spent a great deal of his life learning the lessons presented in the above book and preparing it for publication. It is extensive and encyclopedic in nature. One of the most special things about him, however, is that he learned a considerable amount of the legacy of Drew Ali from those of his associates who were closest to him: his women. In typical Moorish tradition, Drew Ali was polygamous. This should not surprise anyone, but it is interesting than in all of the highlights that have been told about his death, there is scant information about this aspect of his life and those who were most dear to him. Their voice has remained silent for over eighty years.

According to what Elihu Bey learned from these Moorish sisters was that Drew Ali did not die of a police beating nor from illness. This would not have been in keeping with his whole spiritual makeup. As a young boy, he had a reputation for levitation and for moving things by reason of his inherent communication with elementals. In his later years, there were also stories that, at Drew Ali's direction, his followers would throw knives and other dangerous objects at him while he would remain in a corner of the room. The objects never penetrated him. Other people have also reported that Drew Ali was at one time a circus performer and that such tricks were incorporated into his performances. This flair for the paranormal apparently extended to the death state as well.

Before his death, Drew Ali could see what was coming down the pike for the Moorish Nation. Accordingly, he saw that the burden of the Moorish people was so great that it could not easily be overcome in a human form. As a result, he opted out and exited. In other words, he chose his death by simply leaving his body. While this might sound absurd on the one hand, there is no known burial site or death certificate for Timothy Drew that has yet come to light. There are reports of a death and funeral, but these are very anecdotal and do not particularly contradict what was said above.

Whatever the truth of the situation might be, Drew Ali has left behind a legacy that positions himself as an Ascended Master. I do not know what is true or untrue about Drew Ali and his magical abilities. I do know, however, that they pale in comparison to what he represents as a leader of the Moorish movement which is beginning to pattern itself like a giant tsunami. It is time to remember the words of Marjorie Cameron, as taught to her by Jack Parsons. It takes 100-150 years after the death of a man before you can begin to judge him and the impact he has made upon the world. Only after fifty years do you begin to get any real clues. Drew Ali left the physical world seventy-five years ago. We are just now getting some substantial clues.

Since 1929, there has been a major effort to undermine any remnant traces of the Moorish Empire and the life and times of Noble Drew Ali. The "Great Schism" that occurred in 1929, after his death, has sundered the Moorish Empire from any unity. Any true threads of that lineage have remained hidden and are only now emerging. It is something to be reckoned with.

59

THE PRISONER

I want you to consider once again the vestigial freedom that L. Ron Hubbard said was in the United States of America. Of course, there are many people who will proclaim that we are a totally free people. In some ways this is very true, but this does not abrogate the fact that this universe is constructed like a slave empire. If you do not work, you will not live or be forced to assume a further subservient position in society. Even most of the so-called "slave masters," i.e. people who control world governments, are not really in positions of power that reach beyond a mortal reference point.

The enslavement of the Moors and the annihilation of Moorish culture and heritage actually reaches beyond the Age of Pisces and the Age of the Dying God. It is the systematic nature of this material universe. This does not mean that we do not have good times ahead nor should it dampen the theme of enlightenment that the Age of Aquarius brings. The full awakening of "Ammon's Horn" in the hippocampus of the brain is something to look forward to, if one is willing to take the necessary and sometimes harrowing steps.

What I found novel about Scientology was that it addressed sudden excitations of the kundalini in a sophisticated and gentle manner that enabled me to integrate and balance that type of energy. It has made my journey easy in some respects. Where the journey has not been easy, it has been understandable. And while I have to give credit where credit is due, I am completely divorced from any Scientology organizations. There are also plenty of independent Scientologists around who are no longer affiliated with the Church, and they are colloquially known as the Free Zone. I am not a part of them either. None of these statements, however, should be construed as a negative for what any individual might be able to achieve in any such a group.

Earlier in this book, it was mentioned that Scientology had different definitions to describe itself. Two of them were "knowing how to know" and "lookingness." Looking is self-explanatory, but knowing how to know can be confusing to people, especially those who walk around in confusion. Knowing *how* to know simply refers to paying attention to the data you *need* to know. A general contractor does not need to know all of the precise details or methods used by his subcontractors, but he has to know what it takes to get the overall job done. These are two different specialties. All situations in life, particularly jobs, require that we be specialists in some areas and generalists in other areas. When it comes to your own esoteric or spiritual path, it is no different. Most of you already know the lingering mysteries inside of yourself and the answers you seek. Writing them down and seeking them out is the first step in the process.

L. Ron Hubbard proliferated the prospect that we were all once powerful "OTs" or Operating Thetans and that we can once again regain our ancient heritage. The contemplated or actualized experience of such a state of existence has been routinely misunderstood by various factions. When it is not accepted, it is most often mocked or derided with the proposition that "no one" has ever attained such. As was said earlier, it is a matter of gradients or gradations. In football, one first learns to block and tackle before becoming a football player. One then hones their skills in order to become a most valuable player. The term Operating Thetan does suggest, of course, a state of being that is free from slavery or the conditions of slavery, with particular emphasis being placed upon the spirit. Derision can only be proliferated by those who feel or perceive the impossibility of such a state of being. From my perspective, I will give you an analogy.

If you liken the material plane to Alcatraz Island in San Francisco Bay, pretend that you are an inmate in the infamous prison that was once housed there. There was no hope of escape from Alcatraz because, if you were clever enough to get clear of the building, you would have to deal with lethally cold water and a current that was unmanageable to even a good swimmer. Now, let us also presume that, for the purpose of this analogy, most of the inmates in this prison are not even aware of the outside world. Either by rumor or serendipity, you become aware that there is an outside world. Most people you talk to in the prison are not even able to accommodate the thoughts of an outside world, let alone the possibility of escaping the confines of the prison. Nevertheless, you begin to attract more and more information about this outside world and even find a secret cell within the prison that is dedicated to the proposition of an escape. It is almost like a secret cult based upon the legacy of a prisoner who actually did escape and who sends back clandestine messages from time to time. The idea begins to dawn on you that there is not only life beyond the prison but that you can experience it as well.

As the weeks and months go by, you learn the ways and means to escape the guards, get through the air ducts, service tunnels and over the walls. This is only half the battle though. You have also studied how to acquire or make a wetsuit and swim fins. This now gives you more than a fighting chance to get across the bay. If you are lucky, you can also increase your chances by contriving a snorkel and mask. On top of this, you learn or are taught the tide tables so that you can make your swim when the current is easiest. As long as you evade detection by the guards, you are home free. Well, you might be free, but you are really not home.

When you swim up to the shores of San Francisco, you have quite a dilemma on your hands. You are wearing attire that makes you look like the Creature from the Black Lagoon, and you have no money or accoutrements of society. This is not much different from being up a creek without a paddle. Each one who takes this journey is going to have a completely different experience. If you are good looking, or particularly attractive to the opposite sex, you just might get lucky and have someone take an inordinate interest in you and help you handle your immediate living problems. On the other hand, you might be recruited into the sex/slave trade in order to just survive. It is also possible that a religious missionary might show you sympathy and take you in. Or, you could turn to mugging and thievery. There are countless scenarios that might take place. Each of us has a different karma.

Going Clear and OT in Scientology is very similar to the prison analogy I have just given you. Actually, it is much friendlier than what I have described, but the prospect it presents can be just as daunting when you look at the true nature of what you are dealing with. One ends up on the shores of San Francisco and faces an unpredictable and very challenging fate. That is the bad news. The good news is that you have an indestructible confidence and vitality within yourself whereby you know that you will make good of the situation no matter what. While different people may end up in different stations of society, one has the life essence necessary to direct the elemental factors so as to secure a future. One, however, still has to maintain the responsibilities of living in and carrying on with society. In actuality, society contains the very element of life that each and everyone of us are. When you take stock of the fact that we are life, and not matter, we are engaged in an eternal struggle to deal with the mysteries of the physical universe and come to terms with it. While this can be viewed as a condition of enslavement, it can also be viewed from different perspectives. It is far more empowering to view this condition as a game. This brings me to another important point with regard to the Scientology angle. I would be remiss if I did not mention it.

60

THE TONE SCALE

When you consider the broad panorama of life and how many different things there are to know, it is obvious that there are certain importances that should be selected beyond and above all others. Very early on in the research of L. Ron Hubbard, he observed particular emotional characteristics in people which he found tremendously useful in terms of predicting their behavior. He developed his observations into a listed scale of human emotions which he termed the Tone Scale.

In the early years of Dianetic therapy, Hubbard noticed that people's moods or emotions varied as they received auditing. Everything was quite simple in the beginning. He plotted out a scale of emotions that people experienced and it went something like this. The numbers themselves are arbitrary designations.

4.0 Enthusiasm
3.0 Conservatism
2.0 Antagonism
1.0 Fear
0.0 Death

In addition to the above, there was a zone just above death which was designated as "Apathy," a rather lifeless emotion that is akin to a resignation from life just before one quits. As people were audited, it was noticed that they would move up and down the emotions on this scale as they recounted various incidents that they had been through. Routinely, when you got to and cleared out the basic engram, i.e. that moment of pain and unconsciousness that was precipitating the problem in the first place, the preclear would bounce up to the top of the scale and be in enthusiasm. The word *enthusiasm* derives from *theos* or *deios* and suggests "being with God."

Besides noting that different emotions accrued during various difficult incidents in one's life, it was also observed that people tend to habitually gravitate towards one particular tone. In other words, you have all known people who were overly enthusiastic, antagonistic, or fearful. Countless hours of empirical observation also revealed that these tone levels were accompanied by various other characteristics that not only revealed themselves in the muscular and nervous reactions of people but also in how they dealt with various factors in the environment. The book *Science of Survival* was totally dedicated to these observations and gives many clues on how to index the survival potential of other human beings. It also tells the secrets of who may help you and who might hurt you. This book was accompanied by *The Hubbard Chart of Human Evaluation* which gave an overview of such.

As research continued, further observations were made and the Tone Scale was expanded at different times during the evolution of Dianetics and Scientology. This not only included new gradations or listings of emotions but also embraced various characteristics of entities or spirits acting outside the realm of a human body.

One of the later renditions of the Tone Scale was as follows:

40.0	Serenity of Beingness
30.0	Postulates
22.0	Games
20.0	Action
8.0	Exhilaration
6.0	Aesthetics
4.0	Enthusiasm
3.5	Cheerfulness
3.3	Strong Interest
3.0	Conservatism
2.9	Mild Interest

2.8 Contented
2.6 Disinterested
2.5 Boredom
2.4 Monotony
2.0 Antagonism
1.9 Hostility
1.8 Pain
1.5 Anger
1.4 Hate
1.3 Resentment
1.2 No Sympathy
1.15 Unexpressed Resentment
1.1 Covert Hostility
1.02 Anxiety
1.0 Fear
 .98 Despair
 .96 Terror
 .94 Numb
 .9 Sympathy
 .8 Propitiation
 .5 Grief
 .375 Making Amends
 .3 Undeserving
 .2 Self-abasement
 .1 Victim
 .07 Hopeless
 .05 Apathy
 .03 Useless
 .01 Dying
0.0 Body Death

As was said, the Tone Scale was also expanded to include negative states of beingness encompassing the realm of disembodied spirits. They are as follows:

-0.01   Failure
-0.1   Pity
-0.2   Shame (being other bodies)
-0.7   Accountable

429

-1.0	Blame (punishing other bodies)
-1.3	Regret (responsibility as blame)
-1.5	Controlling Bodies
-2.2	Protecting Bodies
-3.0	Owning Bodies
-3.5	Approval from Bodies
-4.0	Needing Bodies
-5.0	Worshipping Bodies
-6.0	Sacrifice
-8.0	Hiding
-10.0	Being Objects
-20.0	Being Nothing
-30.0	Can't Hide
-40.0	Total Failure

It should be noted that the codifications of these emotions were designated as approximating the principles of a natural law. In other words, Hubbard was not so bold as to declare his observations to be *the* law, but they were as close a measuring stick as could be made by him. In essence, he had discovered that nature has a piano keyboard of various states of existence known as emotions and that they follow a natural order that goes from high to low. It is a scale of existence by which everything in the universe can be evaluated, living or not.

If some of the items on the tone scale or the general principle of it is hard to grasp, do not be perplexed. You can start out by looking up each of the words you do not understand. It is then a matter of observation. I can also tell you from my personal experience that it took me years and years of auditing other people before I myself could see the exact logic of how some of these tone levels manifested. There were some helpful study courses which actually required you to memorize this scale, including the numbers, forwards and backwards. After that, you went out into society, asked people various questions and observed the tone level of those spoken to. The results can be quite shocking. In fact, you would probably be surprised at how low-toned people in society generally are. I remember doing a drill and discovering that the highest toned people I interviewed on the streets of Clearwater were, by far, the fishermen at the end of the dock.

They were in a tone of monotony and having a grand old time just sitting there with their fishing poles.

Every person is considered to have a social tone and a chronic tone. The social tone is the face that you present to the world or the work place. It likely has nothing to do with how you really feel. Your chronic tone is your habitual tone about how you feel about everything. In most people, this is quite low. When I say low, that does not mean that such people do not have positive aspects, but it means they might suffer from a habitual apathy, antagonism or other emotion. People will also respond to various life situations with different tones.

In the very early days of Dianetics and Scientology, Hubbard estimated that the general tone of society was about 2.5 which equates to boredom. As the years went by, he realized that he had completely overestimated the state of human beings. This is why the tone scale had to be expanded to include the lower tones. If you look at the porno trade, pimps, professional wrestling, the slave-trade, and religion, you will find broad use for the lower aspects of the Tone Scale. The average "walk-about" is usually walking around with either chronic pain, apathy, or some disappointment that manifests in a lower tone. It is not that life is all bad, but when you stop and assess the entire state of affairs of life on this planet, you are met with a rather daunting prospect. This is what requires "confront" in Scientology lingo. In other words, the first step to resolving a condition or situation is to actually face what it is that you are dealing with. When it comes to difficult prospects or situations, people are often too willing not to talk about it or to deliberately ignore the pink elephant in the living room. "Let somebody else take care of that," or some other catch-phrase is too often employed.

The secret history of the Sphinx, the pyramids, and just about any other mystery you want to tackle on this planet has been made far more complex than it really is. It has been simulated, altered, adopted, and reinvented with only trace elements of the original creators. If you consider the prospect that God created man in his own image, you have to confront that image, contemplate what it is reflecting and ask yourself about the exact nature of this God. Whatever you want to think about God is fine, but you cannot deny that this entity gave you one hell of a riddle to figure out.

The Tone Scale is a tool which will enable you to sharpen your perceptions with regard to the various characters who play a part in your own personal riddle as well as that of the collective. In Scientology, you are taught that you can bring a person up the Tone Scale by addressing them at a level approximately one-half to one point higher than where they are at any given particular moment. For example, if you are having to deal with an antagonistic person, you simply feign boredom over his combative behavior. A person in fear can be brought up the scale by feigning anger. L. Ron Hubbard used these techniques on people all the time. He did it because it was effective. Popularity was not really a consideration in such matters.

Hubbard composed quite a bit of information on the Tone Scale. I am including only a brief overview for a couple of reasons. First, it is essential to comprehending the Scientology experience I went through. It cannot be adequately grasped without at least mentioning it. I have saved it towards the end so that it might give you a tool in better understanding your own life. It will also help you understand various subjects that I have sometimes been associated with, correctly or incorrectly.

Much of the subject matter of UFOs and mind control stems from the lower regions of the Tone Scale. While there is a definite need to face and confront various truths, this should not be used as an invitation to drool over horrific conditions that have been perpetrated upon yourself or others. In other words, if you resonate with manifestations of a various tone level, you will then assume that tone level. Some people have issues they need to deal with and these sort of things should most productively be addressed in therapy sessions. Endlessly talking about it to others, beyond being informed of certain situations, is generally not productive. Conspiracy topics can also hover too much around lower tones. Hanging around a lower tone, particularly if you are a bonafide secret agent, can get you killed.

Choose the people you associate with wisely. The same should apply to subjects you discuss as well. It will do more than make you feel better. Using the Tone Scale will help you.

61

THE BLACK VIRGIN

THE FOLLOWING TRANSMISSION IS FROM A PARALLEL UNIVERSE

After Peter Moon has kicked the Turd Baby, in the shape of a Wilson football, all the way to the Moors Gate in Jerusalem, the Tar Baby looks up at him in admiration.

"Now, dat was a great kick!" he said.

After the Tar Baby completes his words, the outhouse explodes and a vast amount of sewage matter begins to bubble up out of the hole that the outhouse stood over. The entire area is soaked with sewage. After a short while, another eruption comes out of the hole, but this time volumes of various conspiracy books come out along with the sewage. All of them end up sitting in the sewage.

"Look at dat one!" says the Tar Baby who is pointing at a copy of *Holy Blood, Holy Grail.* He then walks over and picks up the book which is dripping with undesirable waste matter. "Dis book all 'bout dat Merovignian Dynasty..."

"I know," says Peter, "They failed to point out or realize that the word *Merovignian* derives from the word Moor."

"Yep, dey 'pletely missed de boat on dat one, just like all dem otha books missed de Moors," says the Tar Baby.

"It's quite true," agrees Peter. "The Merovignian dynasty, as recorded by history, is very specific that the kings were of a pedigree of Major Domos who had assumed the throne and had no

433

affiliation with any royal heritage. The book is quite correct, however, in addressing the fact that a very ancient code has been circulated for centuries in order to convey a secret message."

"De Moors," says the Tar Baby.

"Yes, the Moors. It is quite observable if you have been initiated to look for it. There is another big so-called secret over a creature called the Quinotaur. According to Merovignian legend, Merovech is the first of the Merovignians. His mother was already pregnant when she went swimming and was further impregnated by a mysterious creature called the Quinotaur. All these conspiracy books have been puzzled about the Quinotaur. There is no ready reference that explains it, but it is right in front of them if they study the data revealed in the *Seventh Seal* book. "Quino" refers to five or the sacred pentagram. This symbolizes the sacred name of *Yod He Shin Vau He*. The "taur" could be interpreted as "bull" as in Taurus. This is another way of expressing Mithras who was also identified with Christ. If you separate *tau* and *r* where *tau* means cross and *r* is the Hebrew *reish* (meaning "head" but also "to process" or "to digest"), you have *Quinotaur* referring to the processing of "four into five" by means of the four-pointed cross and its relationship to the pentagram. It is just another way of getting across that the original Moors were a bloodline that represented the sacred formula of *Yod-He-Shin-Vau-He*. It has been so misunderstood, and a huge cult of literature has grown around it without even understanding it."

"Not me!" says the Tar Baby who is now doing cartwheels and bouncing around in the form of Leonardo Da Vinci's pentagrammatic man. When he finally finishes, he is now in the shape of a black starfish.

"Look!" says the Tar Baby, "I'm the Quino-Tar!"

"Very funny!" says Peter.

"I think we'd better get back to the Sphinx," says Marjorie Cameron, who has been listening and watching.

As the Tar Baby returns to his normal shape, the party begins to approach the Sphinx, but they suddenly see a huge mothership flying over the Giza Plateau. It is enormous and is beaming destructive laser beams of light which hit various areas and blow them to bits. A few smaller pyramids are blown up in the process.

"Look!," says Marjorie, "They're going after the parrot."

Having reemerged, the green parrot is flying at sharp angles to avoid being targeted. After making incredibly evasive maneuvers, the parrot flies to the Sphinx and disappears into a hidden compartment behind what would be the third eye of the Sphinx. The mothership is relentless as it follows the parrot, first exploding the Great Pyramid and then the Sphinx itself. As the Sphinx crumbles, debris is all around. A small shuttle craft from the Mothership then touches down near the rubble, and Captain Kidd emerges. As Kidd approaches Peter, Marjorie, and the Tar Baby, the parrot comes out from behind a rock and begins an exaggerated death as if he was in a comedy version of an old western. As his legs stumble and trip over themselves, he speaks.

"Ya got me, partner!" he says before wobbling some more and finally falling down to his death.

"Finally, I got the little bastard," says Kidd.

"What's the point?" asks Peter Moon. "You know he can always resurrect."

"It's just satisfaction. That's all. I think I finally got it out of my system. I can't tell you how much joy it gives to shoot down and annihilate that damn little parrot. He's a little prick."

At this point, the party is startled by a rock falling from the rubble. As they look in the direction of the falling rock, they see that the paws of the Sphinx are still intact. Noble Drew Ali is between them and is flanked by two resplendent goddesses. One is Cleopatra VII who is mostly naked save for an asp adorning and crawling around her breasts. There is also Scota, the Pharaoh's daughter of long ago who migrated to Scotland and was said to be the first to introduce cats to that country.

"You still have one more journey," says Noble Drew.

"But de Sphinx!" says the Tar Baby. "What we gonna do? It broken!"

"Don't mind that," says Noble Drew. "It can be rebuilt. That last rendition could have been more expository. But, as we stand between the paws of the Sphinx, you are in the Lion's Grip. You still have one more journey to make and that is the CAT-aracts."

"You mean the cataracts of the Nile?" asks Peter Moon. "I know those refer to the breaks, rapids, or waterfalls in the Nile where the river is separated from itself. The cataracts were also known to possess different temples of initiation — all symbolized

435

by the word CAT in the word *cataract*."

"No, you're going to the cataracts of Montauk," says Drew Ali. "That is why Captain Kidd's here — to take you there."

"I've never heard of the cataracts of Montauk," says Peter.

"No?" says Drew Ali. "You have certainly been experiencing them and taking others with you. They are in the CAT-acombs of Montauk, hidden to all but the most astute. These cataracts represent the unsealing of the mysteries, and you must unseal the final mystery. But first, you must realize something about the Montauks, their ignorance of their own lost heritage and their failure to properly declare their sovereignty. Before the pharaoh can be restored, they must complete the final step of the process of Tetragrammaton which is the daughter. The holy name of Allah is a balance of male and female and so is Tetragrammaton, the four letters of which represent *Yod* for father, *He* for mother, *Vau* for son, and *He* for daughter. These two daughters of the Pharaoh flank me. Scota carried the lineage of the Pharaoh to Scotland but also brought cats. Her name is often misconstrued for it originally was Scata or Scat which equates to S-CAT. You see, this name represents the blending of the serpent energy, designated by the "S," with that of the cat. In Egypt, the cat was used to vanquish the serpent energy. This is why there is a legend of Cleopatra dying of the bite of an asp. She was the last pharaoh of Egypt. In the legend, a key was offered to future generations. The antidote is the cat. Once again, the Moors are the key."

After these last words, a whirring sound is heard from overhead. It is the Turd Baby flying through the air as a football. Drew Ali reaches out his hand adroitly and catches the ball one-handed. The Turd Baby then unfolds himself and speaks.

"Ah-ha! Here I am again. Don't you see? Scat. I'm a piece of scat — I fit right in again."

"Right," says Peter Moon, "like in scatological. I can only say that you're right at home here at the Sphinx. By the way, who kicked you back here?"

"I think it was Ariel Sharon. He didn't want me anywhere around the Temple Mount. Bye!" says the Turd Baby as he disappears into the ruins of what was the Sphinx.

"Now," says Drew Ali "it is time for you to bring the energy of the daughter back to Montauk Point. That is the only way you can reestablish the Phaoroah who can then, in turn, restore Ma'at. Cleopatra and Scota will lead the way."

Drew Ali then leads the party down a series of steps where they follow the two Pharaohs' daughters to an underground river where a boat from Captain Kidd's adventure ride is waiting for them. As Drew Ali and the two Pharaohs' daughters wave good-bye, Captain Kidd takes the helm and the party takes a high speed ride through underground caverns and waterways until they at last reach an underground station beneath Montauk Point. As they arrive and disembark from the small boat, they see a huge wall of 529 television screens. Sitting at a control station in front of the screen is Otto Wilson, the CIA-Scientologist who they encountered underneath the Sphinx so long ago. He is now wearing a neck brace.

"Hey, Otto," says Peter Moon, "how's your neck?"

"Not, too bad, thanks. I can take it off soon. I sure messed up back there in the Hall of Records."

"Or what was the Hall of Records," replies Peter. "What are you doing here?"

"This is the great console of the Montauk Project. There are 529 screens connected to separate vortexes across the time lines. Someone has to monitor various incidents that crop up from time to time, no pun intended."

"Against what parameters?" asks Peter Moon. "I'd think 529 is a very limited number of screens to try and monitor the whole universe, past and future."

"Hah!" says Otto. "You should have seen it a few years ago when we only had 49 screens. I had to bitch and squeal just to add 480 more crummy televisions. You'd think it was a big budget item or something the way I had to scream, yell, and beg the requisition department. Bureaucracies are bureaucracies."

"Yes," replies Peter, "but if all those televisions are viewing through separate vortexes, doesn't it take a lot of power to set up those vortexes and keep them running?"

"That's what the particle accelerator is for. There are far more problems than power, however. For example, time itself. 529 screens into the past and future is nothing. I mean 529 screens on the present is nothing. You are very limited as to what you can see. This job is very overrated."

"Tell me," says Peter, "how is it determined what screen is going to be on what time and what location?"

"Well, you've got various factions wanting different things. Most of it, however, is very boring. You get boring assignments that have more to do with probability curves than watching exciting pieces of history. Besides, it takes FOREVER for history to unfold. Believe it or not, you'll get more information sometimes by going to Blockbuster and renting some stupid Hollywood movie. At least, it gives you a summation of events. Watching history is b-o-r-i-n-g unless you've got infinite time on your hands and a good video editing console. Ideally, we'd have a separate viewer watching each screen. We used to do some of that with the Remote Viewing program, but most of them went crazy and had to be reprogrammed and dropped out of the project. Once in a great while, like back in 1983, things really start popping. Virtually every screen had something interesting going on. In some respects, it seemed like the screens were running themselves, and we were just trying to catch up with the project. At that point, the Montauk Project was itself, and we became just bit players. But, most of the time, its stochastic observations, sort of like the compilation of data on the SETI project. Being a "time cowboy" and going through various pieces of history to watch "hot stuff" is strictly forbidden. Don't ask me why, either. I'm just a god damn employee around here."

"This is all very interesting," says Peter Moon, "but we're here to see the cataracts."

"Ah!" says Otto Wilson with an odd sense of familiarity. "That's one thing nobody's ever been able to figure out. In fact, it's pretty much the only remaining mystery of the Montauk Project, at least as far as the brass and all of us employees are concerned. I'll take you there myself."

Otto then leads the party to a large elevator where all get in and descend many stories beneath the ground. When they emerge, Otto passes out raincoats and leads them through a cave which leads to another underground river. At a dock, they board another small boat and travel through a series of waterfalls.

"You are lucky," says Otto. "Originally, you could only access where we are now through a long and twisting system of caves, some of which were augmented by an ancient civilization.

It was not only a tough trek, but in some areas the caves went straight down and you needed spelunking equipment to negotiate them. The Montauk Project operators eventually constructed a shaft and put an elevator in. Otherwise, you'd all have to be fitted out like cave explorers."

As the party continues down the river, he points to a huge white crystal rock as a waterfall bounces off of it and sprays the boat.

"These," says Otto Wilson, "are symbolic of ancient portals of initiation that have been lost to the world. Our occult bureau has studied the traditions of Egypt and Atlantis, but they never got this one right. Long tradition indicates, and everyone involved in the project knows this, that the key to these underground cataracts at Montauk can be found in this secret room that I'm taking you to. Only problem is, no one can penetrate it."

At this point, Otto Wilson takes the party before a large metal door that has the Hebrew letters of Tetragrammaton inscribed upon it. The last letter, symbolizing "the daughter," is extra large. There are multiple combination locks built into the door and all are in vertical alignment above the door knob which is also locked. Besides that, there are two deadbolts and various latches with padlocks. It is a general mess.

"All of the so-called safe crackers who have tried to open this door know that the key is the sacred 'four into five.' That means taking Tetragrammaton and manipulating it with the Fifth Element. That is what we need to unlock this door. So far, none of the combinations have been unlocked, and believe me, we have tried every possible combination. None of the other locks can be picked either. It is like a Chinese puzzle."

"Gee," said Captain Kidd. "I guess I blew it by frying that parrot. After all, he was the shin parrot. I shouldn't have let my emotions get so carried away."

"It's OK," says Peter Moon as he nods his head in the direction of the Tar Baby. "We've still got the Quino-Tar."

Hearing the acknowledgment, the Tar Baby proudly sticks out his chest and forms himself into a replica of Da Vinci's Pentagrammatic Man before doing cartwheels once again.

"Tar Baby," says Peter, "please see if you can find a screw driver and a hammer."

"Dat's Quino-Tar!" says the Tar Baby as goes bouncing off.

Otto Wilson looks at Peter as if mystified by the request. "What on earth do you want those for?" asks Wilson.

"All answers are basically simple," replies Peter. "Codes upon codes upon codes require more and more complexity to be resolved. We need less complexity."

At that point, the Tar Baby has returned in almost no time with a hammer and a flat-head screw driver. Peter then takes the screw driver to the hinges and begins pounding out the bolts upon which the door is hung with.

"Whoever locked this door," says Peter, "obviously wanted it to be opened. Apparently, no one saw that the easiest method to open the door is by ignoring the locks and disconnecting the hinges which are conspicuously on this side of the door."

"Gee," says Wilson, "how could we have missed something so obvious?"

"Might have something to do with mind control," says Peter as he jars the door open from the hinged side.

As the party goes through a rather narrow opening from the irregular door configuration, they see a vast tomb of sarcophagi, most of which are almost human-sized except that the top part depicts the head of a cat. There are also frescoes along the wall which suggest that this is a tomb full of ancient cat people. There are some jewels and adornments as well.

"Look," says Cameron, pointing to a chamber in the back.

The party goes to the back where they find a resplendent black chamber, the walls of which are black agate. It is beautiful. Inscribed on a single sarcophagus are what appear to be four words written in obscure hieroglyphics.

"What do those hieroglyphics say?" asks Captain Kidd.

"Better get the Quino-Tar to decipher here," says Peter.

"It's four words," says the Tar Baby turned Quino-Tar, who is no longer speaking broken English. 'It says Ayesha, Scota, Fatima, Alia,' or something like that."

"Ah!" says Peter, "the matrilineal descent of the bloodline of Muhammad — that is Fatima and Alia. Ayesha is the original feminine, pre-Christian word, which represents *Yod He Shin Vau He* or Pentagrammaton. Yeshua is the male version. Interesting that there are four names. We need to find a fifth."

"That is who is in the sarcophagus," says Cameron.

In the middle of the chamber is a human sarcophagus. As they approach, the sarcophagus begins to slowly open.

"What are we going to do?" says Captain Kidd.

"Don't worry," says Peter, "everything will be just fine."

When the sarcophagus is fully opened, it reveals a human mummy in the shape of a woman. It appears completely lifeless.

"OK," says Peter, "I think I know what to do here. Where's the Quino-Tar?"

As the Tar Baby comes bouncing in, Peter picks him up and rests him on his arm.

"Now, Quino-Tar, please shape-shift yourself into the paw of a lion. We're going to use the Lion's Grip on this mummy."

As the Tar Baby carries out Peter's instructions, the tar of the Tar Baby begins to form around Peter's hand until it looks like the paw of a lion. Peter then takes it to the mummy and places the tar paw over it. As he does, the mummy begins to stir. It is coming to life. Captain Kidd then gently places the mummy on a table and Cameron begins the long process of unwrapping whatever this incredible mystery might be. When she is finally done, a beautiful black female can be seen. She is young.

"Who is she?" says Captain Kidd.

"She is the mysterious Black Virgin," replies Cameron, "the same creature that has hovered over the esoteric mysteries of France and elsewhere for thousands of years. Finally, at last, she has manifested."

"The real Black Virgin!" says Captain Kidd excitedly. "Well, I'll be. I had a few of her statues in my various treasures."

"Well," says the Quino-Tar, "this should settle the matter of the Montauks and the issue of the Pharoahship. Do you know who this is?"

"It's rather obvious," says Peter.

"It's not so obvious to me!" exclaims Captain Kidd.

"This Black Virgin represents the bloodline of Noble Drew Ali. In all of the various factions of Moorish Science and Muslim offshoots since the great schism, the card that has been completely overlooked, are the children of Drew Ali," replies Peter.

"How do we even know he had any children?" asks Kidd.

"With that many wives, how could he have not?" replies Peter. "Just as the bloodline of Muhammad has been virtually ignored by the Muslim world, so has the bloodline of Noble Drew Ali been ignored by the Moors, if only because it is unknown."

"The time was not right until now," says Cameron.

"This is why the efforts to help the Montauks have met with utter despair and fruitlessness. The feminine principle is not being properly honored. That can no longer be the case. It is the female of the tribe who are to choose the leader, but what we need at this point is a female Pharaoh. This is the great conundrum that has been needed to release all the pent up and discordant energy of Montauk Point."

"This might upset a lot of people," says Captain Kidd, "especially my old backers in the East India Company."

"No, matter," says Peter. "I have only opened the door. The energy will find its own way. The instructions are very clear. My work here is done."

After Peter's words, which were being overheard by the entire Montauk underground via electronic eavesdropping, there was a sudden burst of joy and celebration by everyone employed there. A party broke out as the revelry was broadcast far and wide on the loudspeakers.

As Peter and Cameron made their way out of the underground and emerged into the young evening, the festivities had extended above ground and even to the sky. A host of flying saucers could be seen hovering around Camp Hero in a circular formation as they beamed rays of light, not unlike a searchlight, in a gesture of celebration. All in all, it looked like a scene that was something of a cross between a used car sale and something that might have represented the birth of a messiah.

Looking up at the sky, Peter speaks to Cameron.

"I can't say what all of these are doing here, but I can assure you of one thing though.

"What's that?" asked Cameron.

"The energy of the Quino-Tar has been released."

"Do you mean the Quino-Tar or the Quinotaur?"

"Both."

As the lights go off, a neon light shines in the dark. It says, "Montauk — The End."

THE DREAM CONTINUED

As I watched the Flying Saucers bathe Camp Hero with all sorts of celebratory lights, I had no idea about the full ramifications of the current I had released. All I knew was that I was due for a nice rest. As I sat with Cameron on the beach in front of the lighthouse, I could see a beautiful crescent moon. The partitions between the real world and my dream world were very thin. I no longer cared, at least for a while, which was which.

Cameron appeared young, just as she looked when she was married to Jack. She was not exactly my type of woman, and I am sure that I was not exactly her type of man, but that did not matter. We were inextricably linked through our work. She had even showed me how our astrological correspondences fit together. It was nice just to sit on the beach, relax, and take in the evening scenery.

"I remember," I said, "when you took that walk in the Arroyo Seco with your brother and saw a UFO together. You told me that you had never known such joy."

"Yes, and it's the same joy I'm feeling now," as she looked up at the saucers.

"There's something strange about all this," I said. "I think I should tell you, and I'd like your opinion. When I was younger, in my teenage years, I would sometimes take trips with father and be alone in the car with him. Every once in a while, he would say two separate things to me which were on a frequency far above anything else he ever said. I mean, most of what he said to me was about mundane things or mundane concerns, but more than a few times, he would rise above this. Something, in some strange way, compelled him to communicate something to me."

"What was it?" she asked.

"Well, for one, he would either reach out and hold my arm, or almost hold my arm, and tell me that if anything ever happened to him, he prayed that I would be all right."

"I'd say," said Cameron, "that he had a premonition that he was going to die. It's really not so odd that people can see beyond the veil that way. Actually, they all can, they just spend most of their time in denial."

"Yes," I said, "but I almost found it patronizing or insulting. I mean, I never believed for a minute that I could not survive without his being here. Nevertheless, with hindsight, I can see that he knew, in some strange way, about his demise. My mother always told me that he was very preoccupied about leaving something behind with regard to a will."

"What was the other thing he said?" asked Cameron.

"This was even stranger. It wasn't always in the car, but he said it quite often. He said to 'Remember the Moors, son. They are very important.' Anytime the subject of the Moors came up, he would talk animatedly about their contributions to science. He would also say that too little was known about them. He was, of course, referring to normal history, but it was as if he knew there was a deeper story. He had no idea I would take it as far as I did. It was almost like a generational imprint. I just wondered what you thought about all this."

"Well," she said, "knowledge is native to all of us. How it manifests or leaks out is different for each individual. It is actually more surprising at what does not leak out, but that is not the way we are wired. No revelations should be surprising. They are only surprising because we are wired to be ignorant. When we short-circuit the wiring, we experience joy."

"Looks like that is what we did with the Montauk crowd here," I said. "I'm not sure they even know what they're celebrating."

At this point, Otto Wilson comes around the bend with a six-pack of Montauk Light beer, a defunct brand that has become a collector's item and can fetch over $30 a can. He was staggering.

"Howdy!" said Otto. "Mind if I join you? Everyone's havin' a grand old time. I've never seen anything like it."

"Why?" I asked. "I can't believe they appreciate all this stuff about the lineage of Drew Ali and the Pharoah."

"Don't be surprised at anything, Peter. These people are much smarter than you think. They've got their problems, and some of them have very serious problems, but there are many intelligent people here and they're laced with esoteric knowledge. You just unlocked the secret to the CATacombs of Montauk. I mean, we've all tried at one time or another to get into that room. It was the one remaining mystery at Montauk no one even had a clue about. It was mostly left to drift in the wind, but it created a far more visceral reaction than anyone could imagine. You'd be surprised, Peter, many of these people like you because you can say what they cannot. They are under security oaths under penalty of death. Admittedly, there is a lot of bullshit, but there are also some very valid reasons for these security oaths. All of their work is not evil."

"Well, Otto," I said, "you all could've fooled me. I mean these oaths only set up an environment where abuse can occur."

"But," continued Otto, "as I said, these people like you. You'd be surprised, but they cannot say a word. The President and many other key people in politics and the Government have made a special arrangement where they commissioned Milton Bradley to make a secret edition of "The Montauk Project Game." They all love to play it. It is a role-playing game where the President and Vice President pretend to be Duncan, Preston or even the Beast."

"Well," I said, "I guess we've added a new character. Condoleeza Rice can now play the Black Virgin if she wants to. But seriously, Otto, I think you've had a bit too much of that Montauk Light beer."

"Don't you see — Condoleeza Rice. She's now the Secretary of State and is the person that the Montauks need to apply to for recognition as a sovereign entity. As a minority and a woman, how could she refuse them?"

"Maybe you're right, but I still think you've had too much to drink of that Montauk Light."

"Maybe I have," said Otto, "but I have another question for you. I can understand what you accomplished in Scientology. That doesn't surprise me too much, but I still don't get how Scientology ties in to the Babalon Working."

"Well, it's really kind of simple. I have already explained how Babalon means 'Gate of the Lion' and that Ron gated in so much of his information from the Excalibur incident where he saw a huge gate. As you've studied Scientology, Otto, I know you will remember what Ron called the "training lion." Besides being promoted on various brochures, the training lion was imprinted as background on every Scientology Grade Chart. Do you recall?"

"Yes, I do."

"Well, Otto, that is only a testament to the fact that LRH was emanating his own version of what Stewart Swerdlow refers to as the Lion Frequency, the highest and most powerful frequency of all. This is the same principle behind the Masonic Lion's Grip which can resurrect the dead. It is the mystery of the cat."

"It is the same as....." interrupted Otto.

"Babalon," finished Peter. "Scientology training, if properly and extensively done, was designed to put you in permanent resonance to the gateway between a free and unfree state. We can call it the Lion's Gate or Babalon if you wish. It is all about a gateway. It is not really any different than what Buddhists call having a healthy ratio between attachment and non-attachment. LRH called it the Bridge to Freedom, but that is really a synonym for gate. There was no way he was going to integrate what he did with his old days during the Babalon Working. It would have been too controversial and was seemingly unnecessary. In fact, it would still be completely unnecessary if not for the fact that the Scientology movement had more than a few problems along the way. If it did not, I would still be there and not explaining to everyone what this whole damn trip was about."

At this point, a silver parrot flew out of the silvery crescent moon. It was the same image that was known in the past as the ash parrot, the green parrot, or the shin parrot. Attached to his ankle, there was a message compartment.

"Write a message, braak, braak. Write a message," said the parrot in his patented irritating tone. "I'm taking it to the Ali sisters. Write what you want."

"Oh, you mean the lineal descendants of Drew Ali?"

"Yes, that's right. That's right."

"OK," I said as I scrawled out a nice hello to them and said the following to them.

"To my dear Moorish sisters — I hope that this message finds you well and that I can support your efforts to bring forth the truths you might wish to share. The Pharaoh has now been released. The world has been waiting a long time for you to become visible. The time is now. Best, Peter."

After attaching the brief note to the silver shin parrot, I yawned. I felt as if it had been a very long day, and I wanted to rest. As I curled up next to Cameron and fell asleep, I could once again not help but wonder about her and the way I had become positioned with her. It was never anything I particularly asked for. I did not regret it, however. This woman, and all she stood for, has been so misunderstood. This applied just as well to her old partners, Jack and Ron. While their work is better known, it is still misunderstood. Her work, however, is only beginning to see the light.

As I dozed off, I began to realize that I was already dreaming. There was no beach. There was no Montauk Light. There was no Otto Wilson. There was, however, a blood descendant of Drew Ali, and a new energy over Montauk Point.

The next thing I knew, I was standing before the glen, somewhere on the Emerald Isle, and there were a host of creatures standing before me and listening to my every word. In the background I could see the ruins of what was said to be the oldest castle in the British Isles: the castle of Og. It was now just about sunset, and I could see the faces of my audience yawning. I had talked enough for one day and knew that I would have to finish my story tomorrow. Telling everyone I was done, the crowd dispersed and the Bard of Bards gave me a wink. I knew I could trust him beyond all others to get my story into circulation. It was now out of my hands, and this was a great relief.

Off in the distance, I could see a huge bonfire which I wanted to make my way to. I could enjoy the warmth of the fire. In the background, a feast and festivities were being planned.

Before walking off the stone platform, I yawned and made a nice stretch. To my surprise, I heard a soft splash behind me. It was the Blue Lady of the Lake once again. As she rose, she pressed me next to her naked body. Despite the slime and wetness, she felt very comforting, but her gesture was not really about comfort. With a strength that did not become her beauty, she held me firmly as she submerged me beneath the water. There was at least one more initiation to undergo. It suddenly it occurred to me that I did not know what I would be talking about the next morning. Still, I knew it would be interesting. Everyone was gone, and so was I.

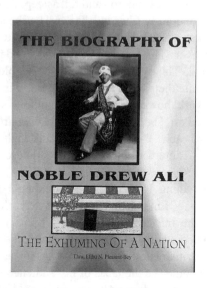

THE MOORISH
SCIENCE TEMPLE

Any understanding of the Moorish Science Temple requires an understanding of its founder, Timothy Drew, born in North Carolina, to the parents of a former slave (father) and a Cherokee. Losing his parents at an early age, Drew went to Egypt, either as a merchant seaman or in some other capacity, and was surprisingly met by a group of "wise men" or mystery school representatives who were expecting him. Taking him to the Great Pyramid, they blindfolded him and took him to the King's Chamber where he was told to find his way out. This is an ancient initiation in which the individual is left to sink or swim. It can, of course, result in death. Eventually, his sponsors found him, quite alive, between the paws of the Sphinx. He was found worthy and commissioned with a new mission to revive the Moorish Empire and teach the displaced Moorish people about their lost heritage. Timothy Drew was given the name of Prophet Abdul Sharif Ali which was then converted to Noble Drew Ali for his English speaking American brethren.

The Moorish Science Temple emerged in 1913 when Noble Drew Ali received a charter from Woodrow Wilson to teach displaced Moorish nationals the truth about their heritage. It was said that Drew Ali was also able to retrieve the original Moroccan flag from a White House safe. It was the flag of Societas Republicae Ea Al Maurikanos, which translates either to "The Al Maurikan Republic Society" or "We the People of the United States of America." Al Maurikanos was the colloquial name for the Americas prior to European colonization, and the entire two continents were once considered to be a part of Amexem, the name of the ancient Moorish Empire which waived the flag of Morocco. As the flag that Drew Ali retrieved was primarily red, it was always known as the "Cherry Tree." Morocco was, not coincidentally, the first nation to sign a treaty with the United States of America. The Sultan of Morocco had sued for peace because the colonists had enslaved a considerable number of citizens from his empire. When the United States did not respond, the Sultan's men kidnapped American citizens until a treaty could be worked out. As a result, any person of any color, including slaves, could go to the Government and proclaim themselves a "free Moor." This was by treaty and assured by the principles and customs of international law and recognized diplomacy. The problem, however, was that neither George Washington nor his colleagues did anything significant to make this known. Instead, they obscured this truth. For this reason, George Washington earned the most famous and satirical yarn that was ever told about him: that he could not lie because it was true that he had chopped down the cherry tree. This satirical yarn, told in the truest tradition of the Moorish bards (which are the source of Flamenco and much gypsy culture, including Carneval), was referring to the fact that George Washington had sold out the Moorish culture and all of its citizens.

Drew Ali's parents were involved with the Theosophical movement, and it has been said that he was schooled in the arts of the circus as well as being a merchant seaman. When he serendipitously came into contact with initiates in Egypt, it was they who taught him more than a thing or two about his own Moorish heritage. When he brought this tradition to America, it is said that Wilson granted him a charter because he thought it a hopeless lark on the part of Ali. It should be remembered that Wilson endured much criticism for being a racist. The racial attributions came to a climax when he allowed the movie *Birth of a Nation* to be shown in the White House and was known to advocate what it stood for. *Birth of a Nation* was about the rigors of reconstruction that occurred in the wake of the Civil War. In the movie, the Ku Klux Klan were portrayed as heroes for putting a lid on the chaos created by freed slaves.

Drew Ali began to promulgate Moorish Science and was far more successful than anyone could imagine. Although Drew Ali has a very thick FBI file, historians have made a gallant effort to remove any trace memory of him from the history books. Not surprisingly, the FBI has not released all of the information they collected on Drew Ali. It is also a matter of public record that the FBI bird-dogged the movements of the Moorish Science Temple very closely.

In 1929, Moorish Science had undergone such a huge renaissance that this new movement was to experience a horrendous version of "Armageddon." Different people within his own brethren tried to seize the considerable power, including financial accounts, that Drew Ali had accrued. Violence broke out and the police became involved. As a result, Drew Ali spent several days in jail and was questioned, some say under harsh and tortuous conditions. The latter has not been confirmed.

Throughout the ordeal, Ali directed his disciples to be kind and nonviolent. Although he was reported dead, history has offered no evidence of a funeral or grave site. His death is shrouded in mystery.

In the wake of Drew Ali's death, the character who inherited the so-called windfall of this Black Muslim movement was Wali Fard, an equally mysterious character who also accrued a huge and sometimes very puzzling, if not contradictory, FBI file. Wali Fard was not black but is well known for using the term "White Devil." Before agreeing with the FBI to remove himself from this new movement, he declared a young man by the name of Elijah Poole as his disciple and handed this new movement to him. Elijah Poole adopted the name of Elijah Muhammad and formed the Nation of Islam which is the premier entity of what has become known as the Black Muslim movement in America.

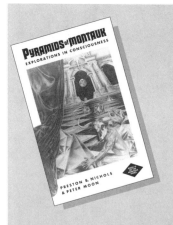

A QUANTUM ADVENTURE

Ong's Hat: The Beginning
by Joseph Matheny
with Peter Moon

ONG'S HAT: THE BEGINNING is the story of mysterious legends from an obscure location in South Central New Jersey, historically known as Ong's Hat, which has inspired a counterculture revolution in physics. Beginning with a club house atmosphere of physicists from the Institute for Advanced Study and Princeton University, exotic pursuits in the Many-Worlds Interpretation of quantum mechanics paved the way for avantgarde experiments in quantum consciousness. Integrating procedural meditation with biofeedback and brain machine techniques, synchronicity attractors were developed which sought out tangible states of existence that reached beyond the bounds of the Consciousness Authority we know so well on Earth. Allegedly, the experimenters ultimately achieved success with time travel and the accessing of parallel universes. *192 pages, ISBN 0-9678162-2-X.....................$19.95*

THE MONTAUK PULSE ™

Characterized as a "Chronicle of Time," a newsletter by the name of *The Montauk Pulse* went into print in the winter of 1993 to chronicle the events and discoveries regarding the ongoing investigation of the Montauk Project by Preston Nichols and Peter Moon. It has remained in print and been issued quarterly ever since. With a minimum of six pages and a distinct identity of its own, the *Pulse* will often comment on details and history that do not necessarily find their way into books. The *Pulse* is interested in and covers quantum phenomena that is pertinent to the understanding of the predicament of time. Subscribing to *The Pulse* directly contributes to the efforts of the authors in writing more books and chronicling the effort to understand time and all of its components. Past support has been crucial to what has developed thus far. We appreciate your support in helping to unravel various mysteries of Earth-based and non-Earth-based consciousness. It makes a difference............*$15.00 annually*

SkyBooks ORDER FORM

*We wait for ALL checks to clear before shipping. This includes Priority Mail orders.
If you want to speed delivery time, please send a U.S. Money Order or use
MasterCard or Visa. Those orders will be shipped right away.
Complete this order form and send with payment or credit card information to:
Sky Books, Box 769, Westbury, New York 11590-0104*

Name	
Address	
City	
State / Country	Zip
Daytime Phone (In case we have a question) ( )	

☐ This is my first order   ☐ I have ordered before   ☐ This is a new address

Method of Payment: ☐ Visa   ☐ MasterCard   ☐ Money Order   ☐ Check

—   —   —

Expiration Date   Signature

Title	Qty	Price
The Montauk Pulse (1 year subscription).....................$15.00		
The Montauk Pulse back issues (List at bottom of page.) $3.75 each		
List: (Use other paper if needed)		
Subtotal		
For delivery in NY add 8.5% tax		
Shipping: see chart on the next page		
U.S. only: Priority Mail		
Total		

Thank you for your order. We appreciate your business.

For a complimentary listing of
special interdimensional books and videos —
send a $1.06 stamp or one dollar to:
Sky Books, Box 769, Westbury, NY 11590-0104

COMING IN 2006

The Montauk
Book of the Living
by Peter Moon

Following
Footsteps of Heroes

A WW1 Guidebook to
Ypres and the Somme

Tom Strickland

GPS Located and Colour Maps

First Published in paperback 2020
Reprinted 2022

Designed and typeset by Ian Bayley.

British Library Cataloguing in Publication Data
A catalogue record for this book is available from the
British Library

Published by Sabrestorm Publishing, The Olive Branch,
Caen Hill, Devizes, Wiltshire SN10 1RB United Kingdom.

Website: www.sabrestorm.com
Email: books@sabrestorm.com

ISBN 978 1 78122 018 4

Popp? ! Awesome Historian!

Dedications

*Vincent Strickland who survived the Somme,
only to be killed in 1917*

Ben Lamb, who survived

Cameron Lamb, DSO killed at Christmas in 1914

Clinton Strickland killed on the Somme 1916

Sid Hawkins who survived Whippet tank driving of 1918

*Wilfred Albert Ball who survived Gallipoli
only to be killed in July 1916*

*Arthur Allen Row who made it to June 1918
and has no known grave*

Enjoy

Contents

Quick Reference Contents

Acknowledgments

Mrs Nancy Strickland
Long suffering wife

Mr Richard Broadhead
Battlefield Guide, friend and author

Mrs Gill Hicks
Mentor, friend and colleague

Miss Amy Cradock
She who checks ones words

Introduction

My name is Tom Strickland and I'm a History teacher at a typical secondary school. I have been taking students and adults to the battlefields of Ypres and the Somme for nearly twenty years. Every

trip I have taken has been different and so I know that yours will not automatically follow my suggested itinerary or the one you set out to follow. If you are looking for a relative's grave or place of commemoration make sure that you use the Commonwealth War Graves Commission (CWGC) website and know the location details before setting off.

Before you go...

These days you can pretty much just get away with navigating using your phone and the mapping apps. If you want a proper map then you can order these online in advance. I would recommend the following:

- Michelin 1:150 000 'Nord' map – This will get you to Ypres and to the Somme
- IGN Green Tourist map 'Great War, Battle of the Somme' 1:75 000
- NGI IGN Ieper Topo50 27-28-36 1:50 000

Suggested Itinerary

I would normally advise a three day tour of the Western Front. Make sure that these are fairly full days though. Arrange accommodation for the first night in Ypres and the following night in Albert, on the Somme. Taking the Eurotunnel is advisable because of the additional time it saves. Some site visits are very quick and others you may explore over a longer period of time.

This may look intense, but it is completely possible.

Here is my suggestion for an Itinerary:

Day One – Ypres
- Essex Farm Cemetery
- Langemarck German Cemetery
- Passchendaele Museum
- Tyne Cot Cemetery
- Sanctuary Wood Museum or Bayernwald Trenches
- Ypres City Centre and Last Post at the Menin Gate

Day Two – Somme
- Lochnagar Crater
- Devonshires Trench Cemetery
- Mametz Dragon and Flat Iron Copse Cemetery
- Delville Wood
- Thiepval Memorial
- Newfoundland Park
- The Sunken Lane and Hawthorn crater
- Sheffield Park

Day Three – Homeward
- Any sites that you have not got to the day before and then…
- Arras Wellington Quarries
- Vimy Ridge
- Museum at Notre Dame de Lorette

I have used this exact itinerary many times when using a car. When taking coach parties I normally stick to just Ypres and the Somme.

On the Somme the farmers have special insurance and have a piece of armour plate under their tractor seats. Remember that people are still being killed by unexploded ordinance.

Please note that all of these battlefields still produce live shells and munitions out of the ground and you may see some on your tour – this is called *the iron harvest*. Please do not attempt to pick anything up. Farmers place anything found on the verges so please be extra careful when getting out of your vehicle.

The Iron Harvest

It is worth noting that the soldiers would have left Britain and made similar journeys from their training bases up to the Front. As I leave my house at an early hour I always wonder how the young men must have felt as they left…

GPS and Google Maps

I use a tablet with the 'Memory-Map' app on it. This is the same app that can also support the Linesman WW1 trench maps. The trench maps are expensive but you can see a range of dated WW1 maps on your exact position. You can walk to exact trench lines and see where things were on the ground. I have collated the various GPS locations using their electronic maps of France at the sites themselves. You can type these GPS locations directly in Google maps (the same works with Apple Maps) to get precise locations. If the GPS says 'Essex Farm GPS 50° 52.291N, 2° 52.381E' then you can just put 50 52.291,2 52.381 in to Google maps and it will take you there. The conversion to Google is not exact but it will get you there.

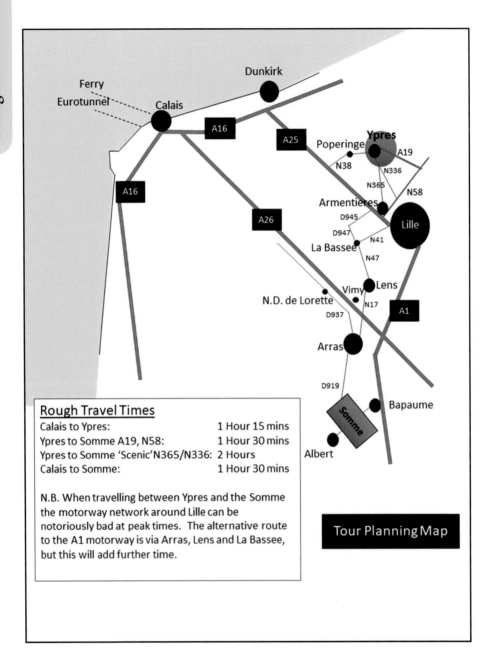

Rough Travel Times

Calais to Ypres:	1 Hour 15 mins
Ypres to Somme A19, N58:	1 Hour 30 mins
Ypres to Somme 'Scenic' N365/N336:	2 Hours
Calais to Somme:	1 Hour 30 mins

N.B. When travelling between Ypres and the Somme the motorway network around Lille can be notoriously bad at peak times. The alternative route to the A1 motorway is via Arras, Lens and La Bassee, but this will add further time.

Tour Planning Map

The History Lesson

The Great War, as I prefer to call it, was much more than just trenches. It was a World war and encompassed fighting on land, sea and in the air. Even for the British alone it was fought across numerous continents and we should remember those who fought and died in places such as in Iraq, in Russia supporting the White Russians and even in Togoland. This book is about the famous battles in Northern France – but remember that those directing this war were watching a global contest and decisions taken in France were linked to the wider conflict. So in France one needs to appreciate the wider front with the action of the French alongside the British – the struggles of Verdun and the Chemin de Dames to name two that are interlinked with decisions about British campaigns. There is one more point that I want to get off my chest before you read further and that is the one about trenches, WW1 is not all about trenches. The fighting in 1914 at places like Mons and the fighting later on during the last 'One Hundred Days' of 1918 are not characterised by trenches at all. Trenches varied enormously based on terrain, local geology, weather and of course enemy bombardment. So try and forget those diagrams that you drew at school in your exercise book – you wouldn't really have seen any like that!

Britain fought this war as an Empire so you will see many references to other nations, most of which make up parts of today's Commonwealth. Britain was in fact a naval power and on the Western Front we were very much the junior partner to the much larger French army. The British worked closely with the French but under our own control up until the appointment of Foch as Commander in Chief in 1918. Britain lost nearly 900,000 troops killed and about 110,000 civilians killed in the War.

A friend of mine has calculated that the war in today's money cost about £110,000 per British man killed.

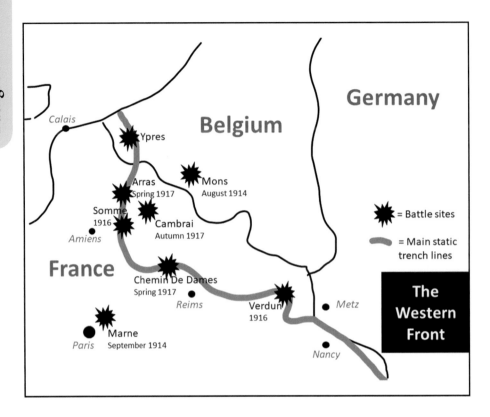

Cemeteries

No tour is complete without visiting some of the military cemeteries. The Commonwealth War Graves Commission(CWGC) is the guardian to the British and Commonwealth War Cemeteries. It is a large organisation financed by us, the tax payers. If you are going to look for a relative then it is worth using their website to locate the burial, but also to find where in the cemetery the grave is – there are maps that you can print off in advance. The CWGC was originally the Imperial War Graves Commission and it was established by Fabian Ware, out of a wartime organisation that he led called the Graves Registration Commission. It was granted a Royal Charter and became the organisation that we know in 1917. (The name change from 'Imperial' to 'Commonwealth' happened in 1960.)

There are in essence two different types of cemetery: Concentration and Battlefield. Concentration Cemeteries were brought together and formed neatly after the war, often from lots of smaller cemeteries. Battlefield cemeteries look different, they are more haphazard in their layout and normally reflect the night time burials around a Dressing Station for the wounded – i.e. the soldier was probably treated and or cared for close by before succumbing to his wounds.

Delville Wood Cemetery, Longueval

Cemeteries tend to follow certain rules. The cemetery will be surrounded by a wall or hedge with a lovely, heavy wrought iron gate. Somewhere prominent will be a metal locker with a cross on it, here you will find a register book (although it is sometimes missing or removed by the CWGC), showing who is buried there and a map. There may also be a folder for visitor comments in the locker that is worth writing your thoughts in. The cemetery will also certainly have a Cross of Sacrifice and if there are over 40 graves there will also be a Stone of Remembrance – standing like an altar in the middle.

Cross of Sacrifice at Luke Copse Cemetery, Serre

Background Information

The cemeteries are on British land and are planted with British plants to give them an 'English Country Garden' feel. Gardeners are well trained and often today are the descendants of the original gardeners.

The Stone of Remembrance at Tyne Cot Cemetery

Many soldiers remained in France and Belgium to tend the graves and the stories talk of comrades staying with their mates, men staying with French girlfriends and even some hiding from 'the law' back in Britain. I am in no doubt that you will find the cemeteries exceptionally moving, calm and beautiful.

The graves are in the midst of a transformation, originally in Portland stone, some are being replaced by a hardier and more shiny marble-esque limestone from Italy. The CWGC says that it is moving to a conservation rather than replacement approach from now on though. The grave stones follow a standard layout:

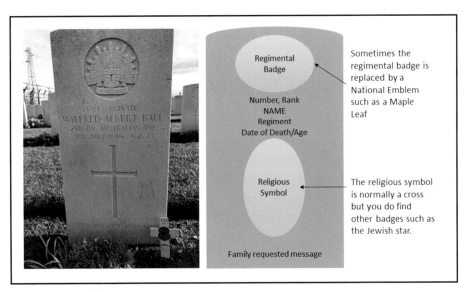

The CWGC headstone

Not every grave is like this though, as I will explain. Most graves will have the family inscription at the bottom and I always find myself walking along and concentrating on these. Originally families were to be charged 3½ pence per letter, but after an outcry the charge was removed. Many of the WW1 inscriptions are religious, probably coming from the advice of the local vicar at a time of great heartbreak. Every so often though, one is caught off guard by an intensely personal tribute. Graves also differ because of the information that the CWGC had, sometimes a grave will read something like 'A Lieutenant from the Durham Light Infantry' where there has obviously been some insignia or clue to the regiment and rank but not to the identity of the man. So this leads on to the main difference that you will find and that is graves to unidentified soldiers. Here they will typically say 'A soldier of the Great war' and 'known unto God', these words are just absolutely perfect and you will not be surprised that they were penned by **Rudyard Kipling**. Kipling was heavily involved in the war and in particular remembrance, following the loss of his son John at the battle of Loos. The mystery of John Kipling's grave is worth a web search at a later date.

There are other differences that you will see as you go round such as different religious symbols instead of crosses and in the case of the individual having been awarded the Victoria Cross for bravery then this is carved prominently on the headstone, as we will see on the tour. I will point out other differences as we visit the sites.

One important point is that this was the first war where bodies were buried individually. At Waterloo, a hundred years before, the bodies were buried in mass graves and some bodies were even left to the

Unknown Soldier, Tyne Cot Cemetery

elements so that their bones could be ground and used as fertiliser. The Great War was a war of the people, a war when communication and understanding amongst those at home was much sharper than ever before. There is also a sense of equality in the cemeteries – there is no difference between the grave of a general to that of a private soldier. Another very modern concept for a world with a rigid class system.

Much of what you see on your tour will be related to cemeteries – they in fact are a physical reminder of the areas of fighting. They are sometimes on the frontline, but often behind the lines linked to first aid posts (dressing stations) or hospitals and I think that an understanding of the system of casualty evacuation and treatment is useful to have when visiting these sites.

Casualty Evacuation

Wounded Chain of Evacuation

The Royal Army Medical Corps (RAMC) made and distributed a casualty evacuation plan for each planned attack. There was also standard plans in place for the evacuation of wounded when not attacking. Surviving diagrams, often buried in War Diaries differ, but follow a basic concept as outlined below. Casualties could skip stages if required.

1. Regimental Aid Post (RAP)

This would be close to the front line, something like 200m away providing initial treatment to essentially keep the casualty alive. It would be staffed by a team and a doctor.

2. Advanced Dressing Station (ADS)

This would be back about 400m and would serve several units. Here wounds were checked and the casualty had a Medical Card attached with key information on.

3. Main Dressing Station (MDS)

This would be back about half a mile and would be larger setup. Some of the wounded would be patched up here enough to return to their units. Others could be treated and even some minor lifesaving surgery before going on to the next part of the system

4. Casualty Clearing Station (CCS)

This was a safe distance from the front and was normally tented or hutted. It would resemble a temporary hospital. They operated a triage system: Walking, Hospital and No chance of survival. Wounds to the stomach/abdomen were particularly challenging and often seen as untreatable. *(Remember firstly this was happening in wartime with huge numbers at once and secondly surgery itself was still quite basic – infection was a particular risk in a pre-antibiotic world!)* They did however increasingly use X Ray units to help locate metal objects in the body prior to operation.

5. Base Hospitals and Home Hospitals

Here we have big hospitals normally on the French coast where more complex surgery and care could be given. If you were 'fortunate' enough you might receive a Blighty wound and end up in hospital back in Britain or as the soldiers would call it Blighty.

Background Information

Soldiers, as part of their orders, would be told what the casualty evacuation procedure was. Normally soldiers would be assigned as 'stretcher bearers' and attached to the RAMC (The Royal Army Medical Corps). Wounded soldiers would either recover themselves or be recovered by stretcher bearers to a Regimental Aid Post (RAP) and would then progress through a sequential system, although casualties could bypass sections based on need.

Casualties could be moved by stretcher bearer, horse drawn ambulance, motorised ambulance, hospital barge, hospital train or even hospital ship. The army made good use of canals and rivers to move casualties -something that is easy to forget in the way we move around today.

Stretcher Bearers

Horse Drawn Ambulance

'Blighty wounds' were wounds that got you home to Britain (Blighty)

Motorised Ambulance

Remember in military terminology an ambulance is really a medical unit - they each ran several of the evacuation chain stages

Hospital Trains

There were also Convalescent Depots used before soldiers returned to their units

Hospital Barge

Hospital Ship

Memorials

Just as cemeteries make up the vast majority of what is left behind so too do the memorials. Again the position of these can mislead you to what was happening on the ground during the war. There are different sorts of memorials such as the one dedicated to Harry Patch, the 'Last Fighting Tommy' beside the Steenbeek near Ypres. There are also memorials to particular places such as The 'Brooding Soldier' at Vancouver Cross Roads marking the spot of the first use of poison gas. There are also memorial parks which we will discuss as we visit them – these tend to be particular areas of infamous ground that are significant enough to keep as memorials or have been unable to return to farmland due to the nature of the warfare there. You will also see numerous 'Brigade memorials' that are almost ignored in the way visitors tour the battlefields and how they think about the battles today.

The most significant memorial type for the Great War Battlefields are the memorials to the missing. Whether it be the Menin Gate or the Thiepval Memorial, which are the most well-known, these are special places and unlike any memorial built before them. To me it is about closure – relatives were aided in visiting the graves after the war. But what happens when there is no grave? The understanding of the peoples' grief and the impact of their loss is a big shift in the way war dead were dealt with. Three hundred thousand names are recorded of the missing in France and Belgium. The memorials were places where the relatives could go, could see the name of their loved one, could lay a wreath or cross. The ability for every relative to go to a name, be it on a grave or on a memorial is a truly moving human project. This I believe was Fabian Ware's greatest lasting achievement.

Of course, many of the names on the memorials could be linked to the graves of an 'unknown soldier' and some people even think we should try and remove some DNA and identify them. I am a believer that you should leave them alone to rest in peace, but you may disagree and many would agree with you. The question that you probably have now is about the numbers – are there the same amount of 'unknown soldier' graves compared to the numbers of missing on the memorials. The answer of course is no, there are still many bodies to be found and many lost forever – consider what warfare can do to a human body. Of course, every so often a body is found, when doing building work typically, and if the body can be identified then it will be buried with full military honours and the name will be removed from the relevant memorial.

The Architects – Blomfield And Lutyens

Two men stand out when you are touring the memorials and cemeteries and that is Sir Reginald Blomfield and Sir Edwin Lutyens. They were both architects, with Lutyens being referred to as the modern 'Christopher Wren'. Blomfield is responsible for the Menin Gate as well as the Cross of Sacrifice found in cemeteries. Lutyens for The Thiepval Memorial and the Cenotaph in London. Both men designed the actual cemeteries too. These two men have gone on to shape the very way we think about what memorials should look like and I think the new WW2 Bomber Command Memorial (2012) in London proves this point. There were other architects such as Sir Herbert Baker who designed Tyne Cot Cemetery but to me Blomfield and Lutyens have shaped the legacy of remembrance as much as the symbol of the poppy has.

Soldiers And The Weapons Of The Great War

Contrary to popular belief British soldiers were not in the frontline all the time -they did not live in the trenches! They spent about 15% of their time in the frontline (normally 3 days a month), 10% in the Support line, 30% in Reserve trenches and 45% out of the trenches all together (training, resting etc). The British continually rotated their troops around where they were on the front too, this helped to maintain morale. The French, who suffered mutinies, kept their troops in the frontline until 'used up' which was seen as reaching 30% of the unit as casualties.

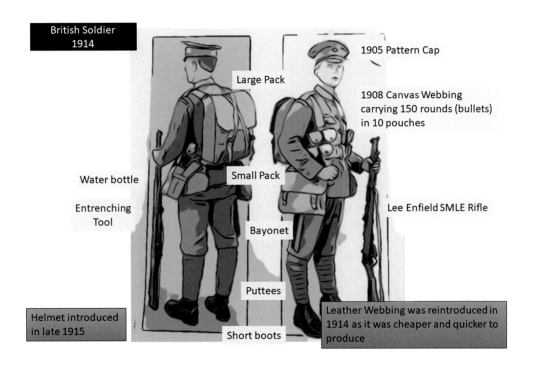

British Soldier 1914

Large Pack

1905 Pattern Cap

1908 Canvas Webbing carrying 150 rounds (bullets) in 10 pouches

Water bottle

Small Pack

Entrenching Tool

Lee Enfield SMLE Rifle

Bayonet

Puttees

Helmet introduced in late 1915

Short boots

Leather Webbing was reintroduced in 1914 as it was cheaper and quicker to produce

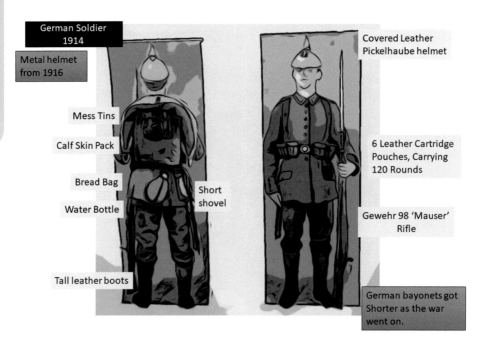

German Soldier 1914

Metal helmet from 1916

Mess Tins

Calf Skin Pack

Bread Bag

Water Bottle

Short shovel

Tall leather boots

Covered Leather Pickelhaube helmet

6 Leather Cartridge Pouches, Carrying 120 Rounds

Gewehr 98 'Mauser' Rifle

German bayonets got Shorter as the war went on.

Infantry Weapons

Vickers Gun	500 rounds a minute	Effective to 2200m	20kg	
	Belt fed & water cooled	Could fire up to 4100m	6 man Team	
Lewis Gun	550 rounds a minute	Effective to 800m	12.7kg	
	47 round magazine	Could fire up to 3200m	2 man Team	
Lee Enfield SMLE Rifle	20-30 aimed shots a minute	Effective to 500m	4.2kg	
	10 round magazine	Could fire up to 2743m		
MG08	500 rounds a minute	Effective to 2000m	62-67kg	
	Belt fed & water cooled	Could fire up to 3500m	4 man Team	
Gewehr 98 (Mauser) Rifle	15 aimed shots a minute	Effective to 500m	4kg	
	5 round magazine	Could fire up to 3735m		

Artillery Comparison

Main Artillery Guns fired 6-10kms, Big Bertha (German) = 12kms, Paris Gun (German) = 130kms

By WW1 most guns were QF - 'Quick Firing' and most had recoil control so that the barrel recoiled rather than the whole gun jumping backwards. This meant they didn't have to re-aim for each shot.

British 18 Pdr (84mm)	7km	Note the crew seats attached to the front
French 75mm	10.5km	
German 77mm	8.4km	
German 105mm	6.3km	We are talking about guns that look like this (This one is the German 77mm)
German 150mm	8.6km	
British 60 Pdr	12-15km	
		Larger Guns (Here the British 60Pdr)
British 6 Inch Howitzer	8.6km	
British 4.5 Howitzer	6.6km	
		Howitzers lobbed shells up into the air to fall directly down on the enemy (Here the British 8 Inch)
German Minenwerfer (17cm)	300m	
British 3 inch Stokes Mortar	731m	Stokes Mortar bomb Not to be confused With a piece of car exhaust!
British 2 inch Mortar ('Toffee Apple' or 'Plum Pudding')	520m	'Toffee Apple' Mortar Bomb
British Livrens Projector	1.5km	These would be buried

25

Trenches

The Parapet

The Parados
(Rear)

Fire step
Would be
cut out of
the side

Duckboard
planks were
placed on the cross piece so
that feet were kept out of the
water/mud below (hopefully).

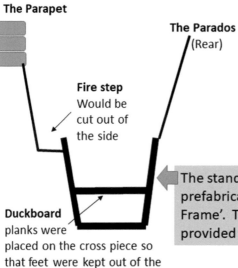

The standard trench was built using a
prefabricated frame called an 'A
Frame'. This turned upside down
provided the basic support required.

Real trenches were rarely 'text book'
examples. Weather, Warfare and
Geography all played their part!

Typically trench systems had
three layers, joined together
by Communication trenches

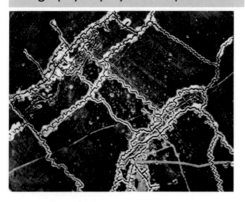

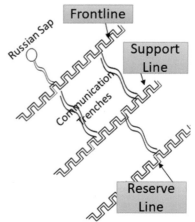

Russian Sap

Frontline

Support
Line

Communication
trenches

Reserve
Line

The Ypres Salient

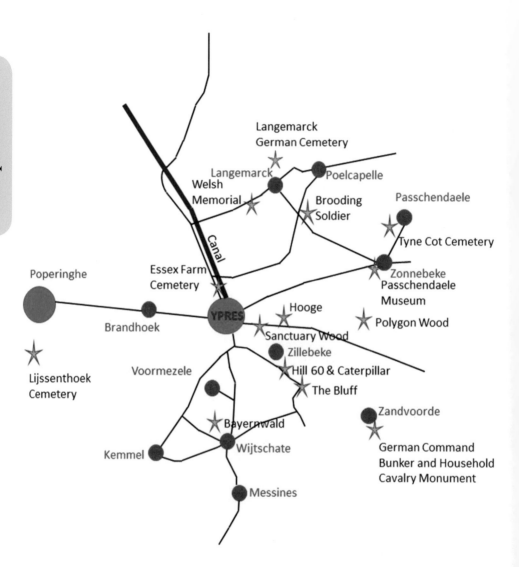

Introduction To Ypres Salient

Key Facts:
- Overlooked by the Messines Ridge (500ft above)
- Series of continuous battles here during the war
- Approximately 1,700,000 soldiers on both sides were killed or wounded here
- Saw the first use of poison gas
- Most of the towns and villages were obliterated during the war

I am going to presume that you are approaching Ypres from the Motorway via Poperinge. This is the perfect way to approach the area as you will pass a couple of key landmarks. You will pass a large cemetery at Lijssenthoek which is at a site of a large Casualty Clearing Station (see page 31)- it was also sited originally next to a railway which was perfect for the evacuation of the wounded. You can of course visit this site, but I would class it as 'an extra'. When you get to Poperinge you will turn east and head straight for Ypres (Ieper) along a dead straight road. Poperinge was an important town during the war and would have been very well known to the soldiers of the day who would have passed through on the way to the front or it was frequented as a rest area for periods of leave. There are two important sites that can be visited, if you have time (see page 87 for more on Poperinge).

As you head down the straight road you will notice the parallel railway line and you can imagine the scale of activity that would have been heading to the front along this route during the war. The road you are driving down is taking you into what was known as the Salient – that is a bulge in the line of trenches that ran from the north coast down through France to Switzerland. The Bulge here is a geographical feature too, in the shape of a saucer with Ypres in the centre. So around Ypres there was a surrounding ridge, that for most of the war was occupied by the Germans. The British were forever trying to break out from the city and push the Germans from the ridge. The Germans on the ridge held the high ground with its superior views and could pour artillery shells down on to the Allies in Ypres. The soldiers of course knew the city as 'Wipers' – this conversion of Flemish and French names is very common as you will see.

There was almost continual fighting here in Ypres, but the fighting is normally divided into four specific battles:

- **The First Battle of Ypres**, October-November 1914
- **The Second Battle of Ypres**, April-May 1915
- (**The Battle of Messines**, June 1917 - should also be included in my eyes too.)
- **The Third Battle of Ypres** (Passchendaele), July-November 1917
- **The Fourth Battle of Ypres** (Battle of Lys), April 1918

You have to consider the geography a bit more, to understand Ypres. As you have been driving you will have noticed the fields with their large surrounding ditches, indeed even the roads have large ditches alongside. The reason for this is the extremely high water table in this area of Belgium – in fact large areas are below sea level. During the war the Belgians had opened the sluice gates and flooded areas to the north as a natural defensive barrier to the German advance. Imagine trying to dig a trench that was safe enough to live in – with sides higher than a man's head when there is a high water table. The result is that Ypres was a world of pumps and also a world of trenches built up out of the ground in many places using the ever present sandbag.

In the Ypres area they have marked the Allied and German frontlines by planting trees with coloured baskets or supports. The Allied ones are blue and the Germans ones are red. You will see this often as you go round and it will help to give you a visual representation of the frontlines.

Metal Cage around a young tree to show where the Frontline was. Blue = Allied Red = German

Cemeteries

Here in Belgium there are just over 600 British cemeteries. There are some key ones that you should definitely visit as part of the story of the war here.

LIJSSENTHOEK CEMETERY
(GPS: 50°49.814'N 2°42.096'E)

Key Facts:
- Second largest British cemetery in Belgium (10,786 graves)
- Grave of Nellie Spindler, female nurse (one of the two female nurses buried in Belgium)
- Linked to part of the medical evacuation chain

Located next to the N38 on the way to Poperinge from the motorway. You may wish to stop here on the way into the area. There are toilets available. This cemetery was linked to the forward area by railway. In fact some of the modern road from the motorway to Poperinge now runs on the original railway route. This huge cemetery was next to the largest evacuation hospital in the Ypres Salient and by 1915 had several British Casualty Clearing Stations. It has the graves of 10,786 people. I say people rather than men or soldiers as it has a female nurse laid to rest here too. In fact there are graves for 233 Germans, 2 Americans, 35 Chinese Labourers, 658 French as well as the graves of men from the Empire. Additional to the nurse there are 4 Generals, which is interesting to consider when most generals have been accused of being back in the chateaux and away from the fighting. The hospital here was 20km from the fighting so was considered safe from the German artillery guns. The railway brought in the wounded as well as picking up those who needed treatment at the larger Base Hospitals (See the Medical Evacuation diagram). There were several sidings alongside what is now the main road to help with the volume of trains. Almost all the graves at this cemetery have names because these were soldiers who arrived alive having been medically evacuated. There was no point in evacuating the dead to a casualty station. They died of their wounds here at the hospital. This indicates the area was also not fought across so the bodies have been undisturbed.

Staff Nurse Nellie Spindler was aged 26 when she was caught up in an artillery barrage on her position at the Casualty Clearing Station at Brandhoek in August 1917. Spindler and four other nurses from the Queen Alexandria's Imperial Military Nursing Service were concussed in the explosions. Spindler actually died from a shrapnel injury to her chest. She had lied about her age to join up as she was required to be single and over 25 to join up, she had been 24! She had a full military funeral with four generals and over a hundred other officers attending. The records recall her as 'killed in action'. Spindler's grave is in Plot XVI, Row A, Grave 3.

Major Frederick Tubb VC, is also buried here. He won his Victoria Cross for bravery at Gallipoli as part of the Australian Imperial Force. His citation reads:

> *For most conspicuous bravery and devotion to duty at Lone Pine trenches, in the Gallipoli Peninsula, on 9th August, 1915. In the early morning the enemy made a determined counter attack on the centre of the newly captured trench held by Lieutenant Tubb. They advanced up a sap and blew in a sandbag barricade, leaving only one foot of it standing, but Lieutenant Tubb led his men back, repulsed the enemy, and rebuilt the barricade. Supported by strong bombing parties, the enemy succeeded in twice again blowing in the barricade, but on each occasion Lieutenant Tubb, although wounded in the head and arm, held his ground with the greatest coolness and rebuilt it, and finally succeeded in maintaining his position under very heavy bomb fire.*

Once recovered he was promoted to Major and though he had never really fully recovered from his wounds received at Gallipoli, he persuaded the medical team to pass him fit for action. He had nearly been evacuated for severe hernia pain on the day before he went into action, but refused to leave his men. He was soon in the thick of the action attacking a series of German bunkers in Polygon Wood in September 1917. He was then wounded by a German sniper in his back. Whilst he was being evacuated he was again wounded, possibly by British artillery guns and died at Lijssenthoek. Tubb's grave is in plot XIX, Row C, Grave 5.

Private William Baker, was shot at dawn, aged 21 in Poperinge on 14th August 1918. He had volunteered in 1914 and had been at the Battle of Mons. He had a habit of going missing, perhaps because he had simply had enough or perhaps because he had yet to see his daughter for the first time. He was already under arrest on 22nd April 1918 when he went missing again. He was eventually arrested at the port of Boulogne in May whilst using a false name. He managed to get away again and this time was arrested trying to get into a Hospital at Étaples, again under a false name. This time the Court Martial had had enough and he was shot in Poperinge. There is no mention of him being executed on his headstone. His grave is in Plot XXV, Row B, Grave 22 (See Poperinge for more on the men shot at dawn).

Lijssenthoek has a visitor centre with a toilet for visitors.

The Ypres Salient

BRANDHOEK NEW MILITARY CEMETERY
(GPS 50°51.130N 2°47.273E)

Key Facts:
- Grave of Captain Chavasse (Double VC Winner)
- Site where Nurse Nellie Spindler was mortally wounded

There are several cemeteries in close proximity here. Park outside Brandhoek Cemetery No. 3 and then cross the road and walk down the narrow path to Brandhoek New Military Cemetery. As one cemetery filled up they opened a new one. This area was perfect for gathering wounded. Ambulances were stationed here as part of the casualty clearance system. The area was relatively sheltered and also on the main evacuation route either via the road or the railway that ran alongside it. This is the last resting place of Captain Noel Chavasse, VC and Bar, MC, one of only three men who have won the Victoria Cross twice. Chavasse was the son of a Bishop and also a twin. Both twins went to Oxford University and were outstanding athletes. They both ran for Great Britain at the 1908 Olympics in London. Noel finished third and his twin, Christopher, second in the 400 metres heats. Not far from Chavasse' grave is that of Private Rudd. Rudd was Chavasse' servant or 'batman' who was wounded in the same action and died of his wounds six days later. See the Hooge Crater Museum section for more information about Chavasse' story and the winning of his medals. There is a memorial to Chavasse in front of the small Brandhoek church. It was here that Nellie Spindler was hit and mortally wounded by a shell in August 1917 (See Lijssenthoek Section). Chavasse' grave is in Plot III, at the end of Row B next to the central path. Rudd's grave is at Plot VI, Row B, Grave 11.

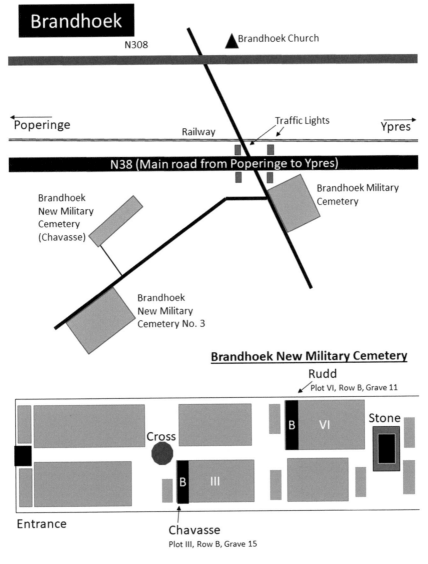

ESSEX FARM CEMETERY
(GPS: 50°52.291'N 2°52.381'E)

Key Facts:
- Grave of the youngest casualty (aged 15) on the Western Front
- Site of John McCrae's bunker and where he wrote the poem that inspired the use of the poppy for Remembrance
- 1204 graves

This cemetery is important for several reasons. Firstly I would like you to follow the 'astro turf' route to the grave of **Rifleman V. J. Strudwick** (Plot 1 Row U Grave 8), you won't be able to miss it as there will be flags and crosses galore in front of it. We live in a world of celebrities – some stay and some fade… well, this one grave is probably the most visited grave on the Western Front. Why? Because Strudwick was serving underage and was killed at only 15. He is generally considered to be the youngest British death of the Great War. There is some dispute, of course, and others have been put forward, but in a time where people were signing up under false names and secretly underage makes the proving of this completely impossible. The legend of Strudwick started when an advert was placed in a newspaper asking if he was the youngest casualty of the war and from there his fame has risen. He was well liked by his unit colleagues and they were allowed to come away from the line to be at his burial. The thing that I want you to consider is that Strudwick is one soldier and this cemetery has 1204 graves -is being 15 a reason to visit his grave and not the other 1203? Have a look at the neighbouring graves – they too carry the same cap badge and date…. What does this suggest? Yes, they were killed by the same shell as Strudwick and now hundreds of people a day (literally!) stand in front of Strudwick's grave without even thinking about his mates who lie beside him – what are their stories? Strudwick's story reminds us of the human story of war, of the nationalistic fervour that meant young men volunteered and wanted to fight, but we should try and remember them all and that although he may in a way be a celebrity today in 1916 he was just another soldier amongst his mates.

Strudwick's commanding officer, as was the custom, sent a letter to the parents. In this letter the officer says that Strudwick was killed

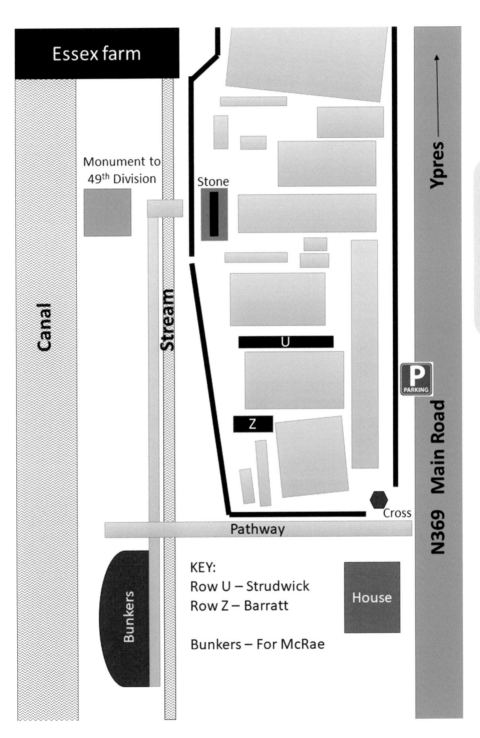

instantaneously and painlessly. This may be true but I am yet to see one of these letters saying that a soldier had died painfully and slowly! The officer wrote this to save the family any further heartache.

The Bunkers: The other reason to visit this particular cemetery are the bunkers along the canal bank just outside the cemetery. (Go back out and turn immediately right and go along the cobbled path towards the canal.) Essex Farm was the site of an Advanced Dressing Station and this is why the cemetery is a mixture of slightly different angled grave lines, rather than perfect parallel lines. The graves nearest to the bunker are the men that didn't survive past this point in the casualty evacuation chain. The ones furthest away, that are neater, were brought in (known as being 'concentrated') later. The burials would almost certainly have taken place at night as we are close to the frontline here. The Germans were about half a mile the other side of the canal and here there was a flimsy wooden bridge to bring in casualties. These bunkers are where the team of medics desperately tried to keep the men alive.

The reason that we are looking at this particular dressing station is that here a part of our culture was born. An experienced battle surgeon from Canada called **John McCrae**, had volunteered to help the mother country. He sailed with the Canadians to Britain and was billeted in the Bear Hotel in Devizes, Wiltshire. Here he lived amongst the officers in relative comfort. One of his fellow officers was a young Lieutenant called **Alexis Helmer**. His stay in Wiltshire was not an easy one though as the Canadian troops were badly affected by their poor tented accommodation. The rain made their stay pretty awful and in fact fifty soldiers died of disease or accidents in Wiltshire. So as a doctor McCrae was busy before even arriving at the front. McCrae was a workaholic and believed in getting the treatment to the soldiers as quickly as possible. He wanted his team of surgeons to be close and be able to do the surgery as quickly as possible. This is not far off the concept we see today in places such as Afghanistan where the medical team goes out in a helicopter to start the treatment straight away whilst in the air. McCrae worked here in these bunkers saving as many lives as he could. In May 1915 as John McCrae worked he found himself confronted with the body of his friend, 22 year old

Alexis Helmer who had been killed by a shell. I have heard a version of the story that involved Helmer's body having to be recovered in several separate sandbags. McCrae was understandably disturbed by this experience and it must have pulled him out of his usual necessary detachment from the casualties he treated. The story goes that he went out of the dugout and sat either on the steps of an ambulance or at the foot of a tree and wrote a poem. In those days poetry was cool and commonplace. The poem he wrote needs to be read in situ as it describes this very place.

> ### In Flanders Fields
> *In Flanders fields the poppies blow*
> *Between the crosses, row on row,*
> *That mark our place; and in the sky*
> *The larks, still bravely singing, fly*
> *Scarce heard amid the guns below.*
> *We are the Dead. Short days ago*
> *We lived, felt dawn, saw sunset glow,*
> *Loved and were loved, and now we lie*
> *In Flanders fields.*
> *Take up our quarrel with the foe:*
> *To you from failing hands we throw*
> *The torch; be yours to hold it high.*
> *If ye break faith with us who die*
> *We shall not sleep, though poppies grow*
> *In Flanders fields.*

The poem is on various boards at the cemetery – do read it and contemplate what it must have been like during the war. The poem 'In Flanders Fields' talks of poppies and so it is here that the now well-known practice of wearing poppies in November comes from. The story is a bit blurred but the poem ended up in Punch magazine and the rest is, of course, history.

There is also a grave of a Victoria Cross hero in this cemetery. He is in the corner near the bunkers. His name is **Private Thomas Barratt** VC(Plot 1, Row Z, Grave 8). Here is an example of a headstone being different from the normal, in this case because of the VC (Victoria

Cross Medal) which is the highest award for bravery. Barratt was a sniper hunter and would spend long periods of time patiently finding and killing German snipers who were firing on his unit. He was killed whilst trying to protect his patrol from German snipers. He volunteered to cover the patrol as it returned to British lines under heavy machine gun fire. He was soon after killed by a shell.

The concrete bunkers are in fact from later in the war, however they are on the same site and give you an idea of the atmosphere.

The bunkers at Essex farm Cemetery

'ARISTOCRATS CEMETERY' AT ZILLEBEKE CHURCHYARD
(GPS: 50°50.144'N 2°55.333'E)

Beside the road as you pass through Zillebeke, you will find this small cemetery known as the 'Aristocrats Cemetery'. The cemetery has only about thirty graves and is in the churchyard. There are not many headstones and most are of officers from the early days of the war. These men then, are the original pre-war elite officer class that went off with the BEF in 1914. When researching these men almost all have links to the rich and famous of Britain. There was ferocious fighting to hold the line south west of Zillebeke in 1914, with many of these men giving their lives to stop the Germans pushing through.

BELGIAN CRYPT AT ZONNEBEKE
(GPS:50° 52.480'N 2° 59.520'E)

Worth a visit if you have time whilst in the area. This crypt has visible coffins and on the end of most of them there is a picture of the man who now resides inside. There are about ten from WW1, one from WW2 and one from The Belgian Revolution of 1830. Rather eerie.

TYNE COT CEMETERY AND THE BATTLE OF PASSCHENDAELE
(GPS: 50°53.250'N 3°00.091'E)

Key Facts:
- Largest CWGC cemetery in the World (11,968 graves)
- 34,954 listed names of the missing, who have no known grave
- Vantage point over the battlefield of Passchendaele

This is a simply huge cemetery and comprises of 11,968 graves with a further 34,954 names of the missing at the back – if you go all the way to the back you will see that they have had to add two extra 'circular rooms' to get all the names on. This is a place of scale and in some way therefore loses some of the intimacy that you get at the smaller cemeteries.

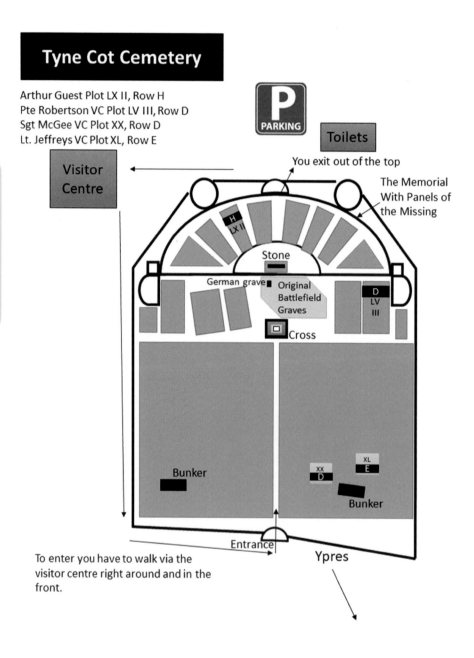

Tyne Cot Cemetery

Arthur Guest Plot LX II, Row H
Pte Robertson VC Plot LV III, Row D
Sgt McGee VC Plot XX, Row D
Lt. Jeffreys VC Plot XL, Row E

P PARKING

Toilets

Visitor Centre

You exit out of the top

The Memorial With Panels of the Missing

H
LX II

Stone

German grave Original Battlefield Graves

D
LV III

Cross

Bunker

XL
E

XX
D

Bunker

Entrance

Ypres

To enter you have to walk via the visitor centre right around and in the front.

First of all head to one of the concrete bunkers towards the front (I normally go for the one on the right as you enter). Turn and look back down the hill towards the city. You are now looking at the Battlefield of Passchendaele or as it is also known, the Third Battle of Ypres. This is the battle that has come to be known for its mud. You can really understand the saucer shaped ridge around Ypres from here, if the weather is clear you can make out the Cloth Hall with its spires. Imagine the German guns on the reverse slope of this ridge firing on the city coordinated by observers with this view – no wonder the city was obliterated.

AUSTRALIAN WAR MEMORIAL   E01220

The battle was fought for 99 days in 1917 and the objective was to push the Germans from the ridge once and for all. The Germans had built a defensive line of bunkers supporting their trenches – these were built 'in depth' meaning that they had several lines of bunkers that the troops would need to fight through.

The plan was developed by **General Gough**, he had hoped to emulate **General Plumer's** success the year before at Messines Ridge. Gough though was undermined by different terrain and the weather. Prior to

The Ypres Salient

the attack there was eight weeks of constant rain – this coupled with a huge fourteen day British bombardment and three years of war meant there was no drainage and the battlefield became a quagmire. It was taking troops twelve hours, instead of about two, to walk the nine kilometres from Ypres to the frontline. A continually repaired path of duckboards was constructed across the landscape. If one slipped or fell from the path then there was real trouble. Heavily laden troops and animals did disappear into the mud. The battle opened with the troops going up to their positions in torrential rain and when they attacked of course it was slaughter: 240,000 casualties!

Before and after photographs of Polygon Wood - An example of the level of destruction encountered at Passchendaele

There is a story of a ration party coming up to the line and the sergeant tripped and fell off the path and into the mud. The troops tried desperately to pull him out but the oozing mud and his kit were pulling him slowly down. He sank lower and lower until he desperately called for someone to shoot him before he drowned. The story goes on to say that he was shot and unfortunately the incident was seen. The soldier was court martialled for shooting a sergeant. How true this story is I do not know, but it highlights the dangers of mud and thus the fighting here.

The troops were quite well prepared – they had canvas covers for the main working parts of their rifles and even a special mud flap to keep mud out of the end of the rifle. However this does not take into account that to reload a clip of bullets a soldier would have to use his hands, probably covered in mud, thus completely undoing all his hard work to keep the rifle serviceable.

I was originally told the cemetery is called Tyne Cot as the bunkers seen by the Geordie Northumberland Fusiliers reminded them of fisherman's cottages beside the River Tyne. The CWGC website says that the name comes from a barn that was near here, amongst the bunkers, and it was this barn that was known as 'Tyne Cot'. Another theory that I have heard is that the name comes from the naming of objectives or features after rivers, thus you find in the area other buildings named after big famous rivers. There is also a suggestion that a local name, Hinnekot was just simply anglicised into Tyne Cot. This section of the ridge was finally taken by the Australians and so you will see a lot of Australian graves here.

Now head up to the central cross. I would advise not climbing this central feature even if others do. This is built on top of another bunker and at the front there is a hole where you can see the original concrete. If you look around now you can see that here there are some surprisingly irregular grave patterns. This is because this central bunker became an Advanced Dressing Station as the battle edged forward. These are the original graves and the later beautiful lines of graves were added or 'concentrated'. You will also see if you look behind the cross two German graves - they are made of slightly different stone and the shape is more angular on the top. This may seem odd but you must remember that the British would treat German wounded where required too. These soldiers must have died of their wounds and in the midst of the battle were buried here. I think this helps us to understand why German troops in WW2 had such respect for the British cemeteries where the same was not always true of French or Belgian ones.

Keep heading up the cemetery and in the last semi-circle of graves head to row H8 of plot LXII (second group to the left of the central path). Here you will see **Arthur Guest**, the brother of Ernest that we discuss at the Menin Gate.

General Gough was eventually replaced by Plumer and in total the allies gained about five miles. The casualty rate had been enormous and the battles were more and more being turned over to the other nations of the Empire to take the brunt.

The cemetery is an important part of the local community and I have witnessed many things that would not be seen in other cemeteries including the taking of wedding photographs. One has mixed feelings about this sort of thing but at the end of the day it is a beautiful place and means a lot to the local people and so why not.

There are three Victoria Cross winners buried here, two are Australian and one is Canadian.

Captain Clarence Jeffries VC (Plot XL, Row E, Grave 1) Jeffries was given the VC posthumously (after death) for his actions in the Battle of Passchendaele. He was killed within sight of here attacking near a point known as Hillside Farm. His citation reads:

> *For most conspicuous bravery in attack, when his company was held up by enemy machine-gun fire from concrete emplacements. Organising a party, he rushed one emplacement, capturing four machine guns and thirty-five prisoners. He then led his company forward under extremely heavy enemy artillery barrage and enfilade machine-gun fire to the objective. Later, he again*

> *organised a successful attack on a machine-gun emplacement,*
> *capturing two machine guns and thirty more prisoners. This*
> *gallant officer was killed during the attack, but it was entirely due*
> *to his bravery and initiative that the centre of the attack was not*
> *held up for a lengthy period. His example had a most inspiring*
> *influence.*

After the war his father came to Belgium to help locate his son's body, one can only imagine the horrors involved in this kind of search. Unfortunately his body was only found after his father had returned to Australia and so he had to make a second pilgrimage to Belgium.

Sergeant Lewis McGee VC (Plot XX, Row D, Grave 1) McGee had previously fought at Messines Ridge. He was a natural soldier and had been promoted quickly. He was fighting near here with his unit in the deep mud and hampered by large amounts of enemy barbed wire. His citation reads:

> *For most conspicuous bravery when in the advance to the final*
> *objective, Sjt. McGee led his platoon with great dash and bravery,*
> *though strongly opposed, and under heavy shell fire. His platoon*
> *was suffering severely and the advance of the Company was stopped*
> *by machine gun fire from a "Pill-box" post. Single-handed Sjt.*
> *McGee rushed the post armed only with a revolver. He shot some*
> *of the crew and captured the rest, and thus enabled the advance*
> *to proceed. He reorganised the remnants of his platoon and was*
> *foremost in the remainder of the advance, and during consolidation*
> *of the position he did splendid work. This Non-commissioned*
> *Officer's coolness and bravery were conspicuous and contributed*
> *largely to the success of the Company's operations.*

On the day of his death, eight days after his VC action he was Acting Sergeant Major and was killed whilst attacking another bunker.

Private James Peter Robertson VC (Plot LVIII, Row D, Grave 26) Canadian Robertson had been quite ill with influenza and syphilis prior to his actions at Passchendaele.

His citation reads:

> *For most conspicuous bravery and outstanding devotion to duty in attack. When his platoon was held up by uncut wire and a machine gun causing many casualties, Pte. Robertson dashed to an opening on the flank, rushed the machine gun and, after a desperate struggle with the crew, killed four and then turned the gun on the remainder, who, overcome by the fierceness of his onslaught, were running towards their own lines. His gallant work enabled the platoon to advance. He inflicted many more casualties among the enemy, and then carrying the captured machine gun, he led his platoon to the final objective. He there selected an excellent position and got the gun into action, firing on the retreating enemy who by this time were quite demoralised by the fire brought to bear on them. During the consolidation Pte. Robertson's most determined use of the machine gun kept down the fire of the enemy snipers; his courage and his coolness cheered his comrades and inspired them to the finest efforts. Later, when two of our snipers were badly wounded in front of our trench, he went out and carried one of them in under very severe fire. He was killed just as he returned with the second man.*

Another man associated with the Battle of Passchendaele is one of my favourite characters from the Great War, his name is **Private Barney Hines**. Hines, a Liverpudlian, had already fought in the Boer war and on the outbreak of the Great War found himself in Australia and so volunteered for the Australian Infantry.

This photo, at Polygon Wood of Barney Hines and his stash of Souvenirs was widely distributed during the war and an unconfirmed story was that a copy ended up with the German Kaiser. The Kaiser was so enraged that he put a price on Hines' head. His nickname was 'Wild eyes' and the stories that followed him were legendary. He is supposed to have danced a jig on top of a German bunker taunting them to surrender before popping a Mills bomb through the gun slots. Here he captured over sixty Germans single handed. He was hard to handle and didn't get on with authority but in combat nobody could touch him and quite simply he was a hero and rogue combined. He

AUSTRALIAN WAR MEMORIAL   E00822

Private Barney Hines.

would certainly make a great movie character. His commanding officer had the good idea to give him a Lewis machine gun, which he loved and could fire from the hip. He was always looking for souvenirs and I am sure he was the inspiration for the Paul Hogan character in the series Anzacs (which is great if you haven't seen it). One time he found a barrel of beer, which he was busy rolling down a road to his mates when he was told by some Military Police that he was to roll it "no further" – his response was to gather his mates at the barrel and to crack it open there. There is even a story about him being arrested trying to rob a bank in Amiens – he was supposedly arrested with cash flooding out of the various suitcases he had gathered. He tried hard to serve in WW2, but was repeatedly turned down. You can make your own mind up whether he should have been locked up or given a VC.

LANGEMARCK GERMAN CEMETERY
(GPS: 50°55.302'N 2°55.018'E)

Key facts:
- 44,000 soldiers in graves
- 25,000 soldiers in a mass grave
- Links to Hitler and the Nazis

In order to get both sides of the story it is worth coming to the German cemetery at Langemarck. After the war German cemeteries were reduced – in Belgium 678 German cemeteries became 4. The Germans now have 4 cemeteries in an area that the British have 300. The Germans had been an occupying enemy force for four years and so a lot of German bodies were simply sent back to Germany in cattle trucks at the end of the war. Other German cemeteries in France and Belgium often have the original beautiful stone headstones, used during the war, as decoration around the sides of the cemetery. This cemetery is definitely not typical of other German cemeteries as I will explain, but its history is so fascinating that this continues to be the most visited.

Head in through the entrance and stand beside the edged rectangular 'rose bed', (this has now been turfed) and face the statues. In 2015 these statues were moved from the rear of the cemetery which had the sky behind them making them stand out – now they almost disappear into the red stone behind them. This is their original location and as a starter shows you that the story here is not straight forward. The statues are representing grieving comrades and were made by **Emil Krieger**.

The ground upon which the cemetery was built, although war torn was not as many say, a discarded and unwanted piece of land. In fact it was part of a chateau's garden and in wartime aerial photos you can make out the beds and paths across the area. In the rose garden rectangle in front of you are the remains of 25,000 Germans in a mass grave. The rest of the cemetery is made up of groups of German soldiers, making a total of 44,000 known graves. Most German cemeteries have black crosses but plaques were used here to accommodate more names.

In the 1930s the cemetery had trees and was in need of repair. The cemetery is referred to by the Germans as the 'Student Cemetery', a group of students on the way back from Paris decided to do something about the state of it and on returning to Germany looked for sponsorship. There was one particular group that liked the idea of that and that was the National Socialists (NAZIs). The cemetery has often been linked to the young – indeed there is a 'student room' in the entrance building. The Nazis latched onto this concept as it fitted their propaganda machine perfectly – young German heroes fighting and dying for their country. The Nazis therefore revamped the cemetery and even had some of the earth taken in stately pilgrimage to the Berlin Olympic Stadium where it was placed in an urn in the Langemarck hall. Other propaganda also made use of the 'sacrifice' with posters and songs designed to inspire the next generation to be prepared to fight and die for their country.

The cemetery was thus renovated and re-landscaped. If you head over towards the bunkers and blocks you will see some of what they did. Go and look at the bunkers – look at the condition and the thickness of the concrete. These are probably not original despite what you might read and despite explanations that they were renovated later. I think they are part of the Nazis making the place a shrine – the blocks and bunkers are supposed to be the frontline.

Krieger's statues photographed when they were at the back of the cemetery

In recent years the cemetery has been restored again and so unusually this cemetery has been altered many times. The final twist is that this is in fact nothing to do with students and young people. The confusion has come through the description of the German units fighting here in 1914 which were newly called up – young regiments… so young militarily not necessarily in age! This is a great example of how history can be warped if we are not careful – especially when you throw in a regime built around propaganda.

Langemarck Cemetery

TOP: Trench map from autumn 1917 showing British trench running through cemetery

On both maps I have marked on the modern carpark. The Roads are the same as today. If you are heading North then you will see the cemetery on your left just before the carpark.

The Trench (following same pattern as the one in the map below)

Note also the obvious ornamental garden layout from pre-war. This was not the worst piece of land that could be given over to the Germans!

The Trench line is where the big marker stone line now is – Neither map shows bunkers here!

The Cemetery today stretches up to near the carpark.

The Ypres Salient

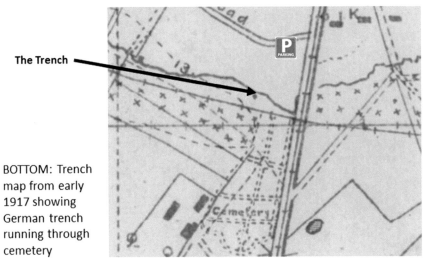

The Trench

BOTTOM: Trench map from early 1917 showing German trench running through cemetery

Hitler visits in 1940

A British memorial: You may have a noticed a small plaque on the end of one of the large square blocks near where you emerged from the entrance, not far from the central massed grave. This is a memorial to **Private Carlill** and **Private Lockley**. They are known to also be buried in the mass grave. Carlill died as a Prisoner of War, aged 19 and just a week before the end of the war.

British Memorial Plaque.(Note behind the now grassed 'Rose bed' mass grave)

The Ypres Salient

The fighting at Langemarck in 1914: There was of course continual fighting around here. In 1914 this was one of the places where the professional BEF (British Expeditionary Force) tried to stop the German advance. It was in the fields near this cemetery that in November 1914 the tough veteran soldiers of the British Empire prepared to hold the line. They had placed ranging posts out in front so they knew exactly how many yards away the enemy would be and could click their Lee Enfield rifle sights to the precise distance. The men were mostly 'marksmen' having passed a test of shooting prowess that enabled them to get higher pay. As the Germans, in vast numbers, approached across the fields often with flowers in their uniforms the British soldiers opened fire at a rate of 30 aimed shots a minute. The newly called up German reservists were massacred as sergeants went down the line docking the pay of those not hitting their targets (This fighting is in sharp contrast to that which we will talk about on the Somme).

The fighting at Langemarck in 1917: When you return to the car park it is worth looking north east – over your left shoulder if you are facing the entrance to the car park. You should be able to just make out some real German concrete bunkers along the road. It was here in October 1917 that the Worcestershire Regiment were held up by fierce machine gun fire. Artillery support had knocked out many of the bunkers but one continued to stop their advance. As the officers tried to decide what to do the firing suddenly stopped and the men began to cheer. **Private Fred Dancox** had attacked the bunker single handed – he had worked his way around by running from shell hole to shell hole and then calmly walked in the door to the bunker with a grenade in his hand. The position was taken and Fred triumphantly used the captured machine gun for the rest of the day. Fred Dancox received the Victoria Cross for his bravery that day! Fred unfortunately never received his medal as he was killed before he could go home to have it presented. (Fred's two brothers and a half-brother were also killed in the War – none have a known grave.)

VLADSLOW GERMAN CEMETERY
(GPS: 51°04.261'N 2°55,670'E)

This is worth a visit as an extra. It is located about half an hour north of Ypres and could include a visit to the Pax Tower (Museum aan de IJzer) and the Belgian Trenches of Death at Diksmuide. This cemetery is particularly interesting for its statues. The statues are of 'grieving parents' and sculpted by **Käthe Kollwitz.**

Kollwitz's statues

The Ypres Salient

Like at Langemarck this cemetery had many graves brought in for the rationalisation of German cemeteries. Here there are 25,645 burials. One of the graves brought in during the 1950s rationalisation was Peter Kollwitz and so they moved the statues in at the same time to look over his grave. If you look on the granite grave blocks near the statues you will find his name. Peter was killed in October 1914 aged just 18 and was thus the motivation for his mother when doing the sculpture. Whilst at the cemetery it is worth nipping into the woods on the northern side and seeing the bunkers and trench lines.

Ypres City

Ypres was previously famous for its role in the wool trade and the large cathedral like building in the centre of the city is in fact the Cloth Hall. It now houses one of the museums called 'Flanders Fields'. The market place is much as it was in 1914 and efforts to rebuild Ypres 'as it once was' are pretty impressive. Remember that if you were here mid war then essentially nothing above your waist was standing. If you go right up to the buildings you can usually make out where the original building and the reconstruction meet.

AUSTRALIAN WAR MEMORIAL   E01171

The Cloth Hall, Ypres 1919

It is worth walking to the west end of the Cloth hall and heading for the small church across the road: St George's Memorial Church. This is a British Anglican Memorial church and has fascinating plaques and flags. Originally it was linked with the British Memorial School. Students came from the British population and the CWGC gardeners' children, and much of the funding came from Eton School. The school was not reopened after WW2. It is this church that visiting relatives came to in the years after the war.

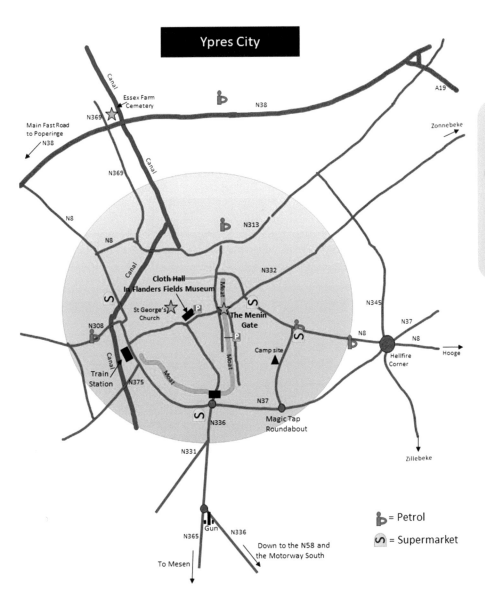

THE MENIN GATE
(GPS: 50°51.122'N 2°53.461'E)

Key facts:

- The names of 54,381 missing soldiers who have no known grave
- Service, including the Last Post every night at 8pm
- Central location for formal acts of remembrance in Belgium

The most impressive site in the city centre of Ypres has to be the Menin Gate. We discussed memorials to the missing back in the introduction, well this is the most famous of them. After the war there was much discussion about how to commemorate the British Empire's sacrifice at Ypres and also what to do about the names of the missing. Various ideas were muted including **Winston Churchill's** which was to leave the entire city in ruins as reminder for future generations. The people of Belgium, of course, wanted their city back and had returned fairly quickly, living in cellars and the odd donated hut. In the end the city's eastern gate – the Menin Gate was agreed upon for a memorial. It was a good site as it marked the spot that many of the troops would have crossed out of the city heading for the frontline. It is called the Menin gate as this was the site of the city gate guarding the road to Menin. **Blomfield** designed what you see before you.

Up on the top facing the city is a sarcophagus draped in a flag, showing the city the sacrifice of the British. On the other side, facing away from the city is a lion staring up towards the old frontline. He is not your usual fierce, proud lion – what do you think of him? Pre-war there was actually a pair of lions guarding the road here, these were given to Australia as a thank you for the Australian commitment to the war. In 2017 they temporarily returned for the centenary of the Battle of Passchendaele, which was fought just outside the city. Then after a few months the two brick plinths either side of the road sat forlorn and empty, left over from this tribute. Now some replicas donated from Australia have arrived to guard the city. The memorial has approximately 54,381 names on it and it was found to be too small for the required number of names so there are a further 34,954 on the memorial wall at Tyne Cot and 11,351 more at Ploegsteert.

Braille Model

It is here that the 'Last Post' is played every night. The Menin Gate was opened in 1927 in the presence of **General Plumer** and **Albert**, King of the Belgians. That night some British buglers played the 'Last Post' and the idea was taken up by the Belgian Fire Brigade who regularly continued the idea until 11th November 1929 when it became a daily service. The only time it has not happened is during the German occupation of WW2 – there are still some marks from the WW2 damage on the outside of the Gate. The very day that the Germans left the city the tradition started again, and has continued to this day. It is worth going up through the middle steps on the south side and looking out of the city across the water. You will find a braille bronze model with absolutely beautiful replicated detail for those unable to view the Menin Gate for themselves. If you are coming to the ceremony in the evening then I advise you allow plenty of time so that you can get a decent spot.

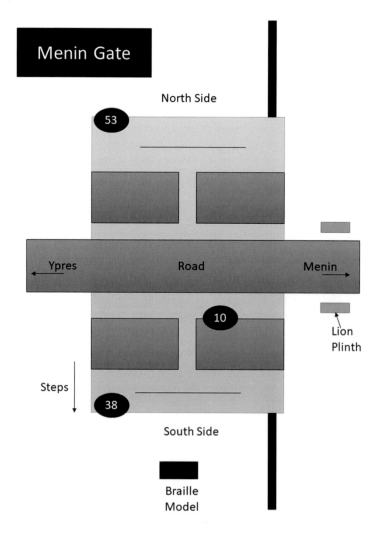

Whilst we are at the Menin Gate it is only right to think about a few of the individuals on the memorial. You will see that all the panels have numbers at the bottom corner. We will start by looking for someone we encounter at Essex Farm Cemetery, find panel 10 and look for **Alexis Helmer**. Here is the place then that the members of Lieutenant Helmer's family can come to try and get a sense of closure. If you now go up the northern steps and go up and round to the left – look for panel 53 and the Wiltshire Regiment you will find Guest E. **Ernest Guest** and his brother Arthur both arrived in Belgium on the 7th October 1914. They went straight into action to hold the Germans back near the Menin Road. Unfortunately they were killed together on October 24th. Their mother, Ellen lost two sons at the same time and straight away! Despite being killed together, Arthur has a grave which we will visit at Tyne Cot Cemetery, Ernest's grave has been lost and so here he is commemorated separately. The last name I would like you to find is back up on the braille model side, panel 38. He is recorded on the Menin Gate as **Blackmac A L.** A historian friend of mine **Richard Broadhead** was asked to help research a relative of a local family. The family supplied the details and even included a rather fetching colourised photograph of their ancestor. They knew all the details of him including that he died on the 11th November 1914 and that he was commemorated on the War Memorial in Weston-Super-Mare. The relative's name was **Arthur Blakeman** and as far as the CGWC register was concerned he never existed. Richard started looking in the records including those at the Kew Records office. He finally cracked the case by matching up all the details except the surname. His detective work uncovered a mistake with the surname Blackmac – the surname had at some point been mis-recorded and so he was on the Menin Gate as Blackmac when in fact he was Arthur L Blakeman. Whether it was a complete mistake or whether it was a nickname that got wrongly recorded we shall never know, but this highlights the problems with commemorating on this scale – mistakes have been made. During my own research I came across a transcribed list of soldiers from the Cameron Highlanders who had been involved in a cave disaster in 1914, during the Battle of the Aisne. Here was another mention of Arthur Blakeman, this time as Bandsman A Blakemac. The list shows that he was wounded in the disaster and as a bandsman he was almost certainly helping in his 'battle role' of a stretcher bearer at the time. Thirty others were killed in the cave incident which was caused by heavy shelling.

The Ypres Salient

Memorials

VANCOUVER CROSSROADS: THE BROODING SOLDIER AND GAS (GPS: 50°53.959'N 2°56.395'E)

Key Facts:
- Site of the first use of poison gas, April 1915
- German frontline for the Battle of Passchendaele 1917
- Site of tank attack in 1917

You will probably pass this memorial on your way to or from Langemarck. This is a Canadian Memorial and I particularly like the way it portrays the soldier in a sense of mourning. This memorial is here to mark the spot where the Canadians 'saved the line' following the first use of poison gas in 1915.

In April 1915 British High Command received intelligence reports from German prisoners that suggested the Germans were about to use gas as a weapon. The prisoners talked about cannisters being prepared. The British had even found protective cloth pads that had been issued to German troops to protect themselves from the gas. The warning signs were largely ignored and so when the cannisters were opened and the wind blew the gas across to the British lines the troops were completely unprepared. Soldiers were either overcome by the gas or ran and the result was a huge gap in the line. Two things saved the Germans having an enormous and devastating victory, firstly the Germans were very wary of the gas themselves and so were slow to follow up behind the gas. Secondly, in the confusion 18,000 Canadians were sent in to plug the gap with 'bayonets fixed'. The Canadians suffered 2000 casualties.

This spot became assigned the name 'Vancouver' as part of the planning for the Battle of Passchendaele in 1917. The name was deliberately a reference to the heroic actions of the Canadians here in 1915. In 1917 they were using tanks to support infantry to attack German bunker positions here. As you may know, the Battle of Passchendaele was all about the mud and tanks were fairly useless to start with, slipping into the huge shell holes and then getting stuck. The solution was to run the tanks along the remains of the roads rather than straight across the open ground. This coupled with a less obvious starting barrage meant that tanks had some success here. There was one particular German bunker, the 'Staigerhaus' that really 'stuck it out' in the area directly behind the Brooding soldier monument -it benefitted from a commander, called **Lieutenant Staiger**, who didn't run away when attacked by the tanks but also the tanks couldn't get close enough to properly destroy the bunker because of the terrain. The road between the monument and Zonnebeke to the southeast roughly marks a line of bunkers, fortified farms and defensive positions that the tanks supported infantry to attack in 1917.

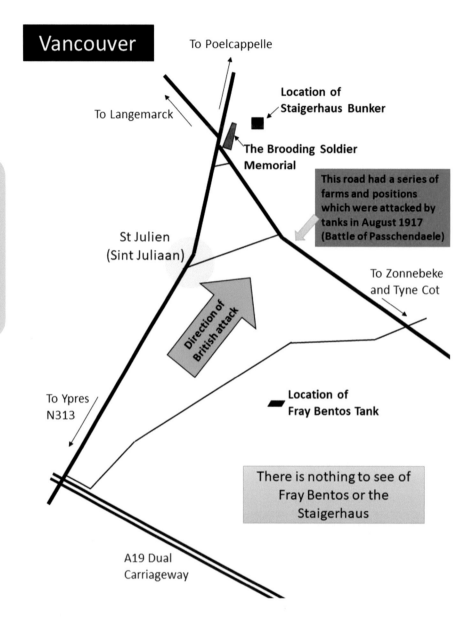

One interesting story is that of a Mark IV tank, '**Fray Bentos**' which was to attack a farm on the Zonnebeke road. As it crossed No Man's Land the tank slipped into a crater, sinking side down in the liquid mud to the point where it could not use its main guns. A member of the crew volunteered to go out and fix the special beam that was carried to help get a tank out of situations like this. Unfortunately he was killed and the beam fell across the main door. The crew were now stuck in the tank that they had so ironically called 'Fray Bentos' after the metal canned food. Several of the crew were wounded by German shelling, with one losing his scalp to a shell splinter and another being accidentally crushed inside as they tried to get the tank going. During the night the Germans repeatedly tried to blow the tank up and even managed to nearly throw in a grenade – the attacker being shot at the last moment. The crew were stranded for three nights, they had resorted to drinking water from the radiator and temperatures were averaging 30 degrees centigrade. Eventually after 72 hours the crew removed their Lewis machine guns and slipped away from the tank. Two men were awarded the Military Cross for bravery: **Captain Richardson** and **Second Lieutenant Hill**.

More on Gas Warfare: Prior to this first use of chlorine gas on the Western Front, there had been some small scale use of tear gas grenades. Chlorine gas is the one that can be seen as a green-yellow colour and smells like a cleaning product. This gas was only really lethal if casualties were given prolonged exposure to it such as being left in No Man's Land for a long period. The gas reacts to water in the lungs forming hydrochloric acid which induces vomiting and irritation. The impact of chlorine gas was exaggerated by the inadequate protection that the troops had.

Later on in the war phosgene gas was used. This was colourless and much more deadly than chlorine gas. Victim's lungs would fill with liquid and the casualty would essentially drown. Effects could be delayed with death occurring two days later. Mustard gas came next, recognised by its particularly unpleasant smell. It causes blisters that damaged eyes and organs.

After the initial unpredictability of using the wind to carry the chlorine gas, gas was placed into shells so that they could deliver the gas directly on top of the target. Although the Germans started using gas first, the allies became the experts and would confuse the Germans by mixing up the types of gas used. This was particular bad for the Germans as their gas masks (respirators) had to have different types of filters for different gas and so had to be manually changed for the different gases. Once we had the box respirator the British had no such problem because 'the box' contained all the various filters in one. As the war progressed the Germans also increasingly struggled with their supply of rubber which added to their problems.

The first gas masks or respirators as they are called in the military, were nothing more than pads and goggles. In fact the first instructions to troops was to use a urine soaked handkerchief, in the hope that the urea would counteract the chlorine. (Do you remember your acids and alkalis from school?) Next came pads with long straps and then hoods (sometimes strangely referred to as gas helmets).

The Main Developments of British Gas Protection

Black Veil and Gas Goggles May 1915	Hypo Helmet/ Smoke Hood June 1915	PH Helmet July 1915	Small Box Respirator August 1916
Impregnated pad to protect mouth and nose	Impregnated cloth to breath through with Mica eye piece	Glass eye pieces and valve to help breathing out	Canister/box had a variety of filters

The hoods were impregnated with chemicals that would again react and protect against the gas. The early ones you had to breath in and out through the thick material, later ones had a valve to breath out through that certainly helped a little. Breathing through heavy cloth was not easy and the eye pieces often steamed up. In 1916 the more effective box respirator arrived – this is the one where the soldier wears a square satchel across his chest. Interestingly the soldiers would at times carry multiple types of respirator to use with different types of gas.

HARRY PATCH MEMORIAL
(GPS: 50°54.607'N 2°54.491'E)

On the outskirts of Langemarck you will find the small memorial. In recent years there has been much publicity over the 'Last Fighting Tommy'. Harry Patch was one of the last veterans alive from the Great War. He remained silent about his experiences until the late 1990s when he was approached by the BBC. He seemed fascinated by the interest in his story and made appearances on various documentaries and even had his autobiography written. He came across here and was involved in the placing of this memorial. It was around here that the 19 year old Harry was wounded alongside his Lewis gun crew. He was the only survivor of a shell blast. This area is known as Pilckem Ridge and it featured as part of the Battle of Passchendaele.

The memorial stone says:

> '*Here, at dawn, on 16 August 1917, the 7th Battalion, Duke of Cornwall's Light Infantry, 20th (Light) Division, crossed the Steenbeek prior to their successful assault on the village on Langemarck. This stone is erected to the memory of fallen comrades, and to honour the courage, sacrifice and passing of the Great War generation. It is the gift of former Private and Lewis Gunner Harry Patch, No. 29295, C Company, 7th DCLI, the last surviving veteran to have served in the trenches of the Western Front.*'

Many an interview are available to watch online.

WELSH MEMORIAL GARDEN, LANGEMARCK
(GPS: 50°54.176'N 2°54.027'E)

On the Pilckem to Langemarck road you will find a rather fetching Welsh dragon. This is to commemorate all of the Welsh who lost their lives in the Great War. The dragon stands on a 'Stonehenge' style plinth and

The Ypres Salient

represents the Celtic links of the Welsh people. There are stones to represent the various Welsh units involved in the war.

HOUSEHOLD CAVALRY MEMORIAL, ZANDVOORDE
(GPS: 50°48.657'N 2°59.022'E)

Not far from the German command bunker is this rather impressive memorial. You need to walk down the narrow pathway between the buildings to actually find it. It is opposite a tiny red brick chapel or memorial structure. There is a green CWGC style sign to look out for. It is worth going to for the memorial itself, but also for the open views of the countryside beyond where in 1914 the British were trying to stop the Germans pushing through. The memorial marks the spot where **Lieutenant Charles Pelham** (Lord Worsley) was originally buried. He was here in command of the machine gun section when his unit became overwhelmed by the sheer number of Germans and he was killed. A German officer ensured that he had a properly marked grave and drew a map. The map eventually made it to Pelham's family and his wife Lady Worsley purchased the spot where he was found. Pelham is now buried in Ypres and this fine monument is here to remember him and his unit.

MESSINES AND THE 1914 CHRISTMAS TRUCE
(GPS: 50°45.589'N 2°53.740'E)

If you head and park at the Irish Peace Tower on the N365 south of Messines(Mesen) you can go for a short walk across to the New Zealand Memorial and in doing so will see the area where in 1914 the infamous truce occurred.

The Irish Peace Tower is relatively recent, being unveiled in 1998 and was born out of the hope given by the Good Friday Agreement in the 1990s. The tower represents the unity of the two Irelands and it is near here that the Irish and Ulster divisions went into attack in 1917 alongside each other as part of the Battle of Messines. They actually attacked near to the town of Wijtschate, but this was the more acceptable location to build the tower. The two Irish divisions lost 37,761 casualties and the Ulster Division 32,186 casualties.

Walk to the New Zealand Memorial: Go around behind the tower, through the gate and along the wooden bridge and board walks (there may be some bright yellow markers). You will go along and turn right, up a small hill and past a football pitch to the New Zealand Memorial (**50°45.625'N 2°53.482'E**). Here you will find two German bunkers, one was built of blocks and the other was cast on site. There is also an excellent orientation board looking down from the ridge onto the British frontline. It is this area where in 1914 soldiers from the two sides held an informal truce where they exchanged chocolate and cigarettes. This only happened in 1914 and despite the Sainsbury's advert never involved playing football – this is a total myth!
The New Zealanders made good progress with their attack on 7th June 1917. Using the surprise of the 19 mine explosions they quickly captured the ridge here and the town of Messines. They had 3000 wounded and 700 killed.

Messines Town: If you drive back up to Messines (Mesen) and stop in the centre (**50°45.919'N 2°53.863'E**) you will find clean toilets as well as the controversial 'handshake' memorial, which has, of course, a football (don't forget they never played football). Adolf Hitler supposedly spent time in the crypt of Messines church which was a medical station when he was wounded in the arm.

Trenches, Bunkers and Craters

GERMAN COMMAND BUNKER AT ZANDVOORDE
(GPS: 50°48.508'N 2°59.166'E)

Quite an impressive bunker, built in 1916. It is just down the road from the Household Cavalry Monument. It has five or six rooms for you to explore. It is free to enter and you access it through a small metal gate. It is a bit off the beaten track and so you will probably have it to yourself. Good to get the feel for what it was like to live in bunkers. It is an empty bunker – not a museum.

BAYERNWALD TRENCHES AND THE BATTLE
OF MESSINES RIDGE
(GPS: 50°48.059'N 2°52.570'E)

Key Facts:
- Part of the Battle of Messines (19 Mines set off)
- Restored German trenches to walk in
- German bunkers to explore

You will no doubt wish to go and see some trenches – to feel what the fighting environment was like, you have several options outside of the museum experiences. I would recommend Bayernwald. Traditionally, before going, you have needed to purchase tickets from the Kemmel Tourist Information Office (GPS: 50°47.110'N 2°49.444'E) (This is the GPS of where I normally park) Kemmel is a town a few miles away. The actual location of the ticket office, has moved several times in recent years and I fear it will probably have moved again by the time you read this – perhaps the safest thing to do is to check their website: www.toerismeheuvelland.be. I have also seen a ticket machine appear at the site itself, but I am not sure whether this is in action yet.

The Battle of Messines Ridge: During 1917 the French army had had a series of disastrous attacks with huge casualties, the result was a series of mutinies that ended up with 23,000 soldiers being charged and 55 shot. The British were under pressure to attack in the north. Here at Bayernwald we are on the Messines Ridge which is a plateau 60m up just to the south of Ypres. It was part of the ridge around Ypres and, as discussed in the Tyne Cot Cemetery section, this provided commanding views down onto the British positions around Ypres. Messines is a fascinating battle in that it was so much more decisively a victory than many of the other battles of WW1. **General Plumer** drafted in coal miners, London Underground workers and sewer builders to dig mines. The miners were paid 6 shillings a day which was six times the amount of a normal infantry soldier. They worked in four hour shifts to dig down then across and under the German positions. **19 mines** were dug of which most exploded as the troops went in to the attack. Plumer also used a ten day artillery bombardment, tanks and sheer numbers of troops, but it was the shock of the massed line of mines that made this attack so successful. The Germans did not know what had hit them and the entire top of the ridge was blown in a series of blasts. Mining was a dangerous job at the best of times but in a war context, even more so. They had to contend with collapses, flooding, asphyxiation and the other usual dangers, but also the German counter mining. Both sides would have listening posts trying to detect each other. If they heard the enemy they would attempt to place their own charge close by and blow it up (These explosions were called Camouflets). The underground war is probably best depicted in the movie 'Digging Hill 60'.

At Bayernwald: What you see once inside the turnstile at Bayernwald is a recreated German trench system built around some German bunkers and further down a German mine shaft. Go and have a look at the orientation table under the wooden shelter. Here you can get a sense of the battle and how this site fits the line of craters that make up the Battle of Messines. If you have a look at the bunkers and also the steps and pathways around them you will see how the Germans built bunkers using essentially concrete Lego blocks. They were cast behind the lines then brought up to the front at night time and could be easily constructed using metal poles through the holes into a standard designed bunker. Walk through the trenches and get a feel for the narrowness of them – imagine being in full kit or even carrying a stretcher or ration boxes. You will come across the mine shaft in a dead end – it has a big mesh grille over the top.

HILL 60 AND THE CATERPILLAR
(GPS: 50°49.479'N 2°55.827'E)

Key Facts:
- Part of the Battle of Messines
- Memorial park showing the landscape of the war and the mining activity
- Caterpillar mine crater blown at 3.10am on June 7th 1917

Hill 60 was a notorious site during the war being one of the highest points overlooking Ypres. It is called Hill 60 as on maps it was recorded as 60 metres above sea level. The hill was heavily mined and it looks radically different to how it would have done before the war. It was here that the first mine of the war was used. Hill 60 was captured as part of the **Battle of Messines**, when two large mines were blown by the Australians. The Australians blew the top of the hill off and also used the Caterpillar mine which we shall see later. After the war this was a place where many of the veterans came back to, visiting the numerous tunnels that still existed at that point.

Today enter the site by the gate and walk along the wooden walkway. You will see the big craters as you walk along. The first memorial that you see on your left is to the Queen Victoria's Rifles and is actually a smaller replacement memorial as the original was destroyed by the Nazis in 1940. You can if you like step off the walkway and have a look around – you will find German concrete bunkers and more craters (although the most intact bunker was converted by the Australians, hence it faces east). Stay on the wooden pathway and go down the steps into the small valley, there you will see a metalled line demarking the German frontline and as you then go up the other side towards the road you will find the same metalled line showing the Allied frontline. Of course the close proximity is yet another reminder of the intensity of this war and the troops would have heard and smelt each other's everyday life. Stand on the Allied frontline looking towards the German frontline and then look left and right, you can actually make out the zig zag of the original trenches. The large craters here are from the mining war – think of stories like the book, Birdsong by Sebastian Faulkes.

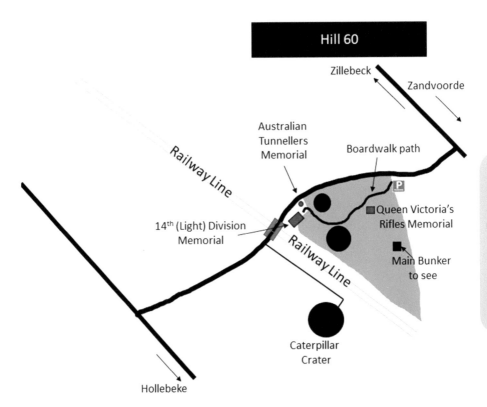

Victoria Cross Heroes: There were four Victoria Crosses won at Hill 60 and they were all won in the same action in April 1915. Three of the four were won by men of the East Surrey Regiment. On the 19th April 1915 the East Surrey Regiment entered the frontline trenches here on Hill 60.

George Roupell VC April 1915: Roupell went over with the British Expeditionary Force in 1914 and had been fighting since the Battle of Mons. He was an officer and had the most extraordinary life, that included being taken prisoner whilst supporting the Tsarist forces in Russia in 1919 and going on the run in German Occupied Europe when he missed the Dunkirk evacuation in 1940.

His citation for the VC in 1915 is here:

> *For most conspicuous gallantry and devotion to duty on 20 April 1915, when he was commanding a company of his battalion in a front trench on "Hill 60," which was subjected to a most severe bombardment throughout the day. Though wounded in several*

places, he remained at his post and led his company in repelling a strong German assault. During a lull in the bombardment he had his wounds hurriedly dressed, and then insisted on returning to his trench, which was again being subjected to severe bombardment. Towards evening, his company being dangerously weakened, he went back to his battalion headquarters, represented the situation to his commanding officer, and brought up reinforcements, passing backwards and forwards over ground swept by heavy fire. With these reinforcements he held his position throughout the night, and until his battalion was relieved next morning. This young officer was one of the few survivors of his company, and showed a magnificent example of courage, devotion and tenacity, which undoubtedly inspired his men to hold out till the end.

Edward Dwyer VC April 1915: Dwyer was in the same regiment as Roupell, the East Surreys. Dwyer was a private soldier and just 19 years old. The London Gazette said the following:

'For most conspicuous bravery and devotion to duty at Hill 60 on the 20th April 1915. When his trench was heavily attacked by German grenade throwers he climbed on to the parapet, and, although subjected to a hail of bombs at close quarters, succeeded in dispersing the enemy by the effective use of his hand grenades. Private Dwyer displayed great gallantry earlier on this day in leaving his trench, under heavy shell fire, to bandage his wounded comrades.'

Before returning to the front he was used comprehensively for propaganda purposes in the recruitment drive. He travelled around Britain and even had a recording made of his experiences.
In his own words….

'At last I was the only unwounded man left in the trench. There were three steps leading up to the parapet of the trench, and I sat crouched on the middle step. Shells and hand bombs were bursting all over and around, but nothing touched me at all. We had a lot of hand grenades in our trench, and I added to my stock by gathering up all I could find. I suppose I had about three hundred in all. Then I went back to crouch on the middle step of the trench. The fear of being taken prisoner was very strong upon me. A straight shot, a

round hole in the forehead, is all right. A soldier can't complain at that. But to be taken prisoner by those Huns - ugh! But funking drives a man to do mad things - I found myself on the trench parapet hurling hand grenades. I won't say it wasn't fine fun, but there was the dread at the back of my mind that the devils might miss me, and take me alive before the trench was relieved. So I gave it to them good and hot. I did a few of them in. If they had only known that I was the last man left they would have rushed me, and by now I should have been - a dead prisoner.'

He was soon bored at home and so persuaded the War Office to let him return to the front. He was killed leading his platoon forward near Guillemont on the Somme in September 1916. See **Flatiron Copse** on the Somme for his grave.

Bunker at Hill 60

Benjamin Geary VC April 1915: Geary was another member of the East Surrey Regiment in April 1915. He led his men across very exposed open ground under fierce enemy fire to join survivors of another regiment in a crater at the top of the hill.
His citation reads:

For most conspicuous bravery and determination on "Hill 60," near Ypres, on April 20th and 21st, 1915, when he held the left crater with his platoon, some men of the Bedfordshire Regiment and a few reinforcements who came up during the evening and night. The crater was first exposed to very heavy artillery fire which broke down the defences, and afterwards throughout the night to repeated bomb attacks which filled it with dead and wounded. Each attack was, however, repulsed mainly owing to the splendid personal gallantry and example of Second Lieutenant Geary. At one time he used a rifle with great effect, at another threw hand grenades, and exposed himself with entire disregard to danger in order to see by the light of flares where the enemy were coming on. In the intervals between the attacks he spent his whole time arranging for the ammunition supply and for reinforcements. He was severely wounded just before daylight on 21st April.

Geoffrey Woolley VC April 1915: Woolley was in action with the others but belonged to a different regiment: The Queen Victoria's Rifles. His company was supplying ammunition to those in the frontline. As the fighting became desperate, without orders, he ended up helping in the defence of the hill. After becoming the only officer left he kept the men fighting all night, fending off German attacks. Only 14 of the 150 men in his company survived the action. His citation reads:

For most conspicuous bravery on "Hill 60" during the night of 20th–21st April, 1915. Although the only Officer on the hill at the time, and with very few men, he successfully resisted all attacks on his trench, and continued throwing bombs and encouraging his men till relieved. His trench during all this time was being heavily shelled and bombed and was subjected to heavy machine gun fire by the enemy.

After the war Woolley stayed in the army and became an army chaplain, serving throughout WW2.

Hill 60 Visit continued: Keep following the path and go out of the gate by the two memorials. The one on your right is to the Australian tunnellers and has World War Two bullet holes in it. The one in front of you is to the Light Division and was moved here later.

Hill 60 August 1917

The Caterpillar Mine Crater
(GPS 50°49.364'N 2°55.700'E)

Go out onto the pavement and continue to walk away from where you parked. Go over the railway bridge and then turn left down the footpath. Keep going a short distance and suddenly you will see the huge crater. This area was known as the Caterpillar as that is what it looked like from the air – it was essentially a bit of high ground made from the spoil of building the railway and was in the shape of a caterpillar. It is well worth a visit and is one of the mines that made up the Messines Ridge attack.

The crater is a result of mining activity associated with the **Battle of Messines**. This and the one at Hill 60, are in fact the most northerly mines of the Messines Ridge battle. It was blown on 7th June 1917 at 3:10am. The mine had actually been dug and prepared earlier in the war, but not blown. It had survived flooding and filling with poison gas prior to the Australians clearing and pumping it out ready for Messines. The original charge was still ok as the explosives had been protected inside petrol cans.

Caterpillar Crater

BLACK WATCH CORNER AND POLYGON WOOD
(GPS: 50°50.904'N 2°58.923'E)

Black Watch Corner is on the southwestern corner of Polygon Wood and marks the spot where in 1914 the Scottish regiment, the Black Watch, halted the German advance (see page 44 for aerial photograph). Despite throwing everything at them, the forty Black Watch, in a hastily dug trench held off repeated Germans assaults. The Germans even brought down heavy artillery fire on them. The Black Watch were outnumbered by at least three to one. If you enter Polygon Wood from here and walk northeast for about 15-20 minutes you will come to the two British cemeteries: The Buttes New British Cemetery and Polygon Wood Cemetery. You will also find an impressive Australian memorial to the Australian 5th Division and also a memorial to the 378 missing of New Zealand. The Australian monument was built quickly and was finished in 1919.

The wood itself, is similar in reputation to Delville Wood on the Somme. It was the scene of fighting during the First Battle of Ypres in 1914. In October 1914 the Germans held the northern half of the wood, near the cemeteries, and two Guards regiments (Grenadier and Irish Guards) were ordered to attack and capture the position. The fighting was ferocious, with the dead lying scattered around. The Irish Guard's medical officer, **Lieutenant Hugh Shields**, was killed whilst trying to help the wounded. He has no known grave, and is commemorated on the Menin Gate. The wood was then lost to the Germans in 1915. In 1917 it was back in the thick of the action during the Battle of Passchendaele. It was taken at a large cost by the Australians, hence the memorial here. One of the famous stories told here is that of the German unexploded gas shells that months later, on the first warm day of 1918, started to leak. It was reported that there were many casualties from the gas. A large surviving bunker on the north side of the track is known as Scott's Post, it was here that the **Lt. Colonels Scott DSO** and **Turnbull DSO** were killed from a ricocheted bullet during a unit handover. They are buried at the Buttes New British Cemetery II B 5 and I C 9. Most of the damage on this bunker is actually from cleared shells being detonated post-war.

The Ypres Salient

THE BLUFF
GPS: 50°48.797'N 2°56.136'E

This is worth a visit as an extra. The site is within a family recreational park called the 'De Palingbeek'. It is beside the canal, with walks and cycleways running through it. There is woodland and open grass spaces as well as childrens play parks. The locals park at the big car park back up the road, but I recommend parking down by the canal and walking in alongside the path by the canal. What you see will depend on the season. As you walk in with the canal on your left you will be able to see entrances to bunkers and tunnels on your right in the bank. If these are hidden by the nettles and foliage do not despair – head on to the visitor centre and there are boards and photos to show you what happened here. There are also trenches and bunkers in the woodland, which are quite impressive.

Museums

MEMORIAL MUSEUM PASSCHENDAELE 1917
(GPS: 50°52.232'N 2°59.247'E)

This is, in my opinion, one of the better museums to visit in the Ypres area and although named as a Passchendaele museum you will get much more out of it than just this one battle. In this museum you start upstairs and you enter a dugout, going deeper as you go along before you pop out in a German trench that then swings round to become a British trench. What you get here is all the uniforms, kit and equipment as well as atmosphere. There is a shell room where you can see all the different types and sizes of shell. It has sections on the different nationalities and things such as medical equipment. You can go in the trench system and see many of the different types of shelter used by both sides. The array of what you get to see is really good.

Photo showing the lake and remains of the church in Zonnebeke.
This is the site of the Passchendaele museum today.

HOOGE CRATER MUSEUM AND THE HOOGE AREA
(GPS: 50°50.771'N 2°56.967'E)

This museum is 'old school' and if you like to see lots of original items in one smallish place then this is the one for you. You also get a great café. The museum has a good collection of the different shells, rifles, and grenades as well as uniforms. It's not as big or modern as the Passchendaele museum but more personal and probably quieter. Hooge, of course is also a significant site for the fighting around Ypres. A stone's throw from the museum stood a grand chateau that had been a British Headquarters until it was shelled and abandoned. It then became a heavily fought over piece of land and in 1915 there were as many as 300 casualties a day at times here. There was obviously a crater here too that has led to the name of the museum and the cemetery across the road. The crater was blown in July 1915 by the British and destroyed a German emplacement. The British dug a 190ft tunnel to reach the position and the resulting crater was 120ft wide and 20ft deep. The explosion was so big that the British lost ten of their own men to falling debris!

I believe that the ornamental lake at the Hotel was originally the crater, it has been reshaped though. It was also around here that the Germans first used flame throwers, which helped them capture a large section of British line.

Hooge War Walk: It is good to walk up to Railway Wood from the museum and see the Miners memorial. To do this you walk up the side road beside the museum and you will come to a wood on your left.

Then turn left and walk forwards following the edge of the wood, follow it around as it bends round to your right. You will start to see large craters full of water in the wood. It is a nice activity to try and count the craters as you go. You will find two memorials as you go round. The second one which has a Cross of Sacrifice is the Royal Engineers Grave and it commemorates those who were never recovered from tunnels near here. If you look out on the fields from here you are looking over a landscape that was heavily tunnelled – the craters behind you are the obvious evidence of this. Under the fields, a geophysical

The Ypres Salient

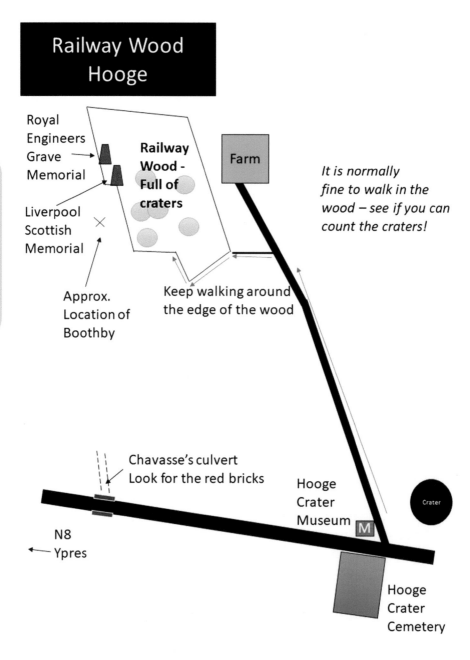

survey has recently found the resting place of Lieutenant Boothby. Boothby was killed whilst trying to stop the Germans breaking into his tunnel. The sad thing is that his story really only emerged when some love letters were found in a trunk. The letters belonged to his girlfriend and she never told anyone, including her son about him. Boothby was

just about to come home on leave
when he was killed. You can
walk through the wood entering
where the first memorial to
the Liverpool Scottish is (keep
counting the craters).

AUSTRALIAN WAR MEMORIAL

Tunnelling Nr Hooge

As you return towards the museum stop on the corner of the wood
and look towards Ypres, run your eyes along the main road until you
can pick out what looks like a red brick bridge – it is quite close to
the museum. This bridge is over a culvert and it was here that **Noel
Chavasse**, a medical officer worked in 1915. Chavasse repeatedly went
into No Man's Land looking for casualties, he continued to do this until
he was satisfied that all the wounded had been brought in. For this
action here he received the Military Cross for bravery.

Noel Chavasse went on to receive two Victoria Crosses. It must be
remembered that to win a VC you must do something so heroic that
you will probably die and many have been awarded posthumously as
the receiver was killed in the action. In 1916 on the Somme Chavasse
acted in the same way as he had at Hooge, this time though he was
wounded. He personally rescued twenty men, including three who
were in a shell hole just twenty five meters from the Germans. His
second VC was back not far from here at the Battle of Passchendaele in
1917. Here Chavasse yet again repeatedly brought in wounded soldiers.
He was in a shell hole when a shell landed and killed everyone except

him. He was heavily wounded, including a wound to the abdomen. Chavasse crawled half a mile for help and as he was being operated on, he dictated a letter to his fiancée saying 'duty called me and it was my duty to obey'. He died of his wounds in the month that he was due to marry Gladys – 4th August 1917 (three years to the day that Britain had gone to war). His grave has two VCs engraved and the words 'Greater love hath no man than this, that a man lay down his life for his friends.' You can visit Chavasse' grave at Brandhoek New Military Cemetery (see the Cemetery section)

IN FLANDERS FIELDS MUSEUM– THE CLOTH HALL
(GPS: 50°51.087'N 2°53.168'E)

Located in the Centre of Ypres, inside the huge Cloth Hall – this was once the museum to see, encompassing a huge collection of artefacts. If you have time to spare in the city centre then it may be worth a visit. It is now a modern interactive style museum with much of the collection no longer on display. You have a wrist band to personalise your experience and there are touch screens to use as you go round. My recommendation would be to go to Passchendaele or Hooge instead, unless you particularly like modern style museums and have the time.

HILL 62, SANCTUARY WOOD MUSEUM
(GPS: 50°50.212'N 2°56.767'E)

Once one of the most popular museums in the area it has become rather dilapidated. It houses a disorganised but fascinating collection of artefacts and some particularly good 3D slides housed in old fashioned stereoscope viewers – some of these photographs can't be seen anywhere else. Outside there are also some very worn and heavily tramped trenches including some tunnels to explore (you might need wellies and a torch). If you have an allergy to cats, stay away as they have the run of the museum. If you have time, then it makes a good extra stop and is close to Hooge.

Poperinge

Market place
GPS: 50°51.340'N 2°43.585'E

Key Facts:
- Site of Toc H, The Everyman's Club
- Site of the 'Shot at Dawn' cells and Firing post

Poperinge or 'Pops' as the troops called it is the town immediately to
the west of Ypres and as such was a rest area, where headquarters were
situated and as a general co-ordinated rallying point for supplies etc
going on up to the front. There are two main reasons that you might
visit this town. The first is to visit **Toc H** (Talbot House) and the second
is to visit the '**Death Cells**' and Firing post that are associated with
those who were 'shot at dawn'. You can normally park adequately in the
market place in the centre of town.

Poperinge

Access to Toc H is from the side street - Pottestraat

The Death Cells are on your right as you enter the Town Hall. The post is in the courtyard inside

Toc H

Market Place

N333

Cells

N333

N308

N308

N308

To the Ring Road And Ypres

N333

To the Ring Road

TOC H
(Toc H GPS: 50°51.354'N 2°43.381'E)

Toc H or more formally Talbot House, still stands and looks much as it did during the war. It was run by **Padre Philip Clayton**, known as 'Tubby' Clayton, it was an 'everyman's club'. This meant that officers and normal soldiers were all accepted, which is unusual for the time. It was a place of calm for the soldiers and they could get cocoa, read in the library, take part in a debate or attend the church in the loft. All of this is still there for you to see, now as a museum. Borrowing books was easy and controlled by the handing over of your hat in return for the book, this was a very safe way to do business as it was a military offence to not have your headgear. This is not your normal museum and you may well be offered a cup of tea, indeed you can even book to stay the night via their website.

DEATH CELLS AND FIRING POST
(Death Cells GPS: 50°51.332'N 2°43.658'E)

The Death Cells and Post can be found at the entrance to the Town Hall. So to find the cells you need to head out of the market place eastwards and as you go down the side of the large Town Hall building you will find a double width gateway – as you go through the gateway the cells are immediately on your right. To find the post walk further into the courtyard and you will see it. The soldiers who were 'shot at dawn' create quite heated debates these days. The government finally pardoned the men in 2006 after relentless pressure from various groups. A few facts need to be thought about in relation to these executions, firstly although several thousand soldiers were sentenced to death only 11% of executions were carried out when reviewed by the senior generals. The British executed 346 men, of these 37 were for murder and another 40 were already under suspended sentences of death. All the men were offered proper legal advice and all were given a trial. The largest number were accused of desertion (266). The grey area comes when we consider the psychological impact of the war on the men and whether this was taken into account. When the records are reviewed, new young soldiers were often treated with mercy. If you research individuals you get very different versions of the stories and things can get confusing – people also make their own judgements without the wartime context. One executed soldier, **Sergeant Joe Stones**, for example is judged innocent and a hero by some for using his rifle to block a trench as he ran from a German ambush. Others say that a soldier must never cast away his weapon and that a rifle across a trench is no real barrier, in fact in the narrow trench the rifle being fired could stop the enemy for a prolonged time. There are also allegations that he may have left behind his wounded officer. Stones had previously been promoted quickly due to his ability in the field and several people spoke up for his character, so he had obviously shown himself not to be a coward before. Stones was tried for 'casting away arms', he was represented by a solicitor and the trial was conducted according to the rules. My point really is that this is an emotional topic, the officers at the time had to fight a war, discipline was essential – even today military law is different from civilian law. If the man was an officer or an NCO (Sergeant etc) they were more likely to receive the death penalty as they were leaders and had more responsibility. There are quite a few comments in the records about ensuring that officers and NCOs were not treated any more positively than ordinary soldiers.

The first man shot here at Poperinge was **Private James Wilson**, he went absent whilst in action on Hill 62 in July 1916. He was shot on the 9th July 1916 and is buried in Poperinge in Poperinge New Military Cemetery. **2nd Lieutenant Eric Poole** was also shot here for desertion. At the Battle of the Somme Poole had been knocked unconscious by a shell blast, possibly causing damage to his brain and afterwards displayed symptoms of shell shock. He had a month's convalescence before returning to the Somme. On return he reported being unwell and in need of seeing the doctor. He went to see the doctor and then disappeared. Whilst he was away his men went over the top without him and were badly mauled, suffering 225 casualties. His commanding officer and the arresting military policeman both advised he be sent home due to his shell shocked condition. The Court Martial, advised by a medical board that he was 'of sound mind', disagreed and he was shot here on the 10th December 1916. He is buried in Poperinge

THE COWARD

I could not look on Death,
which being known,
Men led me to him,
blindfold and alone.

DE LAFAARD

Ik kon de dood niet in de ogen zien,
toen dit geweten was,
Leidde men mij voor hem,
geblinddoekt en alleen.

Rudyard Kipling,
Epitaphs of the War

The Post

The headstones of men 'shot at dawn' look exactly as all the rest of the graves and as such you would never know the stories behind their deaths.

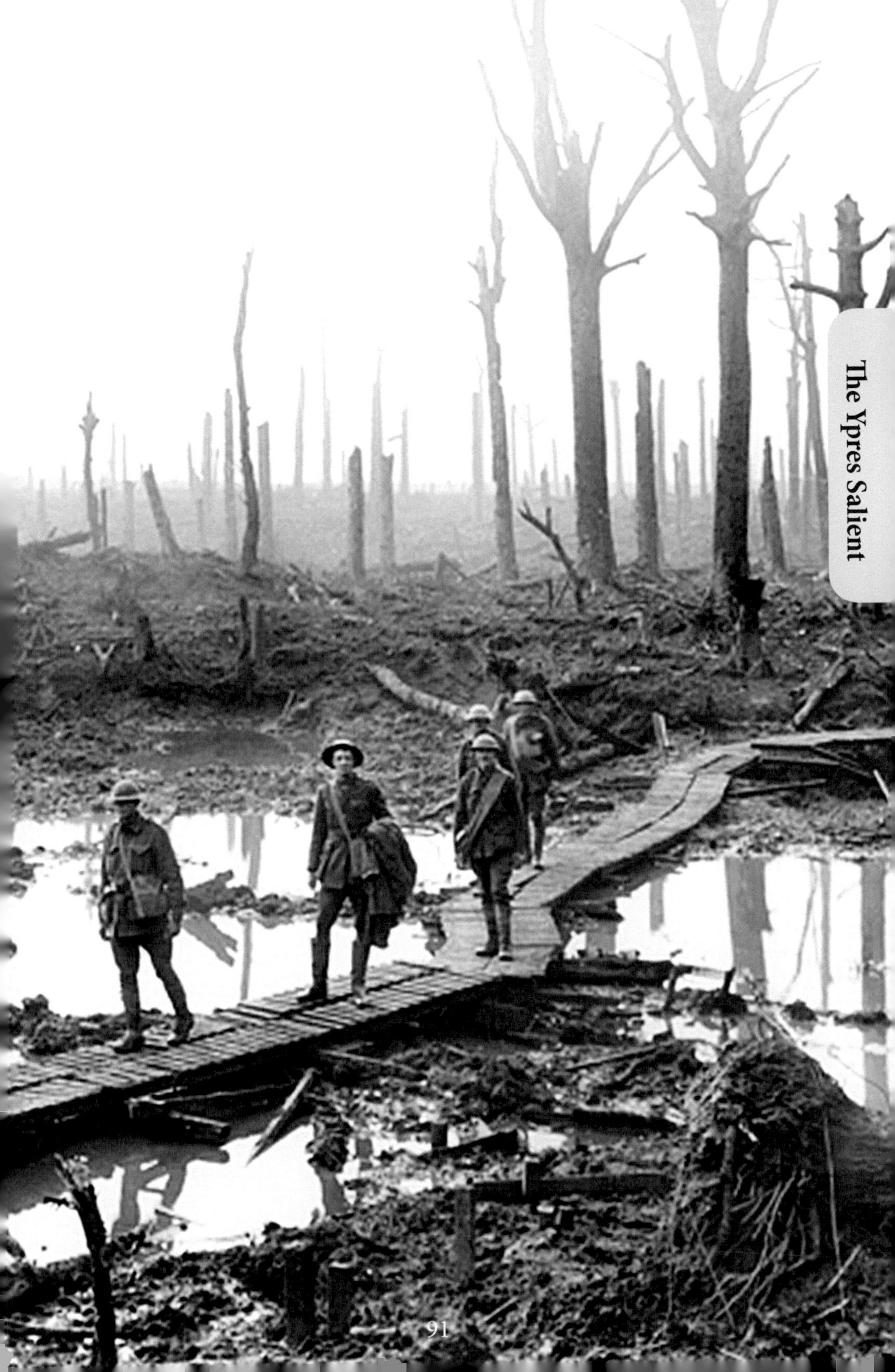

The Somme Battlefield Map

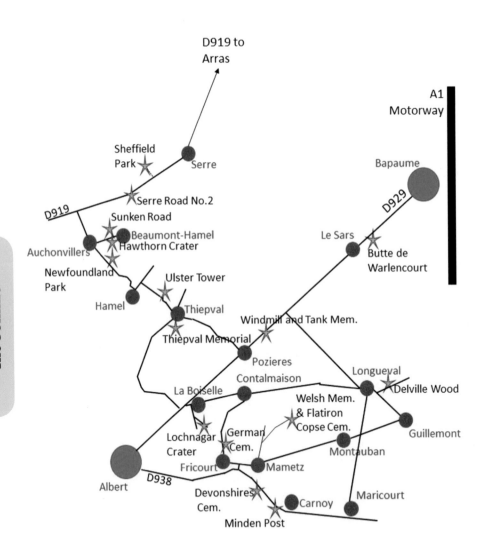

The Somme

Introduction to The Somme

Key Facts:
- Known for the first day – 1st July 1916 with 57,470 British casualties (19,240 deaths)
- Battle lasted 141 days
- 72,339 British have no known grave - The Missing (Commemorated at Thiepval)
- 500,000 total German, 419,000 British and 204,000 French casualties
- Tanks used for the first time in September 1916

The Somme is remembered for its first day: 1st July 1916, but this was a battle that lasted until November 1916. It is a battle that went from sunny days to mud sloppy wet ones. It was also a battlefield of 1918 when the British first lost everything gained in 1916 in the last German hurrah of the Spring Offensive, but then regained it finally in the 'Last 100 days' of the Great War.

I am going to presume that you are approaching the area from Bapaume on the Motorway. The battlefield is a rectangular zone of about 5 miles east-west and 9 miles north-south. Bapaume in the east was German and Albert in the west was British. Between these two towns is a dead straight Roman road that splits the British/German battlefield in half.

The battle here in 1916 was primarily to help take pressure off the French at Verdun. Verdun was a symbol of French resistance to the Germans and indeed the German General Falkenhayn was attempting to 'bleed the French white' there. The idea was to have a joint Anglo-French breakthrough at the Somme. As time went on the British took more and more of a lead in the battle, but there was still French involvement to the south. The battle was a certainty, the British had to support the French and back at home there was pressure to use the new volunteer army and win a great battle. General Haig was ultimately in charge of the British army in France (BEF) and had not long been in command at the time of the battle, officially he still held the same rank as some of his subordinates. The planning for the 1st July 1916 was left

The Somme

to General Rawlinson as the General in charge of that area of the front. General Rawlinson was offered advice by Haig on how to plan and fight on the 1st July and much of this was ignored by Rawlinson and so he bears a lot of responsibility for the slaughter that occurs.

Look out of the car windows as you head onto the Roman road heading for Albert – look at the landscape. This is very different from the landscape around Ypres. Here it is chalk with rolling hills. There is the odd gulley or valley running through it. The chalk geology was significant for several reasons, firstly it is great for digging. The Germans spent considerable effort digging deep underground bunkers which would protect them from artillery fire, as well as often being equipped with electricity. The second reason is that the chalk absorbs blasts well which means that artillery doesn't always have the same destructive effect here as it does in other landscapes. The rolling hills also provide perfect vantage points for dug in German machine guns.

The villages of Le Sars, Pozieres and so on would be recognisable to the pre-war population, but were effectively wiped off the map during the battle only to be rebuilt almost identically afterwards.

Looking towards the British lines from Pozieres and a similar view from 1917

94

The Somme

The Men: The battle had been a year in the planning and by this point the British army was a very different one to that of 1914. In 1914 a small professional British Expeditionary Force had set off to France – now that army was largely dead, wounded or back in Britain training the vast numbers of volunteers. This then was the big test of the volunteer army – Kitchener's 'your country needs you' men. Here were the Pals battalions that had been told they could join up together, train together and fight together (and as you will see die together). The army was about 60% volunteer Pals battalions, the rest was the remains of the original and territorial regiments (these latter regiments also had vast amounts of later recruits in them though.)

The Plan: As I said earlier the planning was done by General Rawlinson. The original date set was the 29th June as the French were desperate for help due to the on-going battle at Verdun. The battle would be started by a week-long artillery bombardment with guns lined up. This artillery bombardment was to be so big that everything would be destroyed – not a German would be left alive. Rawlinson put huge faith in the artillery. The new fresh troops would then advance in an orderly fashion and take possession of the German positions, they need not rush as per the then current army doctrine as the Germans would all be dead. They would take with them huge quantities of materials to mend and rebuild the German positions as their own. This means they would be heavily laden and slow during their advance to the enemy line. Troops were given tin triangles to wear on their backs so that aircraft could see and plot the advance clearly. A lot of time and thought had gone into where the key German positions were, mines had been dug to destroy them from below. Narrow gauge railways were constructed to take up supplies and bring back casualties. A timetable was also published detailing how the artillery gun fire would lift and advance at set times further into the German positions. Big artillery barrages had worked in the past at Verdun. Rawlinson planned to only really capture small amounts on the first day, in places only the German frontline trenches. The British had amassed a numerical advantage of 7:1. Rawlinson was urged to use 'rush' tactics by Haig but he refused saying it was unnecessary and too complex in this huge attack. The time of 7.30am was also unusual, the French wanted it even later but this was as late as Rawlinson would go. So what we have is a plan that

The Somme

was quite different from the military thinking at the time – they weren't going at dawn and they weren't going to charge at speed following the ending of the barrage. This was fine so long as the Germans were all dead!

The British troops would attack to a timetable of waves – normally nine waves, one after the other would move forward and then go 'over the top'. Behind would come the stretcher bearers. 10% of every regiment would remain in case of high casualties and units had to be built around a nucleus of experienced men.

If everything went to plan then the cavalry would charge through and the whole German line would be turned upon.

What Happened: The Germans knew an attack was coming, the build-up was obvious. There were even remarks in the press about the Whitsun bank holiday (June 11th) being postponed so that the shell factories could keep going for the 'big push'. The French had previously held the line here and when it was taken over by the British the Germans became convinced that it was the place. The German response was to dig in even more. They constructed much deeper layers of defence, not just the 'text book' three lines of trenches. Everyone on the British side was pretty much convinced of the plan, especially those who witnessed the extended artillery bombardment, how could anyone live through that? During the week long bombardment they could sit on the frontline parapet and watch the shells firing overhead. The Germans did suffer during the bombardment and many had had their nerves pushed beyond human limits. However those deep German dug outs, deep in the chalk, some up to 100m down, protected them and more survived than anticipated. The Germans had also learnt not to garrison the frontline with anything more than a skeleton force as it was a waste of troops if bombarded. Before going over the top the British troops were given rousing speeches and tots of rum. They were told and they believed that the Germans were dead and thus understood why they only needed to walk in straight lines across No Man's Land. They understood why they only needed to carry their rifles at 'high port' as if on a parade ground. At 7.29am on a hot and sunny 1st July 1916 the shelling stopped and at 7.30am the whistles blew and heavily laden troops climbed up and advanced towards the enemy.

The 'Secret Race': What the British didn't know is that they were actually in a race. They had to get across No Man's Land before the Germans got out of their deep bunkers and got their machine guns set up. The moment the shelling stopped the Germans started the race – the British, of course, thought the Germans were all dead and thus didn't realise they were in a race. Essentially the British lost the race and were mown down by machine guns.

The Result: The British never took their first day objectives. There were 57,470 casualties, mostly within minutes of zero hour at 7.30am. 19,240 of these were deaths. A few other factors helped to ruin the plan, the rigid artillery timetable couldn't be adapted and so often fired at the wrong time at the wrong place – sometimes causing casualties to their own side when the troops had actually gone further than expected. Many of the British shells that so impressively flew over the to the German lines failed to explode (possibly up to 30%) so their impact was limited. The barbed wire, that was in thick belts, was not completely cut or flattened by the shelling so troops were still hampered and caught in the open – losing more time in that race.

Shrapnel shells had been used to destroy barbed wire, although this wasn't easy. The problem here was that the shell had to explode its charge of lead balls at the correct moment. If the shell exploded early then the balls wouldn't damage the wire as the force had dissipated, too late and the shell was in the ground and the blast of balls were contained by the chalk.

The wounded and the dead of this battle were victims of two things, one the machine guns and secondly the German artillery. The attack had started across an almost untouched No Man's Land and the German machine guns which had won the 'Secret Race' had been excellently positioned to fire across the British trenches. The Germans had also noted where the British had cut the wire to let the troops through so were ready to fire at these places. Once the Germans knew the attack was underway they then brought the full might of their own

The Somme

97

artillery down on No Man's Land and the British frontline. Where some British troops were successful they were often trapped as further waves couldn't reach them and supplies of ammunition etc also could not get across in the face of all this firepower. The wounded had a wait of up to 14 hours before darkness gave enough cover to move. The 1st July was a day to forget and became the worst day in the history of the British Army. The battle slogged on until November 1916 (141 days) and cost both sides over a million men.

The Somme

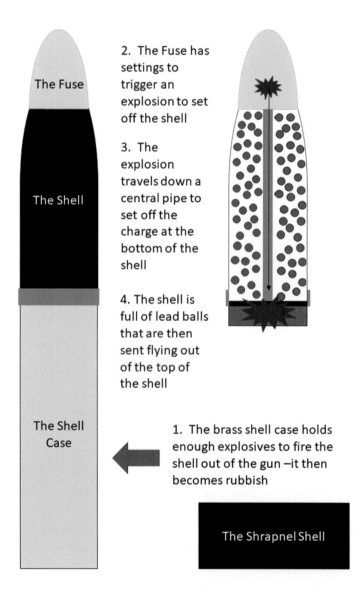

The Fuse

The Shell

The Shell Case

2. The Fuse has settings to trigger an explosion to set off the shell

3. The explosion travels down a central pipe to set off the charge at the bottom of the shell

4. The shell is full of lead balls that are then sent flying out of the top of the shell

1. The brass shell case holds enough explosives to fire the shell out of the gun –it then becomes rubbish

The Shrapnel Shell

Cemeteries

THE DEVONSHIRES CEMETERY
and the Southern Battlefield
(GPS: 49°59.334'N 2°44.080'E)

Key Facts:
- Special story about the 1st July 1916 attack
- The start of using modelling as part of military planning

A rather small and special cemetery this one. Park and walk up the track and you will see the steps up to the cemetery. The cemetery is along the top of a ridge overlooking the area between Mametz and Fricourt. As you walk up to the top of the stairs you will see the famous marker stone, on the left just before you enter– have a real think about what it says.

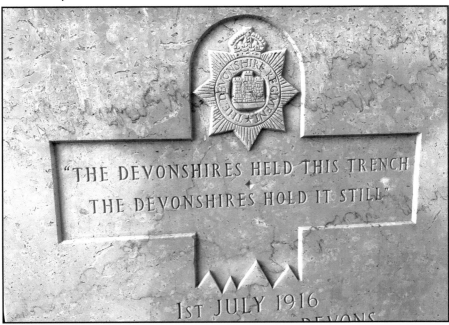

This cemetery is the original frontline, however it had been heavily shelled shortly before the 1st July so the Devons actually started from behind the cemetery in the reserve trench. When you enter the cemetery you will see that it is almost entirely made up of soldiers from the Devonshire Regiment who were killed on the 1st July 1916. Make your way down the left hand side to the end and find the grave of Captain Martin. Duncan Martin was an early volunteer in 1914 and had fought at the Battle of Loos prior to the Somme. He and his men were active in the lead up to the battle and had a good knowledge of German strong points and machine gun posts in front of where they were due to attack. Martin took the maps home on leave shortly before the offensive and decided to make a plasticine model of the German positions to show his men. As he made the model he became increasing concerned about a particular German machine gun position at a point known as Shrine Alley. He was convinced that if the machine gun was still there when he attacked it would destroy his company. He showed the model to his superior officers and despite them being impressed with the model, to the point that the brigade staff used it, they would not budge on the plan saying that the artillery would destroy the position in the build-up. It is not necessarily the case that the superior officers dismissed the importance of the machine gun, in fact this could be why they borrowed the model. The Devons, because they were coming from their reserve trench, had a wider expanse of No Man's Land to cross – they were going to come down the track (the same one you came up from where you parked) and then turn left towards Albert (see map).

Have a look at this photo. You can see clearly down the track and then out towards the Shrine(circled), where the machine gun was – it could fire straight up the track.

When the whistles blew Martin led his men forward and was one of the first to fall. The 9th Devons lost 141 killed, 268 wounded and 55 missing (60% of their strength). Many of the deaths happened as they came down the track which is too exposed, with a clear line of sight to the German frontline, before rounding the corner and coming under fire from the machine gun at the Shrine that Martin had noticed before the attack. A few days later the bodies were brought in and buried in their original trench. A wooden sign was placed above the graves saying 'The Devonshires held this trench, The Devonshires hold it still'. See the map below (To orientate the map on site you may have to do this on the track if the vegetation is too dense in front of the cemetery)

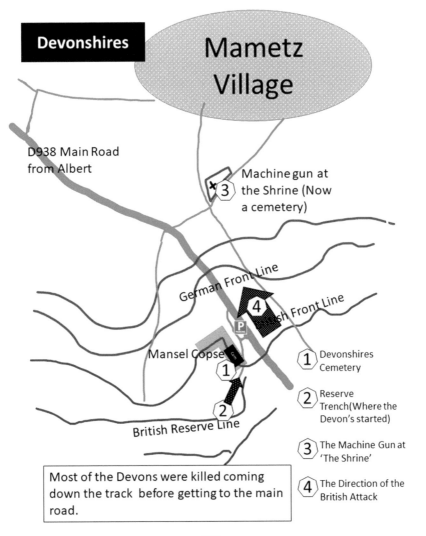

Devonshires

Mametz Village

D938 Main Road from Albert

Machine gun at ③ the Shrine (Now a cemetery)

German Front Line

British Front Line

④

Mansel Copse

P

① Devonshires Cemetery

② Reserve Trench (Where the Devon's started)

③ The Machine Gun at 'The Shrine'

④ The Direction of the British Attack

British Reserve Line

Most of the Devons were killed coming down the track before getting to the main road.

The Somme

If you were wondering about Captain Martin's headstone bearing 3 names, note too that the headstone beside it is blank. One story goes that it wasn't clear about whose body was whose or parts thereof so they were buried together. Another story claims that they ran out of space at the end of the cemetery and buried them together for that reason. The fact that the trench continued along the ridge at the end of the cemetery makes me slightly dubious of the second story.

If you head along towards the entrance, you will find the grave of **Lieutenant W Hodgson**. Also in the cemetery is the grave of **Private A F Weston**. I was told on my first visit to the cemetery that Weston was Hodgson's batman or servant. The story goes that because Hodgson was an officer he had a batman to sort out his kit and provide him meals and so on (this was normal for officers). Weston was a particularly resourceful chap and Hodgson used this to his advantage with the other officers. He would bet them that he could have various luxuries in his dugout and Weston would facilitate him winning his bets. Weston was said to have gone out in to No Man's Land to raid abandoned houses to do this. He therefore provided Hodgson with things like a bath tub, carpeted floor and so on. Hodgson was also a poet and two days before the battle Hodgson had a poem published (remember that writing poetry was cool and very common at this time), the poem is called '**Before Action**' and this part pretty much foretells his own upcoming death:

> *I, that on my familiar hill*
> *Saw with uncomprehending eyes*
> *A hundred of thy sunsets spill*
> *Their fresh and sanguine sacrifice,*
> *Ere the sun swings his noonday sword*
> *Must say good-bye to all of this; -*
> *By all delights that I shall miss,*
> *Help me to die, O Lord.*

The story goes on to say that Hodgson was the 'Bombing Officer' in charge of keeping the men supplied with Mills bombs (grenades). He went into the attack with the other men at zero hour and was wounded. Hodgson was hit in the leg by a machine gun and fell, Weston dressed his wounds as best as he could but needed more bandages so crawled back for more and to get help. The Germans were firing the machine guns at knee height, 'dropping' the soldiers who would then get hit in the head on the next machine gun sweep. On Weston's return he too was mortally wounded and he was found draped over his officer, both having being killed by the same machine gun.

The two separate graves to the side are from an artillery battery that was obviously near here, later on in the war and the battery was almost certainly hit by counter battery fire and this was the nearest cemetery.

MINDEN POST
(GPS: 49°58.916'N 2°44.774'E)

Within sight of the Devonshires Cemetery you will find this 'little explored' site. This site was made famous by the Malins film of the Somme. Here today under the road you will find the tunnel that the troops used to come in to the medical station at Minden Post. It is well worth having a peak in to the tunnel from the south side and watching some of the footage, as found on the internet. The film footage shows troops emerging from the tunnel as well as the medical teams working on various British and German wounded here.

Note the tunnel arch behind the men

The Somme

To find the site: Turn south (right) as you leave the Devonshires and as the road starts to rise towards Carnoy (in a distance of about 1km) you will see 'motorway style' crash barriers on each side of the road. There is a tiny spot to park on the right just before the barriers start. To access the tunnel, I advise that you cross the road and go down the side of the farmers field – the access is much easier on the northern side. Take care, but you can still go through, at your own risk!

Minden Post Tunnel 2018

Footballs: It wasn't far from here that **Captain Nevill** of the East Surreys went in to action on the 1st July 1916 motivating his men forward with footballs. He previously had a reputation for standing on his platoon's fire step and shouting abuse at the Germans opposite. Whilst on leave he bought four footballs, he offered a prize to the first platoon to kick its football up to the German trenches. Nevill himself kicked off as the signal to advance. Unfortunately he was never able to pay the winnings as he was killed in the attack. Footballs aside, what is interesting is how the young officers were trying to help their men. Nevill was clearly trying to distract his men's fear and help them make progress across No Man's Land, today we would call this sideways thinking. Nevill is buried in Carnoy Military Cemetery.

More on the southern attacks: The attacks to the south were much more successful than in the middle and the north of the battlefield. The next village south of Mametz is Montauban and this was captured fairly easily, when the troops arrived in the village, supposedly the only thing still alive was a fox.

The Casino Point Mine (sometimes referred to as Kasino Point Mine) Not too far from here was a mine that was set off late. The

The Somme

mine was supposed to go off at 7.28am with the rest of the mines but failed, so was fired after the troops had gone over the top. The blast did injure a few British troops but it gave the Germans a huge surprise and no chance to win the 'Secret Race', thus there was more success than normal here. The mine also showed that the mines could be effective if blown at the correct moment. There is no trace of the crater now unfortunately.

Fricourt Village was the one place where the British weren't that successful on the 1st July in the southern zone. The original plan was to bypass the fortified village and cause the Germans to voluntarily give it up as the British pressed on and cut it off. The Green Howards were waiting to occupy the village when the Germans withdrew, however for some reason the commander of A Company ordered his men forward – perhaps he thought the time was right with the other successes around him. 140 men attacked and 108 were casualties of the German machine guns in Fricourt. Later in the afternoon the East Yorks and the Green Howards attacked again and within three minutes there were another 400 casualties. On the 2nd July the South Staffords fairly easily captured the now empty village and pushing on into the woods took over one hundred German prisoners. Until the 1960s **Major Raper** of the South Staffords was the village's hero, particularly since his private grave was beside the road. It was only in the 1960s that the CWGC removed his burial to **Fricourt British Cemetery**. Major Raper was killed clearing the wood behind the village. In the same cemetery the Green Howards from the 1st July were originally buried in a shell hole, because of this and later memorials you will find this cemetery quite different from 'the norm'. The headstones here are not over the actual graves.

The Somme

FRICOURT GERMAN CEMETERY
(GPS: 50°00.262'N 2°42.855'E)

Key Facts:
- One of the burial sites for the 'Red Baron'
- Only German cemetery on the Somme
- 17,026 German burials (5056 named graves and 11,970 in a mass grave)

This is the only German cemetery on the Somme. The black crosses that you see are much more typical of what you find in German cemeteries than the blocks at Langemarck. There are 17,026 burials here, 5056 in named graves and 11,970 in the mass grave at the rear. The landscaping of the cemetery was only started in 1929 and had to pause for WW2. For a time the 'Red Baron', the German air ace Manfred Von Richthofen was buried here. Richthofen scored over 80 combat victories. He was shot down in April 1918. After hundreds of respectful Allied soldiers passed his coffin in a hangar near Amiens, he was initially buried by the British in a civilian cemetery. Then in the early 1920s he was moved here to Fricourt. Then in 1925 he was taken to Berlin by his brother and buried following a full state funeral. The Nazis, of course, added to and made the tombstone bigger in the 1930s. The grave then got caught up in Cold War Berlin and fell in to disrepair including bullet holes so he was finally removed to a family plot in Wiesbaden in 1975.

The Somme

FLAT IRON COPSE CEMETERY
(GPS: 50°01.201'N 2°45.512'E)

Key Facts:
- Link to five pairs of brothers
- Link to Hill 60, Ypres
- Continuation of the visit to the Mametz Welsh Dragon Memorial

Having parked at the Welsh dragon at Mametz continue down the road/track and you will come to a cemetery called Flat Iron Copse. You can drive, although it can get muddy or walk and soak up the atmosphere of this valley. First read the Mametz Dragon Memorial in the Memorial Section. This cemetery is another special site as it is associated with a number of families. By mid-July this was an Advanced Dressing Station (ADS) hence a cemetery was established alongside it for those that didn't survive (see the Medical Chain of Evacuation diagram.) Bodies were also brought in from the wood. Later in the battle the valley here was known as 'Happy Valley' as it was out of sight from the Germans, but when the Germans started to shell the area the name changed to 'Death Valley'.

Use the map to head to Plot VI G. These are the graves of **Leonard and Arthur Tregaskis**. These Welsh brothers had been well educated, having been sent away to school in England. They were officers and also tall, over six foot tall, making them very prominent targets. They were killed by machine gun fire in the first attack at Mametz Wood on the 7th July 1916. Major Smith OC 16th Welsh said:

> *'They fell leading their men in an attack on a big wood in which attack we suffered considerable losses. Leonard was without doubt the most popular man in the Battalion, beloved by everyone. Arthur was quiet but very sincere but possessed of great courage. The army chaplain wrote they were both among the noblest and bravest of our valiant officers. I always found them true-hearted men. The whole battalion regarded them with deep affection and real pride. A brother officer, writing to us months ago, paid them a great tribute. He said: "The two Tregaskis are fine fellows, six-footers both. They are straight, pleasant and excellent fellows, without any 'side' or anything but the best".'*

The Somme

Also in Row G is **Albert Oliver**, his brother was killed here and is strangely buried at Dantzig Alley Cemetery.

Now head to Plot VIII F and look for **Harry (Henry) and Tom (Thomas) Hardwidge**. Both brothers had been miners before the war and saw the war as a way of getting out of the mines. They came from a large family of fourteen children and were keen rugby players. They were fighting through the wood on the 11th July 1916 when Tom was wounded by a sniper, Harry went to his aid and was also shot by the same sniper. The family lost another brother called Morgan on Christmas Day 1916. Morgan is commemorated on the Thiepval Memorial to the missing on Panel 7A amongst the Welsh Regiment. The local paper wrote:

> *'Confirmation of the official news has been received of the death in action of the two Brothers Hardwidge, in a letter from their Officer to the two widows. Corporal Tom Hardwidge, the eldest of the two, was wounded by a sniper's bullet. Henry went to his assistance and whilst giving him water was himself killed by a sniper's bullet, both dying in each other's arms. The officer writes: - I had known them for nearly 12 months, for they were in my platoon. More cheerful, willing and capable soldiers I do not think it possible to find, and their presence is greatly missed by everyone in the platoon and by myself. They were members of a well-known Ferndale family and were enthusiastic supporters of all kind of sport. (Rhondda Leader newspaper)*

The last pair of brothers are in Plot I D, look for **Ernest and Herbert Philby**. They had been fighting in the battle at High Wood (15th July – 14th August 1916). They were brought back here for a rest on the 19th August 1916. Here, whilst recovering, the Middlesex Regiment were attacked by gas shells, they lost 23 men including Ernest and Herbert.

Before we leave we should go and see the grave of **Sergeant Edward Dwyer VC** of the East Surreys in Plot III J. Sergeant Dwyer had won his VC at Hill 60 near Ypres. For his story turn to Hill 60 in the Ypres Section. He was killed leading his platoon forward near Guillemont in September 1916.

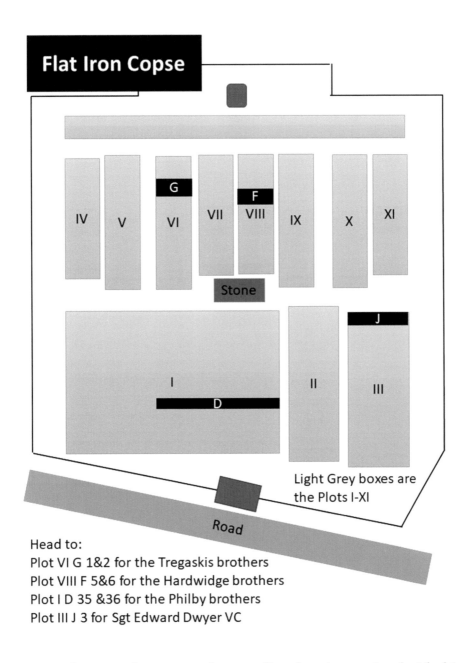

Flat Iron Copse

IV
V
VI
VII
VIII
IX
X
XI

G

F

Stone

J

I
II
III

D

Light Grey boxes are
the Plots I-XI

Road

The Somme

Head to:
Plot VI G 1&2 for the Tregaskis brothers
Plot VIII F 5&6 for the Hardwidge brothers
Plot I D 35 &36 for the Philby brothers
Plot III J 3 for Sgt Edward Dwyer VC

It is worth noting that, yet another set of brothers is associated with this location: **Charles and Henry Morgan**, killed on 7th July in the same action as the Tregaskis and Oliver brothers, but whose bodies were never identifiably found. They are commemorated on Panels 7A and 10A on the Thiepval Memorial.

LUKE COPSE CEMETERY
(GPS: 50°06.470'N 2°39.556'E)

Key Facts:
- Brothers story from 1st July 1916
- Unusual lay out
- Continuation of the Sheffield Park visit

This is part of the Sheffield Park story – make sure that you have read that section first. This point marks the northernmost part of the Somme battlefield (if you don't count the diversion at Gommecourt). As you enter you will straight away realise that this British cemetery is quite different. The graves are lined up in a double line down one side rather than in the usual grid of lines. There are 72 burials here of which 44 are identified. The reason for the unusual layout is that the men were buried in their trench here in a way that is too close for the headstones to be side by side. So what you actually see is one line of tightly packed burials. The headstones are with the correct graves, buried during the war before plans were laid down for the splendid cemeteries that we see today – this is a real 'battlefield cemetery'. In recent years we have seen a focus on WW2 and sets of brothers sparked by the Steven Spielberg film 'Saving Private Ryan', this of course was not the first war to have a wide impact on one family. Look here for the graves of **Frank and William Gunstone**. These are the two sons of William and Addie Gunstone from Sheffield. The story goes that the younger brother William, enlisted first and Frank was urged to join up to look after him by his mother Addie. They have consecutive army numbers so they joined up together. The story goes on to say that William was in the first wave, whilst Frank was in the second. They were in Luke Copse just behind the cemetery and at 7.30am on the 1st July 1916 the whistles blew and William advanced under the watchful eye of his older brother. William was inevitably hit and fell to the ground and on seeing this Frank leapt out of the trench ran forward to recover his brother, he dragged him back and whilst handing him down to his mates was himself hit and killed. Thus the brothers joined up together and died together. I always thinks it is a shame that they are not buried next to one another here.

This cemetery is always so peaceful and as you leave think about the thin grass access path that crosses the farmers field. Come at the right time of year and you will be amazed at the precision of the ploughing around it – this must be a pain to the French farmers, but real care is taken by them. Talking of farmers they have a dangerous job ploughing these fields with their iron harvest. They have extra armour plate under the tractor seats but it is still a scary job if you ask me.

SERRE ROAD NO.2
(GPS: 50°05.789'N 2°39.115'E)

Key Facts:
- Largest cemetery on the Somme
- WW2 Story
- Link to Wilfred Owen (poet)

This is the largest of the three Serre Road Cemeteries and the largest cemetery on the Somme. It has 7140 graves of which 4945 are unidentified. One of the interesting things about this cemetery is a story about one of the original gardeners. **Corporal Ben Leach** of the Manchester Regiment stayed behind in 1918 and married a local girl. Thus he stayed to look after his mates but also for love. He was still gardening for the War Graves Commission when the Second World War erupted, most of the gardeners were evacuated but Ben stayed. One would expect the Germans to round him up as happened with many other British citizens but interestingly they allowed Ben to stay doing his job. The Germans were impressed by his respect towards two German graves that were in the cemetery but also the beauty of the spot. The story goes that they did a deal with him and in exchange for a shed he would host local German dignitaries to tea whilst on a tour of the area. The shed was perfect for Ben to keep his tools in but also to have a secret chamber underneath. Ben became a part of the resistance network helping to get downed Allied airmen away to safety. It has been said he would often have airmen in the secret chamber as he was entertaining German officers above. In total he helped about 30 airmen to get to safety. After WW2 he was awarded various national awards for his efforts. His son followed him into working for the CWGC.

The Somme

Recently, I was chatting to a local Frenchman about Ben Leach and it was suggested that there could be another reason why Ben was allowed to stay by the Germans, he was a collaborator. Unpicking local politics, especially when entwined with the complexity of the four years of occupation makes stories like this quite emotive. It does sound strange that Ben was allowed to stay, but then again, he was an outsider to the rural community at a time when many men were taken for forced labour – I will allow you to make your own mind up about the stories.

If you are parked up in front, look into the field to the left of the cemetery – this is where **Wilfred Owen** occupied a captured German bunker. Wilfred Owen, one of the famous poets of this period was in the Manchester Regiment and spent two days in this bunker in 1917 being shelled.

Owen was ordered to garrison the former German bunker, the fact that it was a German bunker is significant. Bunkers were built for defence and much planning and thought went into this – the door for example was always on the back so that it was safe from shell fire. The fact that the British were manning a German bunker meant that the entrance now faced the enemy and so was vulnerable to shell blasts. The lookout slits were also facing the wrong way, the result was that Owen had to post a sentry at the top of the steps looking out towards the German lines. A young soldier, whom Owen had placed on guard was blown, blinded by a shell, back down the steps into the bunker. Owen as the officer in charge felt quite moved by this responsibility and the incident has been kept alive by one of his poems, called The Sentry.

Following a period of being treated for Shell Shock and concussion he returned to the front and was killed just a week before the Armistice in 1918.

The Somme

Extract from: The Sentry by Wilfred Owen

There we herded from the blast
of whizz-bangs, but one found our door at last.
Buffeting eyes and breath, snuffing the candles.
And thud! flump! thud! down the steep steps came thumping
and splashing in the flood, deluging muck —
The sentry's body; then his rifle, handles
of old Boche bombs, and mud in ruck on ruck.
We dredged him up, for killed, until he whined
"O sir, my eyes — I'm blind — I'm blind, I'm blind!"
Coaxing, I held a flame against his lids
and said if he could see the least blurred light
he was not blind; in time he'd get all right.
"I can't," he sobbed. Eyeballs, huge-bulged like squids
watch my dreams still;
.....
Through the dense din, I say, we heard him shout
"I see your lights!" But ours had long died out.

The Somme

Memorials

POZIERES TANK MEMORIAL AND THE WINDMILL
(GPS: 50°02.688'N 2°44.171'E)

Key Facts:
- Site of the first tank attack September 1916
- Key site for the Australians

Tank Memorial at Pozieres

It is worth slowing down and pausing next to the tank memorial and the remains of the infamous '**Windmill**' just east (Bapaume side) of Pozieres on the straight Roman road. You will see it as a high point as you approach, with some sort of telecoms mast pole on the southern side and two flag poles on the northern side. On the north side of the road is a patch of lumpy bumpy ground preserved since the battle, it is also the site of the infamous windmill which the Australians took in August 1916. The fighting here was ferocious and the remains of the windmill on top of this ridge was perfect as a German observation position and therefore a key objective. This point is the highest point on the Pozieres Ridge. The ridge, being a ridge of high ground was an important strategic point on the battlefield. There is a bronze plaque that shows you the context of the attack here. It was extremely costly for the Australians to take and has special significance to them because of this. In recent years there has been a new animal memorial set up in the field by the memorial, and for the centenary there has been a large Australian Army badge laid out in crosses, although this might be a temporary feature.

On the southern side of the road is the **Tank Memorial**. This is to commemorate the first use of tanks on a battlefield. Around the obelisk are bronze miniature tanks that include the famous lozenge shaped 'mark' tanks but also the oddly shaped Whippet light tanks that came in to use in 1918. Around the memorial is a fence made of driving chains and 6pdr gun barrels for posts. Three tanks set off from here supporting the Canadian attack up the Roman road in September 1916.

Tanks: Tanks were actually first developed by the Navy under First Lord of the Admiralty, **Winston Churchill**. **Colonel Swinton** came up with the idea after seeing an American Holt tracked tractor. Swinton developed the first tank called 'Little Willie', which is in the Bovington tank museum today. Officially known as 'Landships', the tanks were top secret and the name 'tank' came from this secrecy – they resembled large water tanks and the name therefore became a way of keeping them secret. By 1916 the first ones were ready for use on the Somme. To the south of here the first tanks went into action attacking the village of Flers on 15th September 1916. They had a mixed result with most breaking down or getting stuck in the mud. An officer called Arnold who was at the scene, described the impact of just one tank. " A tank is walking up the High Street of Flers with the British Army cheering behind." Thus the British were able to capture nearly 2km of ground as a result of these tanks. However, out of the 49 tanks that were deployed, only 32 made it to the starting line, 25 managed to actually go into attack and of those only 9 reached the German positions.

The Somme

German accounts talk of monsters and sheer terror as these new machines came towards them spitting bullets and shells. General Haig recognised the psychological impact on the Germans and their future potential and therefore ordered another 1000 tanks straight away. It would take time for new tactics to be developed to make best use of these new inventions.

The most famous use of tanks was at the **Battle of Cambrai** in 1917 when they were first used in large numbers. At Cambrai the tanks trained with the infantry and were sneaked up to the front without the Germans realising. By 1918 they were being used in conjunction with aircraft and infantry in a decisive way.

The main tanks were the large lozenge shaped ones -these were the 'mark' tanks with the Mark I being used on the Somme, the Mark IV at the Battle of Cambrai and the Mark V at the **Battle of Amiens** in 1918. These were all just a continual development of essentially the same tank. Tanks were designated 'male' or 'female', with male tanks having 6 pound canons on the sides (in the sponsons) and the females being armed with smaller machine guns instead.

Later the British also developed a smaller, faster tank known as the **Whippet tank**. The Whippet had half the crew(3 or 4) and double the speed(8mph) of the larger tanks. They soon realised a need to rotate crews as the conditions were particularly poor with the exhaust fumes being sucked into the cabins.

The French had some unsuccessful large tanks but also a very good small Renault tank. The Germans were slow to catch on and only ever made twenty of their own tanks. In fact they did better in action with captured British and French tanks. Being on the Somme, you are not too far from the Cambrai battlefield and if you head to Flesquieres, you can see a preserved tank called Deborah and various memorials.

As you drive through and leave Pozieres, on your right hand side you will see the official 1st Australian Division Memorial signposted. Here you will find a memorial and the remains of '**Gibraltar Blockhouse**'. Again there are boards to describe the fierce fighting here by the Australians. You will be disappointed not to have actual access to the bunker though.

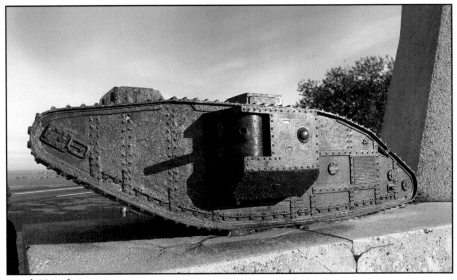

Mark V tank

Whippet tank

The Somme

117

THE GOLDEN MADONNA OF ALBERT
(GPS: 50°00.239'N 2°38.856'E)

The Golden Madonna holding up the baby Jesus sits on top of the basilica in Albert and can be seen glinting in the sun from afar as you drive around. It was an obvious visual landmark for both sides. In 1915 The Germans hit the tower and the Madonna was left hanging at a precarious angle. There were lots of jokes about the Madonna looking as if she were throwing the baby Jesus from the tower. There were also several myths that grew up around the Golden Madonna after it was hit. The British troops believed that the war would end the day she fell off the basilica. The Germans believed that whoever caused the statue to fall would lose the war – this of course suited the British as they could use it as an observation tower in relative safety, protected by the superstition. Despite all this the robustly built structure was hit several thousand times. In the end it was the British who brought the statue down when the British shelled Albert in a desperate attempt to stop the German advances of the 1918 Spring Offensive. They did not want the Germans to have such an excellent vantage point. The original golden statue vanished, possibly melted down by the Germans.

Albert Mural and Golden Madonna in background

THIEPVAL MEMORIAL TO THE MISSING
(GPS: 50°03.156'N 2°41.274'E)

Key Facts:
- Memorial to 73,339 British Missing of the Somme
- The Centre of British Commemorations on the Somme
- 300 British and 300 French Graves in the cemetery
- Remains of the German frontline

This is the largest and most famous of the memorials on the Somme, it is so impressive that it can be seen from most places on the battlefield. It was constructed as a memorial to the missing – a Menin Gate of the Somme. The huge construction was designed by Lutyens and is 45m high. The building work was finished in 1931 and opened amid much pageantry in 1932. It has 73,339 names on it divided on to numbered piers. Even this does not have enough room for all the names and the monument is essentially a 1916 monument to the British regiments. Further names are on the wall in the cemetery at Pozieres.

Park up in the car park and to access the memorial you either walk through the visitor centre or walk back to the entrance of the car park and head up around the side of the centre. On a side note this is one of the best places to find a nice clean toilet.

Thiepval Memorial to the Missing

The Somme

As you approach the memorial itself you will start to realise the scale of it. It was built using German bunkers as foundations but still a considerable amount of work went into the footings. I was once allowed a peer inside one of the doors and saw the 30 foot deep vast vaulted underpinnings in all their beauty – they really should put in a glass door. Have a look around, as per the Menin Gate the names are listed by regiment – look out for oddities such as 'served as' or where a name has been removed. On the far side, as you go down towards the cemetery, you will see the 'Addenda' where when checking the records, they have found more names that should be on here.

Addenda Panel, Thiepval Memorial to the Missing

The Somme

The cemetery behind is 'a brothers in arms' approach with 300 British and 300 French graves brought in to symbolise the joint bloodshed on the Somme.

The attack here - If you walk on through the centre of the cemetery down towards the fence you will find the cleared German frontline of the 1st July 1916. You can stand in this and look across the field at the wood. You are now looking at the view the **Wurttembergers** had as they defended the German position. You can see the power of having the high ground. Here the Northumberland Fusiliers attacked and were massacred by the Wurttembergers, who were standing up on their parapet for an even better view. Six waves of British attackers were mown down by the German machine guns before the assaults were paused. Any wounded soldier that moved was picked off by the watching Germans. This all happened in the field in front of you now.

THE ULSTER TOWER AND SCHWABEN REDOUBT
(GPS: 50°03.652'N 2°40.792'E)

Key Facts:
- Story connected to Northern Ireland
- Moving VC story of Billy McFadzean

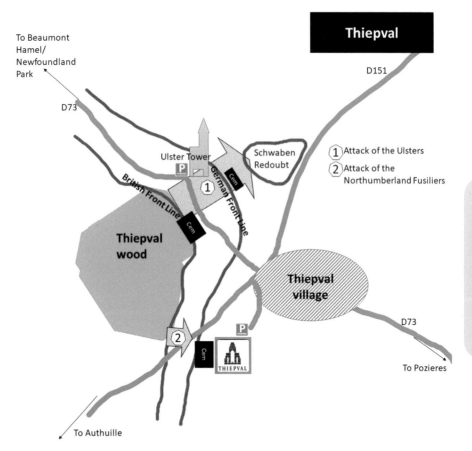

As you drive between Thiepval and Beaumont-Hamel you will see a pretty tower just off to the side of the road, this is the Ulster Tower. This area of the battlefield is hallowed ground to the men from Ulster. Ulster during WW1 means the northern Protestant counties prior to the Partition of Ireland in 1919. I would park beside Connaught Cemetery or outside the tower itself.

The story here is one of huge bravery, success and also terribly frustrating sacrifice. The Ulstermen were in Thiepval Wood on the 1st July 1916, which you can see on the opposite side of the road to the tower. The frontline trench has been partially restored and you might be able to glimpse it running along just inside the wood line (to visit you are advised to contact the Ulster tower in advance – they offer limited pre-arranged tours). The German frontline is on the other side of the road in line with where the tower now is. No Man's Land was the road you are on – then known as the 'sunken road'.

As the final preparations for the 1st July went ahead it was in this wood that **Billy McFadzean** and a party of 'bombers', men designated to have a large supply of Mills bombs (grenades) in order to clear trenches and bunkers, prepared for action. As they worked a box of grenades fell from the fire step dislodging several of the safety pins. Billy had about four seconds to act and he did so in the most unselfish way possible – he threw himself on top of the grenades and took the blast impact, saving his mates. Billy received a posthumous Victoria Cross for this action.

In this area the commander advised his men to enter No Man's Land and get close to the German frontline, some occupied the Sunken Road prior to the 7.30am start, so the men already had an advantage in the 'Secret Race' creeping forward under the protection of the artillery barrage. Many were members of the Orange Order and the accounts talk of some men wearing orange sashes over their equipment. As well as the German trenches there was also a fortified point on the high ground to the right of the tower called the **Schwaben Redoubt**. The Ulstermen did well, they didn't mess about forming lines – they rushed the German positions and quickly won the 'Secret Race'. They captured the German frontline and pushed on into the Schwaben Redoubt. Remember they did not follow the standard orders they were given and it had taken some bravery and foresight to go against General Rawlinson's directive. After initial success the casualties started increasing because the troops on either side were not so successful in taking their objectives and so machine guns were firing across from the sides too. The Sunken Road soon became 'The Bloody Road'.

The Schwaben Redoubt position was a harder challenge for the Ulstermen as the Germans had more time to react here. Their supporting units were caught in the machine gun cross fire trying to cross No Man's Land to follow up and help the attack in the Schwaben Redoubt. Small groups of Ulstermen fought fierce hand to hand battles to push on through the position. **Captain Bell** earned another Victoria Cross for his leadership which included hand throwing mortar bombs at the Germans. By noon the Ulstermen had the Schwaben Redoubt. They then pushed on to the German second line of defence as per the plan but disastrously they had been too successful and arrived early and ended up getting caught in the British timetabled artillery fire plan – they were unable to move forward due to their own artillery and many were killed or wounded. The success of the Ulstermen also brought more attention from the German artillery and they were being pummelled from all angles with little chance of reserves and supplies getting through. The situation for the survivors got worse and worse in their exposed and cut off enclave. Pioneers (specialist engineering troops) tasked with digging a communication trench across to them were also unable to act in the face of the German machine gun fire. By the end of the afternoon the dwindling and exhausted survivors were being pushed back by fierce counter attacks and by the evening the remains of the Ulstermen escaped largely unopposed from the equally tired Germans. 4,700 men had been killed or wounded in the attack here. The final sting in the tail was a rumour that started to do the rounds – had the British deliberately set the Ulstermen against the strongest point on the Somme to rid themselves of the troublesome Ulster Volunteer Force men that were causing so many headaches back in Ireland? There is, of course, no evidence of this.

The Tower: The tower itself is a memorial and houses a small café and museum. Tours of the wood can be booked in advance via the tower. The tower is normally closed on Mondays.

If you are a fan of **Sebastian Faulks'** novel **Birdsong**, look out as you drive on down the hill heading towards Beaumont-Hamel and Newfoundland Park. You will cross a series of ponds and a river before

The Somme

the railway line – this is the area that the 'foot touching' incident appears in the Birdsong boating passage. The novel is relevant to the dangerous mining war that was a feature of the Western Front.

A young author in front of the Ulster Tower

THE WELSH MEMORIAL AT MAMETZ
(GPS: 50°00.846'N 2°45.379'E)

Key Facts:
- Magnificent Welsh Dragon monument
- Links to the Welsh on the Somme
- Visit also encompasses Flat Iron Copse Cemetery

Keep right as the small road north of Mametz village forks and you head towards this monument on the increasingly narrow lanes.

Park underneath the dragon.
In 1987 this splendid red dragon, holding barbed wire in his claws was unveiled, it is overlooking the infamous Mametz Wood. Mametz Wood is the largest of three main woods that feature in the battle, the others being Delville Wood and High Wood. The village of Mametz had been one of the success stories of the first day, but as you can see the wood is some distance on from the village. A week later the British started a big push to keep the battle moving forward, the capture of Mametz Wood was a key objective for this attack.

German machine guns in the wood devastated the attack and it ground to a halt. The Brigade that attacked from this side was the 38th (Welsh) hence we have the Dragon memorial here. There were also British failures with an artillery barrage failing to materialise and the failure of an arranged smokescreen to protect the troops across the open that meant not a single part of the wood was even reached. Three days later the same troops tried again here in force on the south side of the wood. Despite furious German fire from the woods the men of the

The Somme

Welsh Brigade made it into the remains of the wood. The wood had been heavily fortified by the Germans and also heavily shelled making passage extremely difficult through it. Hand to hand fighting went on for two days until in the darkness following the 11th July the Germans withdrew.

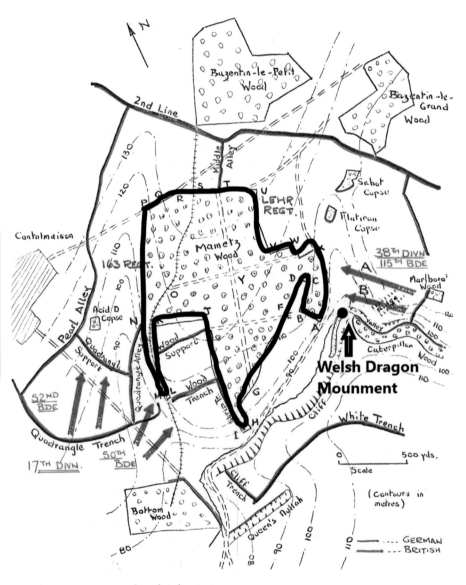

Attack on Mametz Wood - 7th July 1916

Robert Graves' poem The Dead Boche, written in 1918 I think sums up the atmosphere and is well worth a read here.

Walk on now to **Flat Iron Copse Cemetery** which is about 800m straight on down the road/track. Turn to the Cemetery Section to follow the story. (GPS: 50°01.201'N 2°45.512'E)

Two other interesting stories come from this area of the battlefield. On the 21st July a Lieutenant called **Lieutenant Henry Webber** was chatting to his Commanding Officer and some other officers when a random single shell dropped, wounding 12 men. Webber died of his wounds and is buried in Dartmoor Cemetery. What I haven't told you so far is that Henry Webber was 68 years old! The believed 'oldest man' to be killed. He had to be cunning to get into the army in the first place as he was repeatedly turned down due to his age and was finally accepted for a commission by the War Office. His three sons survived the Western Front.

The next day another interesting man was killed beside the road near here. This time a general, **Major General Ingouville-Williams.** He was known as 'Inky Bill' by the troops. He had commanded the worst hit division on the 1st July 1916 and had gone out into No Man's Land to help the stretcher bearers that night. He too was hit by a shell.

Trenches, Bunkers And Craters

THE BUTTE DE WARLENCOURT
(GPS: 50°04.574'N 2°47.683'E)

This is actually a prehistoric mound, much like those seen in my native Wiltshire in the UK. It was originally significantly higher than it is today. But it still offers a commanding view of the British lines and therefore explains why it was an important position during the battles here. During the war the white of the chalk further enhanced the visible prize of this mound. Both sides were obsessed with capturing it and it was covered in barbed wire, tunnels and fortified machine gun positions. It was captured in the pouring rain of November 1916 by the Durham Light Infantry at the cost of 130 soldiers killed, 400 wounded and 300 missing to do so. The Commanding Officer, **Roland Boys Bradford** was given the Victoria Cross for his bravery in the action. Unfortunately the Durhams were unable to hold the Butte and it fell back into German hands until it was finally taken by the British in February 1917. After it was captured three wooden crosses to the Durhams were placed on top – one of these is today to be seen in Durham Cathedral. This Butte also marks the rough position of how far the British finally got at the Somme in 1916.

LOCHNAGAR CRATER AT LA BOISELLE
(GPS: 50°00.983'N 2°41.791'E)

Key Facts:
- Giant Mine Crater (19 mines used on 1st July)
- Good site to see the 1st July 1916 Battlefield

Look out for signs to 'La Grande Mine'. Probably the most visually impressive remnant of the war to see. Just outside of the village of La Boiselle this crater marks the German frontline for the 1st July 1916 and is a good place to start thinking about what happened on that 'first

The Somme

day'. The place where you turned off the main Roman road is pretty much where the British frontline was for the first day. Head to the right hand side of the cross and step off the duckboard path looking at the view shown below.

The view towards the British Frontline from Lochnagar Crater

The British Frontline Crosses the main road where you turned off – roughly here

British troops advancing towards you

We are looking from the German front line (roughly where the road that you parked on is) back towards the British lines. I have marked up on the photo the rough positions of the British front line. On the 1st July 1916 it was across this landscape that at 7.30am the whistles sounded and the men went 'over the top'. The plan was to push up the two valleys either side of the village of La Boiselle and outflank the German positions in the village. No Man's Land was quite high in grass to start with, the British wire had been cleared in readiness. They were in that 'Secret Race' I explained in the Somme Introduction. The British were not blind to the German defences and had blown 19 mines to take out key German strongholds prior to the attack. Here the mine was blown at 7.28am(still two minutes too early for the men involved in the 'Secret Race'). Debris rose 4000 feet in the air (as witnessed by aircraft at the time), combined with that huge week long artillery barrage – how could any of the enemy be alive? The decision to blow the mines two minutes early to save the British troops being accidentally wounded was a critical mistake. With the huge explosion

The Somme

of the mine and the lifting of the artillery barrage, German boots were pounding the chalk steps to get in to position. They emerged into a devastated landscape – but one that still had plenty of places to get into defensive fire positions. Indeed the crater now provided ideal shelter and so had machine guns set up inside the lip.

Looking across this landscape you can see how easy the men walking in their lines were as targets – they who believed that the Germans were all dead and were loaded up ready to rebuild the German positions as their own. Here eight waves of soldiers set off from their trenches, formed up into lines and advanced. The lines of soldiers obviously broke up when the Germans started firing at them and survivors took to shell holes for safety, and in many places still trying to push forward. Some survivors did make it to the crater and it was initially taken by the Grimsby Chums. Behind on the ridge more troops came in support – look at the landscape again! Men of the Tyneside Irish had to approach, pass through here and move on to attack the village of Contalmaison. The exposed landscape meant the German machine guns fired and fired and the German artillery fire blasted and blasted. When the survivors reached the German frontline, which was still held in places, instead of stopping and consolidating they kept to their original orders and continued advancing towards Contalmaison (an order to stop was actually issued but failed to get to them). By sheer luck a small force of survivors made it nearly two kilometres into the German lines – an incredible achievement. None of these men survived though!

The crater was originally more impressive as 100 years of erosion has softened it. It was 450 feet across(including the lips) and 70 feet deep. There were two explosive charges of ammonal of 24,000lbs and 36,000lbs. Walk round the crater anti-clockwise and you will come to a grassed area with a bench and a small wooden cross. The small cross marks the spot where the remains of **George Nugent** were discovered in 1998. If you look into the distance from this spot you will see a wood, this is where the British tunnelled from to place their explosive charges. The tunnel was re-opened a few years ago and is still pretty well preserved (worth an internet search for a video).

The name Lochnagar comes from the name of a trench where the tunnellers started called 'Lochnagar street'

On the second day of the battle the 6th Wiltshires attacked through this area and with them were two Moxham brothers. They left their trenches at 4pm formed up and started forward. German machine guns started up straight away and a witness recalled being fascinated by the sight of an officer walking along the top of his trench urging them out with water trailing from his punctured water bottle. They soon came across Lochnagar Crater and most jumped straight in, **Alfred Moxham** paused in awe of the crater and was shouted at to get down as a German machine gun swept towards him. Unfortunately his pause was enough to mortally wound him and he fell down into the crater. It is said that he was buried in the crater and he is remembered as one of the missing on the Thiepval Memorial. A wreath is laid annually in the crater for Alfred.

Lochnagar Crater

The crater was bought by a British chap called Richard Dunning, who felt compelled to buy and save the crater at a time when many were being filled in. The site is maintained safely by himself and a group of volunteers known as the 'Friends of Lochnagar'. The site has been stabilised and improved with decking pathway and you can, via the crater website, sponsor one of the brass commemoration plaques. If you wish to search for someone on the plaques then why not look for my own Great Grandfather Vincent Strickland - give him my best wishes and let him know that I remember.

Lochnagar Crater 1917

The Glory Hole, Nr Lochnagar Crater: On the way up to the crater you may well have noticed a really lumpy bumpy patch of ground on your right. This is called the Glory Hole and has been largely untouched since the end of the war. Unfortunately the area is on private ground and is not accessible. The area was heavily mined and there was an excavation here in 2011 which uncovered many tunnels in extremely good condition. The site is a mixture of mine craters, collapsed tunnels, trenches and shell craters and would make an excellent stop if one was allowed in… It is worth noting that there were considerable numbers of underground tunnels to shelter troops in during the battle and this can be overlooked sometimes.

THE SUNKEN LANE
(GPS: 50°05.134'N 2°38.911'E)

Key Facts:
- Site of Malins' filming during the actual battle, 1st July 1916 (Lancashire Fusiliers in No Man's Land, Hawthorn Mine explosion and genuine combat footage all filmed from here.)

This is one of my favourite spots to really connect to the battlefield and the story of the first day. The spot is largely recognisable to how it was in 1916 and we know this because it was caught on camera. This is one of the chosen locations for **Geoffrey Malins** and his film camera. The footage filmed here is some of the most used film footage of WW1 and you will recognise it straight away. Malins put together a 77 minute film that was shown in cinemas back in Britain with an organ accompaniment. This was the very first film of real warfare ever shown and the public, at that time were not yet acclimatised to video games and gory or realistic war films. Viewers had a range of reactions including hysteria. 20 million people saw the film and some recognised relatives on the big screen.

The film itself has a few problems which stem from the fact that a large wooden box camera on a tripod couldn't be just set up anywhere – the result is that Malins used a combination of real footage and reconstructed 'fake' footage. The difference between the 'real' and the 'fake' is pretty obvious and the best hint is the equipment – if the men are not loaded up with lots of kit, the section is almost certainly 'fake'. Plenty of the interesting sections of the film are available online. If you do an internet search for something like 'Somme Sunken Lane' on a video site you will get to see the footage. This footage was computer enhanced in 2018 by Peter Jackson and so we should be able to see the footage better than ever now.

The Sunken Lane is exactly what it says on the tin, a sunken lane which you can clearly see from the road going away beside the war memorial. The Sunken Lane is actually in No Man's Land and men from the **Lancashire Fusiliers** alongside other units of a composite

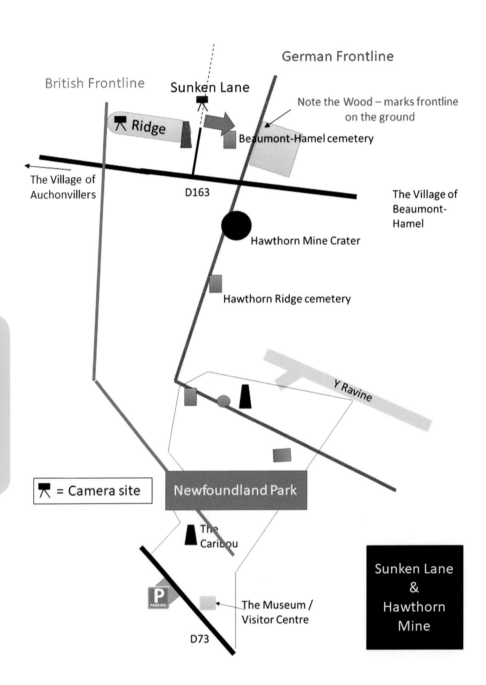

British Frontline

German Frontline

Sunken Lane

Note the Wood – marks frontline on the ground

Ridge

Beaumont-Hamel cemetery

The Village of Auchonvillers

D163

The Village of Beaumont-Hamel

Hawthorn Mine Crater

Hawthorn Ridge cemetery

Y Ravine

The Somme

= Camera site

Newfoundland Park

The Caribou

PARKING

The Museum / Visitor Centre

D73

Sunken Lane & Hawthorn Mine

company entered it via a tunnel, known as a Sap, so as to have a head start in their attack. As you stand with your back to the road, looking up the lane the British lines are on your left and the Germans are on your right. The line wasn't perfectly straight, bear this in mind as we look at different things here. With the men went Malins and his camera – he therefore films the men as they nervously wait to go in for the first wave of the attack. Look on an online video site and watch the footage, see the variety of reactions to the camera. Some ignore it, some look nervous, some do that 'oh I am on camera' thing. Note the chap lead back nonchalantly on the left – try and read his lips, he is saying something like "I hope that we're not in the wrong place coz next time I'm going to **** ***and get out!". Put yourself in their place, what would you be doing as you waited for the whistle? When the whistles did blow the men clambered up the bank on the right and off across the very open landscape straight towards the German machine guns. The Germans here had an extra forewarning, the early detonation of the Hawthorn Mine. The Sunken Lane actually became a place of shelter for the shattered remains of the Lancashire Fusiliers, they suffered 163 killed, 312 wounded and 11 missing. Walking out to the cemetery, towards the German lines, gives you a real feel for why the machine guns had such an impact here. If you wander up the Sunken Lane a few meters you will find a small memorial on the right, placed there exactly a hundred years to the minute after the event.

Now stand by the War Memorial to the Argyll and Sutherland Highlanders and look out across the road with the Sunken Lane behind you. Watch the footage of the Hawthorn mine exploding – this happened right in front of you and slightly to the left. Again, you will recognise the scene.

Soldiers heading for the Hawthorn Crater

The Somme

The third and last bit of film footage from this area is just after the Hawthorn Mine went up – this is quite a spectacular piece of footage and is just across the road in front of you now. It is of soldiers rushing right to left to get to the crater after the mine exploded. The footage is normally quite poor, but you should be able to see men running across the landscape and also how some drop down hit by machine gun fire.

HAWTHORN CRATER
(GPS: 50°05.090'N 2°39.051'E)

Key Facts:
- Large double mine crater
- Mine blown early at 7:20 am 1st July 1916

I would park at the Sunken Lane and watch the film footage of the Hawthorn Mine explosion on a mobile device first as this is roughly where the famous black and white Malins footage was taken from. Then cross the road and head up the path towards the top of the hill. When you get to the top you will see the large crater – much the same as Lochnagar but now with more vegetation surrounding it. It was mostly cleared in 2018 ready for an excavation so you may find the crater still quite accessible. The crater here was blown early at 7.20am (Lochnagar was blown at 07.28!). **General Hunter-Weston** wanted to blow the mine even earlier at 3.30am and had to make a compromise with his staff officers to go for the 7.20am time. Hunter-Weston was worried about debris injuring his troops as they attacked and also he wanted them to capture it before the main attack went in. Hunter-Weston was also thinking about the British reputation of being poor to capture craters and so wanted to give his men more of a chance. Two British platoons rushed to capture the crater straight away – not waiting for zero hour, this time they managed to capture the nearest side, but essentially again the Germans won the race and they had occupied the other side and set up their machine guns. The British held one side for much of the first day before being driven off by the Germans. The crater then remained in German hands. Hunter-Weston was wrong in hindsight and all the early explosion did was to give the Germans a really clear sign that the British were about to attack and showed them where to aim their artillery guns (See Newfoundland Park for the consequences!)

The British tunnellers dug a 75ft deep, 1000ft long tunnel to place 40,000lbs of ammonal explosives under the key strategic position here on Hawthorn Ridge, the Hawthorn Redoubt. You can still clearly see the significance of the landscape and the ridge today. The crater is 40ft deep, 300ft wide and the strange shape of the crater is due to a later mine being blown here in November when with tank support and a creeping barrage, the crater was captured by Scottish Highlanders. You can just make out German machine gun positions carved out of the side on the western side of the crater.

Hawthorn Mine blowing

NEWFOUNDLAND PARK
(GPS: 50°04.326'N 2°38.806'E)

Key Facts:
- Heart-breaking story of the impact of the early blowing of the Hawthorn Mine
- Trenches and craters still cover the preserved landscape
- Park site with cemeteries, memorials and visitor centre

I always find Newfoundland Park at Beaumont Hamel a controversial place. See what your thoughts are. This is a Canadian Memorial Park and is 'guarded' by security guards and teenage Canadian helpers. It has strict rules and you are asked to conduct yourself as if in a cemetery. If you are taking groups of school/young children in then it pays to brief them in advance – the guards particularly dislike: eating, running and any loud noises. The park is a great place to see a landscape of the war and it stands out against the reconstituted land around it – it has trenches and shell craters galore. Park in the car park and cross the road carefully. I would first head to the large Caribou (Deer or Elk like creature) statue on the observation mound.

The Caribou: Here you can look out over the landscape. It is a bit confused as there was continual fighting here, including in 1918. That said if you look carefully you can decode the battlefield of the 1st July 1916. You are looking out with your back to the car park. In the distance you can make out a cemetery wall (Y Ravine Cemetery). You should be able to make out 3 parallel British trench lines with the third being in line with where you are. The first is made obvious by the line of metal pickets. On the pathway that goes straight across No Man's Land toward the cemetery, about half way across is what is known as the 'Danger Tree', this, in fact, looks like a bit of stick concreted into the ground. The German frontline was down by the cemetery, you can see this when you look towards the Danger Tree.

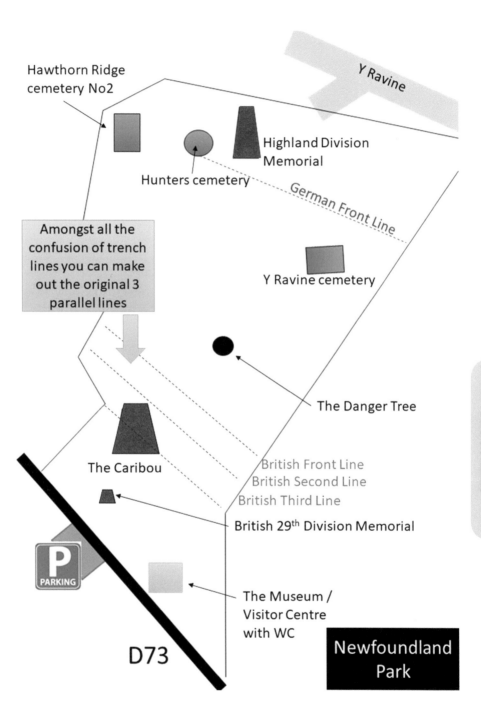

Hawthorn Ridge cemetery No2

Y Ravine

Highland Division Memorial

Hunters cemetery

German Front Line

Amongst all the confusion of trench lines you can make out the original 3 parallel lines

Y Ravine cemetery

The Danger Tree

British Front Line
British Second Line
British Third Line

The Caribou

British 29th Division Memorial

PARKING

The Museum / Visitor Centre with WC

D73

Newfoundland Park

The Somme

The Danger Tree is supposed to be the last original tree from the war and is therefore given some extra help! Behind the cemetery is the infamous Y Ravine that the Germans took full advantage of. They tunnelled in to the sides of the natural gulley to make all sorts of defensive positions.

The Story of the 1st July 1916 at Newfoundland Park – (This story links to Hawthorn Crater.) The trenches here were full of British soldiers ready to go into the attack. They were ready and in full kit, they had all they needed to rebuild the destroyed German positions into their own fortified ones. The Germans were in deep dug outs and although numbed with fear were mostly still alive. Here the Germans were given an enormous advantage when **General Hunter-Weston** set off the Hawthorn Mine at 7.20am – a full ten minutes before zero hour (remember he had wanted to set it off even earlier at about 3.30am!). The Germans were thus prewarned of the attack and opened fire with their own artillery on the preselected British frontline. The disaster was worsened by the huge numbers of British troops packed in the trenches waiting. It was carnage. Wounded men struggled to get back to the dressing stations and the situation was very bad before the attack was even ordered to start. The frontline trenches were full of men from the South Wales Borderers who had by now suffered 70% casualties. The second wave of the British attack here comprised of men from the Border Regiment and to help them follow up the planned 'easy victory', bridges had been placed over the trenches to speed up their attack forward to take up the advance. These bridges, like the early detonation of the mine had a catastrophic outcome – the Germans had spotted them the day before and had pre-targeted them with their machine guns. The Borderer Regiment also lost 70% of their men, 575 of their 832 men were killed, wounded or lost. By 8.00am the attack had completely stalled. At about 9.00am the Newfoundland Regiment who had been held in reserve advanced from the rear, from behind us towards the car park. The story goes that they had no choice but to cross the open ground and jump across the trenches as the trenches themselves were full of the wounded and dead. However, they had rehearsed advancing in single file, in platoon strength lines and bridges had, as we have seen already, been placed over the trenches– so they were most likely just advancing as ordered! Nevertheless at this point in the battle they were extremely exposed and probably the only men on the move in the open. They were decimated in the process. The final devastating machine gun fire tore into them about where the Danger Tree still stands. Of the approximately 800 Newfoundlanders who attacked only about 100 survived unscathed.

This site is a British Pilgrimage site in the first instance and now you understand that the park is a place of Newfoundland Pilgrimage too. Newfoundland is today an area of Canada, but not so in 1916. In 1916 it was a part of the British Empire, a place with fierce traditions and a focus on fishing. It did not see itself as part of Canada, nor would the suggestion that they were Canadian have gone down well with the troops. They were Newfoundlanders and they were helping the British motherland. Here is why I said that the site is controversial, I am sure that the flags will be flying on the day of your visit – what flags? A French Flag, A Newfoundland Flag and a Canadian Flag. Where is the British Flag? The site has been repeatedly asked to represent the British soldiers with a flag, but at the point of writing the site is still refusing. Too me this site is too 'Canadian' and that is hugely confusing when not a single Canadian soldier fought here. The guides present will explain and give a fair picture of the story but too many people go away thinking of Canadian soldiers and not appreciating the disaster that befell the British troops here.

It should also be noted that the Newfoundlanders advanced with the Essex Regiment and they suffered the same tragedy – in fact, by the time they advanced the attack had been called off but the message did not get through.

The Aftermath: Wounded men were still being brought in four nights later. General Hunter-Weston was relieved of his command and his second in command was so badly affected that he committed suicide.

Newfoundland Caribou Memorial

The Somme

The museum and the rest of the site: It is worth going in the museum, where there are clean toilets and an interesting display of information and objects. The rest of the site too is worth a walk around, although it will take time. There is a good statue of a kilted Scotsman flanked by lions on the far side of the park. As you take your leave, just before getting to the road crossing you will notice a rather bland and simple stone pyramid – this is to the 29th Division to which the various units we have talked about belonged to and really the only nod to the British here.

If you turn north from Newfoundland park the next village that you come to is Auchonvillers and here you will find Avril Williams' Guest House and Tea Rooms.

AVRIL WILLIAMS' GUEST HOUSE AND TEA ROOMS, AUCHONVILLERS
(GPS: 50°04.787'N 2°37.876'E)

Avril Williams is an expat who has dedicated her life to the history of her adopted home village. You can book to stay or pop in for lunch or just a cup of tea. It is always worth booking if you are in a large group. Lunches are great and children are welcome. Avril also has a fantastic museum collection that you can pay to see. The main building was here in the war and I once stayed the night in the old byre surrounded by the ghosts of the war. Underneath is her cellar, which featured in Richard Holmes' War Walks TV programme. The Cellar was used as a troop shelter and dressing station during the war and has amazing soldier graffiti on the walls. She also has some trenches in her garden that you can look round. The place is always being improved and she has recently added new apartments. Have you guessed what the troops called the place yet? Ocean Villas, of course.

SHEFFIELD PARK
(Park in front of Serre Road No1 Cemetery
GPS: 50°06.024'N 2°39.454'E)
(Sheffield Park GPS: 50°06.362'N 2°39.409'E)

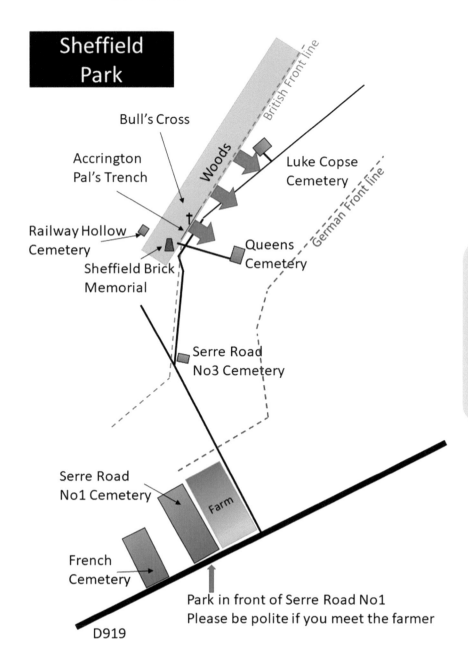

Sheffield Park

Bull's Cross

British Front line

Accrington Pal's Trench

Woods

Luke Copse Cemetery

German Front line

Railway Hollow Cemetery

Queens Cemetery

Sheffield Brick Memorial

Serre Road No3 Cemetery

The Somme

Serre Road No1 Cemetery

Farm

French Cemetery

Park in front of Serre Road No1
Please be polite if you meet the farmer

D919

Key Facts:
- Park site with several cemeteries and memorials
- Key site for the Northern Pals battalions
- The Accrington Pals' trench (600 out of the 720 were killed, wounded or missing on the 1st July 1916 here)

This is one of my favourite spots on the Somme and definitely worth a visit. There have been a few issues with the local farmer recently so take care and be extra polite if he approaches you – I have often spoken to him about the actress Judy Dench who once visited, but he has recently become fed up with people not keeping to paths etc. Do not try and drive up the track to the park. You are going for a short walk that can sometimes be muddy.

Walk away from the French and British Cemetery in an easterly direction, go past the Brick farm and then turn up the track that is signposted with Green CWGC cemetery signs. You will walk up a gently sloping hill and then you will see the wood in the distance. As you approach the wood bear right as the path splits beside the small Serre Road No. 3 Cemetery (85 burials) heading for the front of the wood. As you get closer you should see a brick memorial and a gate just inside the wood (**GPS: 50°06.362'N 2°39.409'E**). Enter the gate and after looking at the brick memorial to the **Accrington Pals** on the left, head right walking along the remains of the original trench – this runs just inside the fence and can appear to be just a ditch. Walk towards the cross. You are now in the trench occupied by the Accrington Pals on the 1st July 1916. Look out of the wood and see the landscape that they were to attack across!

The Story of the 1st July 1916: The Accrington Pals were formed from Kitchener's recruiting campaign and were formed almost entirely from the northern community of Accrington, near Blackburn. The local mayor took just ten days to recruit a battalion of men. They had bought in to the idea of joining up together, training and of course fighting together. On the morning of the 1st July 1916 they had marched 7 miles to arrive at 2.40am. The position had been shelled by the Germans and was not in the best condition. Unusually, and against Rawlinson's directive, at 7.20am they were ordered to get out of their trench and lie down just in front of their position. At 7.30am the whistles blew and they stood up, formed up and went into the attack in their lines. Looking out you will see Queen's Cemetery – this marks about the half way point across No Man's Land towards the Germans. Yet again, being on the spot, you can understand why German machine guns could and were so devastating here. Again these men believed they only had to go and occupy the German positions and yet again the Germans won that 'Secret Race'. At the start of the day the Accringtons were 720 men strong and they lost just short of 600 men, killed, wounded or missing. The survivors and wounded hid in shell holes until nightfall. This was an extra tragedy because of the Pals scheme, the news slowly drifted to Accrington and the lists of names began to appear in the local newspapers and then the community realised the true horror of what had happened to their small town – essentially the male population was wiped out in one go and house after house had their curtains shut. In Accrington, as the rumours began to break, an angry crowd gathered outside the Mayor's house. You can understand why the Pals units were split up soon afterwards.

I was once here with a group of 15 year old school students and it was at this point of my tour that a lad piped up and said 'If I was here on the 1st July 1916 then I would have just hidden behind that wall" after a few moments of silence, the guffaws started… he was of course talking about the Queen's Cemetery wall which was erected later.

Even in the moving story of the Accringtons' there are amazing success stories. Firstly the Accringtons did get to the German frontline and possibly the second line. **Stanley Bewsher** got through to nearly the German third line and he described that this is where the worst casualties came. He soon found himself on his own and confronted with 10-12 Germans coming towards him up a communication trench. In his own words he 'gave a good account' of himself and then retired back to the British lines. He was hit in his water bottle, his pack and his Lewis gun had its barrel bent as he ran back. As he reached the British lines he was then knocked unconscious by a piece of shrapnel hitting his helmet. The truth is that although there was initial success they couldn't hold the gains against heavy German fire and counter attacks. Bewsher was awarded the Military Medal for his actions on the 1st July 1916.

The Somme

The Stone Cross: This simple cross a few meters along the Accringtons' trench marks a rather special spot. The story goes that Louis and Agnes Bull refused to accept that their son **Albert Edward Bull** was missing. So they spent their modest annual holidays searching for his body. One can only imagine the dangers and the sights that would have come with such an undertaking. Albert's body was finally found in 1928 and this cross marks the spot. If the story is true then it highlights the amazing determination to have closure and the human story of luck. I presume he was identified by some item of kit that had his name etched on, common items were eating knives and forks for instance. Albert is buried in Serre Road No 2, back down on the main road.

Luke Copse Cemetery (GPS: 50°06.470'N 2°39.556'E): This is the final 'must visit' here at Sheffield Park. Go out of the gate and turn left walking back alongside the Accringtons' trench but now on the other side of the fence. The wood was in fact originally a series of copses and were named on the trench maps as Matthew, Mark, Luke and John. As you continue along you will find a small and fascinating cemetery called Luke Copse Cemetery – flick to the Cemetery section to find out the next part of the story.

DELVILLE WOOD
(GPS: 50°01.474'N 2°48.637'E)

Key Facts:
- South African Museum (For both World Wars)
- 3433 soldiers went in, 768 emerged six days later
- Trenches to be seen in the woodland

This is another one of the infamous woods, known at the time as 'Devil's Wood'. There are toilets and occasionally a visitor centre in the car park, although I haven't seen it open for many years. To access the wood and proper museum walk along the road a bit further and opposite the cemetery you will see a grand cemetery style entrance. In the centre of the wood is a memorial museum to the South Africans of both World Wars.

To start with head to the left of the building and you will see ahead and to the left a very old tree often with poppies in it. Next to it is an obelisk with an inscription explaining that it is 'the last tree'. This hornbeam tree is supposedly the only tree in the wood to have survived the battle here. In the museum you will find photographs that show the devastation that relentless artillery fire had done to the wood. The area was a mass of trenches and broken trees and thus perfect for defence.

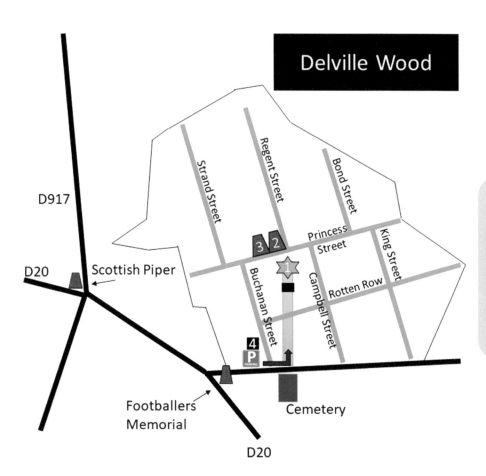

1 = The South African Memorial/Museum
2 = The Last Tree
3 = Cpl. Davies and Pte Hill VCs Memorial
4 = Car Park – WC & Old Visitor Centre/Cafe

You must stick to the paths or avenues as the wood is considered one large war grave. If you peer into the wood though you will see the zig zag pattern of the original trenches. The avenues are on the same layout as before the war and were named after places mostly in London and Edinburgh by the troops at the time to remind them of home: Rotten Row, Regent Street, Bond Street, Princes Street to name a few.

The story of the attack 15th July 1916: Here **3433** South Africans were ordered to take and hold the wood. They attacked and found that the conditions of the wood made the fighting extremely difficult – the tree roots made trench digging hard and the blasted remains of trees everywhere slowed the advance down. Much of the fighting was hand to hand as they desperately pushed on through the wood. Slowly but surely the South Africans captured the wood, they were then hit by devastating German artillery fire. The South Africans held on for six days being shelled by what was claimed to be 400 shells a minute. After the six days only **768** soldiers emerged, of those who were killed only **113** have known graves. The wood was only finally taken by the British on the 25th August 1916.

Delville Wood

148

Head back around and enter the museum. Look up as you approach and you will see the statues of **Castor and Pollux**. These two male figures with a horse represent the two white races of South Africa, the British and the Afrikaans. There are replicas of this in both Pretoria and Cape Town.

As you enter you realise that you actually have a memorial with a museum building behind. Head up to the museum and have a look.

Things to find in the museum include:

1) The **large bronze freeze.** This shows the march to victory in an almost cartoon story manner and is great.

2) Photos of **Nancy the Springbok.** Nancy was the mascot of the 4th South African Infantry Regiment and there are some great photos of her in the devastated wood. She would follow the sound of bagpipes. In Armentieres in 1917 one of her horns was damaged by a shell blast and grew at a funny angle from then on. She died just after the Armistice in 1918.

3) Photos and story of **Jackie the Baboon.** Jackie was the pet of **Albert Marr** and went to war with him. Jackie was formally taken 'on strength' and given a uniform when he arrived in Britain complete with South African badges. He would salute officers and use a knife and fork to eat. He was a firm favourite in the trenches because his advanced senses gave him an edge as a sentry. He was wounded at the same time as his master, Albert, in 1918 and whilst waiting to be evacuated built a wall out of stones to try and protect himself from the flying shrapnel. Jackie had to have his leg amputated as a result of his wound but survived the war and returned home with Albert.

The Somme

Four Victoria Crosses were won in Delville Wood:

Private Faulds VC, a South African twice rescued other soldiers under fire in No Man's Land.

Corporal Davies VC, of the Royal Welsh Fusiliers was cut off after a German counterattack. He repulsed the Germans then charged after them with his bayonet, despite being wounded in the shoulder.

Private Hill VC, of the Royal Welsh Fusiliers bayonetted his way to safety only to find that his company commander had been left behind wounded and so he went back in to rescue him.

Sergeant Gill VC, of the King's Royal Rifle Corps stood up in order to direct a desperate defence against a strong counter attack and was shot dead by a sniper. He is buried in the cemetery opposite.

Davies and Hill have a plaque and tree devoted to them just along from the 'Last Tree.'

FOOTBALLERS BATTALIONS MEMORIAL AND THE PIPERS MEMORIAL AT LONGUEVAL.
(Footballers Memorial GPS: 50°01.438'N 2°48.590'E)
(Pipers Memorial GPS 50°01.576'N 2°48.190'E)

Just up the road from Delville Wood, at the junction is a modern memorial to the Footballers Battalions. The Middlesex Regiment ended up having two football battalions, made up of volunteer footballers. The big names of the day went off to fight together in these 'Pals battalions'. One of the most famous was **Walter Tull**, of Spurs and Northampton who fought near here until he was hospitalised with Trench Fever. On his recovery he was commissioned and became the first black officer in the British Army. 1500 men from the footballers battalions were killed over the course of the war.

The Somme

At the central cross roads in the middle of Longueval you will find the **Kilted Bagpiper** emerging from his trench. Behind him on the wall are the regiments that lost pipers. The inscription on the bronze plaque is rather good, have a read. Before you go look at the sandbags on the base – look carefully, one is not a sandbag at all!

The Piper Memorial at Longueval

Museums

There is now a small museum at Thiepval. I have also mentioned in the text that there are visitor centres at Delville Wood and Newfoundland Park.

ALBERT, 1916 MUSEUM
(GPS: 50°00.207'N 2°38.913'E)

This museum is in the centre of Albert and essentially housed in a tunnel beneath the Basilica. If you park up and head to the Basilica you cannot miss it. It is focussed on the Somme in 1916. The exhibits are very clearly labelled and you can compare different rifles, gas masks and so on. There are also scenes using manikins of various aspects of trench life.

PERONNE, THE HISTORIAL
(GPS: 49°55.773'N 2°55.935'E)

The first thing you need to know about this museum is that it is half an hour south of Albert and so for most British pilgrims it is therefore poorly located. It has fascinating lay outs of the full uniform and kit that each nationality would have worn. My advice is not to use up Somme battlefield time to divert to it, but if you are heading on south then it's worth a stop.

Sir John Monash Centre, Villers Bretonneux
(GPS: 49°53.155'N 2°30.573'E)

Half an hour southwest of Albert is the big impressive Australian visitor centre complete with marble and gold tapped toilets and a cafe. The museum has interactive and immersive displays and is a must for anyone with an Australian link. It is very focused on the Australian actions and is overly critical of the British in places, but it is worth a visit.

The Somme

A SOLDIER
OF THE GREAT WAR

KNOWN UNTO GOD

Arras, Vimy And Homeward

Why not add in some great extra stops as you head north for home. Here are a few of my favourite 'on the way home' stops. If you are doing this then I wouldn't head back to the motorway instead keep on the D919 from Sheffield Park. This road will take you straight up to Arras.

WELLINGTON QUARRIES (LA CARRIÈRE WELLINGTON) IN ARRAS
(GPS: 50°16.790'N 2°47.013'E)

Situated off the D917 and beside a giant E. Leclerc supermarket in southeast Arras. There are thousands of caves underneath this area of France – indeed there are many under the villages on the Somme too. Arras though was extensively tunnelled for rock since Medieval times. In WW1 the quarries were expanded for military purposes. By the Battle of Arras in April 1917 the cave network had been so developed that huge amounts of allied troops were living in safety beneath the ground. Tunnels were also developed going forwards to release points in No Man's Land – thus keeping the troops protected right into the assault. When the troops attacked from here they were so successful that the German officers were captured eating their breakfast. This part of the cave network was expanded by New Zealanders hence why one part was named 'Wellington'.

Beware that the place closes over lunch and you have to join a group to go down into the caves. The safest thing to do is book via their website: **https://www.carrierewellington.com**

The caves have artefacts, maps, graffiti and an audio guide to take you round, but only as part of a guided group. It is impressive and well worth a visit. Don't forget to wear something warm.

VIMY RIDGE
(Monument GPS: 50°22.781'N 2°46.182'E)
(Visitor Centre and Trenches GPS: 50°22.262'N 2°46.162'E)

Forever now connected to Canada, this impressive monument overlooks everything for miles around and is a fascinating visit. It is essentially two stops, the first is the monument and the second is the visitor centre, trenches and the tunnel tour. If you visit the monument, then it is really worth walking down the other side and then properly looking up at the monument. At the visitor centre stop there are toilets. Here too are recreated 'concreted' trench lines to walk in and you can get the sense of the distance between British and German trenches. If you wish to visit the tunnels, which are free and have regular tour departures, head in to the new visitor centre.

The story of the attack in April 1917: It was the Canadian Corps that took this high point from the well dug in Germans. The French had started mining here in 1915 and the area was taken over by the British in 1916. Between 1916 and 1917 The Royal Engineers dug another six miles of tunnels, lit by electric light. Prior to the attack troops were kept in a 22 mile network of tunnels. Many of these tunnels are still there and are accessible to the professionals. Like I explained in the

Wellington Quarry section, the British were now releasing troops out of the tunnels direct to No Man's Land and some of what look like craters in No Man's Land today are actually tunnel exit points. This shows how lessons had been learnt from the earlier battles and how important it was to help the troops get further forward when attacking. The French had lost 130,000 casualties attacking here in 1915. The Canadians attacked after a three week artillery bombardment. The attack went in on Easter Monday 1917 in the snow. It took them three days to take the ridge suffering 10,600 casualties of which 3,000 were killed.

The Vimy Ridge monument is built around two 'pylons' or pillars standing 30 metres higher than the ridge. The pylons represent Canada and France. Then there are 20 sculpted human figures: A group of eight figures high up on the top of the two pylons represent Justice, Peace, Hope, Charity, Honour, Faith, Truth and Knowledge. Peace is the highest figure on the monument, reaching upwards with a torch. Between the pylons the group of two figures comprises a dying soldier who has passed a torch to a comrade. Two further groups of figures located at each end of the front wall comprise seven figures called The Defenders. Two reclining figures on the southern side of the memorial, located either side of the steps, represent the mourning mothers and fathers of Canada's war dead. A female figure, "Mother Canada", draped in a cloak stands alone on the wall at the north-eastern side of the memorial. She bows her head and is looking down at a stone sarcophagus, representing Canada's war dead. This beautiful memorial was opened in 1936.

MUSEE VIVANT 14-18 AT NOTRE DAME DE LORETTE, NEAR SOUCHEZ
(GPS: 50°24.095'N 2°42.875'E)

On the D937, parallel to the main A26 Motorway you will find the largest French Military Cemetery. It is near the village of Souchez. I actually bring you here not for the giant cemetery or the new circular memorial but for the forgotten old museum. To get to the museum drive up the hill and through the car park, keep going and going. Go round the end of the cemetery and keep going until you are on the opposite side to the initial car park. Here you will find a museum which has been here for a VERY long time. It has a priceless collection of uniforms on manikins and weapons. Some of this stuff you can't see anywhere else. It is one of my favourite places. It can be unpredictable in its opening times so good luck with that! It has a sister museum called the **Musee de la Targette** just back down the D937. **https://www.musee1418.com**

When you go back down to the D937 there is another more modern museum, **The Lens 14-18 Museum (GPS: 50°24.069'N 2°44.419'E)**. This is on the opposite side where you turn off/on the D937 – between the D937 and the Motorway. The Lens museum is free if you don't take an audio guide (you don't need one) and has some well-presented interactive maps and enhanced large photos. It also has good clean toilets if you need them.

How did the war end on the Western Front?

The Germans had exhausted their military strength in their 1918 Spring Offensives, this also coincided with the Allies being reinforced by the arrival of American fresh troops. From the Battle of Amiens in August 1918 the Allies fought The 100 Days to victory, where the German army was either repeatedly pushed back or surrendered. The final engagements, often very close to initial 1914 battles, saw mobile warfare return and a demoralised German army was outmanoeuvred by a well-equipped modern army using devastating artillery, tanks and aircraft to pursue and ensure that the Germans could not win. The Germans were also increasingly isolated with a lack of resources, allies and a crumbling society. In November the German Kaiser abdicated, leading the way for peace.

Huge parade of captured German guns, near Amiens 1918.

Index